FOOD&WINE

ANNUAL COOKBOOK 2023

FOOD & WINE MAGAZINE

EDITOR IN CHIEF **Hunter Lewis**
VICE PRESIDENT/GENERAL MANAGER **Michelle Edelbaum**
DEPUTY EDITOR **Melanie Hansche**
EXECUTIVE EDITOR **Karen Shimizu**
EXECUTIVE WINE EDITOR **Ray Isle**
MANAGING EDITOR **Caitlin Murphree Miller**

FOOD & EDITORIAL

RESTAURANT EDITOR **Khushbu Shah**
FEATURES EDITOR **Nina Friend**
FOOD EDITOR **Kelsey Youngman**
ASSOCIATE FOOD EDITOR **Paige Grandjean**
ASSISTANT FOOD EDITOR **Andee Mckenzie**
BUSINESS MANAGER **Alice Eldridge Summerville**
EDITORIAL ASSISTANT **Lucy Simon**
EDITORIAL FELLOW **Alexandra Domrongchai**

COPY & RESEARCH

COPY EDITOR **Erin Clyburn**
COPY EDITOR **Winn Duvall**

ART

CREATIVE DIRECTOR **Winslow Taft**
ART DIRECTOR **James Slocum**
ASSISTANT DESIGNER **Ann Martin Foley**

PHOTO

PHOTO DIRECTOR **Tori Katherman**
PHOTO EDITOR **Dan Bailey**

PRODUCTION

PRODUCTION DIRECTOR **Liz Rhoades**

DIGITAL

SENIOR EDITORIAL DIRECTOR **Sean Flynn**
ASSOCIATE EDITORIAL DIRECTOR, FOOD **Chandra Ram**
EXECUTIVE FEATURES EDITOR **Kat Kinsman**
SENIOR EDITOR **Maria Yagoda**
SENIOR DRINKS EDITOR **Oset Babür-Winter**
SENIOR EDITOR, NEWS AND TRENDING **Adam Campbell-Schmitt**
SENIOR SOCIAL MEDIA EDITOR **Sam Gutierrez**
SOCIAL MEDIA EDITOR **Merlyn Miller**
DIGITAL OPERATIONS EDITOR **Elsa Säätelä**
E-COMMERCE EDITOR **Megan Soll**
PHOTO EDITOR **Alexis Camarena**

CONTRIBUTOR

CULINARY DIRECTOR AT LARGE **Justin Chapple**
EXECUTIVE PRODUCER **Kwame Onwuachi**

MEREDITH OPERATIONS CORPORATION CONSUMER MARKETING

DIRECTOR, DIRECT MARKETING-BOOKS **Daniel Fagan**
MARKETING OPERATIONS MANAGER **Max Daily**
ASSISTANT MARKETING MANAGER **Kylie Dazzo**
MARKETING COORDINATOR **Elizabeth Moore**
CONTENT MANAGER **Julie Doll**
SENIOR PRODUCTION MANAGER **Liza Ward**

WATERBURY PUBLICATIONS, INC.

EDITORIAL DIRECTOR **Lisa Kingsley**
CREATIVE DIRECTOR **Ken Carlson**
ASSOCIATE DESIGN DIRECTOR **Doug Samuelson**
CONTRIBUTING COPY EDITOR **E4 Editorial Services**
CONTRIBUTING PROOFREADER **Andrea Cooley**
CONTRIBUTING INDEXER **E4 Editorial Services**

All of us at Dotdash Meredith Consumer Marketing are dedicated to providing you with information and ideas to enhance your home.

We welcome your comments and suggestions. Write to us at Dotdash Meredith Consumer Marketing, 1716 Locust St., Des Moines, IA 50309-3023.

FRONT COVER

Soppressata Pizza with Calabrian Chilies and Hot Honey (p. 250)
PHOTOGRAPHER **Christopher Testani**

BACK COVER

Chicken Lule Kebab and Charred Jalapeños and Tomatoes (p. 127)
PHOTOGRAPHER **Julie Stotz**

Tropical Jackfruit–Ginger Ale Sorbet with Charred Pineapple (p. 277)
PHOTOGRAPHER **Victor Protasio**

Rigatoni Amatriciana (p. 76)
PHOTOGRAPHER **Antonis Achilleos**

FOOD & WINE

ANNUAL COOKBOOK 2023

AN ENTIRE YEAR OF COOKING

FOOD & WINE
BOOKS

ENMOLADAS DE CALABAZA (P. 204)
OPPOSITE: CITRUS-AND-FENNEL
CHICKEN WITH OLIVES AND CALABRIAN
CHILES (P. 119)

CONTENTS

PINE NUT OLIVE OIL CAKE (P. 285)

FOREWORD

HOW HAVE YOUR NOTIONS OF HOME EVOLVED in the past three years? For many of us here at *Food & Wine*—and for lots of you too, we're sure—home continues to double as a part-time home office some days. But it also continues to be the space where we conduct one of the most vital activities of being human—cooking, creating, and feeding ourselves and our friends and family good food that sustains us not just physically but emotionally and spiritually too.

A common thread in almost all of the stories in *F&W* is the sense of connection fostered by gathering around food, whether we share it in our own homes or at a favorite eatery—and the recipes from the past year bear that out.

After moving to the Midwest from China in the 1960s, the dinner table became the place where the family of writer Lan Samantha Chan shared family recipes that bridged the distance between their new and old homelands. Dishes like their Stir-Fried Flank Steak with Yellow Onions (recipe p. 161), Scallion Pancakes (recipe p. 238), or Chicken Spaghetti Lo Mein (recipe p. 87) retain their power to comfort, all these many years later.

Or experience what chef Kwame Onwuachi's America tastes like, with recipes such as Curried Goat (recipe p. 174), Pollo Guisado (recipe p. 120), or his mother's Red Beans and Rice (recipe p. 221) that reflect his own family's diaspora. Cookbook author Von Diaz opens the door to Boricua Soul, a restaurant in Durham, North Carolina, that became a safe harbor for her during the pandemic thanks to the generosity and community-mindedness of owners Toriano and Serena Fredericks (not to mention their Puerto Rican-meets-Southern cooking). Get the recipe for their Pernil Mac and Cheese—cheesy noodles topped with garlicky, tender shredded pork—on page 83.

We hope this volume brings you moments of discovery, delight, connection, and comfort in your own homes, whether it's perfecting your pizza game (recipes p. 244-253), arranging a beautifully composed Niçoise Salad with Sardines (recipe p. 26) for supper on a warm summer evening, or stirring up Culinary Director at Large Justin Chapple's Short Rib Chili with Pickled Red Onion (recipe p. 61) that he developed for you with cozy nights at home in mind.

—The Editors at *Food & Wine*

STARTERS, SNACKS & APPETIZERS

LEFT: BACON-WRAPPED
WATERMELON RIND PICKLES
(P. 16) BELOW: SMOKED
BLUEFISH SPREAD (P. 16)
OPPOSITE: RADISH TARTINES
WITH GREEN BUTTER (P. 13).

Pão de Queijo

ACTIVE 35 MIN; TOTAL 3 HR 30 MIN
SERVES 14

Pão de queijo is a classic Brazilian snack and breakfast bread. Light and airy, with a delightful chew and savory, cheesy flavor, each puff has a lightly crispy exterior and a tender, bubbly center. Felipe Donnelly's version is a must-have at his New York City restaurant, Cómodo. It's the perfect two-bite snack with hints of cayenne and nutmeg.

- **5 oz. Parmesan or pecorino Romano cheese, grated (about 2 cups)**
- **2 large eggs**
- **2 cups tapioca flour (about 8½ oz.) (see Note) or manioc starch**
- **2 tsp. kosher salt**
- **½ cup plus 3 Tbsp. extra-virgin olive oil, plus more for oiling and shaping**
- **½ cup whole milk**
- **½ cup water**
- **Pinch of ground nutmeg**
- **Pinch of cayenne pepper**
- **Pinch of black pepper**

1. Process cheese and eggs in a food processor until a smooth paste forms, about 1 minute, stopping to scrape down sides of bowl as needed.

2. Combine tapioca flour and salt in bowl of a stand mixer fitted with the paddle attachment. Set aside.

3. Combine oil, milk, and ½ cup water in a small saucepan, and bring to a boil over medium-high. Immediately pour oil mixture into tapioca mixture in stand mixer, all at once, and turn the mixer on at low speed. Beat until dough is smooth and starch is completely incorporated, about 2 minutes. (There will be some oil left in bottom of bowl.)

4. Turn stand mixer off. Add cheese mixture, nutmeg, cayenne, and black pepper to mixture in stand mixer. Beat mixture on low speed until it turns pale yellow, about 10 minutes. (You are trying to develop the structure of the dough by kneading it slowly. Dough should feel a bit sticky and moist.)

5. Transfer dough to a medium bowl; cover with plastic wrap, and refrigerate until dough is chilled and slightly stiffened, at least 2 hours or up to 12 hours.

6. Preheat oven to 350°F. Line 3 large rimmed baking sheets with parchment paper, or oil the baking sheets well.

7. Lightly coat your hands with oil (or flour them with tapioca flour). Pinch off walnut-size pieces (about 1 tablespoon) of dough; roll between your palms into balls. Place 16 to 18 pão de queijo on each prepared baking sheet 1½ to 2 inches apart.

8. Bake in preheated oven, 1 baking sheet at a time, until rolls puff up and are light golden brown, about 20 minutes per batch, rotating baking sheet from front to back halfway through bake time. Remove from oven; place pão de queijo in a basket lined with a napkin. Serve immediately, while they are at their warmest and chewiest. —FELIPE DONNELLY, CÓMODO, NEW YORK CITY

MAKE AHEAD Dough balls can frozen, covered with plastic wrap, on parchment paper–lined baking sheets. Increase bake time by 5 minutes if baking from frozen.

NOTE Tapioca flour can be found at bobsredmill.com.

Chin Chin

TOTAL 1 HR; SERVES 10 (MAKES ABOUT 9 CUPS OF ½-INCH PUFFS)

"The streets of Lagos Island are crowded with street vendors, including the chin chin stalls, generally run by women, which are nearly impossible to resist," says 2019 F&W Best New Chef Kwame Onwuachi, *who shared this snack recipe. "Chin chin are nutmeg-riddled fried puffs of dough, the Nigerian contribution to filling mankind's desire for crunchy, sweet snacks. From behind their tables, the chin chin sellers sold not just these addictive cookies but a whole menagerie of fried foods, foods whose crunch does double duty by helping to maintain their longevity in the hot sun."*

- **3½ cups all-purpose flour (about 14⅞ oz.), plus more for work surface and kneading**
- **¾ cup granulated sugar**
- **½ cup coconut sugar**
- **1 tsp. ground nutmeg**
- **½ tsp. kosher salt**
- **¼ tsp. baking powder**
- **¼ cup unsalted butter, cubed, at room temperature**
- **¾ cup heavy cream**
- **¼ cup unsweetened coconut cream (such as Thai Kitchen)**
- **1 large egg**
- **Vegetable oil, for frying**

1. Whisk together flour, granulated sugar, coconut sugar, nutmeg, salt, and baking powder in a large bowl. Add butter; rub butter into flour mixture using your fingers until well incorporated. (Mixture should look like sand.) Whisk in heavy cream, coconut cream, and egg until a sticky dough ball forms, eventually switching from a whisk to using your hands when mixture becomes too thick to whisk.

2. Turn dough out onto a lightly floured work surface. Knead until smooth, elastic, even in color, and no longer sticky, 2 to 3 minutes, adding up to ¼ cup additional flour, 1 tablespoon at a time, as needed.

3. Divide dough in half. Roll 1 dough piece into a ⅛-inch-thick rectangle about 12×9 inches. (Feel free to use a pasta roller if you have one.) Trim away any uneven edges. Cut dough rectangle into ½-inch squares, occasionally flouring knife blade to prevent dough from sticking. Repeat process with remaining dough piece. (At this point, you can freeze dough squares for later, if you like.) Place cut dough squares in a single layer on a baking sheet lined with parchment paper, and freeze until solid; transfer dough squares to a ziplock plastic freezer bag, and freeze up to 3 months. To cook, let thaw in a single layer at room temperature, and then fry as instructed below.

4. Pour oil to a depth of 3 inches in a large Dutch oven. Heat over medium to 350°F. Working in 6 to 8 batches, add chin chin squares to hot oil. (Don't worry if the chin chin squares are a little stuck together; they'll separate once they hit the oil.) Cook, stirring often using a slotted spoon, until golden, puffed, and crisp, about 1 minute. (This goes quickly, so watch carefully.) Using a spider, transfer chin chin squares to a baking sheet lined with paper towels. Let cool slightly, about 5 minutes. Serve. —KWAME ONWUACHI

MAKE AHEAD Chin chin can be stored in an airtight container at room temperature up to 1 month. Dough can be frozen after being cut up to 3 months.

CHIN CHIN

TANGHULU (CANDIED
FRUIT SKEWERS)

Tanghulu (Candied Fruit Skewers)

⏱ TOTAL 35 MIN; MAKES 5 SKEWERS

The perfect tanghulu—a Chinese street snack—is a skewer of ripe fruit covered evenly in a thin, clear sugar shell. This simple recipe relies on a precise ratio of sugar, water, and corn syrup that produces a crisp, even candy shell. Be sure to thoroughly dry fruit prior to dipping it in the syrup. To add a sweet chew or nutty crunch to these treats, stuff the fruits with red bean paste or walnuts prior to skewering and dunking.

FRUITS

- **15 assorted small fresh fruits (such as hawthorn, crab apples, strawberries, tangerine segments, cherries, and/or grapes), rinsed**
- **Sweetened red bean paste or walnut halves (optional)**

SYRUP

- **¾ cup granulated sugar**
- **⅓ cup water**
- **2 Tbsp. light corn syrup**

1. Prepare the fruits: Stem, core, or otherwise prepare fruit so that each bite-size piece is entirely edible. If desired, stuff fruits with red bean paste or walnuts. Pat outsides of fruit dry with paper towels, and place on a baking sheet lined with paper towels. (Wet fruit will prevent the sugar from sticking.)

2. Slide 3 fruit pieces onto each of 5 (12-inch-long) bamboo skewers, skewering through the center of the fruit. Arrange each piece so fruits are evenly stacked, with bottoms and tops of fruits gently pressed together. Place skewers on a baking sheet lined with paper towels. Set aside.

3. Make the syrup: Combine granulated sugar, ⅓ cup water, and light corn syrup in a shallow pan. Cook over medium, undisturbed, until sugar dissolves and mixture begins to boil, 4 to 5 minutes. (To prevent sugar crystallization, it is very important not to stir.) Reduce heat to medium-low; cook, undisturbed, until syrup reaches 310°F and picks up the faintest golden hue, 15 to 18 minutes. Remove from heat; let syrup stand until bubbles subside, about 30 seconds.

4. While syrup is still hot, tilt pan so that syrup pools on one side. Working with 1 fruit skewer at a time, very lightly touch the side of the fruit skewer onto the surface of the syrup. Carefully and quickly, rotate skewer in one direction, taking care to evenly coat all surfaces of the fruits without submerging the entire fruit into the syrup. Try to do this in 1 rotation. Let excess syrup drip back into pan. Work quickly so that syrup does not cool and thicken. Place skewer, fruit side up, into a heavy cup or other container; let candy stand, untouched, until naturally cooled and fully hardened, about 2 minutes. Meanwhile, repeat process with remaining fruit skewers. If needed, use scissors to trim off any long, hardened strands of syrup from cooled skewers. —LUCAS SIN

MAKE AHEAD The skewers are always best when eaten immediately, but tanghulu can be stored in the freezer. Tanghulu is traditionally wrapped in a thin layer of rice paper for storing, but skewers may also be kept in a ziplock plastic bag.

Radish Tartines with Green Butter

PHOTO P. 8

⏱ TOTAL 40 MIN; SERVES 6

These radish and turnip-topped tartines are a great way to use up radishes and turnips with their greens attached. The radish and turnip greens whipped with sweet butter, garlic, and lemon zest create a delicious, silky spread for the tartines, while the spicy, paper-thin radishes and turnips make the perfect topping. Finished with crunchy sea salt, these make a great appetizer or light lunch.

- **8 medium-size mixed radishes (such as Easter egg, black, watermelon, and Purple Ninja) with tops (about 12 oz.)**
- **2 medium-size Japanese turnips with tops (about 2½ oz.)**
- **½ cup unsalted butter (4 oz.), preferably grass-fed, at room temperature**
- **1 tsp. finely grated lemon zest, plus lemon wedges for serving**
- **½ tsp. flaky sea salt, plus more to taste**
- **¼ tsp. black pepper, plus more to taste**
- **1 small garlic clove, finely grated (about ¼ tsp.)**
- **6 (¾-inch-thick) soft rustic bread slices (about 1¼ oz. each), lightly toasted**
- **Crushed red pepper, for garnish**

1. Remove greens from radishes and turnips; reserve about 1 firmly packed cup greens (about 1½ ounces radish greens and ½ ounce turnip greens). Wash greens, and pat dry. Set aside.

2. Using a mandoline, very thinly slice radishes and turnips (about 1/16 inch thick); transfer to a medium bowl filled with ice water. Let soak 10 minutes. Drain well, and pat dry.

3. While radishes and turnips soak, place reserved 1 cup greens, butter, lemon zest, salt, black pepper, and garlic in a food processor. Process until butter is green and mostly smooth, about 1 minute, stopping occasionally to scrape down sides of bowl. Season with additional salt and black pepper to taste.

4. Spread green butter evenly over 1 side of toasted bread slices (about 2 tablespoons each). Top with sliced radishes and turnips. Season with additional salt to taste. Garnish with crushed red pepper, and serve with lemon wedges. —JUSTIN CHAPPLE

MAKE AHEAD Butter can be made up to 2 days ahead and stored in an airtight container in refrigerator.

WINE Grassy, citrusy New Zealand Sauvignon Blanc: 2020 Craggy Range Te Muna Road

PORK, SHRIMP, AND CHIVE DUMPLINGS

The ideal combination of crispy and chewy, these garlicky pork-and-shrimp-filled dumplings are weeknight-friendly thanks to store-bought wrappers. Before pleating the filled dumplings, moisten the edges just slightly so they stick together.

ACTIVE 45 MIN; TOTAL 1 HR 30 MIN
MAKES 36 DUMPLINGS

DUMPLINGS

- 4 cups roughly chopped napa cabbage (about 5⅓ oz.)
- ½ tsp. kosher salt, divided, plus more to taste
- 8 oz. ground pork
- 1 cup chopped garlic chives
- 4 oz. raw large shrimp, peeled, deveined, and coarsely chopped (about ½ cup)
- ½ cup plus 2 Tbsp. chopped scallions, divided
- ¼ cup plus 2 Tbsp. soy sauce, divided
- 1 Tbsp. oyster sauce
- 1 Tbsp. Shaoxing wine or dry sherry
- 1 Tbsp. cornstarch
- 1 Tbsp. granulated sugar
- 2 tsp. chopped garlic
- 1 tsp. finely chopped peeled fresh ginger
- 1 tsp. sesame oil
- ¼ tsp. black pepper, plus more to taste
- 36 Shanghai-style round dumpling wrappers (such as Twin Marquis), at room temperature
- All-purpose flour, for dusting
- 6 Tbsp. canola oil, divided
- 1½ cups water, divided
- 3 Tbsp. unsweetened rice wine vinegar
- 1 Tbsp. chile-garlic sauce (such as Huy Fong) (optional)

1. Pulse cabbage and ¼ teaspoon salt in a food processor until finely chopped, 8 to 10 pulses. Place mixture on a clean towel; squeeze to remove as much liquid as possible. Place in a large bowl; stir in pork, garlic chives, shrimp, ½ cup scallions, 2 tablespoons soy sauce, oyster sauce, Shaoxing wine, cornstarch, sugar, garlic, ginger, sesame oil, pepper, and remaining ¼ teaspoon salt until combined. Sauté a small amount of filling until fully cooked; taste and adjust seasoning as needed.

2. Working with 1 wrapper at a time and keeping remaining wrappers covered with a kitchen towel, place 1 level tablespoon of filling in center of one wrapper; gently press filling into an oval shape. Lightly wet edge of wrapper with water using an index finger. Place wrapper in 1 hand; bring wrapper sides up around filling to make a taco shape. To make a full or half Buddha belly pleat, see below; otherwise, create a simple scrunch

STEP-BY-STEP

MAKE FILLING Place drained cabbage, ground pork, chopped shrimp, and remaining filling ingredients in a large bowl; stir until combined.

ASSEMBLE DUMPLINGS Place 1 tablespoon filling in center of wrapper; gently press filling into an oval shape. Lightly moisten perimeter of wrapper with water.

FOLD TO ENCASE FILLING Holding a filled dumpling in one hand, bring wrapper sides up around the filling to create a taco shape. Pinch corners together on one side.

CRIMP DUMPLINGS Starting at the pinched corner, use your thumb and index finger to create small, even pleats in the front side of the wrapper.

pleat by pressing to seal edges, creating a crescent shape. Place dumpling on work surface; using both hands, scrunch sealed edges toward center, creating zigzag pleats. Place pleated dumpling on a large rimmed baking sheet dusted with flour, and cover with a damp towel. Repeat process with remaining wrappers and filling.

3. Heat a large nonstick pan over high. Working in 3 batches, add 2 tablespoons oil; swirl to coat pan. Add 12 dumplings, pleated sides up. Pour in ½ cup water to come halfway up sides of dumplings; cover and reduce heat to medium. Cook, undisturbed, until water is evaporated and bottoms of dumplings are golden brown and crispy (sizzling will subside, and dumplings will smell toasty), 12 to 14 minutes (17 to 20 minutes if cooking from frozen). Transfer cooked dumplings to a platter. Repeat with remaining oil, dumplings, and water, wiping pan clean between batches.

4. While dumplings cook, stir together remaining ¼ cup soy sauce, vinegar, remaining 2 tablespoons scallions, and chile-garlic sauce, if using, in a small bowl. Serve dumplings with sauce. —ANITA LO

MAKE AHEAD Freeze uncooked pleated dumplings on a floured baking sheet, uncovered, until fully frozen, about 2 hours. Transfer dumplings to a large ziplock plastic freezer bag. Cook dumplings from frozen.

WINE Tart New Zealand Sauvignon Blanc: 2020 Astrolabe Marlborough

PRESS AND SEAL Continue pleating front side of wrapper, pressing each pleat into back side of wrapper to create a crescent-shaped dumpling.

COOK DUMPLINGS Add dumplings to an oiled skillet, pleated side up. Pour ½ cup water into pan; cover and cook until bottoms are crisp, 12 to 14 minutes.

Smoked Bluefish Spread

PHOTO P. 9

ACTIVE 10 MIN; TOTAL 1 HR 10 MIN
SERVES 6 TO 8

At her summer home on Martha's Vineyard, Jessica B. Harris serves this bluefish spread with crackers as hors d'oeuvres (with a Ti' Punch cocktail) to dinner party guests and at participants in her "five to sevens" —gatherings on the porch with drinks and small bites, so-called because they take place between the hours of five and seven o'clock. Smoky, rich, and creamy, this delicious spread brings together luscious smoked bluefish with light and fluffy whipped cream cheese, tangy whole-milk yogurt, and a dash of acidic hot sauce and horseradish. Don't skip on chilling the dip for at least 1 hour; time in the fridge allows the flavors and textures to meld. Be sure to re-season the bluefish spread with lemon juice and hot sauce after chilling as these ingredients will often mellow over time. The delicate crunch and neutral flavor of lavash or water crackers allow the smoky dip to be the star of the show. Bluefish is a popular and abundant fish on the Vineyard. Another smoked, oily-fleshed fish, such as whitefish, mackerel, or trout, may also be used here.

- 8 oz. plain whipped cream cheese
- 6 oz. boneless, skinless smoked bluefish, whitefish, mackerel, or trout, flaked into small pieces
- ½ cup plain whole-milk strained (Greek-style) yogurt
- 1 Tbsp. prepared horseradish
- 1 tsp. fresh lemon juice (from 1 lemon), plus more to taste
- 1 tsp. hot sauce, plus more to taste
- ¼ tsp. Worcestershire sauce
- Flaky sea salt, to taste
- Black pepper, to taste
- Lavash or water crackers

Stir together cream cheese, bluefish, yogurt, horseradish, lemon juice, hot sauce, and Worcestershire sauce in a medium bowl until well combined. Season to taste with salt and pepper. Cover tightly with plastic wrap; chill until flavors meld, at least 1 hour or up to 2 days. Season with additional lemon juice and hot sauce to taste. Serve with lavash or water crackers.
—JESSICA B. HARRIS

MAKE AHEAD Dip can be made up to 2 days in advance and stored in an airtight container in refrigerator.

NOTE Smoked bluefish can be ordered from shelskys.com.

Bacon-Wrapped Watermelon Rind Pickles

PHOTO P. 9

ACTIVE 15 MIN; TOTAL 40 MIN
SERVES 8 TO 10

Gently rendered, crispy bacon comes together with sweet-and-sour pickled watermelon rind in this salty, tangy, chewy snack. As they bake together in the oven, the bacon takes on the fruity brine, while the watermelon rind takes on the savory, smoky aroma of the bacon. Use standard-cut bacon for the best results; thick-cut slices will not cook evenly. Harris recommends Walnut Creek or Prissy's jarred watermelon rind pickles for their firm texture and not too cloyingly sweet taste. Cut larger pickles in half to form 1-inch squares for even cooking.

- 24 (about 1- × 1-inch) pieces pickled watermelon rind (from 1 [20-oz.] jar), drained and patted dry
- 12 bacon slices (not thick-cut) (about 13 oz.), cut in half crosswise

1. Preheat oven to 400°F. Line a rimmed baking sheet with aluminum foil. Wrap each pickled watermelon rind piece with 1 bacon half; secure with a wooden pick. Arrange wrapped pieces on prepared baking sheet spaced at least ½ inch apart.

2. Bake in preheated oven until bacon is mostly rendered and starting to brown, 20 to 25 minutes. Flip each piece, and continue baking until bacon is browned and crisp on both sides, 5 to 10 minutes. Carefully transfer pieces to a platter, letting excess drippings drip off onto baking sheet. Discard drippings. Serve immediately.
—JESSICA B. HARRIS

MAKE AHEAD Watermelon rind pickles can be wrapped in bacon a day ahead and baked just before serving. Reheat leftover bacon-wrapped pickles at 350°F until heated through, 5 to 10 minutes.

NOTE Jarred pickled watermelon rind can be purchased online at walnutcreekfood.com or prissys.com.

Deviled Eggs

TOTAL 10 MIN; SERVES 14

A heavy dose of mayonnaise gives the filling of these deviled eggs an extra-silky texture and rich flavor, while sharp Dijon mustard and fresh dill add acidity and brightness. Granulated garlic and white pepper impart a subtle complexity without affecting the creamy texture of the yolk filling, and a light dusting of paprika to finish adds a decorative touch and a mildly sweet flavor to balance the richness. Eggs can be boiled up to 1 day in advance and the assembled deviled eggs can be chilled in an airtight container for up to 1 day. When slicing the hard-cooked eggs in half, wipe your knife blade with a damp paper towel in between each egg for clean cuts and to prevent the yolks from sticking to the blade. We recommend a whisk to combine the spice and the yolks: The web of wire loops on a hand whisk not only help to evenly distribute the spices, they work to break apart the hard-cooked egg yolks for a smooth and velvety filling perfect for piping into the egg white boats. Dress up the platter with cornichons and thinly sliced prosciutto, if desired.

- 14 hard-cooked eggs
- 1½ cups mayonnaise
- 1 tsp. chopped fresh dill, plus more for garnish
- 1 tsp. Dijon mustard
- ⅛ tsp. white pepper
- ⅛ tsp. granulated garlic
- Paprika, for garnish

Peel eggs, and cut in half lengthwise. Scoop yolks into a medium bowl. Place egg whites on a platter, and set aside. Add mayonnaise, dill, Dijon mustard, white pepper, and granulated garlic to bowl with egg yolks, and whisk until mostly smooth, about 1 minute. Transfer mayonnaise mixture to a piping bag or a ziplock plastic freezer bag with a ½-inch hole cut in 1 corner. Pipe evenly into egg white halves. Garnish deviled eggs with paprika and additional dill.
—GENOVA DELICATESSEN

MAKE AHEAD Deviled eggs can be prepared up to 1 day in advance and stored in an airtight container in refrigerator.

NOTE Shock hard-boiled eggs in a large bowl of ice water to quickly stop the cooking process.

DEVILED EGGS

FAN TUAN

Fan Tuan

ACTIVE 40 MIN; TOTAL 1 HR SERVES 4

A layer of cooked sticky rice becomes the satisfying wrapper for fan tuan, colorful rolls filled with fried eggs, scallions, pickled daikon, the fried dough sticks called youtiao, and pork floss. "Fan tuan is exercise in textures: chewy sticky rice and crunchy youtiao (Chinese crullers), crisp-tender salted radishes and fluffy rousong (pork floss), all bound by sweet soy sauce and a fried egg," says 2020 F&W Best New Chef Trigg Brown of Win Son, in Brooklyn. "While I first had fan tuan in Taiwan, I really fell in love with the dish when, at the recommendation of chef Eric Sze, I went to Huge Tree Pastry, Lillian Liu's family bakery in L.A. Eddie Huang showed me a technique where you toast the rice in a wok and then massage in oil before cooking it so that the grains remain separate but also stick together. For me, the fan tuan we serve at the bakery represents the collaborative nature of my understanding of Taiwanese food. Without Eric and Lillian and Eddie, I would never get that satisfying multi-textural bite that continues to get me every time I eat it."

- 1½ **cups uncooked white sticky rice (about 10½ oz.)**
- 4½ **Tbsp. canola oil, divided, plus more for frying**
- 1½ **cups water**
- 4 **large eggs**
   Kosher salt, to taste
   Black pepper, to taste
- 4 **(4-×1-×1-inch) pieces youtiao (Chinese cruller) or brioche**
- ¼ **cup rousong (pork floss) or finely chopped spiced firm tofu, divided**
- ¼ **cup thinly sliced scallions (about 2 scallions), divided**
- 4 **tsp. finely chopped pickled daikon or pickled mustard greens, divided**
- 4 **tsp. sweet soy sauce, divided**

1. Toast rice in a dry large saucepan over medium, stirring constantly, until fragrant but not browned, about 4 minutes. Transfer rice to a large metal bowl; stir in 1½ tablespoons oil until evenly coated. Return rice to saucepan, and add 1½ cups water. Bring to a boil over medium-high. Reduce heat to low; cover and cook until water is completely absorbed and rice is tender, about 20 minutes. Remove from heat, and cover to keep warm until ready to use. (Alternatively, place toasted rice and 1½ cups water in a rice cooker. Cook according to manufacturer's instructions. Set aside.)

2. Heat remaining 3 tablespoons oil in a large nonstick skillet over medium-high. Crack eggs into skillet, spacing evenly apart. Season with salt and pepper to taste. Cook until whites are set and beginning to crisp around edges and yolks are still runny, 2 to 3 minutes. Flip eggs, and lightly press on each egg with spatula to break the yolk. Cook until outsides of yolks are set but centers are still soft, 10 to 20 seconds.

Transfer eggs to a plate lined with paper towels to drain. Set aside.

3. Clean skillet, and wipe dry. Pour oil into skillet to a depth of about ½ inch. Heat over medium-high until oil reaches 375°F. Add youtiao, and fry, turning often, until golden brown on all sides, about 2 minutes. Transfer to a plate lined with paper towels to drain. Set aside.

4. Lightly brush a clean work surface (about a 12-inch square) with water. Place a 12-inch square piece of plastic wrap on top of water-coated area. Place about 5 ounces (about ¾ cup) cooked rice in center of plastic wrap; using a wet hand, press rice into a 7- × 6-inch oval with one long side closest to you. Top rice with 1 cooked egg, and lay 1 youtiao piece, lengthwise, on top of egg. Sprinkle with 1 tablespoon pork floss, 1 tablespoon scallions, and 1 teaspoon pickled daikon. Drizzle with 1 teaspoon soy sauce. Using plastic wrap, roll up into a tight log, enclosing the rice around the fillings. Twist ends of plastic wrap to seal rice edges. Using a small paring knife, poke a few holes in plastic wrap to allow air to escape, then roll tighter. Tie both ends of plastic wrap snug against rice to secure; trim excess plastic wrap. Repeat process with remaining rice, eggs, youtiao, pork floss, scallions, pickled daikon, and soy sauce. Cut rolls in half crosswise (leaving wrapped in plastic wrap), and serve. —TRIGG BROWN, WIN SON, BROOKLYN

NOTE Source youtiao at asian-veggies.com and rousong at bokksumarket.com.

NINA'S POTATO SALAD (P. 23)
OPPOSITE: ASPARAGUS AND
SPRING ONION SALAD WITH
SEVEN-MINUTE EGGS (P. 24)

SALADS & SIDES

GREENS, AVOCADO, AND
BLUEBERRY SALAD

Greens, Avocado, and Blueberry Salad

⏱ TOTAL 15 MIN; SERVES 6 TO 8

At her summer home on Martha's Vineyard, food scholar and cookbook author Jessica B. Harris keeps specialty salts and vinegars on hand to bring instant interest to salad dressings. Here, a honey-ginger white balsamic is the backbone of a sweet and fragrant sesame-honey-ginger dressing that adds a mildly piquant kick to the fresh peppery greens and creamy avocado in this colorful side salad. The blueberry-honey sea salt made on Martha's Vineyard is absolutely worth sourcing for both its pleasantly fruity and tart flavor and its stunning purple hue. While these specialty ingredients add an elegant touch, the Food & Wine *test kitchen also came up with a few simple substitutions to make this recipe without them (see Note).*

SESAME-HONEY-GINGER DRESSING

- ¼ cup sesame oil (untoasted)
- ¼ cup honey-ginger white balsamic vinegar (such as LeRoux)
- 1 tsp. herbes de Provence
- ¾ tsp. blueberry-honey sea salt (such as Martha's Vineyard Sea Salt), plus more to taste

SALAD

- 1 (about 3½-oz.) Boston lettuce head, leaves separated (about 4 cups)
- 4 cups loosely packed arugula (about 3 oz.)
- 2 cups loosely packed mizuna (about 2 oz.)
- 1 small red onion (about 6 oz.), thinly sliced (about 1 cup)
- 1 medium avocado (about 6 oz.), chopped into ½-inch pieces (about ¾ cup)
- ¾ cup fresh blueberries (about 4 oz.)

1. Make the sesame-honey-ginger dressing: Whisk together oil, vinegar, herbes de Provence, and salt in a medium bowl until salt is dissolved. Season to taste with additional salt.

2. Make the salad: Toss together lettuce, arugula, mizuna, onion, avocado, and blueberries in a large bowl.

3. Drizzle salad with ⅓ cup dressing, and toss to coat. Drizzle with additional dressing as desired, or serve remaining dressing on the side. —JESSICA B. HARRIS

MAKE AHEAD Dressing can be made up to 2 days in advance.

NOTE Blueberry-honey sea salt can be purchased at mvseasalt.com. Flaky sea salt may be used as a substitute but will not provide the same mild salinity and slight tartness. If you don't have honey-ginger white balsamic vinegar, whisk together 3 tablespoons white balsamic vinegar, 2 teaspoons honey, and 1½ teaspoons grated peeled fresh ginger.

Yountville Caprese Salad

⏱ TOTAL 10 MIN; SERVES 6 TO 8

This simple Italian salad named after the island of Capri is no stranger to a summertime table setting. Sun-ripened farmers market tomatoes are layered with creamy mozzarella and topped with aromatic fresh basil, sweet and tangy balsamic vinegar, and floral lemon zest in this riff on the seasonal favorite.

- 6 medium (5-oz.) heirloom tomatoes
- 2 (8-oz.) fresh mozzarella cheese balls
- 1 tsp. kosher salt
- ½ cup loosely packed fresh basil leaves, thinly sliced
- 3 Tbsp. extra-virgin olive oil
- 2 Tbsp. balsamic vinegar
- 1 lemon
  Freshly cracked black pepper

1. Cut tomatoes and mozzarella in even slices (about ⅜ inch thick). Sprinkle evenly with salt.

2. Arrange tomato and mozzarella slices alternately on a platter. Sprinkle evenly with basil. Drizzle evenly with olive oil and balsamic vinegar. Using a Microplane grater, grate lemon zest directly over tomatoes and mozzarella; reserve zested lemon for another use. Garnish with cracked black pepper. —KERRIN LAZ

MAKE AHEAD Mozzarella can be sliced up to 4 hours in advance and stored in an airtight container in refrigerator. Assemble platter just before serving.

Nina's Potato Salad

PHOTO P. 20

⏱ ACTIVE 15 MIN; TOTAL 30 MIN
SERVES 8 TO 12

"One of our first—and favorite—Horn side dishes is our potato salad," says chef Matt Horn, of his wife Nina's popular recipe. "This is our take on the classic recipe that goes perfectly with barbecue!" This crowd-pleasing side is neither too rich nor too light, hitting the perfect balance of tart and creamy to perfectly complement a smoked brisket.

- 2 lb. 8 oz. red potatoes (unpeeled), cut into ½-inch pieces (about 8 cups)
- 1½ cups mayonnaise
- ¼ cup sweet pickle relish, drained
- 1 Tbsp. kosher salt
- 1 Tbsp. yellow mustard
- 1 tsp. Horn Rub (recipe p. 306)
- 1 tsp. smoked paprika, plus more for garnish
- ¾ tsp. garlic powder
- ¾ tsp. onion powder
- ¼ tsp. black pepper
- ½ cup thinly sliced scallions (from 4 medium scallions), plus more for garnish
- 4 hard-cooked eggs, peeled and chopped

1. Place potatoes in a large saucepan; add salted water to cover by 2 inches, and bring to a boil over high. Reduce heat to low; simmer, partially covered, until potatoes are just cooked through, 8 to 10 minutes. Drain and rinse under cold water. Set aside.

2. Whisk together mayonnaise, relish, salt, mustard, Horn rub, smoked paprika, garlic powder, onion powder, and pepper in a large bowl until well combined.

3. Add potatoes, scallions, and eggs to mayonnaise mixture; stir until well combined. Garnish with additional smoked paprika and scallions. Serve immediately. —MATT HORN

MAKE AHEAD Potato salad can be stored in an airtight container in refrigerator up to 3 days.

Asparagus and Spring Onion Salad with Seven-Minute Eggs

PHOTO P. 21

⟳ ACTIVE 20 MIN; TOTAL 25 MIN; SERVES 4

Spring onions are the sweetest alliums of the year, and they play well in this salad with first-of-the-season asparagus and tender lettuces. Soy and ginger team up with sherry vinegar in the tangy dressing that's perfect with the rich, jammy egg yolks. If spring onions aren't available, you can substitute scallions.

- 2 qt. water
- 2 Tbsp. kosher salt, plus more to taste
- 4 large eggs
- 1 lb. thin to medium asparagus, trimmed and halved crosswise
- 2 small spring onions (about 3 oz.), greens trimmed and thinly sliced crosswise (about ½ cup), bulbs thinly sliced lengthwise (about ½ cup), divided
- ¼ cup plus 2 Tbsp. grapeseed oil
- 3 Tbsp. sherry vinegar
- 2 Tbsp. minced peeled fresh ginger
- 2 tsp. soy sauce
- 3 oz. tender spring lettuces, roughly torn if large (about 6 loosely packed cups)
- Toasted sesame seeds, for garnish
- Whipped feta, ricotta, or labneh, for serving (optional)

1. Fill a large bowl with ice water; set aside. Bring 2 quarts water to a boil in a medium saucepan over medium-high. Stir in salt. Carefully add eggs; cook 7 minutes. Using a slotted spoon, transfer eggs to ice water in bowl.

2. Add asparagus to boiling water; cook over medium-high, stirring occasionally, until crisp-tender, about 2 minutes. Transfer asparagus to ice water with eggs; let cool 3 minutes. Remove eggs, and peel; cut in half lengthwise, and set eggs aside. Drain asparagus, and pat dry; set asparagus aside.

3. Whisk together spring onion greens, oil, vinegar, ginger, and soy sauce in a medium bowl. Toss together spring onion bulbs, spring lettuces, asparagus, and half of dressing (about ½ cup) in a large bowl. Season with additional salt to taste. Top salad with jammy eggs, and garnish with sesame seeds. Serve salad over whipped cheese, if desired. Serve with remaining dressing. —JUSTIN CHAPPLE

WINE Medium-bodied French rosé: 2020 Domaine de Fondrèche Ventoux

Candied Beet Salad with Horseradish-Cashew Cream

ACTIVE 20 MIN; TOTAL 2 HR; SERVES 4

Using a variety of beets, such as red, golden, or Chioggia (sometimes called candystripe), adds stunning color to this vibrant beet salad recipe from London chef Carine Ottou. The beets are cut into wedges and then roasted with garlic and fresh rosemary, which intensifies their earthy sweetness. Nutty and crunchy, the flax, chia, and poppy seed crisps stand in for croutons; soaked and pureed cashews serve as the creamy base of the vegan horseradish sauce that ties the beet salad together.

BEETS

- 2 lb. trimmed multicolored baby beets (from about 3 lb. beets with greens, or 12 to 14 beets), unpeeled, scrubbed, and cut into 1-inch wedges
- 5 unpeeled garlic cloves
- 3 (3-inch) rosemary sprigs
- 1½ tsp. olive oil
- 1¼ tsp. fine sea salt
- ¼ tsp. black pepper

CRISPS

- 2 Tbsp. golden flax seeds or brown flax seeds
- 2 Tbsp. water
- 2 Tbsp. chia seeds
- 1½ Tbsp. poppy seeds
- ⅛ tsp. fine sea salt

CASHEW-HORSERADISH CREAM

- ¾ cup raw cashews, soaked in water at least 1 hour or up to 12 hours
- ¼ cup fresh lemon juice, plus more for serving
- ¼ cup water
- 2 Tbsp. freshly grated horseradish
- 2 Tbsp. apple cider vinegar
- 1 Tbsp. nutritional yeast flakes (optional)
- ¼ tsp. fine sea salt

ADDITIONAL INGREDIENT

Baby salad greens, pea shoots, or torn beet leaves

1. Make the beets: Preheat oven to 350°F. Arrange beets, separated by color, in an even layer in a 13-×9-inch baking pan. Add garlic cloves and rosemary sprigs to pan; drizzle with oil, and sprinkle with salt and pepper. Roast in preheated oven until beets are tender and slightly wrinkled, about 1 hour. Let stand at room temperature until cool, about 45 minutes.

2. Meanwhile, make the crisps: Increase oven temperature to 375°F. Pulse flax seeds in a spice grinder until coarsely ground, 4 to 6 pulses. Stir together ground flax seeds, 2 tablespoons water, chia seeds, poppy seeds, and salt in a large bowl; let stand at room temperature, uncovered, 10 minutes. Spoon mixture onto a baking sheet lined with parchment paper, and top with an additional parchment paper sheet. Roll mixture to ⅛-inch thickness. Remove top parchment sheet. Bake mixture at 375°F until hardened, about 15 minutes. Let cool 15 minutes. Break into about 2-inch pieces.

3. Make the cashew-horseradish cream: Drain soaked cashews. Place cashews, lemon juice, ¼ cup water, horseradish, vinegar, nutritional yeast (if using), and salt in a blender; process until smooth, about 30 seconds.

4. Remove and discard rosemary sprigs from pan with beets. Peel garlic cloves; discard skins. Arrange salad greens on a large platter, and top with beets and garlic. Sprinkle with crisps, and dollop with cashew cream. If desired, sprinkle with additional lemon juice. —CARINE OTTOU

MAKE AHEAD Store leftover cashew-horseradish cream in an airtight container in refrigerator up to 1 week, or freeze up to 6 months.

NOTE Baby beets have a thin skin that gets tender after roasting. If using larger beets, peel before roasting.

CANDIED BEET SALAD WITH
HORSERADISH-CASHEW CREAM

Shaved Beet and Carrot Salad with Citrus-Scallion Dressing

TOTAL 15 MIN; SERVES 4

This gorgeous, colorful salad takes late-winter produce like thinly shaved beets, carrot ribbons, and rounds of juicy clementine and dresses them up for spring with a citrus-scallion vinaigrette so delicious, recipe creator Leah Koenig says, "I sneak it straight from a spoon." Crisp arugula serves as the base for this bright, earthy salad. Topped with nutty almonds and a citrus-scallion dressing balanced with honey, this salad is special enough to serve at a holiday meal (Koenig includes it on her table for Passover, alongside her Chicken, Potatoes, and Leeks with Pine Nut Gremolata) but it is just as delicious as a quick, light lunch.

DRESSING

- 3 medium scallions, roughly chopped (about ½ cup)
- ⅓ cup extra-virgin olive oil
- 2 Tbsp. mild honey
- 2 tsp. Dijon mustard
- 1 tsp. grated lemon zest plus 3 Tbsp. fresh lemon juice (from 1 large lemon)
- ¼ tsp. kosher salt
- ⅛ tsp. black pepper

SALAD

- 1 (5-oz.) container baby arugula
- 2 medium carrots, peeled and shaved into thin strips using a vegetable peeler (about 2 cups)
- 2 small red beets, peeled, trimmed, and very thinly sliced (about 1 cup)
- 4 medium radishes, trimmed and very thinly sliced (about 1 cup)
- 2 medium clementines, peeled and sliced crosswise into ⅛-inch-thick rounds
- ⅓ cup roughly chopped unsalted almonds, toasted
  Flaky sea salt, for garnish

1. Make the dressing: Pulse scallions, oil, honey, mustard, lemon zest and juice, salt, and pepper in a food processor until dressing is creamy and scallions are finely chopped, about 10 pulses, stopping to

scrape down sides as needed. Transfer to a small bowl, and set aside.

2. Make the salad: Arrange arugula on a large, wide salad platter. Layer with carrot strips, beets, radishes, and clementines. Scatter with almonds; drizzle with ⅓ cup dressing. Garnish with flaky sea salt. Serve salad alongside remaining dressing. —LEAH KOENIG

MAKE AHEAD Dressing may be covered and refrigerated up to 2 days.

Niçoise Salad with Sardines

ACTIVE 20 MIN; TOTAL 1 HR; SERVES 4

There's truly no better nor more versatile showcase for spring's bounty than a spin on the classic Niçoise salad. Simple and elegant, it can easily be made vegan or vegetarian, or you can add a good prosciutto or lobster tails for a more indulgent take. This version features sardines, a more sustainable protein than the traditional choice of tuna, but any cooked fish will be delicious.

- ½ cup plus 1 Tbsp. extra-virgin olive oil, divided
- 1 medium shallot, finely chopped (about 3 Tbsp.)
- 3 Tbsp. fresh lemon juice (from 1 lemon)
- 2 Tbsp. Dijon mustard
- 1¼ tsp. kosher salt, divided
- 4 large eggs, at room temperature
- 8 oz. new or baby potatoes, halved if large
- 8 oz. fresh haricots verts (French green beans), trimmed
- 1 (1-lb.) bunch asparagus, woody ends trimmed
- 1 head butter lettuce or other spring lettuce, leaves separated
- 1 (8-oz.) bunch radishes, green tops discarded, radishes cut in half lengthwise
- 1 (6- to 8-oz.) jar or tin sardines in oil
- 1 cup Niçoise olives, pitted
- 2 Tbsp. drained capers
  Crushed red pepper, cracked black pepper, and flaky sea salt, for garnish

1. Preheat oven to 425°F. Bring a medium pot of salted water to a boil over high.

2. While water comes to a boil, whisk together ½ cup oil, shallot, lemon juice, mustard, and 1 teaspoon kosher salt in a medium bowl until well combined. Transfer 6 tablespoons dressing to a small bowl, reserving remaining 6 tablespoons dressing in medium bowl.

3. Prepare an ice bath by filling a large bowl with ice water; set aside. Carefully add eggs to boiling water; cook 6 minutes. Using a slotted spoon, transfer eggs to ice bath. Let stand until completely cooled, about 5 minutes. Remove eggs from ice bath; peel eggs, and set aside.

4. While eggs cool, add potatoes to boiling water; cook until almost tender, about 12 minutes. Add haricots verts to potatoes; cook, stirring occasionally, until potatoes and haricots verts are tender, about 3 minutes. Drain in a fine wire-mesh strainer, and rinse under cold water until cooled, about 1 minute. Transfer potatoes and beans to dressing in medium bowl, and toss to coat; set aside.

5. Spread asparagus evenly on a baking sheet; drizzle evenly with remaining 1 tablespoon oil, and sprinkle evenly with remaining ¼ teaspoon kosher salt. Roast in preheated oven until very lightly charred and tender, about 10 minutes.

6. Cut peeled eggs in half lengthwise. Arrange lettuce leaves in a single layer on a large platter. Arrange potatoes, haricots verts, radishes, eggs, and sardines in loose piles atop lettuce. Drizzle with remaining 6 tablespoons dressing. Top with olives and capers; garnish with crushed red pepper, black pepper, and flaky salt. —LAUREN FRIEL

MAKE AHEAD Dressing can be made up to 5 days ahead and stored, covered, in refrigerator. Eggs can be boiled and kept in their shells in refrigerator up to 2 days ahead.

WINE 2020 Domaine de la Pépière La Pépie Muscadet Sèvre et Maine sur Lie

NIÇOISE SALAD WITH SARDINES

THAI-STYLE BLUEFISH SALAD

Thai-Style Bluefish Salad

ACTIVE 30 MIN; TOTAL 1 HR 10 MIN; SERVES 4

Laap pla duk, a Thai catfish salad, is the inspiration for this flavor-packed dish of flaked bluefish fillets tossed with fish sauce, lime juice, spicy red Thai chiles, and fresh mint and cilantro. Toasted and powdered jasmine rice adds aroma and helps unify the dish, absorbing flavors from the other ingredients. Serve the salad with lettuce leaves, lime wedges, and cooked rice so each diner can assemble their own lettuce wraps. If you can't find bluefish, another fatty fish like mackerel is a good substitute.

FISH

- 6 medium scallions, roots trimmed
- 6 (6-inch) cilantro sprigs
- 1½ lb. skinless bluefish fillets (¾ inch thick)
- ½ tsp. kosher salt
- 2 Tbsp. fresh lime juice

SALAD

- 3 Tbsp. uncooked white jasmine rice
- 6 Tbsp. fresh lime juice (from 3 limes)
- 2 Tbsp. fish sauce
- 2 medium-size fresh red Thai chiles, stemmed and minced (2½ tsp.)
- 1½ tsp. cane sugar
- 1 small red onion (about 5 oz.), halved and thinly sliced lengthwise (about 1¼ cups)
- ½ cup packed fresh cilantro leaves, chopped
- ½ cup packed fresh mint leaves, chopped
- 3 medium scallions, thinly sliced (about ⅓ cup)
- ½ tsp. kosher salt

ADDITIONAL INGREDIENTS

- Cooked white jasmine rice, for serving
- Lettuce leaves, for serving
- Lime wedges, for serving

1. Make the fish: Preheat oven to 350°F. Arrange 3 scallions and 3 cilantro sprigs in a large ceramic baking dish. Arrange fish fillets on top; sprinkle evenly with salt. Place remaining 3 scallions and remaining 3 cilantro sprigs on fish; drizzle with lime juice. Roast in preheated oven until fish flakes easily with a fork, 20 to 25 minutes. Remove from oven; let cool completely, about 15 minutes. Flake fish into small pieces. Discard scallions, cilantro sprigs, and drippings in baking dish.

2. Make the salad: Toast rice in a small skillet over medium, stirring often, until light golden and fragrant, about 5 minutes. Transfer to a spice grinder; let cool about 5 minutes. Grind into a powder. (Alternatively, grind using a mortar and pestle.)

3. Whisk together lime juice, fish sauce, chiles, and sugar in a large bowl. Add fish, onion, cilantro, mint, scallions, salt, and ground toasted rice; stir well. Serve with cooked rice, lettuce leaves, and lime wedges. —JUSTIN CHAPPLE

MAKE AHEAD Bluefish salad can be refrigerated overnight. Let stand at room temperature 15 to 20 minutes, and fold in herbs just before serving.

WINE Dry, lime-inflected Riesling: 2021 Pewsey Vale Dry Riesling

Watermelon Salad with Feta

TOTAL 10 MIN; SERVES 8

Milky, salty feta cheese enhances the floral, sweet, and grassy flavors of juicy watermelon while fresh mint leaves bring a refreshingly cool bite to this simple summer salad. Serve it well chilled to beat the heat, and select a fruity olive oil, such as one made from Arbequina olives, to bring out the honeylike sweetness of the watermelon.

- 1 small seedless watermelon (about 7 lb. 8 oz.)
- ¼ cup extra-virgin olive oil
- ¾ Tbsp. fine sea salt
- ¼ tsp. black pepper
- 7 oz. feta cheese, sliced
- Fresh mint leaves, for garnish

Cut watermelon in half lengthwise; reserve 1 half for another use. Cut remaining watermelon half in half lengthwise. Slice each watermelon quarter into ½-inch-thick wedges (about 16 wedges total). Drizzle watermelon evenly with olive oil, and sprinkle with salt and pepper. Top evenly with feta, and garnish with mint leaves. —JOSH PHELPS

MAKE AHEAD Store sliced watermelon in an airtight container in refrigerator up to 2 days. Top with remaining ingredients just before serving.

Peach Salad

TOTAL 15 MIN; SERVES 4

Spicy chiles and sweet peaches come together in this simple, summery salad. Lemon vinegar and manuka honey lend each bite a sweet-tart zing and silky texture, amplifying the juiciness of fresh peaches. The sweet honey mellows the sharp and punchy lemon vinegar, adding brightness without overpowering the delicate fruit. Long, thin, and vibrantly colored, Holland finger chiles, or Dutch chiles, add a moderate jalapeño-like heat to the fragrant dish. Lean on this stunning salad when peaches are at their prime to showcase the best of summer produce. Freestone peaches, such as July Prince, release cleanly from the pit making slicing a breeze, while clingstone peaches, like Flavorich, are typically smaller, juicier and slightly sweeter but can be more challenging to cut. Top a generous serving with grilled chicken or shrimp for a hearty main course. Infused with peaches and chiles, leftover dressing on the platter makes a great addition to spicy margaritas.

- ⅔ cup lemon vinegar (such as O Citrus Champagne Vinegar) (see Note)
- ⅓ cup manuka honey
- 1 tsp. kosher salt
- 1½ lb. fresh peaches (such as Flavorich or July Prince) (about 4 medium peaches)
- ½ cup blanched raw peanuts (about 2¾ oz.), toasted
- 1 to 2 (½-oz.) fresh Holland finger, cayenne, or red Fresno chiles (to taste), seeded if desired, and thinly sliced (about 3 Tbsp. per chile)
- ¼ cup packed fresh basil leaves (such as Thai, sweet Italian, or African blue basil), larger leaves torn in half
- 1 tsp. flaky sea salt (such as Maldon)

1. Whisk together vinegar, honey, and kosher salt in a large bowl; set aside.

2. Cut peaches in half lengthwise; remove and discard pits. Slice peaches into 1-inch wedges; cut each wedge in half crosswise.

3. Add peaches, peanuts, and chiles to vinaigrette in bowl; toss well to combine and evenly coat. Gently fold in basil. Arrange salad on a platter; sprinkle with flaky salt. —BRANDON CHAVANNES, THE BETTY, ATLANTA

NOTE Lemon vinegar is available online at ooliveoil.com.

Classic Slaw

⏱ TOTAL 20 MIN; SERVES 12

"When you visualize a table loaded with barbecue items, I bet there is a heaping bowl of slaw," says Matt Horn. His slaw recipe is a natural side for smoked meats, with a cooling, creamy, tart-sweet dressing that cuts through the richness of the barbecue. For another pop of color, throw in a shredded carrot or two.

- 1½ cups mayonnaise
- ⅓ cup apple cider vinegar
- 3 Tbsp. honey
- 2 Tbsp. yellow mustard
- 2 tsp. kosher salt, plus more to taste
- 1 tsp. dried dill
- ½ tsp. black pepper, plus more to taste
- 8 cups finely shredded green cabbage (from 1 small [3-lb.] head cabbage)
- 4 cups finely shredded red cabbage (from 1 small [3-lb.] head cabbage)
- 5 medium scallions, thinly sliced (about 1 cup)

Whisk together mayonnaise, vinegar, honey, mustard, salt, dill, and pepper in a large bowl until well combined. Add green cabbage, red cabbage, and scallions; toss to coat. Add additional salt and pepper to taste. Serve immediately. —MATT HORN

MAKE AHEAD Slaw can be stored in an airtight container in refrigerator up to 4 days.

Cherry, Plum, and Black Rice Salad

ACTIVE 25 MIN; TOTAL 1 HR 25 MIN; SERVES 4

Fresh plums and cherries add pops of juicy sweetness to this hearty summer salad. Black rice gives the dish a dark, moody hue and an extra textural bite. The salad builds to a delicious crescendo with its finishing touch: crunchy, craggy, blue cheese–infused breadcrumbs, which provide a lovely textural reprieve to the chewy rice and fruit.

- 2 cups water
- 1 cup uncooked black rice (unrinsed)
- 1 tsp. kosher salt, divided
- 1½ cups chopped baguette, sourdough, or country white bread (about 2 oz.)
- 1 oz. Gorgonzola dolce cheese (about 2 Tbsp.)
- 5 Tbsp. extra-virgin olive oil, divided
- ⅓ cup chopped black walnuts
- 3½ Tbsp. Champagne vinegar
- 1½ Tbsp. honey
- ¼ tsp. black pepper
- ¼ cup finely chopped red onion
- 1 cup halved fresh Bing cherries (from 6 oz. whole pitted cherries)
- 1 cup ¼-inch-thick plum wedges (from 2 [6-oz.] unpeeled plums)

1. Bring 2 cups water, rice, and ¼ teaspoon salt to a boil in a small saucepan over medium-high. Cover, reduce heat to low, and simmer, undisturbed, until water is absorbed, about 35 minutes. Remove from heat. Let stand, covered, 10 minutes.

Uncover and fluff rice with a fork. Spread rice in an even layer on a baking sheet. Let cool completely, about 30 minutes.

2. Meanwhile, preheat oven to 350°F. Line a rimmed baking sheet with parchment paper; set aside. Place bread in a food processor; pulse until pea-size breadcrumbs form, about 12 pulses. Using a rubber spatula, mash together Gorgonzola dolce and 2 tablespoons oil in a medium bowl until smooth. Add breadcrumbs; toss to coat. Stir in walnuts. Spread mixture evenly on prepared baking sheet. Bake in preheated oven until nuts are toasted and bread is golden brown, about 12 minutes, stirring once after 8 minutes. Remove from oven. Let cool completely, about 15 minutes. (Breadcrumbs will become more crisp as they cool.)

3. Whisk together vinegar, honey, pepper, remaining ¾ teaspoon salt, and remaining 3 tablespoons oil in a large bowl; transfer ¼ cup vinegar mixture to a medium bowl. Add rice and onion to vinegar mixture in large bowl; toss to coat. Add cherries and plum wedges to vinegar mixture in medium bowl; toss to coat. Arrange rice mixture on a platter; top with cherry mixture. Sprinkle with ⅓ cup breadcrumb mixture, and serve. —ANN TAYLOR PITTMAN

MAKE AHEAD Prepared rice salad can be stored in an airtight container in refrigerator up to 1 day. Breadcrumbs can be stored in an airtight container at room temperature up to 4 days.

WINE Earthy, natural sparkling wine: 2020 François et Julien Pinon Pétillant-Naturel Brut Rosé

CHERRY, PLUM, AND
BLACK RICE SALAD

BEET AND PEAR SALAD

Beet and Pear Salad

ACTIVE 30 MIN; TOTAL 1 HR 10 MIN; SERVES 4

This crunchy, refreshing salad studded with purple beets, Asian pear, and hazelnuts is complemented by a fragrant dressing of ginger and white miso. "For me, this salad embodies the Japanese saying 'shokuyoku no aki,' meaning 'the appetite of the fall season,' when we look to make dishes a bit heartier and more warming," says chef Shota Nakajima of Taku in Seattle, who shared this recipe with Food & Wine. *"This salad combines the earthy sweetness of beets with the crisp acidity of Asian pear, and the complementary textures of the ingredients will keep you coming back for seconds. Simply dressed with an umami-forward miso-honey dressing and finished with toasted hazelnuts and Parmesan cheese, this dish can incorporate any root vegetables or tree fruits." You can speed up your salad prep by using store-bought sliced cooked beets in place of homemade.*

SALAD

- 2 medium (about 6-oz.) beets
- 2 cups blanched hazelnuts
- 1 Tbsp. olive oil
- 1 Tbsp. shichimi togarashi
- 2 tsp. granulated sugar
- 1 tsp. kosher salt
- 1 large (about 12-oz.) Asian pear
- 10 oz. mizuna (about 10 cups) or arugula
  Shaved Parmesan cheese, for garnish

MISO-HONEY DRESSING

- ½ cup rice vinegar
- ½ cup canola oil
- ¼ cup plus 1 Tbsp. honey
- ¼ cup plus 1 Tbsp. white miso (such as Hikari)
- ¼ cup olive oil
- 1½ tsp. grated peeled fresh ginger (from 1 [2-inch] piece ginger)
- ½ tsp. kosher salt
- 1½ tsp. toasted sesame oil

1. Make the salad: Place beets in a medium saucepan with salted cold water to cover. Bring to a boil over medium-high. Reduce heat to medium to maintain a gentle boil; cook until beets are tender, about 45 minutes. Drain. Let beets cool 10 minutes. Peel beets, and slice using a mandoline into ⅛-inch-thick slices.

2. While beets cook, preheat oven to 350°F. Toss together hazelnuts, olive oil, shichimi togarashi, sugar, and salt on a baking sheet. Spread hazelnuts evenly on sheet. Bake in preheated oven until hazelnuts are lightly toasted and fragrant, 12 to 15 minutes, stirring halfway through bake time. Remove from oven; let cool 5 minutes. Transfer hazelnuts to a cutting board, and roughly chop. Set aside.

3. Peel and core pear; slice crosswise into ¹⁄₁₆-inch-thick slices. Place pear slices in a large bowl filled with lightly salted ice water. Set aside.

4. Make the miso-honey dressing: Process rice vinegar, canola oil, honey, miso, olive oil, ginger, salt, and toasted sesame oil in a blender until smooth, about 30 seconds. Set aside.

5. Drain pear, and pat dry. Toss together mizuna and ¾ cup miso-honey dressing in a large bowl until evenly combined; divide evenly among 4 plates. Top evenly with sliced beets and pear. Drizzle salads evenly with ¼ cup miso-honey dressing. Sprinkle evenly with ¼ cup hazelnuts, reserving remaining hazelnuts for another use. Garnish with shaved Parmesan. Serve with remaining dressing on the side. —SHOTA NAKAJIMA, TAKU, SEATTLE

MAKE AHEAD Dressing can be made up to 3 days in advance and stored in an airtight container in refrigerator.

WINE Melony, crisp white: 2021 Bonny Doon Beeswax Vineyard Picpoul

NOTE Hikari miso paste can be found at Asian grocery stores or online at ratekitchen.com.

Salad of Pink Radicchio, Citrus, and Mushroom Bagna Cauda

⏱ TOTAL 40 MIN; SERVES 8

Melted anchovies and porcini mushroom powder lend a savory depth to nutty brown butter bagna cauda. The sweetness of vibrant Cara Cara oranges mellows the bitter radicchio and adds a pop of color. While this salad is crispy and refreshing, the warmth of the buttery dressing slightly softens the crunchy radicchio leaves and combines with acidic sherry vinegar and orange juice for a balanced bite.

BROWN BUTTER–PORCINI BAGNA CAUDA

½ cup unsalted butter (4 oz.), at room temperature

1 cup extra-virgin olive oil

12 anchovy fillets (from 1 [2-oz.] can), chopped (about 2 Tbsp.)

10 medium garlic cloves, smashed

1 Tbsp. porcini or hen-of-the-woods mushroom powder (see Note)

RADICCHIO SALAD

4 medium-size (6-oz.) Cara Cara oranges or satsuma mandarins

2 medium shallots (about 2¼ oz.), thinly sliced (about ½ cup)

¼ cup sherry vinegar

1 tsp. honey

½ tsp. Himalayan pink salt

1 large (9-oz.) head pink radicchio (La Rosa del Veneto), trimmed and leaves separated

1 large (9-oz.) head Castelfranco radicchio, trimmed and leaves separated

½ tsp. flaky sea salt, plus more to taste

½ tsp. black pepper, divided

2 oz. Parmigiano-Reggiano cheese, shaved (about 1 cup)

1. Make the brown butter–porcini bagna cauda: Melt butter in a small saucepan over medium-low. Cook, stirring occasionally, until butter starts to foam and turn brown, about 8 minutes. Remove from heat, and stir in oil. Let cool slightly, about 1 minute. Return to heat over low; add anchovies and garlic. Cook, stirring occasionally, until garlic softens, about 10 minutes. Add porcini powder, and cook, stirring occasionally, until flavors meld and anchovies melt, about 5 minutes. Remove from heat, and gently mash garlic with a fork to incorporate. Set aside.

2. Make the radicchio salad: Juice 1 orange to yield ¼ cup orange juice. Stir together ¼ cup orange juice, shallots, sherry vinegar, honey, and pink salt in a small bowl. Let stand at room temperature until flavors meld and shallots soften, about 10 minutes.

3. Meanwhile, carefully remove peels from remaining 3 oranges, using a sharp knife to cut along the curve of each orange, removing as little flesh as possible; discard peels. Slice peeled oranges crosswise into ½-inch-thick rounds, and set aside.

4. Place pink radicchio leaves and Castelfranco radicchio leaves in a large bowl. Pour orange juice mixture over radicchio leaves, and toss thoroughly using your hands. Add orange rounds, flaky sea salt, and ¼ teaspoon pepper; gently toss. Season with additional flaky sea salt to taste.

5. Drizzle 3 tablespoons warmed brown butter–porcini bagna cauda evenly over salad. Top evenly with cheese and remaining ¼ teaspoon pepper. Serve salad alongside remaining brown butter–porcini bagna cauda. —EXCERPTED FROM *COOKING WITH MUSHROOMS* BY ANDREA GENTL. ARTISAN BOOKS © 2022

NOTE Mushroom powder adds a rich umami flavor and mild earthiness. Find it at specialty grocery stores or online at thespicehouse.com.

Peanut and Watermelon Chaat

⏱ TOTAL 10 MIN; SERVES 2 TO 4

Every chaat has a little bit of sweetness, a little bit of tartness, a little heat, and a little crunch. This chaat marries the succulent sweetness of watermelon with the hearty crunch and saltiness of peanuts. "It's a very Southern combination that I thought should work," chef Vishwesh Bhatt says. "And it did." Eating watermelon with a sprinkle of salt and a dash of hot sauce is popular in chef Bhatt's hometown of Oxford, Mississippi. This sweet-savory chaat recipe marries that inspiration with a sprinkle of chaat masala, a tangy spice blend often used as a seasoning for fruit in India.

2 tsp. canola oil

1 cup lightly salted roasted peanuts

1 (4-inch) curry sprig

2 tsp. chaat masala, divided

1 cup chopped seedless watermelon (about 5½ oz.)

½ cup thinly sliced cucumber (from 1 small cucumber)

¼ cup finely chopped red onion (from 1 small onion)

¼ cup thinly sliced radishes (from 3 medium radishes)

1 medium-size serrano chile, seeded and finely chopped (about 1½ Tbsp.)

½ tsp. kosher salt

½ tsp. cayenne pepper

2 Tbsp. fresh lime juice (from 1 medium lime)

2 Tbsp. chopped fresh mint

2 Tbsp. chopped fresh basil

2 Tbsp. chopped fresh cilantro

2 Tbsp. cane syrup or sorghum

1. Heat oil in a large skillet over medium-high until shimmering. Add peanuts, curry sprig, and 1 teaspoon chaat masala. Cook, tossing constantly, until well coated and fragrant, about 30 seconds. Set aside to let cool until ready to use.

2. Combine watermelon, cucumber, onion, radishes, serrano, salt, and cayenne in a large bowl, and toss well. Add peanut mixture, lime juice, mint, basil, cilantro, cane syrup, and remaining 1 teaspoon chaat masala. Remove and discard curry sprig. Toss gently and serve. —VISHWESH BHATT

NOTE Chaat masala is available online at spicewallabrand.com.

Soba and Zucchini Salad with Gochujang Dressing

◔ TOTAL 25 MIN; SERVES 4

This soba salad offers bracing heat that's most welcome on a hot day when the coldest beers are at hand. Tender buckwheat noodles and crispy strands of zucchini soak up a pleasantly piquant dressing laced with both gochugaru and gochujang for a double hit of spicy Korean peppers mellowed by a touch of brown sugar. Perfect served chilled or at room temperature, it's an easy make-ahead dish for summer entertaining.

- 8 oz. uncooked soba noodles
- 3 Tbsp. gochujang (see Note)
- 3 Tbsp. rice vinegar
- 2 Tbsp. gochugaru
- 2 Tbsp. light brown sugar
- 2 Tbsp. toasted sesame oil
- ½ tsp. kosher salt
- 1 large garlic clove, grated (about ½ tsp.)
- 3 cups zucchini spirals (about 10 oz.) (from 2 small [6-oz.] zucchini)
- 2 cups thinly sliced red cabbage (from 1 small [2-lb.] head cabbage)
- ½ cup matchstick-cut carrots
- 1 small yellow bell pepper (about 7 oz.), cut into thin strips

1. Bring a large pot of water to a boil over high. Add noodles, and cook according to package directions, being careful not to overcook. Drain and rinse with cold water until noodles are cool. Drain well.

2. Whisk together gochujang, vinegar, gochugaru, brown sugar, sesame oil, salt, and garlic in a large bowl. Add noodles, zucchini, cabbage, carrots, and bell pepper;

toss well to coat. Serve chilled or at room temperature. —ANN TAYLOR PITTMAN

MAKE AHEAD Salad can be prepared up to 1 day in advance and stored in an airtight container in refrigerator.

NOTE Be sure to use real gochujang paste—the miso-thick, glossy-shiny paste sold in tubs in Asian markets. Gochujang sauce, sold in many grocery stores, is thinner and milder and doesn't have as deep a flavor.

Cabbage and Speck Panade

ACTIVE 30 MIN; TOTAL 1 HR 20 MIN; SERVES 6

Tender cabbage is tossed with crispy speck, a cured and smoked ham in this French country stuffing from 2018 F&W Best New Chefs Jess Shadbolt and Clare de Boer of King in New York City. "This Cabbage and Speck Panade is luscious, smoky, and savory," they told us. "It would make a good meal with a leafy salad or an ideal celebratory side, akin to stuffing. The key to good flavor is cooking the speck and rosemary at the start — the pork fat and herbs will flavor the butter and perfume the bread and cream. Allow the panade to sit and settle when it comes out of the oven — it shouldn't be eaten scorching hot. Many like it best the next day!" Pancetta or bacon may also be substituted for the speck.

- ½ cup unsalted butter (4 oz.), divided, plus more for greasing
- 2 oz. Parmesan cheese, grated (about ½ cup), divided
- 1 (1-lb.) head Savoy cabbage, cored and leaves separated
- 10 (6-oz.) speck slices, divided
- 2 large garlic cloves, slivered
- ½ tsp. chopped fresh rosemary
- ½ tsp. black pepper, divided
- 1 (12-oz.) day-old bread loaf (country loaf, pagnotta, or white sourdough), crusts removed and bread torn into 2-inch pieces (about 3 cups)
- 1¼ cups chicken stock
- ¼ cup heavy cream
- Olive oil

1. Preheat oven to 450°F. Grease a 12-inch round frying pan or baking dish with butter, and sprinkle with ¼ cup Parmesan; set aside. Bring a large pot of salted water to a boil over high. Add cabbage leaves; cook until tender, about 3 minutes. Drain and set aside.

2. Cut 5 of the speck slices crosswise into ¼-inch slices; reserve remaining 5 speck slices. Melt ¼ cup butter in a large skillet. When it starts to foam, add garlic, rosemary, and sliced speck; cook, stirring occasionally, until speck is crispy and garlic becomes sticky but before it browns, about 5 minutes. Add cooked cabbage leaves and ¼ teaspoon pepper; cook, stirring occasionally, until cabbage is softened, 4 to 5 minutes. Remove from heat.

3. Combine cabbage mixture and bread pieces in prepared baking dish, using all the cabbage and holding back bread if you have too much. Whisk together stock, cream, and remaining ¼ teaspoon pepper in a measuring cup or small bowl. Pour over the bread-cabbage mixture. Sprinkle with remaining ¼ cup Parmesan. Cut remaining ¼ cup butter into tablespoon-size pieces. Top bread-cabbage mixture evenly with butter pieces. Tuck reserved speck slices attractively on top, and drizzle with olive oil. Bake in preheated oven until nicely browned on top, about 30 minutes. Let stand 5 minutes, and serve. —CLARE DE BOER AND JESS SHADBOLT, KING, NEW YORK CITY

WINE Fragrant, minerally Alto Adige white: 2021 J. Hofstatter Pinot Bianco Weissburgunder

CABBAGE AND SPECK PANADE

**GRILLED PEPPER AND
ONION PANZANELLA WITH
PEPERONCINI VINAIGRETTE**

Grilled Pepper and Onion Panzanella with Peperoncini Vinaigrette

⏱ ACTIVE 35 MIN; TOTAL 40 MIN; SERVES 4

Molly Stevens' panzanella uses grilled sweet peppers and onions in place of tomatoes as the centerpiece of this dinner salad. The charred vegetables are tossed with cubes of grilled bread, drizzled with a peperoncini vinaigrette, and topped with creamy feta and crisp slices of peperoncini, which add pops of flavor and contrasting texture. This is a highly adaptable salad; try incorporating your favorite sweet or hot peppers and grilling other vegetables, such as squash and eggplant planks, alongside the peppers, if you like.

- 10 to 12 oz. rustic bread (such as ciabatta or Pugliese) (from 1 [20-oz.] loaf), sliced 1 inch thick
- 3 small red and/or yellow bell peppers (about 5 oz. each), each cut lengthwise into 4 planks
- 1 large red onion (about 16 oz.), sliced into ½-inch-thick rounds
- ¼ cup plus 1 Tbsp. extra-virgin olive oil, divided, plus more to taste
- 1½ tsp. kosher salt, divided, plus more to taste
- ¼ tsp. black pepper, divided, plus more to taste
- 8 peperoncini, sliced into thin rounds, plus ¼ cup peperoncini brine (from 1 [15-oz.] jar), divided
- 3 oz. feta cheese, crumbled into large pieces (about ½ cup)
- ¼ cup torn fresh basil

1. Preheat grill to medium-high (400°F to 450°F). Brush bread slices, bell peppers, and onion rounds evenly with 2 tablespoons oil, and sprinkle evenly with 1 teaspoon salt and ⅛ teaspoon black pepper. Whisk together peperoncini brine, remaining 3 tablespoons oil, remaining ½ teaspoon salt, and remaining ⅛ teaspoon black pepper in a small bowl; set vinaigrette aside.

2. Arrange bread on unoiled grates; grill, uncovered, until nicely marked and toasted, 2 to 3 minutes per side. Transfer to a cutting board. Grill bell peppers and onion, covered, turning occasionally, until charred and tender, 8 to 10 minutes. Transfer to cutting board.

3. Cut bread into 1-inch cubes, and transfer to a large bowl. Slice bell peppers into thin strips, and separate onion rounds into rings; add to bread in bowl. Toss to combine. Drizzle with peperoncini vinaigrette, and toss again. Add additional salt and black pepper to taste, and add a drizzle of oil if salad seems dry. Top with peperoncini rounds, feta, and basil. Serve panzanella warm or at room temperature.
—MOLLY STEVENS

MAKE AHEAD Salad can be prepared through step 2 up to 2 hours in advance and held at room temperature. Proceed with step 3 just before serving.

WINE Substantial Italian rosé: 2021 Leone de Castris Five Roses Rosato

NOTE Grilling the bread adds a smoky flavor and dries it out, allowing it to absorb the flavorful vinaigrette.

Cheesy Scallion Stuffing with Sesame Seeds

ACTIVE 25 MIN; TOTAL 1 HR 30 MIN, PLUS 12 HR STANDING; SERVES 6 TO 8

Marrying Korean flavors with iconic holiday dressing, cookbook author Eric Kim's incredibly tasty casserole is full of alliums, butter, and cheese, all punctuated with a touch of soy sauce and sesame oil. It echoes the pleasures of eating Korean pajeon (pancakes), white wine–laden cheese fondue, and the crusty top of French onion soup. Want to skip the 12-hour bread drying? See Note for an oven-baked shortcut.

- 1 (1-lb.) sourdough bread loaf
- ¼ cup unsalted butter, plus softened unsalted butter, for greasing
- 1 large (12-oz.) red onion, halved lengthwise and thinly sliced (about 2½ cups)
- 7 large scallions (about 7 oz.), thinly sliced diagonally (about 2 cups)
- 2 medium celery stalks (about 2 oz.), thinly sliced (about 1 cup)
- 1 Tbsp. granulated sugar
- 1 tsp. kosher salt
- 1½ cups turkey stock or vegetable stock
- 6 oz. Parmesan cheese, shredded (about 1½ cups), divided
- ½ cup whole milk
- 2 Tbsp. plus 1 tsp. toasted sesame seeds, divided
- 1 tsp. soy sauce
- 1 tsp. toasted sesame oil
- 2 large eggs, lightly beaten

1. Tear bread into 1- to 2-inch pieces, removing and discarding crusts. (You should have about 9 cups torn bread pieces.) Arrange bread pieces in a single layer on a baking sheet, and let stand at room temperature, uncovered, until bread dries out and becomes crusty, at least 12 hours or up to 24 hours.

2. Preheat oven to 350°F. Lightly grease an 11- × 7-inch baking dish with softened butter; set aside. Melt butter in a large skillet over medium-high. Add onion, scallions, celery, sugar, and salt; cook, stirring occasionally, until vegetables begin to soften slightly but remain bright in color, about 5 minutes. Transfer mixture to a large bowl.

3. Add stock, 1 cup Parmesan cheese, milk, 2 tablespoons sesame seeds, soy sauce, and sesame oil to vegetable mixture, and stir to combine. Add eggs, and gently whisk until mixture is well combined. Add bread pieces, and toss until evenly coated. Let mixture stand at room temperature until bread slightly absorbs excess liquid in bowl, about 10 minutes. Transfer stuffing to prepared baking dish, and top evenly with remaining ½ cup Parmesan cheese and remaining 1 teaspoon sesame seeds.

4. Cover baking dish with aluminum foil, and bake in preheated oven until stuffing mixture is set and liquid is completely absorbed, about 30 minutes. Remove foil, and bake until stuffing is browned and lightly crisp and cheese is melted, 25 to 30 minutes. Let cool 5 minutes, and serve.
—ERIC KIM, *KOREAN AMERICAN: FOOD THAT TASTES LIKE HOME*, PENGUIN RANDOM HOUSE

MAKE AHEAD Assembled stuffing may be covered and stored in refrigerator up to 24 hours. Let stand at room temperature 30 minutes before baking.

NOTE Don't have time to dry your bread for 12 hours? Bake torn bread pieces in a 300°F oven in a single layer on a baking sheet until bread dries out but has not developed any color, 20 to 25 minutes, tossing halfway through baking time. Set bread pieces aside at room temperature until ready to use.

SOUPS & STEWS

SHORT RIB CHILI WITH
PICKLED RED ONION (P. 61)
OPPOSITE: CHILLED
ZUCCHINI SOUP (P. 48)

TIMORESE FISH-AND-
TAMARIND SOUP

Timorese Fish-and-Tamarind Soup

⏱ TOTAL 35 MIN; SERVES 4

This is a vivifying soup, good in warm or cold weather. The chile and ginger gently warm your mouth, while acidic tomatoes and tart tamarind come together in the delicate and fragrant broth, which, while light, is full of flavor and satisfying. The fish gently poaches in the broth during the last minutes of cooking, which infuses both the soup base and the fish itself with aroma and flavor, leaving the fish tender, flaky, and moist.

- 1 lb. boneless, skinless meaty white fish (such as sea bass, cod, or halibut), cut into 1-inch pieces
- 1½ cups plus 1 Tbsp. water, divided
- ¼ cup plus 1½ tsp. Tamarind Water (recipe p. 330), divided
- 1¾ tsp. fine sea salt, divided, plus more to taste
- 3 Tbsp. neutral cooking oil (such as canola or grapeseed oil)
- 2 medium tomatoes (about 10 oz.), stemmed, seeded, and cut into 1-inch pieces
- 1 large shallot (about 2½ oz.), halved lengthwise and thinly sliced (about ½ cup)
- 1 (3½-inch-long) fresh red chile (about ½ oz.), stemmed, shaken to remove seeds, and thinly sliced (about 3 Tbsp.)
- 3 medium garlic cloves, thinly sliced (about 1½ Tbsp.)
- 1 Tbsp. finely chopped peeled fresh ginger
- 5 makrut lime leaves, stemmed and thinly sliced crosswise (about 1 Tbsp.)
- 1 (6-inch) lemongrass stalk
- 1½ cups vegetable stock
- 4 scallions, thinly sliced diagonally (about ⅔ cup)
- ½ cup loosely packed fresh basil leaves, thinly sliced, divided

1. Stir together fish, 1 tablespoon water, 1½ teaspoons tamarind water, and ¼ teaspoon salt in a medium bowl. Set aside.

2. Heat oil in large saucepan over medium. Add tomatoes, shallot, chile, garlic, ginger, lime leaves, and ½ teaspoon salt; cook, stirring often, until mixture is softened and tomatoes are broken down, about 6 minutes. Meanwhile, bruise lemongrass using the back or spine of a chef's knife until softened, and tie into a knot.

3. Add tied lemongrass stalk, stock, scallions, and remaining 1½ cups water to mixture in pan. Bring to a boil over medium-high. Reduce heat to medium-low; simmer, uncovered, stirring occasionally, until flavors meld, about 5 minutes.

4. Stir remaining ¼ cup tamarind water and remaining 1 teaspoon salt into mixture in pan. Stir in fish. Bring soup to a gentle simmer over medium. Reduce heat to medium-low; cook until fish is just cooked through, about 3 minutes. Remove from heat. Stir in about half of the basil (about ¼ cup). Season with additional salt to taste. Remove and discard lemongrass. Ladle soup evenly into 4 bowls. Sprinkle evenly with remaining basil. —LARA LEE

WINE Citrusy coastal Italian white: 2020 Argiolas Costamolino Vermentino di Sardegna

Vichyssoise

ACTIVE 35 MIN; TOTAL 1 HR 15 MIN, PLUS 4 HR CHILLING; SERVES 4

This simple chilled potato soup is packed with buttery, sweet sautéed leeks and pureed for a silky-smooth texture. A swirl of half-and-half adds the perfect amount of richness to cut the starchy potatoes without weighing down the light and creamy vichyssoise. Topped with crunchy garlic croutons, shaved pecorino Romano cheese, and a scattering of sliced scallions, this soup deserves a spot in your summer rotation.

- 3 large (10-oz.) leeks
- ¼ cup unsalted butter (2 oz.)
- 5 cups lower-sodium vegetable broth or chicken broth
- 1 lb. russet potatoes, peeled and chopped (about 2½ cups)
- 2 tsp. kosher salt, plus more to taste
- ½ cup half-and-half
- Black pepper, to taste
- Thinly sliced scallions, garlic croutons, and shaved pecorino Romano cheese, for garnish

1. Trim and discard root ends from leeks. Trim and discard the dark green tops, reserving the white and light green parts of the leeks. Halve leeks lengthwise; rinse them, inside and out, under cool water. Pat leeks dry, and thinly slice crosswise. (You should have about 7 cups sliced leeks.)

2. Melt butter in a large saucepan over medium. Add leeks, and stir to coat in butter; cook, stirring often, until leeks are softened but have not developed any color, about 8 minutes.

3. Add broth, potatoes, and salt to leek mixture; bring to a simmer over medium. Reduce heat to low; simmer, uncovered, until potatoes are tender, about 30 minutes. Remove from heat. Let cool slightly, about 10 minutes.

4. Working in batches if needed, pour leek mixture into a blender. Secure lid on blender, and remove center piece to allow steam to escape. Place a clean towel over opening. Process until completely smooth, about 1 minute. Transfer soup to a heatproof bowl, and refrigerate, covered, until completely cold, at least 4 hours or up to 24 hours. Remove soup from refrigerator, and stir in half-and-half. Taste soup, and season with salt and pepper to taste. Divide soup evenly among 4 bowls. Garnish with scallions, croutons, and pecorino Romano cheese. —MARY-FRANCES HECK

MAKE AHEAD Soup may be kept chilled up to 1 day.

WINE Citrusy, tart French white: 2021 Domaine Delaporte Sancerre

Mashhurda (Mung Bean and Vegetable Soup)

ACTIVE 1 HR 15 MIN; TOTAL 1 HR 30 MIN
SERVES 6

League of Kitchens cooking instructor Damira Inatullaeva learned to make this delectable mung bean soup recipe from her Tajik mother-in-law, who makes it without meat (traditional mashhurda includes beef or lamb) and also uses dried apricots for a flavorful twist. Don't let the list of simple ingredients fool you—this is one of the most complex and delicious vegetarian soups we've ever tasted. The fresh herbs, pepper, and labneh at the finish take it over the top.

- 9 cups water
- 1 cup dried mung beans
- ⅓ cup uncooked Turkish baldo rice
- ¼ cup sunflower oil
- 1 medium-size yellow onion, chopped (about 1¾ cups)
- 1 large carrot, cut into ¼-inch cubes (about ½ cup)
- 2 Tbsp. tomato sauce
- 4 fresh or dried bay leaves
- 2 tsp. table salt, divided
- 2½ cups chopped fresh cilantro leaves and tender stems, divided
- 1¾ cups chopped fresh tender dill fronds, divided
- ¾ cup dried Turkish apricots (preferably unsulfured or organic) (about 5 oz.)
- ½ cup plus 1 Tbsp. labneh or Greek-style yogurt
- ½ tsp. black pepper

1. Bring 9 cups water to a boil in a large saucepan over medium-high. Reduce heat to maintain a simmer.

2. Place mung beans in a small saucepan; add enough cold water to cover. Bring to a boil over high. Reduce heat to medium, and simmer about 6 minutes to remove any small particles and dirt. Drain beans in a colander, and transfer to a fine wire-mesh strainer. Rinse under cool water. Set aside.

3. Place rice in a separate fine wire-mesh strainer, and rinse under cold water until water runs clear. Set aside.

4. Pour oil into a large saucepan; heat over medium-high until shimmering, about 1 minute. Add onion, and cook, stirring occasionally, until onion starts to soften, 1 to 2 minutes. Add carrot, and cook, stirring occasionally, until carrot starts to soften, about 2 minutes. Add tomato sauce, and cook, stirring constantly, until vegetables are well coated and sauce thickens slightly, about 2 minutes. Add 1½ cups of the hot water, and cook, stirring occasionally, until mixture comes to a boil, about 30 seconds. Add 1½ cups hot water, rinsed beans, bay leaves, and 1 teaspoon salt, and return to a boil over medium-high. Reduce heat to medium-low, and simmer, covered, stirring occasionally, 10 minutes.

5. If beans are barely covered with water, add ½ cup hot water. Cover and cook over medium-low, stirring occasionally, until beans have fully softened and are starting to break apart, 10 to 25 minutes, adding hot water, ½ cup at a time, as needed so that water barely covers beans.

6. Add rice, 2 cups cilantro, 1½ cups dill, 2½ cups hot water, and remaining 1 teaspoon salt to bean mixture. Increase heat to medium-high, and cook, stirring constantly, until mixture comes to a boil. Cover and reduce heat to medium-low. Cook, stirring often and adjusting heat as needed to make sure nothing sticks on bottom of pan, until rice is soft and tender, 18 to 20 minutes.

7. Check water level in bean mixture; add ½ cup to 1 cup hot water, if needed, until mixture resembles a thick soup but not quite a stew. Add apricots, and cook over low, stirring often, until apricots have softened but are not completely broken down, about 5 minutes. Cover pan, and remove from heat. Let stand 10 minutes for flavors to meld.

8. Uncover soup. Remove and discard bay leaves. Ladle soup evenly into 6 bowls, and mound about 1 tablespoon cilantro and about 2 teaspoons dill into middle of each bowl. Dollop servings with yogurt, and sprinkle with pepper. —DAMIRA INATULLAEVA

MAKE AHEAD This soup is best served the day it's made; to reheat, add a little water, and cook very gently to avoid overcooking the apricots.

WINE Full-bodied, lightly peppery white: 2018 Rousset Crozes-Hermitage

NOTE Find Turkish apricots and baldo rice at kalustyans.com.

MASHHURDA (MUNG BEAN
AND VEGETABLE SOUP)

HERB GARDEN MATZO BALL SOUP

Herb Garden Matzo Ball Soup

ACTIVE 40 MIN; TOTAL 2 HR 30 MIN
SERVES 6

Matzo ball soup gets a glow-up in this version by cookbook author Leah Koenig, with fresh parsley, dill, chives, and fennel fronds in the matzo balls themselves, plus more herbs, lemon zest, and edible flowers adding color and bright, spring flavors to each finished bowl of soup.

MATZO BALLS

- 4 large eggs, lightly beaten
- 1 cup matzo meal
- ¼ cup seltzer
- ¼ cup neutral vegetable oil
- 2 Tbsp. finely chopped mixed fresh herbs (such as parsley, dill, chives, and fennel fronds)
- 1 tsp. kosher salt

SOUP

- 12 oz. medium carrots, peeled, divided
- 1 (3½-lb.) whole chicken, cut into 8 pieces
- 1 lb. medium-size yellow onions, halved lengthwise
- 1 medium (about 13-oz.) fennel bulb, quartered, ¼ cup packed fennel fronds reserved
- 2 large celery stalks, trimmed and halved crosswise
- ¼ cup loosely packed fresh flat-leaf parsley sprigs
- 6 medium garlic cloves, smashed
- 2 fresh or dried bay leaves
- 10 cups cold water
- 1 Tbsp. plus 1 tsp. kosher salt, plus more to taste
- 1 tsp. black pepper, plus more to taste

ADDITIONAL INGREDIENTS

- ½ cup packed fresh flat-leaf parsley leaves
- ½ cup packed fresh dill fronds
- ¼ cup sliced fresh chives
- 1 Tbsp. grated lemon zest (from 1 large lemon)
- Edible flowers (optional)

1. Make the matzo balls: Stir together eggs, matzo meal, seltzer, oil, chopped mixed herbs, and salt in a large bowl. Cover and refrigerate 30 minutes.

2. Meanwhile, bring a Dutch oven filled with generously salted water to a boil over medium-high. Reduce heat to medium-low to maintain a simmer while you shape the matzo balls.

3. Using lightly moistened hands, scoop out chilled matzo mixture by heaping tablespoonfuls, and roll into balls, carefully adding each ball to simmering water after you shape it. (You will have 18 to 20 balls total.)

4. Cover Dutch oven; simmer matzo balls until tender and puffed, 45 to 55 minutes. To test for doneness, remove 1 matzo ball from water, and cut in half. It should be uniformly pale in color throughout. Remove from heat. Remove matzo balls from water, and transfer to a plate. Let cool 30 minutes. Proceed with making soup, or refrigerate matzo balls in an airtight container up to 1 day.

5. Make the soup: While matzo balls cook, cut 2 carrots in half crosswise, and place in a large stockpot. Add chicken, onions, fennel bulb, celery, parsley sprigs, garlic, and bay leaves to stockpot. Cover with 10 cups cold water. Bring to a boil over high. Reduce heat to medium-low, and gently simmer, partially covered, until chicken is very tender and falling off the bone, about 1 hour and 30 minutes, occasionally skimming any foam that accumulates. Soup should maintain a very gentle simmer; if it starts to bubble too vigorously, nudge the heat down a little.

6. While soup cooks, cut remaining carrots into thin (1½- × ¹⁄₁₆- × ¹⁄₁₆-inch) julienned strips. Set aside.

7. Remove chicken from stock mixture; transfer to a cutting board, and let stand until cool to the touch, about 10 minutes. Meanwhile, place a fine wire-mesh strainer over a large heatproof bowl; pour stock mixture through strainer. Discard solids. Return strained stock to stockpot; stir in salt and pepper. Add julienned carrot strips. Bring mixture to a simmer over medium-low. Simmer, covered, until carrots are tender, about 10 minutes.

8. Remove and discard chicken skin and bones from meat. Shred meat into bite-size pieces. Return shredded chicken to stockpot, and return to a simmer over medium-low. Simmer until warmed through, about 2 minutes. Season with additional salt and pepper to taste.

9. Place parsley leaves, dill fronds, chives, lemon zest, and reserved fennel fronds on a cutting board; roughly chop mixture, leaving some larger pieces intact.

10. Place 3 or 4 matzo balls in each of 6 bowls; top evenly with soup. Generously scatter bowls with herb mixture. If desired, decorate with a few edible flowers. Serve immediately. —LEAH KOENIG

MAKE AHEAD Cooled matzo balls can be stored in an airtight container in refrigerator up to 1 day.

WINE Floral sparkling wine: NV Freixenet Excelencia Kosher Brut Cava

Chilled Zucchini Soup

PHOTO P. 40

ACTIVE 30 MIN; TOTAL 2 HR 45 MIN
SERVES 2 TO 4

"This recipe came about as a happy accident, when my nephew mistook zucchini for cucumbers when we were making a cold cucumber soup," chef Vishwesh Bhatt says of the origins of this dish. More than a decade later, he stands by the result, which has a tangy buttermilk broth that gets subtle vegetal sweetness and a wonderfully smooth, creamy texture from the zucchini. Small, tender zucchini are perfect for this soup. If you're using bigger ones, remove the seeds.

SOUP

- 1 medium-size fresh poblano chile (about 3 oz.)
- 2 Tbsp. neutral cooking oil (such as canola oil)
- ½ cup chopped yellow onion (from 1 small onion)
- ½ cup chopped fennel (from 1 medium fennel bulb)
- 3 medium garlic cloves, finely chopped (about 1 Tbsp.)
- 5 cups chopped zucchini
- 3 cups vegetable stock
- 1 cup buttermilk
- 2 Tbsp. chopped fresh mint
- 1 Tbsp. fresh lemon juice (from 1 small lemon)
- 1 tsp. kosher salt, plus more to taste

VAGHAR (GARNISH)

- 2 Tbsp. neutral cooking oil
- 1 tsp. brown mustard seeds
- 2 whole star anise
- 1 chile de árbol, broken in half
- 1 (4-inch) curry sprig

1. Make the soup: Preheat oven to broil with rack 6 inches from heat. Line a rimmed baking sheet with aluminum foil. Place poblano on prepared baking sheet. Broil in preheated oven until skin is charred all over, about 10 minutes, turning occasionally using tongs. Remove from oven; transfer poblano to a medium bowl. Cover with plastic wrap, and set aside 10 minutes to steam. Transfer poblano to a cutting board; peel off and discard skin. Remove and discard seeds and stem. Chop poblano, and set aside.

2. Heat oil in a Dutch oven or heavy-bottomed pot over medium. Add onion, fennel, and garlic; cook, stirring occasionally, until onion is turning golden and fennel has softened, about 10 minutes. Add zucchini and chopped poblano; cook, stirring constantly, until zucchini starts to sweat, about 2 minutes. Add stock; bring to a simmer over medium. Cover and cook until zucchini is tender, about 10 minutes. Remove from heat. Stir in buttermilk, mint, lemon juice, and salt. Let cool slightly, about 10 minutes. Using an immersion blender, process mixture until completely smooth, about 45 seconds. Chill until cold, at least 2 hours or up to 6 hours.

3. Make the vaghar: Heat oil in a small skillet over medium-high. Add mustard seeds; cook, tossing constantly, until seeds start to pop, 15 to 20 seconds. Add star anise, chile de árbol, and curry sprig; cook, tossing and swirling constantly, until curry leaves start to crackle and wilt, about 1 minute. Pour hot mixture onto soup. Stir, add additional salt to taste, and serve.
—VISHWESH BHATT

MAKE AHEAD Soup can be prepared through step 2 up to 6 hours in advance.

WINE Bright. light-bodied red: 2020 Louis Jadot Beaujolais-Villages

NOTE Serve soup chilled in the summer and hot in the winter.

Chicken Soup with Ginger and Cilantro

ACTIVE 35 MIN; TOTAL 1 HR 40 MIN;
SERVES 6

This seasonal twist on a classic is loaded with summer market finds like tomatoes, zucchini, and bell peppers. Quick-cooking boneless chicken pieces are gently simmered in a ginger-and-cilantro-infused broth.

- 1 lb. boneless, skinless chicken breasts or thighs
- 12 cups homemade or lower-sodium chicken broth
- 2 bunches fresh cilantro, stems only (about 1 cup packed stems), leaves reserved for garnish
- 3 medium scallions (about 1½ oz.), cut in half
- 1 (3-inch) piece fresh ginger (unpeeled), sliced
- 2 tsp. kosher salt, plus more if desired
- 1 medium (9-oz.) zucchini, quartered lengthwise and cut into ¼-inch-thick slices (about 2 cups)
- ¾ cup chopped (½-inch pieces) red bell pepper (from 1 medium [8-oz.] bell pepper)
- 1 small (6-oz.) tomato, roughly chopped (about 1 cup)
- Soy sauce or fish sauce (optional)
- 4 cups loosely packed mixed tender fresh herbs (such as basil, cilantro, shiso, scallions, chives, and tarragon)
- Sliced fresh jalapeños or other chiles, thinly sliced red onion or shallot, and lemon, lime, and orange wedges, for garnish

1. Combine chicken pieces, broth, cilantro stems, scallions, ginger, and salt in a large saucepan; bring to a simmer over medium-high. Reduce heat to medium to maintain a gentle simmer. Simmer, undisturbed, until chicken is cooked through and is easily shredded, 30 to 40 minutes. Transfer chicken pieces to a plate. Let chicken stand until cool enough to handle, about 5 minutes, then shred into bite-size pieces; set aside. While chicken is cooling, increase heat under pan to medium-high, and bring broth mixture to a boil. Boil, undisturbed, until liquid has reduced by one-third, about 15 minutes. Remove from heat. Let cool slightly, about 3 minutes. Pour through a fine wire-mesh strainer into a large heatproof bowl; discard solids.

2. Wipe pan clean; return strained broth mixture to pan. Bring to a simmer over medium. Stir in zucchini and bell pepper; cook, undisturbed, until vegetables are tender, about 6 minutes. Stir in tomato and shredded chicken; cook, undisturbed, until warmed through, about 2 minutes. Season soup to taste with soy sauce or fish sauce and additional salt as desired.

3. Arrange mixed herbs, jalapeños, red onion, and citrus wedges on a platter. Divide hot soup evenly among 6 bowls, and serve alongside aromatic garnishes. —MARY-FRANCES HECK

MAKE AHEAD Soup can be prepared through step 1 up to 2 days ahead. Chill chicken and broth separately in airtight containers.

WINE Crisp, tangy white: 2020 Hugues Beauvignac Picpoul de Pinet

Borscht with Buttermilk and Grated Cucumber

ACTIVE 10 MIN; TOTAL 2 HR 40 MIN SERVES 8

Packed with fresh summer herbs, this chilled beet soup is bright, earthy, and doesn't require turning on your stove. Grated beets are quickly marinated in a pickle juice brine to mellow their earthiness before they are stirred together with grated cucumber and buttermilk for a crisp, cooling bite. The topping of quartered hard-cooked eggs, generous dollops of sour cream, and fresh herbs add textural interest, color, and heft as they help make each bowl a satisfying meal.

- 2 lb. peeled cooked red beets
- ½ cup dill pickle juice
- 2 Tbsp. granulated sugar
- 1 Tbsp. plus 2 tsp. kosher salt, divided, plus more to taste
- 1 large cucumber (about 12 oz.), peeled, halved lengthwise, and seeded
- 1 cup cold water
- ½ cup chopped scallions (from 4 large scallions), plus more for garnish
- ¼ cup finely chopped fresh dill, plus more for garnish
- 1 Tbsp. fresh lemon juice (from 1 lemon)
- 1½ tsp. black pepper, plus more to taste
- 4 cups buttermilk
- 8 hard-cooked eggs, peeled and quartered lengthwise
- 1 cup sour cream
- Chopped fresh herbs (such as chives or flat-leaf parsley), for serving

1. Using large holes of a box grater, grate beets into a large bowl. Add pickle juice, sugar, and 1 tablespoon salt; toss to combine. Let stand at room temperature, uncovered, until flavors meld, about 30 minutes.

2. Using large holes of a box grater, grate cucumber into beet mixture in bowl. Add 1 cup cold water, scallions, dill, lemon juice, pepper, and remaining 2 teaspoons salt; gently stir until mixture is combined. Add buttermilk in 2 additions, gently stirring and folding until soup turns fuchsia and is evenly colored. Stir in additional salt and pepper to taste. (The soup should be assertively seasoned.)

3. Refrigerate soup, covered, until very cold, at least 2 hours or up to 3 days. Serve topped with hard-cooked eggs, sour cream, chopped fresh herbs, and additional scallions and dill. —MARY-FRANCES HECK

MAKE AHEAD Soup can be made up to 1 day ahead and stored in an airtight container in refrigerator.

WINE Light, fruity red: 2020 Louis Jadot Beaujolais-Villages

NOTE Use whole-fat buttermilk for extra richness. Look for pre-cooked beets in the refrigerated produce section. Rub cooked beets with a paper towel to easily remove their skins.

White Asparagus Soup with Pickled Ramps and Hazelnuts

TOTAL 1 HR; SERVES 6

Winemaker and restaurateur André Mack's silky white asparagus soup is buttery and creamy with a mild sweetness from the asparagus and a touch of acidity from the pickled ramps that brightens the entire dish. Roasted hazelnuts and hazelnut oil lend a deliciously nutty body to the soup and make a beautiful garnish. If ramps are out of season, spring onions make a good substitute here. Straining the soup thoroughly is key to its final, silken texture.

PICKLED RAMPS

- 8 oz. fresh ramps or spring onions
- ⅔ cup white vinegar
- ½ cup water
- 3 Tbsp. granulated sugar

SOUP

- 4 cups water
- 1 Tbsp. plus 1 tsp. kosher salt, divided
- 4 lb. fresh white asparagus (about 4 bunches), trimmed
- ½ cup unsalted butter (4 oz.)
- 2 cups whole milk
- 2 cups heavy cream
- ¼ oz. whole mace (5 to 7 pieces)
- 1 Tbsp. ramp vinegar (from Pickled Ramps)
- 1 Tbsp. white soy sauce
- 2 Tbsp. chopped roasted hazelnuts
- 2 tsp. hazelnut oil

1. Make the pickled ramps: Remove greens from ramps, and reserve for another use. Trim white root ends of ramps. Place trimmed ramps in a medium-size heatproof bowl or a rimmed heatproof dish; set aside. Combine vinegar, ½ cup water, and sugar in a small saucepan; bring to a boil over medium-high. Cook, stirring constantly, until sugar has dissolved, about 30 seconds. Remove from heat; pour over ramps in bowl. Cover and refrigerate.

2. Make the soup: Fill a large bowl with ice water; set aside. Place 4 cups water and 1 tablespoon salt in a small saucepan; bring to a boil over high. Cut off tips from asparagus. Add asparagus tips to boiling water. Cook until crisp-tender, about 2 minutes. Drain. Transfer asparagus tips to ice water; let stand 5 minutes to stop cooking process. Drain again, and set aside.

3. Thinly slice asparagus stems. Melt butter in a Dutch oven over medium-high. Add asparagus stems; cook, stirring occasionally, until tender and liquid from asparagus is almost evaporated, about 10 minutes. Add milk, cream, and mace; bring to a simmer. Simmer, stirring occasionally, until asparagus has completely softened, about 10 minutes. Remove from heat; discard mace.

4. Transfer mixture to a blender. Secure lid on blender, and remove center piece to allow steam to escape. Place a clean towel over opening. Process until completely smooth, about 45 seconds. Place a fine wire-mesh strainer over small saucepan. Pour some of the asparagus mixture into strainer, stirring to strain asparagus soup into saucepan. Discard strained solids, and rinse strainer well. Repeat straining process until all soup has been strained. Add ramp vinegar, white soy sauce, and remaining 1 teaspoon salt; stir to combine.

5. Cut pickled ramps in half lengthwise, and chop crosswise into about ¼- to ½-inch pieces. Ladle soup evenly into 6 bowls (about 1 cup each). Sprinkle bowls evenly with chopped hazelnuts and asparagus tips. Garnish with pickled ramps; reserve remaining pickled ramps for another use. Drizzle soup evenly with hazelnut oil. —ANDRÉ MACK

WINE 2020 Maison Noir Wines New Noir

NOTE Sweeter in flavor and lighter in color than regular soy sauce, white soy sauce can be ordered from igourmet.com.

Easy Chicken and Dumplings

ACTIVE 20 MIN; TOTAL 1 HR 20 MIN; SERVES 4

This satisfying one-pot meal of silky chicken and tender dumplings starts with searing chicken thighs to render fat to cook the mirepoix in, building a flavorful base for this classic dish. Self-rising flour, buttermilk, and butter are the only ingredients in the pillowy dumplings, which come together in the final minutes, cooking right in the creamy soup.

- 4 bone-in, skin-on chicken thighs (about 1½ lb.)
- 2 tsp. kosher salt, divided
- ¾ tsp. black pepper, divided, plus more for garnish
- 1 medium-size (9-oz.) yellow onion, chopped (about 1 cup)
- 2 medium carrots (about 6 oz.), peeled and cut into ¼-inch-thick rounds (about 1 cup)
- 2 large celery stalks (about 5 oz.), chopped (about 1⅓ cups)
- ¼ cup all-purpose flour
- 6 cups water
- 1 Tbsp. jarred chicken stock base (such as Better Than Bouillon)
- 1 small bunch thyme sprigs, tied with kitchen twine, plus fresh thyme leaves for garnish
- 1½ cups self-rising flour (about 6 oz.)
- ¾ cup buttermilk
- 2 Tbsp. unsalted butter, melted

1. Sprinkle chicken thighs evenly with 1 teaspoon salt and ½ teaspoon pepper. Place chicken, skin side down, in a medium Dutch oven; cook over medium-high, undisturbed, until skin is browned and crisp, about 10 minutes. Transfer chicken to a plate, reserving drippings in Dutch oven.

2. Add onion, carrots, and celery to Dutch oven. Cook over medium-high, stirring often, until just softened, about 6 minutes. Add all-purpose flour, and cook, stirring constantly, 30 seconds. Stir in 6 cups water, stock base, and thyme sprigs. Return chicken to Dutch oven; bring to a boil over medium-high. Reduce heat to medium-low, and gently boil, stirring occasionally, until vegetables are tender and a thermometer inserted in thickest portion of chicken registers at least 165°F, about 15 minutes. Remove chicken from Dutch oven (keep Dutch oven over medium-low heat), and transfer to a cutting board; let cool 5 minutes. Shred chicken, discarding skin and bones. Remove thyme from Dutch oven; discard. Return shredded chicken to Dutch oven. Stir in remaining 1 teaspoon salt and remaining ¼ teaspoon pepper.

3. Stir together self-rising flour, buttermilk, and butter in a medium bowl until batter is just combined. Bring soup to a boil over medium-high. Drop batter by heaping tablespoonfuls into boiling soup. Cover and reduce heat to medium. Cook, undisturbed, until dumplings are cooked through, about 18 minutes. Garnish with additional pepper and thyme leaves. —ANNA THEOKTISTO

WINE 2019 Au Bon Climat Santa Barbara County Chardonnay

Shrimp Bisque

ACTIVE 35 MIN; TOTAL 1 HR 15 MIN
SERVES 6 TO 8

Sautéed shrimp shells impart a sweet complexity to the foundation of this deeply flavorful bisque. White rice is slowly simmered in the aromatic broth and then pureed to give the soup body and a velvety consistency, without masking the flavor of succulent shrimp. Serve with chopped steamed shrimp and a crusty baguette.

- ½ cup unsalted butter (4 oz.), divided
- 3 large (4-oz.) plum tomatoes, cored and chopped (about 2 cups)
- 1 large (12-oz.) yellow onion, chopped (about 2 cups)
- 1 medium (4-oz.) carrot, peeled and chopped (about ½ cup)
- 1 medium (1½-oz.) celery stalk, chopped (about ½ cup)
- 6 cups uncooked shrimp shells (about 5½ oz.), crab shells, or lobster shells
- ½ cup uncooked white rice (preferably basmati)
- 2 Tbsp. tomato paste
- ½ cup (4 oz.) brandy
- 6 (6-inch) flat-leaf parsley sprigs
- 6 (6-inch) thyme sprigs
- 1 fresh or dried bay leaf
- 9 cups water
- 3½ tsp. kosher salt, plus more to taste
- ½ cup heavy cream
- 1 Tbsp. plus 1 tsp. fresh lemon juice (from 1 lemon), plus more to taste
- 1 tsp. black pepper, plus more to taste
- ⅛ tsp. cayenne pepper, plus more to taste
- Crème fraîche
- Chopped fresh chives (optional)
- Paprika, cayenne pepper, or Old Bay seasoning, for garnish

1. Melt ¼ cup butter in a large stockpot over medium. Add tomatoes, onion, carrot, and celery; cook, covered, stirring occasionally, until vegetables are soft, about 7 minutes. Increase heat to high, and add shrimp shells and rice; cook, stirring often, until shells turn deep red, 2 to 3 minutes. Stir in tomato paste; cook, stirring often, until browned, about 2 minutes. Remove from heat, and stir in brandy. Return to heat over high, and cook, stirring occasionally, until liquid has almost evaporated, 2 to 3 minutes.

2. Tie together parsley, thyme, and bay leaf using kitchen twine to make a bouquet. Add herb bouquet, 9 cups water, and 2 teaspoons salt to mixture in pot; bring to a boil over high. Reduce heat to medium-low; cover and simmer 30 minutes. Remove from heat. Uncover and let cool briefly, about 10 minutes.

3. Remove and discard herb bouquet from soup mixture. Working in 2 batches, pour soup mixture into a blender. Secure lid on blender, and remove center piece to allow steam to escape. Place a clean towel over opening. Process until completely smooth, about 1 minute. Pour through a fine wire-mesh strainer into a 6-quart saucepan; discard solids.

4. Bring bisque in saucepan to a low simmer over medium. Whisk in cream, lemon juice, black pepper, cayenne pepper, remaining ¼ cup butter, and remaining 1½ teaspoons salt until smooth and well combined. Adjust seasoning with additional salt, lemon juice, black pepper, and cayenne pepper to taste.

5. Divide bisque evenly among bowls. Garnish with crème fraîche, chives, and paprika, cayenne pepper, or Old Bay seasoning, as desired. —MARY-FRANCES HECK

MAKE AHEAD Soup can be prepared through step 3 and refrigerated in an airtight container up to 2 days.

WINE Herbal, zesty Sauvignon Blanc: 2021 Massican Napa Valley

NOTE Two pounds of shell-on large shrimp yield about 6 cups shrimp shells.

SHRIMP BISQUE

SINIGANG NA HIPON

Sinigang na Hipon

ACTIVE 35 MIN; TOTAL 1 HR 35 MIN;
SERVES 4

Sinigang is a soup from the Philippines with a tangy broth, often made using sour fruit like tamarind or unripe guava. For her sinigang na hipon (prawn sinigang) chef Melissa Miranda uses fresh grapefruit and lemon juice for the sour notes in the full-bodied fish broth.

SINIGANG BROTH

- 1 (33.8-oz.) pkg. fish broth (such as Aneto)
- 2 medium-size plum tomatoes (about 8 oz.), quartered lengthwise
- 1 small (6-oz.) yellow onion, peeled and halved lengthwise
- 1 (1-inch) piece fresh ginger, peeled and thinly sliced
- 4 medium garlic cloves, smashed
- 1 small (11-oz.) red grapefruit
- 1½ Tbsp. fish sauce, plus more to taste
- 1 tsp. fresh lemon juice (from 1 lemon)
- Fine sea salt, to taste

ADDITIONAL INGREDIENTS

- 12 deveined unpeeled head-on raw large Argentinean prawns (about 1½ lb.) or 1½ lb. deveined unpeeled head-on raw extra-large shrimp
- 1 Tbsp. seasoning salt (such as Johnny's Fine Foods)
- 1 Tbsp. canola oil, divided
- 12 medium shishito peppers (about 3 oz.)
- Small fresh cilantro leaves and thinly sliced watermelon radish, for serving

1. Make the sinigang broth: Bring fish broth, tomatoes, onion, ginger, and garlic to a boil in a medium saucepan over medium. Reduce heat to medium-low; simmer, uncovered, until flavors meld and liquid has reduced to about 3¼ cups (about 6¾ cups including solids), about 45 minutes.

2. Using a Y-shaped peeler, remove grapefruit peel in 6 to 8 long strips. Cut grapefruit in half crosswise, and squeeze to yield ½ cup juice. Discard squeezed grapefruit. Remove broth mixture from heat, and add grapefruit juice and peel strips. Let mixture stand 10 minutes. Pour mixture through a fine wire-mesh strainer set over a medium-size heatproof bowl;

discard solids. Return strained broth to saucepan; stir in fish sauce and lemon juice. Add salt and additional fish sauce to taste. Cover and keep warm over low.

3. Preheat grill to medium-high (400°F to 450°F). Toss together prawns, seasoning salt, and 2 teaspoons oil in a medium bowl. Toss together shishito peppers and remaining 1 teaspoon oil in a separate medium bowl. Arrange prawns and shishito peppers on unoiled grates; grill, uncovered, turning occasionally, until prawns are cooked through and peppers are lightly charred and tender, about 4 minutes per side. (Prawn shells will start to release from the meat when they're cooked through.)

4. Divide sinigang broth evenly among 4 bowls. Arrange 3 prawns and 3 shishito peppers in each bowl. Garnish with cilantro and radish, and serve. —MELISSA MIRANDA

MAKE AHEAD The sinigang broth can be prepared through step 1 up to 3 days in advance and stored in an airtight container in refrigerator. Warm broth over low heat before proceeding with step 2.

NOTE Aneto fish broth is available online at marianafoods.us.

Chicken and Shrimp Laksa

TOTAL 45 MIN; SERVES 4

Top Chef winner Buddha Lo shares this family recipe for the refreshing and brothy noodle dish popular throughout Southeast Asia. Lo's homemade laksa paste — made with fresh lemongrass, pungent shrimp paste, and nutty peanuts — forms the base of this fragrant noodle dish.

LAKSA PASTE

- 3 medium (1-oz.) shallots, chopped (about ¾ cup)
- 4 medium lemongrass stalks (about 4 oz.), sliced (about ½ cup)
- ¼ cup canola oil
- 1 (2-inch) piece fresh ginger, peeled and sliced (about ¼ cup)
- 1 (3-inch) piece fresh galangal, peeled and chopped (about ¼ cup)
- 4 small dried red chiles
- 3 large garlic cloves, smashed
- 1 cup chicken stock, divided
- ½ cup peanuts
- 2 tsp. dried shrimp paste
- 2 tsp. ground turmeric

- 2 tsp. ground coriander
- 1 tsp. palm sugar or brown sugar

SOUP

- 2 Tbsp. canola oil
- 4 cups chicken stock
- 2 cups coconut cream (from 1 [15-oz.] can)
- 2 Tbsp. fish sauce, plus more to taste
- 8 oz. dried rice noodles
- 2 (8-oz.) cooked boneless, skinless chicken breasts, sliced
- 8 unpeeled raw jumbo shrimp, peeled, cleaned, and poached
- 1 cup fresh bean sprouts
- 4 scallions (about 1½ oz.), sliced (about ⅓ cup)
- ½ cup loosely packed fresh Vietnamese mint leaves
- ½ cup loosely packed fresh cilantro leaves
- ¼ cup fried shallots
- 1 lime, cut into 4 wedges

1. Make the laksa paste: Combine shallots, lemongrass, oil, ginger, galangal, red chiles, garlic, and ½ cup stock in a blender; process until mixture forms a thick, smooth paste, about 30 seconds. Add peanuts, shrimp paste, turmeric, coriander, sugar, and remaining ½ cup stock to blender; process until smooth, about 30 seconds.

2. Make the soup: Heat oil in a large Dutch oven over medium. Add laksa paste, and cook, stirring constantly, until fragrant, 4 to 6 minutes. Whisk in stock and coconut cream; bring to a boil. Reduce heat and simmer, covered, 10 minutes. Remove from heat. Whisk in fish sauce.

3. While stock mixture simmers, cook rice noodles according to package directions. Divide rice noodles evenly among 4 bowls. Arrange chicken and shrimp evenly on noodles. Ladle hot stock mixture evenly into bowls. Top evenly with bean sprouts, scallions, mint, cilantro, fried shallots, and lime wedges. —BUDDHA LO, HUSO, NEW YORK CITY

MAKE AHEAD Laksa paste can be made up to 3 days in advance and stored in an airtight container in refrigerator.

WINE Citrusy, off-dry Riesling: 2020 Fritz Haag Estate

NOTE Shrimp paste can be found at Asian grocery stores or online at foodsofnations.com.

Gazpacho

ACTIVE 25 MIN; TOTAL 2 HR 45 MIN
SERVES 4 TO 6

Perfect for sweltering summer days, this refreshing chilled soup is bursting with sweet and juicy peak-season tomatoes. Bright sherry vinegar and shallots balance the silky-smooth vegetable puree while salsa fresca adds a crunchy bite and pops of fresh herbs. Look for plump, bright red tomatoes to give the soup a vibrant color.

GAZPACHO

- 2 lb. red beefsteak tomatoes, cored and chopped (6 cups)
- 1 medium (11-oz.) cucumber, peeled, seeded, and chopped (about 1½ cups)
- 1 medium-size (10-oz.) red bell pepper, stemmed, seeded, and chopped (about 1¼ cups)
- 2 tsp. fine sea salt, plus more to taste
- 1 medium (2-oz.) shallot, chopped (about ½ cup)
- 2 Tbsp. sherry vinegar, plus more to taste
- 1 cup vegetable juice (such as V8)
- ½ cup extra-virgin olive oil

SALSA FRESCA

- 2 cups multicolored cherry tomatoes (from 1 lb. tomatoes), halved lengthwise
- ¼ cup finely chopped shallot (from 1 medium shallot)
- 1 Tbsp. finely chopped seeded fresh jalapeño (from 1 medium jalapeño)
- 1 Tbsp. chopped fresh cilantro
- 2 tsp. sherry vinegar
- 2 tsp. extra-virgin olive oil
- ½ tsp. fine sea salt
- ¼ tsp. black pepper

ADDITIONAL INGREDIENTS

- Fresh herbs (such as cilantro or basil leaves)

1. Make the gazpacho: Toss together beefsteak tomatoes, cucumber, bell pepper, and salt in a medium bowl. Let stand until 1 inch of drained vegetable juice collects in bottom of bowl, about 30 minutes. Meanwhile, place shallot in a small bowl, and drizzle with sherry vinegar; let stand 30 minutes.

2. Pour tomato mixture (with juices), shallot mixture, and vegetable juice into a blender; pulse until finely chopped, about 4 pulses. Process until smooth, about 1 minute. Remove center piece from blender lid; with blender running, slowly drizzle in oil, and process until smooth, about 1 minute. Season with additional salt to taste. (It should taste bright, bracing, and rich.) Chill, covered, until very cold, at least 2 hours or up to 2 days.

3. Make the salsa fresca: Stir together cherry tomatoes, shallot, jalapeño, cilantro, vinegar, oil, salt, and pepper in a medium bowl until well combined. Let salsa fresca stand, uncovered, at room temperature up to 1 hour.

4. Stir gazpacho to blend, and adjust seasonings with additional salt and vinegar to taste. Divide gazpacho evenly among bowls; top with salsa fresca and fresh herbs.
—MARY-FRANCES HECK

MAKE AHEAD Soup and salsa may be kept chilled in separate airtight containers up to 2 days.

WINE Bright Spanish rosado: 2021 Ameztoi Rubentis Txakolina

Parmesan-Braised Gigante Beans with Turkey

ACTIVE 35 MIN; TOTAL 2 HR 35 MIN,
PLUS 12 HR SOAKING; SERVES 4 TO 6

Giant lima beans cooked to al dente complement tender braised leftover turkey thighs and drumsticks in this cozy stew. A rind of Parmesan cheese enriches the broth.

- 2 cups dried gigante beans
- ¼ cup extra-virgin olive oil
- 1 medium-size (8-oz.) yellow onion, finely chopped (about 1⅓ cups)
- 1 medium (2-oz.) celery stalk, finely chopped (about ⅓ cup)
- 1 small (2-oz.) carrot, peeled and finely chopped (about ⅓ cup)
- ¼ tsp. kosher salt, plus more to taste
- ¼ tsp. black pepper, plus more to taste
- 4 medium garlic cloves, finely chopped (about 1½ Tbsp.)
- 2 tsp. fennel seeds
- 8 cups Leftover Turkey Broth (recipe p. 59) or lower-sodium turkey or chicken broth
- 1 (20-oz.) cooked bone-in, skin-on turkey leg quarter
- 1 (4-oz.) Parmigiano-Reggiano cheese rind
- 2 (5-inch) thyme sprigs, plus fresh thyme leaves, for garnish
- 2 (5-inch) sage sprigs
- 2 (5-inch) rosemary sprigs
- 2 fresh or dried bay leaves
- Crushed red pepper, for garnish

1. Place beans in a large bowl or container; add cold water to cover beans. Cover and refrigerate 12 hours. Drain beans, and set aside.

2. Heat oil in a large Dutch oven or heavy-bottomed pot over medium. Add onion, celery, carrot, salt, and black pepper. Cook, stirring occasionally, until vegetables are softened, about 6 minutes. Add garlic and fennel seeds; cook, stirring often, until fragrant, about 2 minutes. Add reserved beans, broth, turkey, cheese rind, thyme, sage, rosemary, and bay leaves.

3. Bring turkey mixture to a boil over high. Cover, reduce heat to low, and simmer, stirring occasionally, until turkey easily pulls away from bones, 1 hour to 1 hour and 15 minutes. Transfer turkey to a plate. Simmer bean mixture over low, uncovered, stirring occasionally, until beans are tender but slightly al dente, 35 to 45 minutes. Remove from heat. Season with additional salt and black pepper to taste. Let beans stand 10 minutes.

4. Meanwhile, remove turkey meat from bones; discard skin and bones. Tear meat into bite-size pieces; stir into bean mixture in Dutch oven.

5. Remove and discard cheese rind and herb sprigs from bean mixture. Divide bean mixture evenly among bowls; garnish with crushed red pepper and thyme leaves.
—JUSTIN CHAPPLE

NOTE If using a separated turkey drumstick and thigh, begin checking for doneness after 45 minutes.

PARMESAN-BRAISED GIGANTE
BEANS WITH TURKEY

Oliaigua (Menorcan Vegetable Soup) with Fig Jam–Topped Toast

ACTIVE 1 HR 15 MIN; TOTAL 1 HR 55 MIN
SERVES 6 TO 8

The name for this simple soup of gently stewed onions, tomatoes, and peppers comes from the Catalan words oli (oil) and aigua (water). The soup can be served warm or chilled, and is customarily eaten with bread, which is topped here with figat (fig jam). The recipe is from chef Felipe Riccio of March restaurant in Houston. To take it to the next level, June Rodil and Mark Sayre, who lead the wine program at March, suggest serving it with a rosé, such as the 2019 Clos Canarelli Corse Figari Rosé, from Corsica, France.

FIGAT

- 1 lb. fresh figs, stemmed and quartered
- ¾ cup granulated sugar
- ¼ tsp. anise seed
- ½ cup plus 2 Tbsp. water
- 1 tsp. grated lemon zest plus 2 Tbsp. fresh lemon juice (from 1 lemon)

OLIAIGUA

- 10 Tbsp. extra virgin olive oil, divided
- 1 small (6-oz.) leek, halved lengthwise and thinly sliced crosswise (about ¾ cup)
- 2 medium garlic cloves, thinly sliced (about 1½ Tbsp.)
- 1¼ cups sliced yellow onions (from 2 small [7-oz.] onions)
- 1 cup sliced sweet green pepper or chile (such as bell pepper, Anaheim chile, or Hatch chile)
- 1 cup sliced sweet mini peppers (from 8 oz. mini peppers)
- 2 tsp. kosher salt, divided, plus more to taste
- ¼ cup drained and chopped sun-dried tomatoes (from 1 [7-oz.] jar)
- 3½ cups chopped fresh tomatoes (from 4 small [6-oz.] tomatoes)
- 2 tsp. smoked paprika
- 4 cups vegetable stock
- ¼ cup chopped fresh flat-leaf parsley
- 2 tsp. grated lemon zest (from 1 lemon)

ADDITIONAL INGREDIENT

- 6 to 8 crusty bread slices, toasted

1. Make the figat: Combine figs, sugar, and anise seed in a large nonreactive saucepan until combined. Let fig mixture rest at room temperature, stirring occasionally, until figs have released their juices, about 20 minutes.

2. Add ½ cup plus 2 tablespoons water to fig mixture, and bring to a boil over medium-high, stirring occasionally to dissolve sugar. Reduce heat to medium, and cook, stirring occasionally, until liquid runs off the side of a spoon in thick drops, 20 to 25 minutes. Add lemon zest and juice, and cook, stirring often, 30 seconds. Remove from heat, and let cool completely, 30 to 45 minutes.

3. Meanwhile, make the oliaigua: Heat 6 tablespoons oil in an 8-quart stockpot over medium-low. Add leek and garlic; cook, stirring occasionally, until garlic begins to brown, about 10 minutes. Reduce heat to low; add onions, peppers, and 1 teaspoon salt; cook, stirring often, until onions and peppers have softened, 4 to 5 minutes. Push mixture to edges of stockpot to create a well in the center.

4. Pour remaining ¼ cup oil into well in stockpot; increase heat to medium-high, and heat until oil is hot and shimmers. Add sun-dried tomatoes to hot oil, and cook, undisturbed, until edges of sun-dried tomatoes start to brown, 2 to 3 minutes. Add fresh tomatoes, smoked paprika, and remaining 1 teaspoon salt to the well in center of stockpot; cook, stirring occasionally, until tomatoes are tender and flavors are well combined, 5 to 7 minutes.

5. Reduce heat to low, and add vegetable stock. Stir entire mixture in stockpot to combine, and bring to a simmer over low. Simmer (do not boil), stirring occasionally, until a white foam begins to form on surface, about 20 minutes. Remove from heat; stir in parsley and lemon zest, and season with additional salt to taste. Divide oliaigua evenly among 6 bowls. Top bread slices evenly with figat, and serve alongside oliaigua. —FELIPE RICCIO, CHEF-PARTNER, GOODNIGHT HOSPITALITY, HOUSTON

MAKE AHEAD Figat can be made up to 5 days in advance and stored in an airtight container in refrigerator.

Yemeni Bulgur Wheat Shurba (Soup)

⏱ TOTAL 45 MIN; SERVES 2 TO 4

Often served with meals during Ramadan, this Yemeni shurba, or soup, is warming and hearty. Shurba usually contains lamb, but Hakim Sulaimani of Yafa Café in Brooklyn makes this vegetarian version, which is rich and satisfying thanks to the savory blend of cumin, black pepper, cinnamon, ground ginger, and bay leaves.

- 1 cup uncooked #3 coarse bulgur
- 5 cups water
- 1 small yellow onion, halved, peeled, and root end trimmed
- 1 small tomato, cored
- 4 medium garlic cloves, peeled
- 1 Tbsp. tomato paste
- 1¾ tsp. kosher salt, divided, plus more to taste
- ½ tsp. ground cumin
- ½ tsp. black pepper
- ¼ tsp. ground cinnamon
- ¼ tsp. ground ginger
- 2 bay leaves
- 2 Tbsp. unsalted butter, melted
- 4 (1½-oz.) sourdough bread slices
- Chives and lemon wedges, for serving

1. Place bulgur in a fine wire-mesh strainer; rinse under cold water 30 seconds. Transfer bulgur to a large saucepan; add 5 cups water, onion halves, tomato, and 2 garlic cloves. Bring to a boil over high. Boil, turning onion and tomato occasionally, until onion is translucent and just tender, 10 to 12 minutes. Remove from heat.

2. Transfer onion halves, tomato, and the 2 garlic cloves to a blender, leaving bulgur and water in pan. Secure lid on blender, and remove center piece to allow steam to escape. Place a clean towel over opening. Process until smooth, about 25 seconds. Return pureed onion mixture to pan with bulgur. Stir in tomato paste, 1½ teaspoons salt, cumin, black pepper, cinnamon, ginger, and bay leaves. Bring to a gentle simmer over medium. Simmer, stirring and scraping bottom of pan occasionally to prevent sticking, until bulgur is tender, soup thickens, and mixture resembles the consistency of porridge, 12 to 15 minutes.

Remove from heat. Remove and discard bay leaves. Season soup with additional salt to taste.

3. While soup cooks, preheat oven to broil with rack about 6 inches from heat. Grate remaining 2 garlic cloves to equal 1 teaspoon. Place grated garlic in a small bowl, and stir in melted butter. Brush butter mixture evenly over both sides of bread slices, and sprinkle evenly with remaining ¼ teaspoon salt. Arrange bread slices on a rimmed baking sheet lined with aluminum foil. Broil in preheated oven until bread is toasted and golden brown, 2 to 3 minutes per side. Garnish soup with chives, and serve with garlic bread and lemon wedges.

—HAKIM SULAIMANI

WINE Light-bodied Alto Adige white: 2020 Cantina Terlano Pinot Grigio

Leftover Turkey Broth

ACTIVE 55 MIN; TOTAL 4 HR 25 MIN; SERVES 8 TO 10

This simple Leftover Turkey Broth recipe from Justin Chapple provides a simple method to making broth from scratch using your leftover roasted turkey carcass.

- 1 roasted turkey carcass (from 1 [12- to 14-lb.] roasted whole turkey)
- 2 medium-size yellow onions (about 11 oz. each) (unpeeled), halved
- 2 small (2-oz.) carrots (unpeeled)
- 2 celery stalks (about 3 oz.)
- 2 small garlic heads, halved
- 1 small (1-oz.) bunch fresh flat-leaf parsley
- 1 small (¼-oz.) bunch fresh thyme
- 2 small dried chiles de árbol
- 2 fresh or dried bay leaves
- 1 Tbsp. black peppercorns
- 6 qt. water

Combine turkey carcass, onions, carrots, celery stalks, garlic heads, parsley, thyme, chiles, bay leaves, and peppercorns in a large stockpot; add 6 quarts water. Bring to a boil over high. Reduce heat to medium-low; simmer, skimming fat from top of liquid occasionally, until stock is golden and very flavorful, about 2 hours and 30 minutes. Carefully pour broth through a fine wire-mesh strainer into a large heatproof bowl; discard solids. Divide broth evenly among 4 (1-quart) airtight containers. Let cool completely, uncovered, about 1 hour. Refrigerate until ready to use.

—JUSTIN CHAPPLE

MAKE AHEAD Refrigerate broth up to 1 week or freeze up to 6 months.

Master Stock

ACTIVE 15 MIN; TOTAL 5 HR 15 MIN
MAKES 8 CUPS

Master stock is a foundational recipe in Cantonese and Fujian cooking. Jonathan Kung's version is packed with savory chicken wings, aromatics, and spices, including dried sand ginger, a rhizome related to galangal, with a bright, citrusy, pine-sap flavor. This salty-sweet and intensely umami stock is perfect for using again and again as a poaching liquid to infuse flavor into various proteins and vegetables. The flavor of the stock will change slightly with each round. Kung recommends poaching meats and vegetables like chicken, beef, pork, tofu, and kohlrabi in it, and avoiding using it to poach fish or gamey meats, which can give the stock a more pungent aroma and flavor.

- 3 (3-inch) pieces fresh ginger (about 6 oz.) (unpeeled), cut into ¼-inch-thick slices
- 1 (2-oz.) bunch scallions, trimmed
- 1½ Tbsp. canola oil
- 3 cups chicken stock
- 2 cups Shaoxing wine
- 2 cups light soy sauce
- 1 cup dark soy sauce
- 15 whole star anise
- 5 (1-inch) dried Chinese licorice root slices
- 5 (3-inch) cinnamon sticks
- 1½ Tbsp. fennel seeds
- 6 (¼-inch-thick) unpeeled dried sand ginger slices
- 3 black cardamom pods
- 20 oz. slab cane sugar, Chinese rock sugar, or light brown sugar (about 4 cups)
- 4 dried tangerine peels (about 1 oz.)
- 1½ lb. chicken drumettes
- 3½ cups sliced sweet onion (from 1 large [1-lb.] onion)

1. Preheat oven to broil with rack 4 to 5 inches from heat. Line a rimmed baking sheet with aluminum foil. Toss together fresh ginger slices, scallions, and oil on prepared baking sheet until coated. Spread mixture in an even layer. Broil in preheated oven until lightly charred, about 3 minutes. Remove from oven.

2. Pour chicken stock, wine, light soy sauce, and dark soy sauce into a large saucepan; set aside. Place star anise, licorice root, cinnamon sticks, fennel seeds, sand ginger slices, and cardamom pods in middle of a 4-×5-inch piece of cheesecloth, and secure using kitchen twine.

3. Bring stock mixture to a simmer over medium-high. Add sugar, and stir to dissolve. Add tangerine peels, charred ginger and scallions, and cheesecloth bundle with spices. Reduce heat to medium-low; gently simmer, stirring occasionally, until mixture is fragrant and full-bodied, 45 minutes to 1 hour. Remove from heat.

4. Remove and discard cheesecloth with spices from stock mixture. Pour mixture through a fine wire-mesh strainer into an 8-cup glass measuring cup; discard solids. Pour strained stock mixture into a 6-quart slow cooker; add chicken drumettes and sweet onion. Cover and cook on low until chicken is fork-tender, about 3 hours.

5. Pour stock mixture through a fine wire-mesh strainer into a large heatproof bowl. Discard chicken pieces, or reserve for another use. Let stock cool at room temperature 1 hour; transfer to an airtight container, and store in refrigerator up to 1 week or in freezer up to 3 months.

—JONATHAN KUNG, DETROIT

NOTE A fine wire-mesh sieve or tea wand may be used to remove the spices instead of cheesecloth. Find Chinese licorice root, dried sand ginger slices, and slab cane sugar at most Asian grocery stores or tsemporium.com.

POSOLE ROJO

Posole Rojo

ACTIVE 25 MIN; TOTAL 1 HR 20 MIN; SERVES 8

Edgar Castrejón's posole rojo recipe from his cookbook Provecho *is velvety and rich. His mom sometimes used turkey (see Note) for a Thanksgiving rendition, but Edgar's vegan version smartly employs mushrooms for earthy flavor and slight chew. The result is just as satisfying as a meat-laden posole, and leftovers are fabulous.*

- 8 guajillo chiles (about 1½ oz.)
- 4 California chiles (dried Anaheim chiles) (about 1 oz.)
- 4 cups water
- 3 Tbsp. avocado oil
- 1½ lb. fresh oyster mushrooms or lion's mane mushrooms, trimmed and roughly chopped or torn (about 8 cups)
- 1 medium-size white or yellow onion (about 9 oz.), halved lengthwise and thinly sliced (about 1½ cups)
- 3 dried bay leaves
- 5 medium garlic cloves
- 5 cups drained and rinsed canned white hominy (from 4 [15.5-oz.] cans)
- 1½ tsp. Himalayan pink salt, plus more to taste
- 6 to 8 cups vegetable broth (such as Zoup!), divided
- 5 cups thinly shredded green cabbage (from 1 small head cabbage)
- 8 medium radishes (about 5 oz.), thinly sliced (about 1 cup)
- 4 limes, cut into wedges
- 2 cups chopped fresh cilantro (leaves and tender stems)
- Corn tortilla chips or corn tortillas, for serving

1. Trim stems from chiles; cut chiles lengthwise but not all the way through, and remove seeds. Transfer chiles to a small saucepan, and add 4 cups water. Bring to a boil over high; boil until softened, about 8 minutes. Set aside.

2. While chiles cook, heat avocado oil in a 6-quart pot or Dutch oven over medium-high. Add mushrooms, onion, and bay leaves, and cook, stirring often, until onion is translucent and mushrooms start releasing liquid, about 5 minutes. Reduce heat to medium, and cook, stirring often, 5 minutes. Remove from heat.

3. Drain chiles, reserving 2 cups soaking liquid. Place chiles, reserved soaking liquid, and garlic in a high-powered blender. Secure lid on blender, and remove center piece to allow steam to escape. Place a clean towel over opening. Process chile mixture until smooth, about 45 seconds.

4. Pour chile mixture through a fine wire-mesh strainer directly into mushroom mixture in pot; discard strained solids. Add hominy, salt, and 6 cups broth; stir to combine. Bring to a boil over medium-high; reduce heat to medium. Cover pot, and boil posole, undistined, 35 minutes. Season with additional salt to taste; add up to remaining 2 cups broth as needed if posole is too thick. Cover and continue cooking posole over medium, undistined, 10 minutes.

5. Remove pot from heat, and let posole rest, covered, 10 minutes. Remove and discard bay leaves. Serve with cabbage, radishes, lime wedges, cilantro, and chips or tortillas. —EDGAR CASTREJÓN. *PROVECHO: 100 VEGAN MEXICAN RECIPES TO CELEBRATE CULTURE AND COMMUNITY,* TEN SPEED PRESS

MAKE AHEAD Blended chile mixture can be made up to 1 day in advance and stored in an airtight container in refrigerator.

WINE Rich, full-bodied California red: 2018 Buehler Napa Valley Zinfandel

NOTE For a turkey version of this recipe, replace the vegetable broth with lightly salted turkey stock or chicken broth. Cook the onion and bay leaf until soft and translucent, 5 to 6 minutes. Add 2 cups strained chile liquid, hominy, 1½ to 2 pounds raw boneless turkey thighs (cut into 8-ounce pieces), salt, and 4 cups turkey stock. Cook, covered, at a swift boil 30 minutes. Remove turkey pieces, partially cover pot, and continue cooking posole 15 minutes. When turkey is cool enough to handle, shred turkey meat; discard or slice the skin. Add turkey to pot, let stand 10 minutes, and serve.

Short Rib Chili with Pickled Red Onion

PHOTO P. 41

ACTIVE 50 MIN; TOTAL 3 HR 15 MIN
SERVES 6 TO 8

Fresh jalapeños, smoky chipotles in adobo, and fruity ancho chile powder give this thick, meaty short rib chili layers of heat, while red wine and tomato add acidity to balance out the richness of the tender short ribs. For a more budget-friendly option, substitute cubed beef chuck roast for the short ribs. Homemade pickled red onions provide a colorful, tasty, crunchy topping.

CHILI

- 2 Tbsp. canola oil
- 3½ lb. boneless beef short ribs, trimmed and cut into 1-inch cubes
- 5 tsp. kosher salt, divided, plus more to taste
- 2½ tsp. black pepper, divided, plus more to taste
- 1 medium-size red onion, finely chopped (about 2¼ cups)
- 2 jalapeño chiles, stemmed, seeded, and finely chopped (about ½ cup)
- 10 garlic cloves, finely chopped
- ½ cup tomato paste
- ¼ cup ancho chile powder
- 1 to 2 chipotle chiles in adobo sauce, finely chopped
- 2 tsp. dried oregano
- 1½ tsp. ground cumin
- 1½ tsp. ground coriander
- 1½ cups dry red wine
- 1 (28-oz.) can crushed tomatoes
- 3 cups lower-sodium chicken broth

PICKLED RED ONION

- 1 small red onion, thinly sliced lengthwise (about 2½ cups)
- 1 cup distilled white vinegar
- 1 cup water
- 2 Tbsp. granulated sugar
- 1 Tbsp. kosher salt

ADDITIONAL INGREDIENTS

- Crumbled queso fresco, for serving
- Fresh cilantro leaves, for serving

1. Make the chili: Heat oil in a large enameled Dutch oven over medium-high. Toss together beef, 4 teaspoons salt, and 2 teaspoons black pepper in a large bowl.

continued on page 62

continued from page 61

Working in 3 batches, add beef to hot oil, and cook, turning occasionally, until browned on all sides, 8 to 10 minutes per batch. Using a slotted spoon, transfer beef to a medium bowl.

2. Add chopped onion, jalapeños, garlic, remaining 1 teaspoon salt, and remaining ½ teaspoon black pepper to drippings in Dutch oven. Cook over medium, stirring occasionally, until onion is softened and lightly browned, about 8 minutes. Stir in tomato paste, chile powder, chipotles, oregano, cumin, and coriander; cook, stirring constantly, until mixture is fragrant and vegetables are evenly coated, 1 to 2 minutes. Add wine; cook, scraping up browned bits from bottom of Dutch oven, until liquid is slightly reduced, about 2 minutes. Add crushed tomatoes and broth; bring mixture to a simmer over medium-high. Stir in beef and any juices in bowl. Reduce heat to low; cover and simmer, stirring occasionally, until beef is very tender, 2 hours and 30 minutes to 3 hours, uncovering during final 30 minutes of cook time. Season with additional salt and black pepper to taste.

3. Make the pickled red onion: While chili cooks, place sliced red onion in a medium-size heatproof bowl; set aside. Combine vinegar, 1 cup water, sugar, and salt in a small saucepan. Bring to a boil over medium-high, stirring often to dissolve sugar. Pour hot vinegar mixture over onion, pressing onion pieces with a spoon to keep submerged. Let stand at room temperature 10 minutes. Cover and chill at least 1 hour or up to 3 days.

4. Serve chili topped with queso fresco, cilantro, and drained pickled onion
—JUSTIN CHAPPLE

MAKE AHEAD Chili can be made up to 3 days ahead and stored in an airtight container in refrigerator.

WINE Light, earthy red: 2018 Domaine Rolet Arbois Poulsard

Cataplana (Portuguese Fish Stew)

ACTIVE 30 MIN; TOTAL 50 MIN; SERVES 4 TO 6

This Cataplana from F&W's Culinary Director-at-Large Justin Chapple is his version of a savory feast of shellfish and smoky linguiça hailing from the Algarve in Portugal. Named for the vessel it is traditionally cooked and served in, the stew gets lots of flavor from the Portuguese linguiça included, but you can substitute Spanish-style chorizo or even kielbasa in a pinch.

- ¼ cup extra-virgin olive oil
- 8 oz. linguiça, cut into ¼-inch slices
- 1 large yellow onion (about 1 lb.), cut in half lengthwise and thinly sliced lengthwise (about 3 cups)
- 2 medium-size fresh Cubanelle chiles, halved lengthwise, seeded, and sliced crosswise (about 1½ cups)
- 4 large garlic cloves, sliced (2 Tbsp.)
- ½ cup dry white wine
- 1 (14½-oz.) can whole peeled tomatoes, crushed by hand and juices reserved
- 2 cups clam juice
- 2 bay leaves
- 1½ tsp. paprika
- ½ tsp. saffron threads, crushed
- 2 cups packed chopped kale
- ½ tsp. kosher salt
- ¼ tsp. black pepper
- 8 littleneck clams (about 9 oz.), scrubbed
- 8 oz. peeled and deveined tail-on raw large shrimp (about 12 shrimp)
- 4 oz. cleaned small squid tentacles (12 to 15 small tentacles), rinsed
- 8 mussels (about 4 oz.), scrubbed and debearded
- Portuguese rolls, warmed

1. Heat oil in a large Dutch oven over medium-high. Add linguiça; cook, stirring often, until fat just starts to render, about 3 minutes. Add onion, chiles, and garlic; cook, stirring often, until vegetables are just softened, 5 to 7 minutes.

2. Add wine to mixture in Dutch oven; cook, scraping up any browned bits from bottom of Dutch oven, until nearly evaporated, about 2 minutes. Add crushed tomatoes and juices, clam juice, bay leaves, paprika, and saffron. Bring to a boil over medium-high. Cover and reduce heat to medium-low; simmer 15 minutes.

3. Stir kale, salt, and black pepper into stew. Nestle clams, shrimp, squid, and mussels into stew. Cover and increase heat to medium-high; cook until mussels and clams open and shrimp and squid are just cooked through, 4 to 6 minutes. Discard any closed clams or mussels. Remove and discard bay leaf. Serve with warm rolls. —JUSTIN CHAPPLE

WINE Tropical-fruited Portuguese white: 2019 Quinta da Fonte Souto Branco

CATAPLANA (PORTUGUESE FISH STEW)

PASTA &
NOODLES

LINGUINE AND SHRIMP WITH
SAUCE VIERGE (P. 67)
OPPOSITE: RIGATONI
AMATRICIANA (P. 76)

MAFALDINE WITH PEA SHOOT–
MEYER LEMON PESTO

Mafaldine with Pea Shoot–Meyer Lemon Pesto

⏱ TOTAL 30 MIN; SERVES 4

Fresh pea shoots, parsley, and dill make a verdant pesto balanced with salty ricotta salata cheese and nutty roasted sunflower seed kernels. The bright sauce clings beautifully to ruffled mafaldine pasta, but any textured pasta shape will work well. Sommelier Raquel Stevens of Leeward in Portland, Maine, provided the inspiration for this dish. She loves to pair it with Colle Trotta Q500 Passerina, a complex white wine from Abruzzo made from the Passerina grape. "The bright green pea shoots and salty sheep's milk cheese are balanced beautifully by the Colle Trotta Passerina's notes of ripe peach and wildflower honey," she says.

- ½ cup plus 2 Tbsp. extra-virgin olive oil, divided
- 2 garlic cloves
- 1 cup fresh breadcrumbs
- ¾ tsp. kosher salt, divided
- ½ tsp. grated Meyer lemon zest plus ¼ cup fresh Meyer lemon juice (from 1 large lemon or 2 medium lemons), divided
- 4 cups loosely packed fresh pea shoots, plus more for garnish, if desired
- ½ cup packed fresh flat-leaf parsley leaves
- ½ cup loosely packed fresh dill fronds
- 2 oz. ricotta salata, grated (about ½ cup)
- ¼ cup salted roasted sunflower seed kernels
- ¼ tsp. crushed red pepper
- 16 oz. uncooked mafaldine pasta
- 1 oz. pecorino Romano cheese, grated (about ¼ cup)
- 2 Tbsp. unsalted butter

1. Heat 2 tablespoons oil in a large skillet over medium-high. Using a Microplane grater, finely grate 1 garlic clove to yield about ½ teaspoon garlic. Finely chop remaining garlic clove, and set aside. Add grated garlic to skillet; cook, stirring constantly, until fragrant, about 30 seconds. Add breadcrumbs; cook, stirring constantly, until golden brown and crisp, 6 to 8 minutes. Remove skillet from heat; stir in ¼ teaspoon salt and ¼ teaspoon lemon zest, and set aside.

2. Combine pea shoots, parsley, dill, ricotta salata, sunflower seed kernels, lemon juice, reserved chopped garlic, and remaining ¼ teaspoon lemon zest in a blender. Pulse until mixture is finely chopped, 12 to 15 pulses. With blender running, add remaining ½ cup oil to mixture in a thin stream, and continue processing until smooth and emulsified, about 2 minutes. Stir in crushed red pepper and remaining ½ teaspoon salt. Set aside.

3. Bring a large pot of salted water to a boil over high. Add pasta, and cook according to package directions for al dente. Drain, reserving 1 cup cooking liquid.

4. Return pasta to large pot; add pea shoot pesto, pecorino Romano, butter, and ⅔ cup reserved cooking liquid, stirring until butter is melted and pasta is nicely coated, adding remaining ⅓ cup cooking liquid if needed to loosen sauce. Sprinkle with toasted breadcrumb mixture. If desired, garnish with additional pea shoots. —ANNA THEOKTISTO

WINE 2019 Colle Trotta Q500 Passerina

Linguine and Shrimp with Sauce Vierge

PHOTO P. 65

ACTIVE 30 MIN; TOTAL 1 HR 45 MIN; SERVES 4

Sauce vierge, named after England's Queen Elizabeth I (also known as the Virgin Queen), is a fresh chopped tomato sauce with roots in southwestern France. Whether referred to as "virgin" due to being uncooked or because of the addition of extra-virgin olive oil, this sauce is a wonderful example of how minimal preparation and perfect seasoning allow seasonal ingredients to shine. Briny capers, sweet shallots, and fragrant lemon zest pair together to add bright complexity to acidic, sun-kissed tomatoes. Seek out very ripe, juicy tomatoes for the best flavor in this summery sauce. Try it spooned over grilled fish or simply scooped up with warm, crusty bread.

- 1 lb. beefsteak tomatoes, cored and finely chopped (about 3 cups)
- ½ cup extra-virgin olive oil
- 1 large shallot, minced (about ¼ cup)
- 3 Tbsp. capers, drained
- 2 garlic cloves, minced (about 2 tsp.)
- 2 tsp. coriander seeds (not ground), finely crushed
- 1 tsp. grated lemon zest plus 2 Tbsp. fresh lemon juice (from 1 lemon)
- 1 tsp. crushed red pepper
- 1½ tsp. kosher salt, divided
- ¾ tsp. black pepper, divided
- 12 oz. uncooked linguine
- 1 lb. peeled and deveined raw large shrimp
- ¾ cup sliced (¼- to ½-inch pieces) fresh chives
- ½ cup chopped fresh basil
- Freshly grated Parmigiano-Reggiano cheese, for serving

1. Stir together tomatoes, oil, shallot, capers, garlic, coriander, lemon zest and juice, crushed red pepper, 1 teaspoon salt, and ½ teaspoon black pepper in a large heatproof serving bowl until well combined; let stand at room temperature 1 hour.

2. Bring a large saucepan of salted water to a boil over high. Add linguine; cook, stirring occasionally, 8 minutes. Add shrimp to pasta; cook, stirring occasionally, until linguine is al dente and shrimp are just cooked through, about 4 minutes.

3. Drain pasta-shrimp mixture; immediately add to tomato mixture in bowl. Vigorously toss to coat well. Fold in chives and basil; sprinkle with remaining ½ teaspoon salt and remaining ¼ teaspoon black pepper. Serve, passing Parmigiano-Reggiano at the table. —JUSTIN CHAPPLE

WINE Brisk Italian white: 2020 Marchesi Antinori Tenuta Guado al Tasso Vermentino

Malfatti in Parmesan Broth

ACTIVE 2 HR; TOTAL 3 HR; SERVES 4

Traditional Italian malfatti are delicate dumplings made mostly of mild cheese; here, 2021 F&W Best New Chef Trey Smith of Saint-Germain in New Orleans makes them with a blend of cream cheese, lemon zest, egg, and spices. "Finding great ingredients and letting them shine is a philosophy that many cooks share," Smith says. "Being a small tasting-menu restaurant, we are able to really push this ideal. This Malfatti in Parmesan Broth was built around some particularly delicious Parmesan that we came across. It was a natural idea to season dumplings with it to focus on the nutty richness of the cheese. We then found that making a broth with the remaining pieces and rind highlighted its acidity and umami." To create a richly savory Parmesan broth for the fluffy, creamy malfatti, Smith uses coffee filters to transfer the flavor of the cheese into a water broth without leaving any melted rinds behind.

- 1 lb. Parmesan cheese (as 1 single wedge or multiple wedges)
- 1 lb. cream cheese, softened
- 1 large egg
- 1 tsp. grated lemon zest plus ¾ tsp. fresh lemon juice (from 1 small lemon), divided
- ¾ tsp. kosher salt, divided, plus more to taste
- ½ tsp. ground white pepper, plus more to taste
- ⅛ tsp. freshly ground whole nutmeg (about 10 grinds)
- 1½ cups Italian-style 00 flour or all-purpose flour (about 6⅜ oz.)
- ¼ cup thinly sliced fresh chives
- 4 cups plus 1 Tbsp. water, divided
- ½ tsp. granulated sugar
- 2 Tbsp. cold unsalted butter, cut into pieces
- 2 Tbsp. chopped fresh flat-leaf parsley

1. Using a Microplane grater, grate 1½ loosely packed cups (about 1½ ounces) of the Parmesan; set aside. Cut remaining Parmesan, including rinds, into 1½- to 2-inch cubes; set aside.

2. Beat cream cheese, egg, lemon zest, ½ teaspoon salt, white pepper, and nutmeg with a stand mixer fitted with the paddle attachment on medium-high speed until light and smooth, about 3 minutes, stopping to scrape down sides and bottom of bowl with a rubber spatula as needed. Reduce mixer speed to low; gradually beat in flour. Increase mixer speed to medium; beat until mixture forms a thick and tacky batter, about 3 minutes. Add chives and grated Parmesan; beat on medium speed until grated cheese is incorporated, about 1 minute. Scrape mixture into a piping bag or a heavy-duty ziplock plastic bag. Cut a ¾-inch opening in one corner of bag. Let batter rest at room temperature 1 hour.

3. Divide Parmesan cubes evenly among 6 (12-cup) coffee filters. Working with 1 coffee filter at a time, gather filter up and around cheese cubes; secure with kitchen twine to keep from opening. Place cheese bundles in a 3-quart saucepan; add 4 cups water. Bring to a simmer over medium. Reduce heat to low; gently simmer, stirring occasionally, until you can smell the aroma of Parmesan, about 1 hour. Pour Parmesan broth through a fine wire-mesh strainer into a small saucepan. Gently press on cheese bundles in strainer using back of a spoon; discard bundles. (If desired, freeze Parmesan cubes, and use to make another broth.) Stir sugar, ¼ teaspoon lemon juice, and remaining ¼ teaspoon salt into strained Parmesan broth. Set aside until ready to use.

4. While Parmesan broth simmers, bring a large pot of lightly salted water to a boil over high. Carefully pipe batter straight down into boiling water, cutting into pieces at ¾-inch lengths using scissors and piping in batches of about 15 malfatti (batter pieces) at a time. For clean cuts, dip scissors in boiling water as needed. Cook until slightly firm but set, about 3 minutes per batch. Using a spider or slotted spoon, transfer cooked malfatti to a baking sheet lined with plastic wrap. Let last batch of cooked malfatti cool 5 minutes.

5. Transfer cooked malfatti to a large skillet; add butter and remaining 1 tablespoon water. Cook over medium, gently stirring occasionally, until malfatti are heated through and lightly glazed in butter mixture, 4 to 5 minutes. Remove from heat; stir in parsley and remaining ½ teaspoon lemon juice. Season with additional salt and white pepper to taste. Divide malfatti evenly among 4 shallow bowls; top evenly with hot Parmesan broth. —TREY SMITH, SAINT-GERMAIN, NEW ORLEANS

WINE Herbal, medium-bodied Italian white: 2020 Villa Bucci Verdicchio dei Castelli di Jesi Classico Superiore

NOTE Source high-quality aged Parmesan cheese. If using a less flavorful cheese, add a few drops of lemon juice to the broth before serving to give it a boost.

AGNOLOTTI DEL PLIN

Agnolotti del Plin

ACTIVE 2 HR; TOTAL 3 HR 15 MIN; SERVES 8

These tiny, meat-filled Piedmontese agnolotti (the name translates as "agnolotti with the pinch") originated as a means of using up braised meat. In this version from Casa di Langa's Fàula Ristorante, the agnolotti are stuffed with a pork, chicken, veal, and vegetable filling bound with butter and cheese. The pasta is typically served on special occasions with a reduced sauce made from meat drippings, but at the restaurant, they finish it in a simple butter sauce. If you can't find Grana Padano, Parmigiano-Reggiano is a good substitute.

PASTA SHEETS

- 2 cups fine semolina flour (about 10¾ oz.) (such as Caputo), plus more for dusting
- ⅓ cup 00 flour (about 1⅝ oz.) (such as Caputo), plus more for dusting
- ½ tsp. fine sea salt
- 10 large egg yolks
- 2 large eggs

FILLING

- 2 Tbsp. extra-virgin olive oil
- 2 (about 9-oz.) veal osso buco, meat cut into ¾-inch pieces and bones reserved
- 8 oz. boneless, skinless chicken thighs, cut into ¾-inch pieces
- 8 oz. boneless pork loin chops, cut into ¾-inch pieces
- ⅓ cup dry white wine
- 1 cup vegetable broth (such as Zoup!)
- 4 cups packed fresh spinach (about 4 oz.)
- 2½ cups roughly chopped Savoy cabbage (about 4 oz.) (from 1 small cabbage)
- 1¼ tsp. fine sea salt, plus more to taste
- ¾ tsp. black pepper, plus more to taste
- ¾ cup unsalted butter (6 oz.), chilled and cut into ½-inch pieces
- 2 oz. Grana Padano cheese, finely grated (about ½ cup)

ADDITIONAL INGREDIENTS

- 1 large egg, beaten
- 4 qt. water
- ¼ cup fine sea salt
- ½ cup unsalted butter (4 oz.), divided
  Shaved Grana Padano cheese
  Cracked pepper and flaky sea salt (optional)

1. Make the pasta sheets: Whisk together semolina flour, 00 flour, and fine salt in a large bowl; transfer mixture to a clean large work surface. Make a well about 4 inches in diameter in center of flour mixture. Add egg yolks and whole eggs to well, and whisk using a fork to break yolks and mix eggs together. Using fork, push some of the flour mixture from inside edge of well into eggs to combine. Continue incorporating flour mixture into egg mixture, kneading with hands until a shaggy dough forms.

2. Knead dough, adding additional 00 flour 1 teaspoon at a time as needed if dough sticks to work surface, until dough is smooth and elastic, about 10 minutes. Shape dough into a ball; wrap tightly in plastic wrap, and let rest at room temperature at least 1 hour or up to 3 hours.

3. Make the filling: Heat oil in a large saucepan over medium-high. Working in 2 batches, add osso buco meat and bones, chicken, and pork; cook, stirring occasionally, until browned on all sides, 8 to 10 minutes per batch. Return all browned meat to pan. Add wine; cook, stirring to scrape up browned bits from bottom of pan, until wine has reduced almost completely, about 4 minutes. Add broth; cook, stirring occasionally, until liquid has reduced to about ¼ cup, 15 to 20 minutes. Remove and discard osso buco bones. Stir in spinach and cabbage. Cook, stirring occasionally, until wilted, about 3 minutes.

4. Transfer hot filling mixture to a food processor. Add fine salt and pepper; process until finely chopped, about 10 seconds, stopping to scrape down sides of bowl as needed. With processor running,

gradually add butter, processing until well combined after each addition. Process until mixture is smooth and creamy, about 30 seconds. Add cheese; pulse to combine, 10 to 12 pulses. Season with additional fine salt and pepper to taste. Transfer filling to a large piping bag or a ziplock plastic bag with a ½-inch hole cut in 1 corner. Set aside.

5. Divide pasta dough evenly into 4 portions. Working with 1 dough portion at a time (and keeping remaining portions covered with a towel), flatten dough to ⅓-inch thickness. Roll flattened dough through a pasta machine with rollers on widest setting, dusting with 00 flour as needed to prevent sticking. Fold dough in half crosswise, and reroll through pasta machine until dough is as wide as the pasta machine (about 5½ inches). Continue rolling dough through pasta machine, reducing width of rollers 1 setting at a time, until dough has been rolled through setting 0 (the thinnest setting), dusting dough with 00 flour as needed to prevent sticking. Fold pasta sheet in half lengthwise, and press gently along the fold to create a crease; unfold. Using a fluted pastry wheel, cut pasta sheet in half lengthwise along the crease; trim ends to form 2 (about 36- × 2½-inch) sheets. Transfer pasta sheets to a clean work surface, and cover loosely with plastic wrap. Repeat process with remaining 3 dough portions.

6. Lay 1 pasta sheet lengthwise on a clean work surface with fluted side on top. Starting ½ inch from the left edge, pipe filling in a line running lengthwise across pasta sheet, about ¼ inch above the long edge closest to you, and leaving a ½-inch gap on the right edge. Brush exposed dough above filling lightly with some of the beaten egg. Starting at long edge of pasta sheet closest to you, roll the dough edge over the line of filling just until the filling is fully enclosed in a tube of dough, leaving about ½ inch of dough sheet unrolled at the top. Using thumb and index finger, pinch the filled dough tube every 1½ inches to form small pillows (about 20 per pasta sheet);

continued on page 72

continued from page 71

pinch to seal ends. Using a pastry wheel, cut between pillows to separate and seal ends. Dust 4 baking sheets with semolina flour. Arrange agnolotti in a single layer on prepared baking sheets; cover with plastic wrap. Repeat process with remaining 7 pasta sheets and filling, arranging agnolotti evenly among the 4 baking sheets.

7. Bring 4 quarts water to a boil in a large pot over medium-high. Stir in fine salt, and return to a boil. Add half of the agnolotti; cook, undisturbed, until al dente, about 2 minutes. While agnolotti cooks, melt ¼ cup butter in a large skillet over medium. Transfer cooked pasta to butter in skillet, and add ⅓ cup pasta cooking liquid. Cook, stirring constantly, until sauce thickens and coats pasta, about 2 minutes. Transfer to a serving bowl. Repeat process with remaining agnolotti, butter, and pasta cooking liquid. Garnish with shaved Grana Padano and, if desired, cracked pepper and flaky salt. —FÀULA RISTORANTE, CERRETTO LANGHE, ITALY

MAKE AHEAD Uncooked agnolotti can be covered tightly on a lightly floured baking sheet and refrigerated up to 1 day or frozen on a baking sheet, transferred to ziplock plastic freezer bags, and frozen up to 3 weeks. (Add frozen agnolotti to boiling water, and increase cook time by 1 to 2 minutes.)

WINE Earthy, elegant Nebbiolo: 2019 Vietti Perbacco Langhe Nebbiolo

NOTE Find semolina and 00 flour at most specialty stores and online at italianfoodonline.com.

Parmesan-Herb Gnudi

ACTIVE 35 MIN; TOTAL 50 MIN, PLUS 12 HR REFRIGERATION; SERVES 6 TO 8

These savory, cheesy, herb-flecked Italian dumplings are a simple and elegant early spring dinner. The fresh ricotta and parmesan gnudi are buried in semolina flour overnight (or up to a few days), which allows a thin skin to form around each dumpling. That skin helps these delicate dumplings hold their shape while they simmer.

- 1 lb. Homemade Fresh Ricotta (recipe p. 180) or store-bought fresh ricotta, drained
- 2 oz. Parmigiano-Reggiano cheese, grated with a Microplane (about 1¼ cups)
- ½ cup finely chopped mixed fresh herbs (such as chives, parsley, basil, and tarragon), plus more for garnish
- 2 large eggs
- 1 large egg yolk
- ¼ cup plus 1¼ tsp. kosher salt, divided
- ¼ tsp. ground nutmeg
- ½ cup all-purpose flour (about 2⅛ oz.)
- 4 cups fine semolina flour (such as Caputo), plus more for dusting
- 4 qt. water
  Extra virgin olive oil, for drizzling
  Flaky sea salt, for garnish

1. Stir together ricotta cheese, Parmigiano-Reggiano, chopped herbs, eggs, egg yolk, 1¼ teaspoons kosher salt, and nutmeg in a large bowl until well combined. Stir in all-purpose flour until just incorporated. Transfer dough to a large ziplock plastic bag with a 1-inch hole cut in one corner.

2. Sprinkle 2 cups semolina on a large rimmed baking sheet. Pipe dough into 8 (12-inch-long, 1-inch-thick) logs onto semolina on baking sheet. Using scissors, cut each log crosswise into 5 (about 2½-inch-long) dumplings; arrange dumplings ½ inch apart. Cover dumplings with remaining 2 cups semolina, ensuring each dumpling is completely buried. Chill, uncovered, until dumplings form a thin skin, at least 12 hours or up to 72 hours.

3. Remove dumplings from refrigerator, and let stand at room temperature 15 minutes. Meanwhile, bring 4 quarts water to a boil in a large pot over medium-high. Stir in remaining ¼ cup kosher salt.

4. Lift half of dumplings from semolina, and dust off excess. Add dumplings to boiling water, and reduce heat to medium-low. Adjust heat as needed to maintain a low simmer. Cook dumplings until set, puffed, and tender, 3 to 4 minutes. (Continue cooking dumplings for 30 to 45 seconds after they float to the surface.)

5. Using a spider or large slotted spoon, transfer dumplings to serving bowls. Drizzle with olive oil; garnish with flaky sea salt and additional chopped fresh herbs. Serve immediately. Repeat steps 4 and 5 with remaining dumplings. —PAIGE GRANDJEAN

MAKE AHEAD Shaped dumplings can be refrigerated up to 2 days before cooking.

WINE Crisp, herbal Italian white: 2020 La Spinetta Toscana Vermentino

PARMESAN-HERB GNUDI

RAGÙ DI SALSICCIA (SAUSAGE RAGÙ) WITH TAJARIN

Ragù di Salsiccia (Sausage Ragù) with Tajarin

ACTIVE 1 HR 5 MIN; TOTAL 2 HR 30 MIN
SERVES 4 TO 6

Sausage and veal come together in a lightly sweet and aromatic ragù with tajarin — a Piedmontese fresh pasta that gets its gold color from a high ratio of egg yolks to flour. At Casa di Langa in Piedmont, chef Daniel Zeilinga uses tomato water made from fresh tomatoes strained overnight in the ragù; this streamlined version uses a mixture of tomato juice and water, making the dish achievable on any evening at any time of year. One pound of purchased fresh egg spaghetti or about 12 ounces of dried thin spaghetti may be substituted for the tajarin. A final drizzle of olive oil adds a rich finish to the lean meat sauce. To give the tajarin the best color, use pasture-raised or free-range eggs, which have deep-orange yolks.

RAGÙ

- 1 Tbsp. extra-virgin olive oil, plus more for serving
- 10 oz. mild Italian sausage, casings removed
- 6 oz. 90% lean ground veal
- 1 small (6-oz.) white onion, finely chopped (about 1½ cups)
- 3 medium celery stalks (about 4 oz.), trimmed and finely chopped (about ¾ cup)
- 2 small carrots (about 3½ oz.), peeled and finely chopped (about ½ cup)
- 1 tsp. fine sea salt, plus more to taste
- ½ tsp. black pepper, plus more to taste
- ⅓ cup dry white wine (such as Arneis)
- 1¾ cups water
- ¾ cup tomato juice (such as Campbell's) (1 [5½-oz.] can)
- 3 (5-inch) thyme sprigs
- 2 fresh bay leaves
- 1 (5-inch) sage sprig
- 1 (5-inch) rosemary sprig

TAJARIN

- 1⅓ cups fine semolina flour (such as Caputo) (about 7¾ oz.), plus more for dusting
- ¼ cup 00 flour (such as Caputo) (about 1⅛ oz.), plus more for dusting
- 14 large egg yolks

ADDITIONAL INGREDIENTS

- 4 qt. water
- ¼ cup fine sea salt

1. Make the ragù: Heat oil in a medium-size Dutch oven over medium. Add sausage and veal; cook, stirring often to break meat into small crumbles, until meat is browned, 6 to 8 minutes. Add onion, celery, carrots, salt, and pepper; cook, stirring often, until vegetables are softened but not caramelized, about 8 minutes. Add wine; cook, stirring to scrape up browned bits from bottom of Dutch oven, until almost completely evaporated, about 2 minutes. Stir in 1¾ cups water and tomato juice. Using kitchen twine, tie together thyme, bay leaves, sage, and rosemary to form a bouquet garni; add to Dutch oven. Bring to a boil over medium. Reduce heat to low; cover and simmer, stirring occasionally, until flavors meld, about 2 hours. Remove and discard bouquet garni. Season with additional salt and pepper to taste. Keep ragù warm over low until ready to use.

2. Make the tajarin: While ragù cooks, whisk together semolina flour and 00 flour in a large bowl; transfer to a clean large work surface. Make a well about 5 inches in diameter in center of flour mixture. Add egg yolks to well, and whisk using a fork to break yolks. Using fork, push some of the flour mixture from inside edge of well into eggs, and whisk with fork until just incorporated. Continue incorporating flour mixture into eggs and whisking with fork until a shaggy dough forms.

3. Knead dough until smooth and elastic, about 10 minutes. Shape into a ball, and wrap tightly in plastic wrap; let rest at room temperature at least 1 hour or up to 3 hours.

4. Unwrap dough, and divide evenly into 4 portions. Working with 1 dough portion at a time (and keeping remaining portions covered with a towel), flatten dough to ⅓-inch thickness. Roll flattened dough through a pasta machine with rollers on widest setting. Fold dough in half crosswise, and reroll through pasta machine until dough is as wide as the pasta machine (about 5 to 5½ inches). Continue rolling dough through pasta machine, reducing width of rollers 1 setting at a time, until dough has been rolled through setting 3 (the fourth-thinnest setting), dusting dough with 00 flour as needed to prevent sticking.

5. Dust both sides of dough with 00 flour, and fold in half crosswise. Starting at the folded edge, very loosely roll up dough into a log to form long coiled strands. Cut log crosswise into ⅛-inch-wide pieces. Unroll log; sprinkle with 00 flour, and cut pasta strands in half crosswise to form pieces about 12 to 14 inches long. Form pasta strands into small bundles or nests, and transfer to a rimmed baking sheet dusted with semolina flour; cover with plastic wrap. Repeat process with remaining 3 dough portions.

6. Bring 4 quarts water to a boil in a large pot over medium-high. Stir in salt, and return to a boil. Add tajarin; cook, stirring occasionally, until al dente, 2 to 3 minutes. Using a spider or fine wire-mesh strainer, remove tajarin from water, and add to ragù in Dutch oven. Cook, uncovered, over medium, stirring often, until ragù thickens slightly and coats tajarin, 2 to 3 minutes. Divide mixture evenly among 4 to 6 bowls. Drizzle lightly with additional oil, and serve immediately. —FÀULA RISTORANTE, CERRETTO LANGHE, ITALY

MAKE AHEAD Ragù can be made up to 2 days in advance and stored in an airtight container in refrigerator. Uncooked tajarin can be placed on a flour-dusted baking sheet, covered tightly, and refrigerated up to 1 day or frozen in ziplock plastic freezer bags up to 3 weeks. (Pasta can be cooked directly from frozen.)

WINE Lively, berry-inflected Barbera: 2019 Fontanafredda Briccotondo

NOTE Find semolina and 00 flour at most specialty stores or online at italianfoodonline.com.

Rigatoni Amatriciana

PHOTO P. 64

TOTAL 55 MIN; SERVES 4

Amatriciana sauce typically calls for cured pork, traditionally guanciale. Here, we've substituted fatty pancetta for easier sourcing. It comes together with tomatoes, pecorino Romano cheese, sweet onion, and crushed red pepper to make a rich, jammy, pleasantly spicy sauce. Finishing the pasta in the sauce, along with a splash of starchy cooking water and nutty shredded cheese, helps the sauce thicken and emulsify, while infusing each bite of pasta with rich flavor. The recipe is inspired by sommelier Arjav Ezekiel, co-owner of Birdie's in Austin, who loves to pair the rich pasta with a Nero d'Avola from Martha Stoumen. "It is delightful, especially with a good chill, which brings out the bright fruit and smoked tomato on the nose, making it an ideal pairing with zingy and rich amatriciana," he says.

- 2 Tbsp. olive oil
- 1 medium-size (9-oz.) yellow onion, finely chopped (about 1½ cups)
- 1 (4-oz.) pkg. chopped pancetta
- ¼ tsp. crushed red pepper
- 1 (28-oz.) can whole plum tomatoes
- ¼ tsp. kosher salt
- 1 lb. uncooked rigatoni pasta
- 1½ oz. Parmigiano-Reggiano cheese, finely shredded (about ⅔ cup), plus more for serving
- ¾ oz. pecorino Romano cheese, finely shredded (about ¼ cup), plus more for serving
- 2 Tbsp. unsalted butter
  Finely chopped fresh flat-leaf parsley, for garnish

1. Heat oil in a large, deep skillet over medium-high. Add onion, and cook, stirring often, until softened, about 4 minutes. Stir in pancetta; cook, stirring often, until pancetta begins to render, about 5 minutes. Stir in crushed red pepper. Using your hands or a wooden spoon, crush tomatoes; add tomatoes and their juices to skillet. Bring to a boil over medium-high; reduce heat to medium-low, and simmer, stirring often, until flavors meld and mixture thickens, about 20 minutes. Stir in salt. Remove from heat.

2. While sauce cooks, bring a large pot of salted water to a boil over high. Add rigatoni, and cook according to package instructions for al dente, about 13 minutes. Drain, reserving ½ cup cooking liquid.

3. Add rigatoni, reserved ½ cup cooking liquid, Parmigiano-Reggiano, pecorino Romano, and butter to sauce in skillet. Cook over medium, stirring constantly, until sauce thickens and coats pasta, about 2 minutes. Remove from heat, and garnish with parsley. Serve with additional Parmigiano-Reggiano and pecorino Romano cheeses. —ANNA THEOKTISTO

WINE 2019 Martha Stoumen Nero d'Avola

Spanish-Style Pasta Salad with Tuna and Marinated Tomatoes

ACTIVE 30 MIN; TOTAL 1 HR 30 MIN; SERVES 6

Spanish pantry staples like mildly spicy and sweet piparra peppers and tangy sherry vinegar bring bold flavor to this hearty pasta salad from 2015 F&W Best New Chef Katie Button of Cúrate in Asheville, North Carolina. "I love this pasta salad because it incorporates fresh summer ingredients, like tomatoes and herbs, with staples I already have on hand in the pantry, including imported Spanish tuna and pasta," says Button. "It's a perfect low-cook dish that you can make ahead in large batches and eat on for lunches and dinners all week; it keeps getting better with time. This is a go-to salad in my house, and when I pack it for a picnic or a hike, it feels like I've won. It's hearty and easy to make, and my kids love it, too." Feel free to riff with what's on hand in your own cupboard; Button likes adding artichokes or hearts of palm and swapping in boquerones (white Spanish anchovies) for the tuna.

- 1½ lb. small tomatoes, cored and chopped into 1-inch pieces (about 5 cups)
- ¼ cup extra-virgin olive oil, plus more to taste
- 1½ Tbsp. sherry vinegar, plus more to taste
- 2 medium garlic cloves, minced (about 1½ tsp.)
- 3 Tbsp. plus 1½ tsp. kosher salt, divided, plus more to taste
- 3 qt. water

- 8 oz. uncooked lumaconi, conchiglie, or galet pasta
- 3 large hard-cooked eggs, peeled
- 1 (4-oz.) can solid white tuna in olive oil, drained and flaked
- ½ cup pitted black olives (preferably Empeltre olives)
- 10 jarred piparra peppers (from 1 [6.4-oz.] jar), quartered lengthwise (or ¼ cup drained capers)
- 2 Tbsp. fresh flat-leaf parsley leaves, roughly torn, plus more for garnish
- 1 Tbsp. fresh tarragon leaves, roughly torn, plus more for garnish

1. Toss together tomatoes, oil, vinegar, garlic, and 1½ teaspoons salt in a medium bowl. Cover with plastic wrap, and let marinate in refrigerator at least 1 hour or up to 8 hours. (The longer the tomatoes marinate, the better the flavor will be.)

2. Bring 3 quarts water to a boil in a large pot over high; stir in remaining 3 tablespoons salt. Add pasta, and cook according to package directions for al dente. Drain and rinse pasta with cold water to stop the cooking process until pasta is cool to the touch.

3. Cut eggs into eighths by slicing them in half lengthwise and then cutting each half in half crosswise and lengthwise. Add eggs, tuna, olives, peppers, parsley, tarragon, and cooked pasta to tomato mixture in bowl; gently toss to combine. Adjust seasonings with additional olive oil, vinegar, and salt to taste.

4. Transfer salad to a large bowl or platter. Garnish with additional parsley and tarragon, and serve. —KATIE BUTTON, CÚRATE, ASHEVILLE, NORTH CAROLINA

MAKE AHEAD Tomatoes may be marinated up to 8 hours in advance. Pasta salad may be kept chilled up to 3 days.

WINE Fruity Spanish rosé: 2021 Bodegas Muga Rosado

NOTE Piparra peppers may be found at curateathome.com.

SPANISH-STYLE PASTA SALAD WITH
TUNA AND MARINATED TOMATOES

CRISPY RICE CAKE LASAGNA

Crispy Rice Cake Lasagna

TOTAL 50 MIN; SERVES 6

For this creative take on lasagna, chewy, tender Korean rice cakes are coated with a spicy sauce of sweet Italian sausage, fennel seeds, crushed red pepper flakes, gochujang, ssamjang, and kimchi. A caramelized, bubbly, stringy provolone topping helps temper the heat. Find tubular Korean rice cakes, which are sold partially cooked and vacuum-sealed, in the freezer section at Korean markets or online.

SWEET ITALIAN SAUSAGE

- 1 tsp. fennel seeds
- ¼ tsp. coriander seeds
- 1 lb. ground pork
- 1½ tsp. black pepper
- 1½ tsp. granulated sugar
- 1½ tsp. kosher salt
- 2 garlic cloves, minced (1½ tsp.)
- ¼ tsp. crushed red pepper
- ¼ cup red wine

LASAGNA

- ½ cup vegetable oil, divided
- 1¾ cups gochujang
- 2 lb. Korean rice cakes (tubular shape)
- 2 cups dashi
- ¼ cup tomato sauce
- 1 Tbsp. ssamjang
- 1 Tbsp. sesame oil
- 2 cups kimchi, drained (liquid reserved) and chopped
- 4 cups thinly sliced scallions (from 10 large scallions)
- ½ cup unsalted butter (4 oz.), cut into ½-inch pieces
- 1 oz. Parmesan cheese, grated (about ¼ cup)
- 12 oz. provolone cheese, shredded (about 3 cups)

1. Make the sweet Italian sausage: Cook fennel seeds and coriander seeds in a small skillet over medium, stirring often, until seeds are toasted and aromatic, 2 to 3 minutes. Remove skillet from heat; let stand at room temperature until toasted seeds have cooled completely, 2 to 3 minutes. Grind toasted seeds in a spice grinder until finely ground, 30 to 45 seconds. Stir together ground seeds, ground pork, black pepper, sugar, salt, garlic, and crushed red pepper in a medium bowl until combined. Add wine, and stir until well combined.

2. Make the lasagna: Heat ¼ cup vegetable oil in a shallow saucepan over medium-low. Add sweet Italian sausage; cook, stirring constantly using a whisk, until mostly cooked, 3 to 4 minutes. (Using a whisk is a chef's trick to break up chunks of meat as it cooks. The sausage should not get any color or char.) Stir in gochujang; cook, stirring constantly using whisk, until sausage is completely cooked, 2 to 3 minutes. Transfer sausage mixture to a large heatproof bowl. Set aside until ready to use.

3. Heat remaining ¼ cup vegetable oil in a large skillet over medium-high. Working in 2 batches if needed, add rice cakes to skillet; cook, flipping occasionally, until cakes are crispy on all sides, 6 to 8 minutes. Transfer rice cakes to a plate lined with paper towels, reserving oil in skillet.

4. Preheat oven to broil with rack about 6 inches from heat. Add dashi, tomato sauce, ssamjang, sesame oil, and reserved kimchi liquid to reserved vegetable oil in skillet. Bring mixture to a boil over medium-high. Boil, stirring occasionally, until mixture is reduced by half, about 5 minutes. Add crispy rice cakes and chopped kimchi to mixture, and gently stir to combine. Reduce heat to medium-low; stir in scallions, butter, and Parmesan. Cook, stirring constantly, until sauce is emulsified, turns a creamy orange color, and coats rice cakes, 2 to 3 minutes. Remove from heat.

5. Transfer rice cake mixture to reserved pork mixture in bowl; gently stir until well combined. Transfer mixture to an ungreased 13-×9-inch broiler-safe baking dish; sprinkle evenly with provolone. Broil in preheated oven until provolone is melted and golden brown, 4 to 5 minutes. Serve immediately. —CHRISTINE LAU

MAKE AHEAD Sweet Italian sausage can be made up to 3 days ahead and stored in an airtight container in refrigerator.

WINE Fruit-forward, spicy Zinfandel: 2019 Marietta Cellars Román

SAVORY CARROT MOCHI

Spring carrots are celebrated three ways in this recipe from 2021 F&W Best New Chef Gaby Maeda: rolled into chewy mochi dumplings, pickled, and roasted. Using the signature method she came up with at State Bird Provisions in San Francisco, Maeda makes bouncy carrot mochi from scratch by combining fresh carrot puree with mochiko, sweet rice flour, then fries them in butter to give them a crispy-chewy texture. Served alongside her pickled carrots, pistachio dukkah, and roasted carrots, the dish is a riot of color, texture, and flavor. You will only need 1 tablespoon of the dukkah for this recipe. Try the rest sprinkled on top of steamed rice or roasted vegetables, or transform a simple green salad by mixing in a few tablespoonfuls of this crunchy, aromatic seasoning.

ACTIVE 50 MIN; TOTAL 1 HR; SERVES 4 TO 6

MOCHI

- 8 oz. carrots, peeled, trimmed, and cut crosswise into ½-inch pieces (about 1¼ cups)
- ¾ cup plus 3 to 4 Tbsp. carrot juice, divided
- 3 Tbsp. plus ¾ tsp. kosher salt, divided
- 1 cup mochiko (sweet rice flour) (such as Koda Farms Blue Star) (about 5 oz.), plus 1 Tbsp. more, if needed
- 3 qt. water
- 1 Tbsp. extra-virgin olive oil
- 2 Tbsp. unsalted butter

ADDITIONAL INGREDIENTS

- Roasted Carrots (recipe p. 182)
- ¼ cup drained Pickled Carrots plus 2 Tbsp. pickling liquid (recipe p. 303)

- 2 tsp. extra-virgin olive oil
- ¼ cup loosely packed mixed fresh herbs (such as dill, mint, and sorrel), torn if large
- 1 Tbsp. Pistachio Dukkah (recipe p. 303)
- Flaky sea salt (optional)

1. Make the mochi: Bring carrots, ¾ cup carrot juice, and ¼ teaspoon kosher salt to a boil in a small saucepan over medium-high. Reduce heat to medium-low; cook, stirring and skimming foam from surface often, until carrots are very tender and liquid has almost completely evaporated, 18 to 24 minutes.

2. Transfer carrot mixture to a blender, and remove top insert in lid to allow steam to escape. Add 3 tablespoons carrot juice, and place a clean towel over opening. Process until mixture is very smooth, about 2 minutes, stopping to scrape sides as

needed. Add remaining 1 tablespoon carrot juice, ½ tablespoon at a time, if needed to thin mixture just enough for the blender to process.

3. Transfer carrot mixture to a medium bowl. Stir in 1 cup mochiko until just combined, and knead in bowl until a smooth, tacky dough forms, 1 to 2 minutes, adding remaining 1 tablespoon mochiko if needed to prevent dough from sticking to hands.

4. Divide dough into ½-ounce (about 1-tablespoon) pieces (22 to 24 pieces total). Roll each piece between your hands to form a 1-inch ball. Bring 3 quarts water to a boil in a large saucepan over medium-high. Stir in 3 tablespoons kosher salt. Fill a medium bowl with ice water, and set aside.

5. Add mochi balls to boiling water; cook, stirring occasionally, until no longer grainy in center, 6 to 8 minutes. (Mochi balls

STEP-BY-STEP

COOK THE CARROTS Simmer fresh spring carrots in carrot juice until carrots are tender and juice is reduced for a double dose of carrot flavor.

MAKE A PUREE Puree the cooked carrots with an additional splash of fresh carrot juice to form a silky-smooth puree.

MAKE THE MOCHI DOUGH Stir mochiko—a sweet, glutinous rice flour that lends a bouncy, chewy texture—into carrot puree; knead until smooth.

ROLL THE MOCHI Working with 1 tablespoonful of mochi dough at a time, roll dough between palms to form smooth 1-inch balls.

will float after about 4 minutes; continue cooking.) To test for doneness, remove 1 ball from water, cut in half, and taste for graininess. Using a spider, transfer mochi balls to prepared ice water, and let cool 2 minutes. Drain well, and transfer to a large bowl. Add oil, and toss to coat. Mochi balls can be used immediately or stored in an airtight container in refrigerator up to 24 hours. Bring to room temperature before using.

6. Melt butter in a large stainless steel skillet over medium-high. Cook, stirring occasionally, until butter is lightly golden, about 2 minutes. Add mochi balls, and sprinkle with remaining ½ teaspoon kosher salt; cook, stirring often, until balls are lightly crispy and golden, 3 to 4 minutes. Transfer to a rimmed platter; spoon brown butter in skillet over top.

7. Assemble the dish: Arrange roasted carrots around mochi balls on platter, discarding garlic and thyme. Sprinkle with drained pickled carrots. Drizzle with pickling liquid and oil. Sprinkle with herbs, pistachio dukkah, and flaky sea salt, if desired. Serve immediately. —GABY MAEDA

MAKE AHEAD Mochi can be prepared through step 5 and stored in an airtight container in refrigerator up to 24 hours.

WINE Fruity, citrus-edged rosé: 2020 Domaine de la Mordorée La Reine des Bois Tavel Rosé

NOTE Find Koda Farms mochiko at Asian markets or online at bokksugrocery.com.

BLANCH AND SHOCK THE MOCHI Cook mochi dumplings in boiling salted water to set the dough, and then cool in an ice bath. (The mochi can be made ahead to this step.)

CRISP THE MOCHI Pan-fry mochi in brown butter to crisp the exterior of the dumplings while maintaining the fun and classic mochi texture within.

BUTTERY SPAETZLE WITH ROASTED
CAULIFLOWER AND SHALLOTS

Buttery Spaetzle with Roasted Cauliflower and Shallots

⏱ ACTIVE 25 MIN; TOTAL 45 MIN;
SERVES 6 TO 8

Like tiny gnocchi, German spaetzle are delicious simply blanched but spring to a whole new level when crisped with butter in a pan.

- 1 small (2-lb.) head purple or regular cauliflower, cut into 1-inch florets (about 6½ cups)
- 2½ cups thinly sliced shallots or red onion
- ¼ cup extra-virgin olive oil
- 4½ tsp. kosher salt, divided, plus more to taste
- 1 tsp. smoked paprika
- 1 tsp. black pepper, plus more to taste
- 2½ qt. water
- 10 oz. dried spaetzle (such as Bechtle Hofbauer)
- ½ cup unsalted butter (4 oz.)
- 1 tsp. grated lemon zest plus 2 Tbsp. fresh lemon juice
  Dill sprigs, sour cream, and crushed red pepper, for garnish

1. Preheat oven to 425°F. Toss together cauliflower, shallots, oil, 2 teaspoons salt, paprika, and black pepper on a large rimmed baking sheet. Spread mixture in a single layer. Roast until cauliflower is tender and browned in spots, 30 to 35 minutes.

2. Meanwhile, bring 2½ quarts water to a boil in a large pot. Stir in remaining 2½ teaspoons salt. Cook spaetzle according to package directions. Drain, reserving ½ cup cooking liquid. Wipe pot dry.

3. Add butter to pot, and heat over medium, stirring often, until lightly browned and foamy, 3 to 5 minutes. Add cauliflower mixture, spaetzle, and reserved cooking liquid; gently toss to combine until spaetzle is coated with brown butter. Remove from heat; stir in lemon zest and juice. Season to taste with additional salt and black pepper. Garnish with dill, sour cream, and red pepper as desired. —JUSTIN CHAPPLE

WINE Crisp, lightly earthy German white: 2019 Villa Wolf Pinot Blanc

NOTE Find dried spaetzle at specialty grocery stores or online at thetasteofgermany.com.

Pernil Mac and Cheese

ACTIVE 45 MIN; TOTAL 1 HR 30 MIN, PLUS 4 HR REFRIGERATION AND 5 HR ROASTING
SERVES 10 TO 12

At their Durham, North Carolina, restaurant Boricua Soul, Serena and Toriano Fredericks serve this garlicky pernil—a Puerto Rican-style pork shoulder—on top of a rich and creamy mac and cheese.

PERNIL

- 1¼ cups peeled garlic cloves (from about 4 garlic heads)
- 3 Tbsp. dried oregano
- 3 Tbsp. white vinegar
- 2 Tbsp. coarse kosher salt (such as Morton's)
- 1 Tbsp. plus 1½ tsp. sazón with coriander and annatto (such as Badia)
- 1 Tbsp. adobo all-purpose seasoning powder with pepper
- 1 (7- to 9-lb.) bone-in, skin-on pork shoulder

MAC AND CHEESE

- 3 qt. water
- 1 Tbsp. plus 2 tsp. coarse kosher salt (such as Morton's), divided
- 1 lb. uncooked elbow macaroni
- 4 large eggs
- 2 cups heavy cream
- 1 tsp. seasoned salt (such as Lawry's)
- 1 tsp. black pepper
- 1½ lb. sharp cheddar cheese, shredded (about 6 cups), divided
  Cooking spray

1. Make the pernil: Process garlic, oregano, vinegar, salt, sazón, and adobo seasoning in a food processor until mixture forms a paste, about 45 seconds, stopping occasionally to scrape down sides of bowl. Alternatively, crush mixture using a mortar and pestle to form a paste.

2. Using a sharp knife, score pork skin and fat cap about ¼ to ½ inch deep in a diamond pattern, spacing cuts 1¼ inches apart. Cut 8 (2½-inch-deep) slits into bottom and sides of pork. Rub garlic paste over roast, pushing into the slits and scores in fat cap. Place seasoned pork on a rimmed baking sheet; cover tightly with plastic wrap, and refrigerate 4 to 12 hours.

3. Preheat oven to 350°F with rack in lower third position. Unwrap pork shoulder. Place pork, skin side up, in a medium-size roasting pan; let rest at room temperature while oven preheats. Roast pork, uncovered, in preheated oven until a thermometer inserted in thickest portion of meat registers 200°F, 5 to 7 hours, tenting with aluminum foil after 1 hour and 45 minutes if needed to prevent burning. After about 2 hours of roasting, begin basting pork with pan drippings every hour. Transfer cooked pernil to a cutting board, and let rest 30 minutes. Reserve drippings in pan. Do not turn oven off. Carefully position oven rack in middle of oven.

4. While pork roasts, make the mac and cheese: Bring 3 quarts water to a boil in a large pot over medium-high. Stir in 1 tablespoon kosher salt. Add pasta, and cook according to package directions until al dente. Drain pasta, and rinse well under cold water. Whisk eggs vigorously in a large bowl until frothy, about 1 minute. Whisk in cream, seasoned salt, black pepper, and remaining 2 teaspoons kosher salt. Stir in 5 cups cheese until well combined. Gently fold in cooked pasta. Spoon mixture into a 13-×9-inch baking dish lightly coated with cooking spray. Sprinkle evenly with remaining 1 cup cheese. Cover and refrigerate unbaked mac and cheese until pork has finished roasting.

5. While pernil rests, uncover mac and cheese. Place on middle rack in oven; bake at 350°F until light golden brown on top, about 45 minutes. During final 15 minutes of baking mac and cheese, remove skin from pernil, and finely chop. Shred meat into bite-size pieces. Transfer shredded meat and chopped skin to a large bowl; toss to combine. Discard pork bone, or reserve for stock. Pour pan drippings into a fat separator or a measuring cup; skim and discard fat. Season pernil to taste with skimmed pan drippings. Divide mac and cheese among bowls; top with pernil. —TORIANO FREDERICKS

MAKE AHEAD Mac and cheese can be made up to 1 day ahead, covered, and refrigerated up to 12 hours. Let come to room temperature before baking.

BEER Crisp Puerto Rican lager: Medalla Light

NOTE Find sazón at Latin markets or online at amigofoods.com.

Mushroom-and-Tofu Pad Thai

🕐 ACTIVE 30 MIN; TOTAL 40 MIN; SERVES 2

This Thai noodle dish is a delectably sweet, salty, and sour sauce that's seasoned with fish sauce, sugar, tamarind, and lime juice. Lara Lee's meatless pad thai heroes hearty, savory fresh oyster and shiitake mushrooms, which suffuse the dish with earthy flavor and combine beautifully with chewy noodles, golden-fried tofu, fresh, crisp bean sprouts, lightly spicy long red chiles, and crunchy peanuts. Tamarind sits firmly at this pad thai's center, balancing the dish and holding it all together with its delightfully sour high note. When you prepare the dish, be sure to wash and dry the skillet after browning the mushrooms to prevent the fond from burning while cooking the tofu and peanuts. To make it vegetarian, use a vegan fish sauce, such as Ocean's Halo, and swap mushroom sauce for the oyster sauce.

SAUCE

- ¼ cup superfine sugar
- 2 Tbsp. fish sauce
- 2 Tbsp. oyster sauce
- 2 Tbsp. Tamarind Water (recipe p. 330)
- 4 tsp. fresh lime juice (from 1 lime)
- 1 fresh long red chile (about ⅜ oz.), finely chopped (about 1 Tbsp.)
- 1 medium garlic clove, finely chopped (about 1 tsp.)

PAD THAI

- 5 oz. uncooked rice noodles (about ⅓ inch wide)
- 5 Tbsp. neutral cooking oil (such as canola oil), divided
- 6 oz. mixed fresh mushrooms (such as king oyster, thinly sliced crosswise into ¼-inch pieces; shiitake caps, sliced into ⅓-inch pieces; or oyster mushrooms, torn if large)
- ¾ tsp. fine sea salt, divided, plus more to taste
- 6 (2½-×1¾-×¼-inch) firm tofu slices (from about 3 oz. tofu, drained and patted dry)
- 2 Tbsp. peanuts, chopped
- 2 large eggs, beaten
- 4 medium-size fresh Chinese chives or 1 scallion, cut crosswise into 1-inch pieces
- 1 cup fresh bean sprouts, divided
- ¼ cup loosely packed fresh cilantro leaves and stems

1. Make the sauce: Stir together superfine sugar, fish sauce, oyster sauce, tamarind water, lime juice, chile, and garlic in a small bowl. Set aside.

2. Make the pad thai: Soak noodles in boiling water according to package directions. Drain. Transfer to a medium bowl. Add 1 tablespoon oil, and toss to coat. Set aside.

3. Heat 1 tablespoon oil in a large stainless steel skillet over high. Add mushrooms and ½ teaspoon salt; cook, stirring occasionally, until mushrooms are tender and golden brown, 3 to 5 minutes. Transfer to a small bowl; set aside. Wash and dry skillet.

4. Return skillet to heat over medium-high, and add 2 tablespoons oil. Add tofu slices to hot oil in a single layer; sprinkle evenly with ⅛ teaspoon salt. Cook, undisturbed, until golden on bottom, 1 minute and 30 seconds to 2 minutes. Carefully flip using a thin metal spatula. Sprinkle evenly with remaining ⅛ teaspoon salt. Cook until golden brown on other side, 1 minute and 30 seconds to 2 minutes. Transfer to a plate lined with paper towels. Set aside. Wipe skillet clean.

5. Return skillet to heat over medium-low, and add 1½ teaspoons oil. Add peanuts, and sprinkle with salt to taste. Cook, stirring constantly, until peanuts are fragrant and toasted, 1 to 2 minutes. Transfer to a mortar, and coarsely grind using a pestle. (Alternatively, transfer to a cutting board, and finely chop.) Set peanuts aside, and wipe skillet clean.

6. Return skillet to heat over high, and add remaining 1½ teaspoons oil. Add eggs; cook, undisturbed, until bubbly and mostly set, about 15 seconds. Scramble eggs, and break into large pieces; push scrambled eggs to back edge of skillet. Add Chinese chives and ⅔ cup bean sprouts to center of skillet. Cook, stirring constantly, until softened, about 30 seconds. Add noodles and half of the sauce (about ¼ cup). Cook, stirring constantly, until ingredients in skillet are well incorporated and noodles have separated into individual strands, about 30 seconds. Stir in cooked mushrooms, tofu, and remaining sauce (about ¼ cup). Cook, stirring constantly, until well combined and noodles are shiny and well coated, about 20 seconds. Immediately divide noodle mixture between 2 bowls. Top evenly with ground peanuts, cilantro, and remaining ⅓ cup bean sprouts. —LARA LEE

WINE Crisp Côtes de Provence rosé: 2020 Château Miraval

MUSHROOM-AND-TOFU PAD THAI

CHICKEN SPAGHETTI LO MEIN

Chicken Spaghetti Lo Mein

ACTIVE 50 MIN; TOTAL 1 HR 10 MIN;
SERVES 4

Lan Samantha Chang's family adds even more savory flavor to their favorite lo mein recipe with dried shiitake mushrooms, soy sauce, and Shaoxing wine. Baking the noodles with the mushroom soaking liquid and soy sauce infuses them with rich flavor, complemented by the stir-fried chicken, eggs, and celery that complete the dish.

- 4 oz. dried shiitake mushrooms (about 3 cups)
- 4 cups hot water (170°F)
- 7 oz. uncooked spaghetti
- 1 Tbsp. plus 1 tsp. toasted sesame oil
- 5 Tbsp. plus 1 tsp. soy sauce, divided
- 6 Tbsp. plus 1 tsp. vegetable oil, divided
- ½ tsp. black pepper, plus more to taste
- 2 (7-oz.) boneless, skinless chicken breasts, sliced diagonally into ⅛-inch-thick strips
- 2 Tbsp. Shaoxing wine
- ½ tsp. cornstarch
- 4 large eggs
- ¼ tsp. kosher salt
- 2 cups (2-×¼-inch) celery strips

1. Place mushrooms in a medium-size heatproof bowl. Pour 4 cups hot water over mushrooms; weigh down using a small plate to keep submerged. Let soak until mushroom caps are softened, about 30 minutes. Drain mushrooms, reserving ¼ cup soaking liquid. Remove stems, and discard. Slice mushroom caps into ⅛-inch-wide slices; set aside.

2. Preheat oven to 300°F. Bring a large saucepan of lightly salted water to a boil over high. Add spaghetti, and cook according to package directions for al dente; drain. Transfer spaghetti to a 13-×9-inch baking dish. Drizzle spaghetti with reserved mushroom soaking liquid, sesame oil, 2 tablespoons soy sauce, and 1 tablespoon vegetable oil; sprinkle with pepper. Add additional pepper to taste. Toss using chopsticks to evenly coat, and spread in an even layer. Cover dish tightly with aluminum foil, and bake in preheated oven 20 minutes.

3. Meanwhile, combine chicken, Shaoxing wine, cornstarch, 1 tablespoon plus 1 teaspoon soy sauce, and 1 teaspoon vegetable oil in a medium bowl; stir to combine using chopsticks, and set aside. Using chopsticks, beat eggs and salt in a small bowl until well blended; set aside.

4. When spaghetti has baked about 10 minutes, heat 2 tablespoons vegetable oil in a wok over medium-high until fragrant and shimmering. Add mushroom slices;

cook, stirring often, until beginning to brown in spots, about 3 minutes. Add 1 tablespoon soy sauce; cook, stirring constantly, 10 seconds. Add celery; cook, stirring often, until celery is just crisp-tender, about 3 minutes, adding remaining 1 tablespoon soy sauce after 1 minute. Transfer mushroom mixture to a large bowl. Do not wipe wok clean.

5. Add 2 tablespoons vegetable oil to wok; heat over medium-high until shimmering. Add chicken mixture; cook, stirring often, until chicken is no longer pink and is cooked through, about 3 minutes. Return mushroom mixture to wok; cook, stirring constantly, until warmed through, about 1 minute.

6. Remove baking dish from oven, and remove foil. Stir spaghetti using chopsticks until starch from pasta thickens any remaining liquid in baking dish. Spread chicken mixture evenly over spaghetti.

7. Add remaining 1 tablespoon vegetable oil to wok; heat over medium-high until a drop of egg added to wok immediately bubbles up in oil. Add eggs; cook, undisturbed, until eggs begin to puff up and set along edges of wok, about 30 seconds. Continue to cook, stirring constantly, until eggs are set, about 1 minute. Spoon eggs over chicken mixture, and serve immediately. —LAN SAMANTHA CHANG

WINE Red-fruited, medium-bodied Pinot Noir: 2019 Sokol Blosser Evolution Willamette Valley

PANCIT MIKI BIHON

Pancit Miki Bihon

ACTIVE 50 MIN; TOTAL 1 HR 30 MIN;
SERVES 4 TO 6

For Carlo Lamagna, a F&W 2021 Best New Chef, and the owner of Magna Kusina in Portland, Oregon, this pancit recipe equals comfort. "When I first started working in the restaurant industry, I would come home late at night around 2 am, exhausted from working a shift," he says. Tired and hungry, I would often find a plate of food left out for me by my mom and dad. Pancit was in regular rotation and really hit the spot after a long day. When I would pop the plate in the microwave to heat up, I would often hear footsteps coming down the staircase, and it was either my mom or dad making their way to the kitchen to check in and make sure that I wasn't eating alone. That is true love of a parent."

MIKI NOODLES

- 1⅓ cups unbleached bread flour (such as King Arthur) (about 5¾ oz.), plus more as needed
- 3 Tbsp. nutritional yeast
- 2 qt. plus ⅓ cup plus 5 tsp. water (as needed), divided
- 2 Tbsp. kosher salt

BIHON NOODLES

- 1 (8-oz.) pkg. bihon rice stick noodles (such as Excellent)
- 2 Tbsp. neutral cooking oil (such as vegetable oil)
- 8 medium garlic cloves, finely chopped (about 2½ Tbsp.)
- 1 (1-inch) piece fresh ginger, peeled and finely chopped (about 4 tsp.)
- 3 Tbsp. chicken stock
- 2 Tbsp. fish sauce (such as Red Boat)
- 2 Tbsp. soy sauce (such as Silver Swan)

ADDITIONAL INGREDIENTS

- ¼ cup neutral cooking oil (such as vegetable oil), divided
- 1 cup shredded Savoy cabbage (from 1 small [2-lb.] cabbage), divided
- 1 large (3½-oz.) carrot, peeled and cut into ⅛- × ⅛- × 2-inch strips (about ⅔ cup), divided
- 1 cup shredded cooked chicken (about 5 oz.), divided
- 2 tsp. fish sauce (such as Red Boat), divided, plus more to taste
- 2 tsp. soy sauce (such as Silver Swan), divided, plus more to taste
- Lemon wedges, for serving
- Thinly sliced scallions, fried chopped garlic (such as Maesri), fried shallots (such as Maesri), and chicken skin chicharrones, for garnish (optional)

1. Make the miki noodles: Stir together flour and nutritional yeast in a medium bowl. Stir in ⅓ cup water. Add up to 5 teaspoons water as needed, 1 teaspoon at a time, stirring well to combine after each addition, until a shaggy dough forms and dry ingredients are just incorporated. (Dough should not be sticky.) Turn dough out onto a clean work surface, and knead until smooth and springy to the touch, 10 to 12 minutes. Wrap dough tightly in plastic wrap, and let rest at room temperature until dough is slightly softer (touching it with a finger should leave an easy indentation), at least 30 minutes or up to 4 hours.

2. Unwrap dough, and cut in half. Set rollers of a pasta machine to widest setting. Working with 1 dough half at a time (keeping other half covered with plastic wrap), flatten dough using your hands to ⅓-inch thickness. Roll dough through pasta machine. Fold rolled dough in half crosswise, and reroll through pasta machine. Continue refolding and rerolling dough until it is as wide as the pasta machine (about 5 inches), 1 or 2 additional times. Once appropriate width is reached, continue rolling dough through pasta machine, reducing width of rollers 1 setting at a time, until dough has been rolled through setting 4 (spaghetti thickness, or fourth-thinnest setting), flouring dough as needed to prevent sticking. Cover rolled dough sheet with a towel. Repeat process with remaining dough half.

3. Attach a spaghetti cutter to pasta machine. Cut each rolled dough sheet crosswise into 6- to 8-inch-long sections. Pass each dough piece through cutter, flouring dough as needed to prevent sticking. (Alternatively, roll dough by hand to ⅟₁₆-inch thickness and cut into ⅛-inch-wide, 8-inch-long noodles.) Sprinkle cut noodles with flour, and place on a lightly floured rimmed baking sheet; cover with a towel to prevent drying out. Repeat process with remaining dough pieces.

4. Bring remaining 2 quarts water to a boil in a large saucepan over medium-high. Stir in salt, and return to a boil. Fill a medium bowl with ice water, and set aside. Add miki noodles to boiling water; cook, stirring occasionally, until noodles are just tender, 1 minute and 30 seconds to 2 minutes. Using a fine wire-mesh strainer or a spider, remove noodles, and transfer to prepared ice bath. Let stand until cold, about 3 minutes. Drain well, and set aside.

5. Make the bihon noodles: Soak noodles in hot water according to package directions until tender, about 3 minutes. Drain well, and set aside. Heat oil in a 14-inch wok over medium-high. Add garlic and ginger; cook, stirring constantly, until fragrant, about 30 seconds. Stir in noodles, chicken stock, fish sauce, and soy sauce. Reduce heat to medium; cook, stirring often, until noodles absorb liquid and become tender, about 2 minutes. Transfer mixture to a large bowl; set aside.

6. Add 2 tablespoons oil to wok; heat over medium-high. Add half of the cabbage (about ½ cup) and half of the carrot (about ⅓ cup). Cook, stirring constantly, until tender, about 30 seconds. Add half of the chicken, half of the miki noodles (about 1½ cups), half of the bihon noodles (about 2½ cups), 1 teaspoon fish sauce, and 1 teaspoon soy sauce. Cook, tossing often, until mixture is evenly combined and hot, 1 to 2 minutes. Season with additional fish sauce and soy sauce to taste. Transfer pancit to a larger platter.

7. Repeat cooking process with remaining oil, cabbage, carrot, chicken, miki noodles, bihon noodles, fish sauce, and soy sauce.

8. Serve pancit immediately with lemon wedges. If desired, garnish with scallions, fried garlic, fried shallots, and chicken skin chicharrones. —CARLO LAMAGNA

MAKE AHEAD Homemade miki noodles can be prepared through step 4 up to 1 hour in advance.

NOTE Store-bought miki noodles, such as Fiesta Pinoy dry miki noodles or fresh Wah Nam noodles, found at most Asian grocery stores, can be substituted for homemade noodles. Start recipe at step 4, and cook miki noodles according to package directions.

FISH &
SHELLFISH

SHRIMP WITH ROASTED CORN, LEEKS,
TOMATOES, AND BASIL (P. 106)
OPPOSITE: SHAOXING-STEAMED STEELHEAD
TROUT AND MUSHROOMS (P. 97)

**POACHED SALT COD SALAD
WITH SWEET PEPPERS**

Poached Salt Cod Salad with Sweet Peppers

ACTIVE 45 MIN; TOTAL 1 HR 25 MIN, PLUS
12 HR SOAKING; SERVES 4

Pieces of slightly sweet, pleasantly chewy poached salt cod feature in this hearty salad of sweet peppers, purslane, herbs, and cherry tomatoes. After soaking in water to rehydrate and remove salt, the fillets of salt cod get poached in a bath of olive oil, garlic, bay leaf, and thyme, infusing them with flavor and giving the fish some succulence. The cooled oil and aromatics are then strained and used in a parsley puree to dress the salad and to blister the sweet peppers, layering flavor into every element of the dish. 2004 F&W Best New Chef Melissa Perello of Octavia and Frances in San Francisco, who shared her recipe with Food & Wine, *suggests using Jimmy Nardello peppers here if you can find them. "One of my favorite markers of the season is seeing sweet peppers pop up at the farmers market, and Jimmy Nardellos are some of my favorite peppers to work with. (If you're local to the Bay Area, Full Belly Farm's are excellent.) In this hearty salad, the peppers complement the poached cod with rich sweetness and acidity."*

- 1 (10½-oz.) skinless salt cod fillet
- 12 medium garlic cloves (from 2 garlic heads), peeled
- 4 (4-inch) thyme sprigs
- 1 fresh or dried bay leaf
- 2 to 3 cups olive oil, as needed
- 1 cup chopped fresh flat-leaf parsley leaves and tender stems (from 1 bunch parsley)
- 1 Tbsp. capers, drained and rinsed
- ½ tsp. crushed red pepper
- 2 tsp. grated lemon zest plus 3 Tbsp. fresh lemon juice (from 2 lemons)
- 1 tsp. kosher salt, divided, plus more to taste
- 12 medium-size sweet mini peppers, Jimmy Nardello peppers, or shishito peppers (6 to 8 oz.)
- 8 cups fresh purslane, sorrel, or watercress (about 8 oz.)
- 12 Sun Gold cherry tomatoes (about 6 oz.), halved lengthwise
- 1 Tbsp. white wine vinegar or Champagne vinegar

  Toasted breadcrumbs (optional)

1. Rinse cod under cool water to remove as much salt as possible. Place cod in a large container, bowl, or pot; add water to cover cod by 2 inches. Cover and let cod soak in refrigerator at least 12 hours or up to 24 hours, changing water about 4 times throughout.

2. Remove soaked cod from water; discard water, and gently pat fish dry with paper towels. (The fish should have softened considerably.) Place fish in a small saucepan just large enough for it to fit snugly. Add garlic, thyme sprigs, and bay leaf. Add oil as needed to just cover the fish, and make sure the pan is tall enough that there are a few inches of space remaining to prevent any oil spilling over as it cooks. Bring cod mixture to a gentle simmer over low; simmer, covered, until cod is tender and flakes easily with a fork, 20 to 30 minutes. (If your fish is very thin, check after 15 minutes.) Transfer cod to a medium bowl; gently flake into bite-size pieces with a fork, and place in refrigerator until ready to use. Let oil mixture cool at room temperature 10 minutes.

3. Pour cooled oil mixture through a fine wire-mesh strainer into a heatproof bowl; reserve garlic cloves, and discard bay leaf and thyme sprigs. Transfer strained oil to refrigerator, and let chill completely, about 30 minutes.

4. Pulse parsley, capers, crushed red pepper, 6 poached garlic cloves, and 1 cup reserved poaching oil in a food processor until mixture is coarsely chopped and blended into a salsa-like texture, 8 to 10 pulses. Stir in lemon zest and juice; season with salt to taste. Set puree aside, uncovered and at room temperature, until ready to use.

5. Heat 2 tablespoons reserved poaching oil in a 12-inch skillet over high. Add half of the peppers to skillet; cook, stirring occasionally, until peppers blister and begin to pop, 1 to 2 minutes. (If you have a splatter guard, this is a great time to use it.) Transfer blistered peppers to a plate, and sprinkle with ½ teaspoon salt. Repeat cooking process with remaining peppers, adding more poaching oil as needed and sprinkling blistered peppers with remaining ½ teaspoon salt. Reserve remaining poaching oil for another use.

6. Toss together purslane, tomatoes, vinegar, flaked cod, peppers, and remaining 6 poached garlic cloves in a large bowl to combine; season with salt to taste.

7. Drizzle ¼ cup parsley puree on a plate or platter; arrange salad mixture on plate. Garnish with breadcrumbs, if desired, and serve with remaining ¾ cup parsley puree on the side for drizzling. —MELISSA PERELLO, OCTAVIA AND FRANCES, SAN FRANCISCO

WINE Light, peppery Italian red: 2020 Castello di Verduno Basadone Pelaverga

Ginger-Ponzu Salmon Poke

TOTAL 20 MIN; SERVES 4

Salmon is tossed with ponzu and ginger to make a poke that is perfect served over cooked rice. Ask your fishmonger about sushi-grade salmon suitable for poke.

- 2 Tbsp. ponzu (such as Poi Dog Maui Lavender Ponzu), plus more to taste
- 2 Tbsp. finely chopped scallions (from 2 medium scallions), plus more to taste
- 1 Tbsp. finely sliced fresh shiso (Japanese or Vietnamese) (about 6 leaves), plus more to taste
- 1 Tbsp. crushed unsalted roasted macadamia nuts, plus more to taste
- 2 tsp. perilla oil, plus more to taste
- 1½ tsp. grated peeled fresh ginger (from 1 [2-inch] piece), plus more to taste
- 1 lb. skinless sushi-grade salmon fillet

  Alaea sea salt or Maldon sea salt, to taste

  Toasted shiso seeds (perilla seeds) or white sesame seeds

  Cooked short-grain white rice, fried wonton skin chips, or gim (dried seaweed), for serving (optional)

1. Stir together ponzu, scallions, shiso, macadamia nuts, perilla oil, and ginger in a medium bowl. (Mixture will be slightly creamy.)

2. Cut salmon into bite-size (about ¾-inch) cubes using a sharp knife. Add salmon to ponzu mixture in bowl; gently stir together until well coated.

3. Season with salt to taste. Adjust flavors with additional ponzu (umami tang), scallions (pungency), shiso (brightness), macadamia nuts (creaminess), perilla oil (velvety richness), ginger (heat), and/or salt (texture) to taste. Garnish with shiso

seeds; serve immediately with desired accompaniments. —KIKI ARANITA

MAKE AHEAD Poke can be made up to 1 day in advance and stored in an airtight container in refrigerator. Re-season before serving.

WINE Substantial, spicy rosé: 2021 Domaine de la Begude Bandol Rosé

NOTE Perilla oil is available at Korean markets and online at gothamgrove.com. Poi Dog Maui Lavender Ponzu is available online at poidogphilly.com. Alaea sea salt is available online at thespicehouse.com.

Sizzling Garlic Salmon with Sheet Pan Potatoes

ACTIVE 15 MIN; TOTAL 50 MIN SERVES 4

For this sheet pan dinner, baby potatoes, red onion, and spring onions get a head start in a hot oven, before they are joined by a side of salmon, slathered with mustard and drizzled with toasted garlic oil, which cooks alongside the vegetables for a seamless final presentation. Sommelier Erin Miller, of Charlie Palmer's Dry Creek Kitchen in Healdsburg, California, who provided the inspiration for this dish, notes that it tastes even better when served with a great wine. She recommends a glass of Hirsch Vineyards Raschen Ridge Sonoma Coast Pinot Noir, noting, "The bright acidity of the Hirsch Pinot Noir is a perfect foil for the fresh, fatty fish and flavors of garlic and lemon."

- 1½ lb. baby yellow potatoes, halved lengthwise
- 1 large red onion, cut into ½-inch wedges
- 5 spring onions (about 6 oz.), trimmed and halved lengthwise
- ⅓ cup plus 2 Tbsp. extra-virgin olive oil, divided

- 2 tsp. kosher salt, divided
- ½ tsp. black pepper, divided
- ¼ cup Dijon mustard, divided
- 1 (2-lb.) skin-on or skinless salmon side
- 3 garlic cloves, thinly sliced (about 1½ Tbsp.)
- 2 Tbsp. chopped fresh tarragon
- 2 Tbsp. chopped fresh chives

  Lemon wedges, for serving

1. Preheat oven to 425°F. Toss together potatoes, red onion, spring onions, and 2 tablespoons oil on a large rimmed baking sheet; spread in an even layer. Sprinkle evenly with 1 teaspoon salt and ¼ teaspoon pepper. Roast in preheated oven until vegetables begin to brown, about 20 minutes. Remove from oven, and reduce oven temperature to 325°F.

2. Add 1 tablespoon mustard to vegetable mixture on baking sheet; toss to coat. Push vegetables to long edges of baking sheet. Place salmon, skin side down, lengthwise in middle of baking sheet. Spread salmon with remaining 3 tablespoons mustard; sprinkle with remaining 1 teaspoon salt and remaining ¼ teaspoon pepper.

3. Heat remaining ⅓ cup oil in a large skillet over medium-high. Add garlic; cook, stirring often, until garlic is fragrant and light golden brown, about 2 minutes. Pour hot oil mixture over salmon on baking sheet. Roast at 325°F until salmon flakes easily with a fork and vegetables are tender, 12 to 15 minutes. Remove from oven. Transfer salmon to a platter; sprinkle with tarragon and chives. Transfer vegetables to a bowl. Serve salmon and vegetables with lemon wedges. —ANNA THEOKTISTO

WINE 2014 Hirsch Vineyards Raschen Ridge Sonoma Coast Pinot Noir

**SIZZLING GARLIC SALMON
WITH SHEET PAN POTATOES**

BRANZINO WITH MESCLUN AND TOMATO—HERBES DE PROVENCE VINAIGRETTE

Branzino with Mesclun and Tomato–Herbes de Provence Vinaigrette

TOTAL 30 MIN; SERVES 4

Branzino, known as loup de mer, or "wolf of the sea" in French, is mild and sweet. Its delicate flavor pairs nicely with a summery tomato–and–mixed herb vinaigrette. Scoring the fish skin before cooking prevents the fillets from curling in the pan.

- 1 small beefsteak tomato (about 6 oz.), halved crosswise
- ½ cup extra-virgin olive oil, divided
- 3 Tbsp. Champagne vinegar
- 2 tsp. herbes de Provence
- 2 tsp. kosher salt, divided
- ¾ tsp. black pepper, divided
- 1 small garlic clove, finely grated (about ¼ tsp.)
- 4 (5-oz.) skin-on branzino fillets
- 5 oz. mesclun greens (about 10 cups)
- 1 cup loosely packed fresh flat-leaf parsley leaves
- ½ cup sliced (¼- to ½-inch pieces) fresh chives
- ⅓ cup loosely packed fresh tarragon leaves
- 1 tsp. fresh chervil leaves (optional)

1. Grate cut sides of tomato halves on small holes of a box grater into a medium bowl until only tomato skin remains in your hand; discard tomato skins. Add 6 tablespoons oil, vinegar, herbes de Provence, ½ teaspoon salt, ¼ teaspoon pepper, and garlic to grated tomato in bowl; whisk until well combined. Set vinaigrette aside.

2. Place 1 branzino fillet, skin side up, over rim of a plate. Gently fold fillet over the rim to pull the skin taut. Using a sharp paring knife, score only the skin by making 3 to 4 shallow slashes, being careful not to cut too deep into the fillet. Repeat scoring process with remaining 3 fillets. Sprinkle both sides of fillets evenly with 1 teaspoon salt.

3. Heat remaining 2 tablespoons oil in a large nonstick skillet over medium-high. Add fillets, skin side down, to skillet; using a fish spatula (see Note), gently press each fillet to flatten. Cook, undisturbed, until skin is browned and crisp, about 4 minutes. Flip fillets; cook until just cooked through, 30 seconds to 1 minute. Transfer fillets, skin side up, to plates or a platter.

4. While fillets cook, toss together mesclun, parsley, chives, tarragon, and, if using, chervil in a large bowl to combine. Add ⅓ cup tomato vinaigrette, remaining ½ teaspoon salt, and remaining ½ teaspoon pepper; toss well to coat.

5. Serve salad alongside branzino fillets, passing remaining vinaigrette (about ½ cup) at the table. —JUSTIN CHAPPLE

WINE Medium-bodied Oregon Pinot Gris: 2020 Ponzi Willamette Valley

NOTE The large surface area and flexible paddle of a fish spatula make it perfect for pressing fish fillets flat as they cook.

Shaoxing-Steamed Steelhead Trout and Mushrooms

PHOTO P. 90

ACTIVE 20 MIN; TOTAL 30 MIN SERVES 4

Oyster, beech, and shiitake mushrooms cook alongside fatty, succulent steelhead trout fillets in a bath of steam from the Shaoxing wine simmering in the wok beneath the steamer. Serve the fish alongside cooked rice to soak up the aromatic sauce.

- 1 small fresh red Fresno chile or serrano chile (unseeded), stemmed and finely chopped (about 1 Tbsp.)
- 1 Tbsp. granulated sugar
- 2 tsp. very finely chopped peeled fresh ginger (from 1 [½-inch] piece)
- 2 small garlic cloves, very finely chopped (about 1½ tsp.)
- 2 tsp. kosher salt, divided
- 4 (5- to 6-oz.) skin-on steelhead trout fillets
- 8 oz. mixed fresh mushrooms (such as oyster mushrooms, beech mushrooms, and shiitake mushroom caps) (about 4 cups)
- 1 cup Shaoxing wine
- 1 cup water
- 1 Tbsp. fresh lime juice
- 2 medium scallions (about ¾ oz.), cut crosswise into 2-inch pieces and thinly sliced lengthwise (julienned)

1. Combine chile, sugar, ginger, garlic, and 1 teaspoon salt in a medium-size heatproof bowl; set aside. Line each of 2 trays of a 14-inch bamboo steamer with a 6-inch square of parchment paper, leaving space around sides of parchment square for steam to rise. Sprinkle trout evenly with remaining 1 teaspoon salt. Place 2 fillets, skin side down, in each steamer tray on parchment paper. Tear mushrooms into large bite-size pieces, if needed; scatter mushrooms between and around fillets. Stack steamer trays; cover basket with lid.

2. Pour wine and 1 cup water into a nonreactive 14-inch flat-bottomed wok. Bring to a boil over medium-high. Place prepared steamer over wok. Steam until fish is just cooked through and mushrooms are tender, 5 to 6 minutes.

3. Remove bamboo steamer from wok. Immediately ladle ¼ cup of the boiling wine mixture from wok over chile mixture in bowl, and stir in lime juice. The sauce should be sharply flavored, tart, salty, and a little sweet. Discard remaining wine mixture in wok.

4. Arrange trout fillets, skin side down, on a platter. Scatter mushrooms on top of and around fish. Pour chile-ginger sauce over fish and mushrooms, and sprinkle with scallions. —ANDREA SLONECKER

WINE Minerally, lightly off-dry Riesling: 2020 Peter Lauer Senior Fass 6

Grilled Mahi-Mahi with Lemongrass-Lime Aioli

PHOTO P. 344

◷ TOTAL 25 MIN; SERVES 4

Sweet, mild grilled mahi-mahi harmonizes with an aioli featuring lemongrass and lime. The creamy aioli comes together in seconds using an immersion blender, resulting in a silky texture that's less likely to break and adding richness and zest to a classic summer meal.

- 1 large egg yolk
- 1 Tbsp. grated lemongrass (grated using a Microplane, see Note)
- 1 tsp. grated lime zest plus 2 Tbsp. fresh lime juice (from 1 lime)
- 1 large garlic clove, grated (about ½ tsp.)
- ¾ tsp. fine sea salt, divided
- 3 Tbsp. avocado oil or other neutral cooking oil
- 5 Tbsp. extra-virgin olive oil, divided
- 4 (6-oz.) skinless mahi-mahi fillets
- ¼ tsp. black pepper

1. Preheat a grill to medium-high (400°F to 450°F). Combine egg yolk, lemongrass, lime zest and juice, garlic, and ¼ teaspoon salt in a 1-pint mason jar. Place an immersion blender inside jar, and process until mixture is well incorporated, about 3 seconds. Stir together avocado oil and 3 tablespoons olive oil in a small bowl; with immersion blender running, drizzle oil mixture into egg yolk mixture, processing until smooth and combined, 10 to 15 seconds. Set aside.

2. Brush fish fillets evenly with remaining 2 tablespoons olive oil; sprinkle evenly with pepper and remaining ½ teaspoon salt. Arrange fillets on oiled grill grates; grill, covered, until fish flakes easily and is just cooked through, 4 to 5 minutes per side. Transfer fillets to plates or a large serving platter; serve alongside aioli. —ANN TAYLOR PITTMAN

MAKE AHEAD Aioli can be made up to 1 day in advance and stored in an airtight container in refrigerator.

WINE Bright, citrusy white: 2020 Adelaida Vineyards Picpoul Blanc

NOTE To grate lemongrass on a Microplane and easily break down the fibrous herb, peel away the tough outer leaves, and trim off the root end with a serrated knife. Grate the pale, softer bottom of the stalk, and reserve the woodier tops (about two-thirds of the way up the stalk) for infusing in broths, soups, and stews.

Grilled Halibut with Roasted Red Pepper Sauce and Summer Squash

◷ ACTIVE 15 MIN; TOTAL 35 MIN; SERVES 4

A generous five cloves of garlic give this punchy, well-balanced sweet roasted red bell pepper sauce (made using jarred, roasted red peppers) a mildly spicy bite. It's a terrific marinade for mild white fish, infusing fillets with flavor without making them tough. When marinating the fish, be sure to first set aside a generous portion of the marinade, which does double duty here as a sauce for the cooked fish. Serve with crusty bread for sopping up extra sauce, with juicy grilled squash on the side.

- 1 (16-oz.) jar roasted red bell peppers, drained
- 5 garlic cloves
- 1 Tbsp. sherry vinegar
- 2 tsp. honey
- 1 tsp. kosher salt
- ¼ tsp. black pepper
- ½ cup olive oil
- 4 (6-oz.) skin-on halibut fillets
  Grilled summer squash, fresh parsley leaves, and crusty bread, for serving

1. Process bell peppers, garlic, vinegar, honey, salt, and black pepper in a food processor or blender until smooth, about 45 seconds. Transfer mixture to a bowl; whisk in oil. Measure 1 cup sauce into a large ziplock plastic bag; add halibut fillets. Seal bag; turn to coat fillets in sauce. Let marinate in refrigerator 20 minutes. Reserve remaining sauce for serving.

2. Preheat a grill to medium-high (400°F to 450°F). Remove halibut from marinade, scraping off excess. Discard remaining marinade. Arrange fillets on oiled grill grates; grill, covered, until fish flakes easily and is just cooked through, 4 to 5 minutes per side. Transfer fillets to serving plates or a large platter. Serve alongside grilled summer squash, parsley, crusty bread, and reserved sauce. —KELSEY YOUNGMAN

MAKE AHEAD Sauce may be stored in an airtight container in refrigerator up to 3 days.

WINE Full-bodied California rosé: 2020 Marietta Cellars OVR Old Vine Rosé

NOTE Alternatively, to broil the fish: Arrange marinated fish fillets, skin side down, on a greased baking sheet. Broil 4½ inches from heat source until fish flakes easily and is just cooked through, 6 to 8 minutes.

**GRILLED HALIBUT WITH
ROASTED RED PEPPER SAUCE
AND SUMMER SQUASH**

CHÁO B`ÔI (VIETNAMESE
PORRIDGE WITH SEAFOOD)

Cháo Bồi (Vietnamese Porridge with Seafood)

ACTIVE 1 HR MIN; TOTAL 1 HR 30 MIN; SERVES 8

In this light, savory Vietnamese porridge, shrimp, crab, and mushrooms are suspended in a silky soup of rice and tapioca pearls.

- 8 oz. unpeeled raw large shrimp, tail-on
- 3 medium scallions (about 1½ oz.), cut into 3-inch-long strips and smashed
- 1 (½-inch) piece unpeeled fresh ginger, thinly sliced and smashed (about 1 Tbsp.)
- 12 cups lower-sodium chicken broth, divided
- 1 (6-oz.) boneless, skinless chicken breast
- 1 cup uncooked long-grain white rice
- 6 dried wood ear mushrooms
- 2 Tbsp. canola oil or other neutral cooking oil
- ½ cup thinly sliced shallot (from 1 large [2-oz.] shallot)
- 8 oz. crabmeat (fresh, thawed frozen, or canned), drained and picked
- ⅓ cup uncooked small pearl tapioca (about 2 oz.)
- Kosher salt, to taste
- Thinly sliced scallions (light green and dark green parts only)
- Roughly torn fresh cilantro

1. Peel and devein shrimp; place shells and tails in a medium saucepan. Cut each shrimp in half lengthwise. Place shrimp on a plate, and refrigerate until ready to use.

2. Add smashed scallions, ginger, and 4 cups broth to shrimp shells. Bring to a rolling boil over medium-high. (Remove chicken from refrigerator, and let stand at room temperature while broth comes to a boil.) Boil, stirring occasionally, until flavors meld, about 5 minutes. Add chicken breast. Cover saucepan tightly with lid, and remove from heat; let stand until chicken feels firm yet still yields a bit to the touch and a thermometer inserted in thickest portion of meat registers 155°F, about 20 minutes. Using a slotted spoon, transfer chicken to a plate, and loosely cover with aluminum foil; set aside. Pour broth through a fine wire-mesh strainer into a large (5-quart) pot; discard solids. Cover and set aside.

3. Rinse medium saucepan, and fill halfway with water. Bring water to a boil over high; add rice, stirring to separate grains. Boil over high, undisturbed, until tender but still firm, about 8 minutes. Drain rice, and set aside. Rinse and dry saucepan.

4. While rice cooks, soak mushrooms in hot water until softened, about 15 minutes. Drain and cut into thin (⅛-inch-wide) strips.

5. Add remaining 8 cups chicken broth to warm broth in pot. Bring to boil over high; stir in mushrooms and reserved rice. Reduce heat to medium-high; gently boil, undisturbed, until rice grains are plump and start to split at ends, about 10 minutes. Remove from heat.

6. While rice cooks, heat oil in a medium saucepan over medium. Add shallot, and cook, stirring occasionally, until fragrant and soft, 3 to 5 minutes. Add reserved shrimp; cook, stirring often, until shrimp are just cooked and turn opaque, about 2 minutes. (Shrimp will curl into a corkscrew shape.) Remove from heat, and add crabmeat to shrimp mixture. Hand-shred reserved chicken into saucepan. Set aside.

7. Place tapioca pearls in a fine wire-mesh strainer, and rinse briefly under cold water. Stir tapioca pearls into rice mixture in pot; return to heat over medium-high, and cook, undisturbed, until soup is slightly thickened and opaque tapioca pearls have expanded and are mostly clear, about 10 minutes.

8. Stir chicken mixture into soup in pot; cook over medium-high, undisturbed, until heated through, about 1 minute. Season with salt to taste. Add up to 1 cup water as needed for soup to reach desired consistency. Remove from heat, and ladle soup evenly into 8 individual bowls or a large bowl or tureen; garnish with sliced scallions and cilantro. Serve immediately.

—ANDREA NGUYEN

WINE Tart, minerally white: 2021 Lieu Dit Santa Maria Valley Melon de Bourgogne

NOTE Dried wood ear mushrooms impart an earthy quality and can be purchased at nuts.com.

Fritto Misto With Calabrian Chile Aioli

ACTIVE 50 MIN; TOTAL 1 HR 20 MIN
SERVES 4 TO 6

A festive mix of shrimp, calamari, anchovy-stuffed olives, and paper-thin lemon slices are dredged in a Pernod-spiked batter and fried to crispy, golden perfection. Jarred Calabrian chiles add a fruity heat to the creamy aioli dipping sauce.

CHILE AIOLI

- 2 Tbsp. finely chopped jarred Calabrian chiles in oil (from 1 [10-oz.] jar), or more to taste
- 2 Tbsp. sherry vinegar, plus more to taste
- 1½ tsp. whole-grain mustard (such as Maille)
- 1½ tsp. tomato paste
- 1 garlic clove, finely chopped (about 1 tsp.)
- 1 large egg yolk
- ¾ cup grapeseed oil
- Kosher salt, to taste

FRITTI

- 1 lemon, cut crosswise into ⅛-inch-thick slices, seeds removed
- 1 tsp. kosher salt
- 12 pitted Castelvetrano olives (from 1 [8-oz.] jar)
- 4 anchovy fillets in oil (from 1 [3.3-oz.] jar), drained, each fillet torn crosswise into thirds
- 1 medium (11-oz.) fennel bulb, trimmed and cut lengthwise into ½-inch-wide strips (about 2 cups), fronds reserved for batter
- 6 oz. tail-on peeled and deveined raw large shrimp (about 12 shrimp)
- 6 oz. calamari tubes and small tentacles, cleaned, tubes sliced crosswise into ½-inch-thick rings (about ¾ cup)
- 4 scallions, white and light green parts only, cut into 1½-inch pieces (about ½ cup)
- ½ cup loosely packed fresh flat-leaf parsley leaves
- Canola oil, for frying

BATTER

- 1 cup all-purpose flour (about 4¼ oz.)
- ½ cup cornstarch (about 2⅜ oz.)
- 1 Tbsp. finely chopped fresh tarragon
- 1 tsp. baking powder
- 1 tsp. kosher salt, plus more to taste
- 1¼ cups club soda, chilled
- ¼ cup (2 oz.) anise-flavored liqueur (such as Pernod)

1. Make the chile aioli: Combine chiles, vinegar, mustard, tomato paste, garlic, and egg yolk in a food processor, and process until well combined, about 45 seconds. With food processor running, gradually drizzle in grapeseed oil in a slow, steady stream, processing until mixture is thickened and smooth, about 2 minutes, stopping to scrape down sides as needed. Transfer mixture to a medium bowl, and season with salt and additional vinegar to taste; set aside.

2. Make the fritti: Arrange lemon slices on a paper towel–lined plate, and sprinkle both sides evenly with salt. Let stand at room temperature 30 minutes. Rinse and pat dry using paper towels; set aside. While lemons stand, stuff each olive with 1 torn anchovy piece; set aside. Place fennel strips, shrimp, calamari, scallions, and parsley each in separate bowls; set aside.

3. Pour canola oil into a large Dutch oven to a depth of 2 inches; heat over medium to 350°F. Place a baking sheet fitted with an oven-safe wire rack in oven; preheat oven to 200°F. Line a second baking sheet with several layers of paper towels; set aside.

4. Make the batter: Just before oil reaches target temperature (about 340°F), finely chop reserved fennel fronds to measure 1 tablespoon. Whisk together fennel fronds, flour, cornstarch, tarragon, baking powder, and salt in a medium bowl. Gradually pour in club soda and anise-flavored liqueur, gently whisking just until combined but not smooth.

5. Working in batches with 1 fritti ingredient at a time (and quickly so batter stays cold), use your hands to dip lemon slices, stuffed olives, fennel strips, shrimp, calamari, scallions, and parsley in batter, letting excess batter drip off. Add fritti ingredient to hot oil; fry, turning occasionally, until golden brown and crisp, 1 to 3 minutes for each ingredient. Using a spider, transfer to prepared paper towel–lined baking sheet to drain; season with additional salt to taste. Place fried fritti ingredient on baking sheet in oven to keep warm. Repeat process with remaining fritti ingredients, 1 at a time, letting oil come back up to 350°F and skimming off any floating bits of batter in between batches. Transfer fritti to a platter, and serve with aioli. —CARLTON MCCOY

MAKE AHEAD Aioli can be made up to 3 days in advance and stored in an airtight container in refrigerator. Fritti ingredients can be prepared through step 2 and refrigerated, covered, in separate bowls up to 1 day.

WINE Elegant, focused Napa Valley white: 2018 Stony Hill Vineyard Chardonnay

NOTE Jarred Calabrian chiles are available at specialty grocery stores or online at delallo.com.

FRITTO MISTO WITH
CALABRIAN CHILE AIOLI

Summer Squash and Shrimp Fricassee

⟳ TOTAL 20 MIN; SERVES 2 TO 4

"Once the summer starts, there are inevitably big baskets of zucchini and yellow squash that we just don't know what to do with," says Oxford, Mississippi-based chef Vishwesh Bhatt. "This fricassee is a terrific place to use them. It's really light, it's really quick, and it's really easy to cook a big batch of it, making it an ideal centerpiece for summer gatherings." Fricassee is a cross between a quick sauté and a stew. This recipe calls for a habanero chile, which can be very hot but has beautiful floral notes that you can't replicate with other peppers. If you take care to remove the seeds, the heat will be more manageable. "This recipe is inspired by a dish my friend Nina Compton served us for dinner one night at her restaurant, Compere Lapin," Bhatt says. It's a great one to reach for in summer, but because good quality frozen shrimp and yellow squashes can be found year-round in grocery stores, this dish can be thrown together almost any time of the year.

2 (5-oz.) bunches scallions

2 Tbsp. olive oil

6 medium garlic cloves, thinly sliced (about 2½ Tbsp.)

2 fresh or dried bay leaves

1½ cups fresh corn kernels (from 2 ears corn)

1 lb. peeled and deveined raw large shrimp, tail-on

½ cup shrimp stock or fish stock

1 small fresh habanero chile (about ½ oz.), seeded and minced (about 1 tsp.)

1 lb. summer squash, chopped into ¼-inch pieces (about 3⅔ cups)

1 medium tomato (about 8 oz.), finely chopped (about 1 cup)

½ cup dry white wine

3 Tbsp. chopped fresh flat-leaf parsley

2 Tbsp. fresh thyme leaves

2 Tbsp. fresh lemon juice (from 1 lemon)

2 tsp. kosher salt

1 tsp. black pepper

2 Tbsp. unsalted butter

1. Thinly slice scallions, dividing the white and light green parts from the dark green parts. Set dark green parts aside.

2. Heat oil in a Dutch oven over medium-high. Add white and light green scallion parts, garlic, and bay leaves; cook, stirring occasionally, until scallions just soften, about 2 minutes. Add corn; cook, stirring constantly, 1 minute. Add shrimp, shrimp stock, and habanero; cook, stirring constantly, until shrimp just start to turn opaque but are not cooked through, about 45 seconds. Add squash, tomato, wine, parsley, thyme, lemon juice, salt, and black pepper. Cook, stirring constantly, until shrimp are just cooked through, about 1 minute. Add butter; cook, stirring vigorously, until butter melts and makes a creamy sauce, about 1 minute.

3. Remove from heat. Stir in dark green scallion parts. Serve immediately.
—VISHWESH BHATT

WINE Lemony, medium-bodied Chardonnay: 2019 Roserock Eola-Amity Hills Chardonnay

NOTE Wear gloves when seeding and mincing the habanero chile.

Shrimp with Roasted Corn, Leeks, Tomatoes, and Basil

PHOTO P. 91

⏲ TOTAL 30 MIN; SERVES 4

Showcasing late-summer produce, this simple sauté is a perfect shoulder-season weeknight dinner. Marinating sweet cherry tomatoes in vinegar and salt tenderizes them and draws out their juices, creating a light sauce. "I love how quickly this dish comes together!" says chef Cassidee Dabney of The Barn at Blackberry Farm in Walland, Tennessee, who shared this recipe with Food & Wine. *"If you have the leeks and corn prepped ahead of time, you can have this dish finished and on the table in about 15 minutes. It's convenient and delicious and just begging to be enjoyed alfresco with a glass of white wine. It's an ideal dish for a casual dinner party with friends. Another tip: Use the best shrimp available. Chat with your local fish market and find quality product — you'll taste the difference."*

- 3 small fresh leeks (about 11 oz.), trimmed, sliced into ¼-inch rounds, and rinsed thoroughly (white and light green parts only) (about 1½ cups)
- ½ cup unsalted butter (4 oz.), plus more for serving
- 2 tsp. kosher salt, divided, plus more to taste
- 2 cups multicolored cherry tomatoes, halved lengthwise
- 2 Tbsp. red wine vinegar
- 1 Tbsp. plus 1 tsp. neutral cooking oil (such as canola oil or vegetable oil)
- 5 cups fresh corn kernels (from 8 ears)
- 1½ lb. peeled and deveined raw extra-large shrimp
  Black pepper, to taste
- 1 cup loosely packed fresh basil leaves, torn if large
  Crusty bread and flaky sea salt, for serving

1. Cook leeks, butter, and 1 teaspoon kosher salt in a small saucepan over low, covered, uncovering often to stir, until leeks are very tender, 15 to 20 minutes. Remove from heat.

2. While leeks cook, stir together tomatoes, vinegar, and remaining 1 teaspoon kosher salt in a small bowl; let marinate at room temperature at least 10 minutes or until ready to use.

3. Heat oil in a large skillet over high. Add corn; cook, stirring often, until corn is warmed through, 3 to 4 minutes. Add shrimp; cook, stirring often, until shrimp turn pink and are cooked through, 3 to 5 minutes. Remove from heat.

4. Add leek mixture and tomato mixture (with juices in bowl) to shrimp mixture in skillet; stir to combine. Season with pepper and additional kosher salt to taste. Sprinkle with basil. Serve with warm crusty bread smeared with a thick layer of butter and a sprinkle of flaky sea salt. —CASSIDEE DABNEY, THE BARN AT BLACKBERRY FARM, WALLAND, TENNESSEE

WINE Rich, lightly oaky Chardonnay: 2021 Hahn Monterey County

Buttery Shrimp with Peas and Potatoes

⏲ TOTAL 30 MIN; SERVES 4

Unlike their larger, late-season siblings, baby veggies are supremely quick to cook. Creamy new potatoes add substance to this quick one-pan skillet dinner of tender shrimp, fresh shelling peas, and dill, which come together in a sweet and buttery broth laced with cream.

- 5 cups water
- 2 Tbsp. plus 1 tsp. kosher salt, divided, plus more to taste
- 8 oz. baby gold potatoes, cut into ¼-inch-thick slices (about 1¾ cups)
- 8 oz. shelled fresh or frozen English peas (about 1½ cups)
- ¼ cup unsalted butter
- ¼ cup extra-virgin olive oil
- 1 medium shallot, finely chopped (about ⅓ cup)
- 1 medium-size fresh Fresno chile, stemmed, seeded (if desired), and finely chopped (about 2 Tbsp.)
- 4 medium garlic cloves, finely chopped (about 4 tsp.)
- ⅓ cup dry white wine
- 12 oz. peeled and deveined tail-on raw large shrimp
- ¼ tsp. black pepper, plus more to taste
- 1 cup lower-sodium chicken broth
- ¼ cup heavy cream
- ⅓ cup chopped fresh dill
  Crusty bread, for serving

1. Bring 5 cups water to a boil in a 12-inch skillet over medium-high. Stir in 2 tablespoons salt. Add potatoes; cook, stirring occasionally, until barely tender, 5 to 7 minutes. Using a slotted spoon, transfer to a plate. Add peas to boiling water; cook, stirring occasionally, until crisp-tender, 2 to 3 minutes. Remove skillet from heat. Drain peas in a colander; rinse under cold water until cool to the touch, about 15 seconds. Set aside.

2. Wipe skillet dry using paper towels. Add butter and oil to skillet; cook over medium-high until butter is melted. Add shallot, chile, garlic, and ½ teaspoon salt; cook, stirring often, until mixture is fragrant and softened, 2 to 3 minutes. Add wine; cook, stirring occasionally, until wine is almost completely reduced, about 2 minutes.

3. Add shrimp to skillet in a single layer; sprinkle with black pepper and remaining ½ teaspoon salt. Cook, undisturbed, until shrimp are partially opaque, about 2 minutes. Flip shrimp, and immediately add broth and potatoes to skillet. Bring to a simmer over medium-high; simmer, stirring occasionally, until shrimp are almost cooked through, about 1 minute. Add peas and cream; cook, stirring occasionally, until heated through, about 30 seconds. Remove from heat. Season with additional salt and black pepper to taste. Sprinkle with dill, and serve with crusty bread. —JUSTIN CHAPPLE

WINE Crisp, steely California Chardonnay: 2020 Balletto Vineyards Teresa's Unoaked

A PROPER SHRIMP BOIL

Food & Wine editor-in-chief Hunter Lewis grew up in North Carolina obsessed with peel-and-eat shrimp, especially those fished out of pots of Frogmore stew in the South Carolina Lowcountry and those cooked and spiced like Maryland crab farther north. Now, he lives in the Deep South, where his shrimp boil has taken on a slight Cajun accent. It still bobs with corn and potatoes, but the Italian sausage is andouille, the Old Bay spice mix is sometimes Zatarain's, and the wild shrimp is always sweet, plump, and scooped from the Gulf. While all of those ingredients are essential, Lewis says the real flavor from a boil comes from a potent cooking liquor, loaded with alliums, lemon, spices, and a bottle each of white wine and clam juice.

ACTIVE 20 MIN; TOTAL 1 HR 30 MIN
SERVES 8

- 2 lemons
- 6 Tbsp. unsalted butter (3 oz.)
- 1 Tbsp. Cajun seasoning or Old Bay seasoning, plus more for serving
- 2 garlic cloves, minced (about 2 tsp.)
- 5 Tbsp. plus ⅛ tsp. fine sea salt, divided
  Hot sauce (such as Tabasco), to taste
- 11 qt. water (44 cups)
- 1 (750-ml.) bottle dry unoaked white wine (such as Pinot Grigio)
- 1 (8-oz.) bottle clam juice (such as Bar Harbor)
- 1 large yellow onion (about 12 oz.), quartered lengthwise, root intact

- 2 garlic heads, halved crosswise
- 8 dried bay leaves
- 1 Tbsp. dried thyme
- 2 (3-oz.) pkg. boil-in-bag crawfish, shrimp, and crab boil (such as Zatarain's) or ¼ cup Old Bay seasoning
- 2 lb. small yellow, red, or gold potatoes
- 8 (8-oz.) shucked ears fresh corn, halved crosswise
- 3 lb. fresh or smoked sausages (such as Italian sausage, bratwurst, or andouille) (about 8 [6-oz.] sausages or 16 [3-oz.] sausages) (see Note)
- 4 lb. unpeeled raw large wild shrimp
  Cocktail Sauce (recipe p. 312), for serving
  Whole-grain mustard, for serving

1. Grate zest from 1 lemon to measure 2 teaspoons. Set grated zest aside. Cut zested lemon and remaining lemon into quarters; set aside. Melt butter in a small saucepan over low. Stir in Cajun seasoning, minced garlic, ⅛ teaspoon salt, hot sauce to taste, and reserved lemon zest. Remove from heat; cover to keep warm.

2. Place a 24-quart pot on an outdoor propane burner. Add 11 quarts water, wine, clam juice, onion, garlic heads, bay leaves, thyme, quartered lemons, and remaining 5 tablespoons salt to pot; cover and bring to a boil over high flame. Stir in crab boil packets; cover and cook 10 minutes. Place a fitted strainer inside pot.

3. Add potatoes to strainer in pot; cover and cook 5 minutes. Stir in corn and sausages; cover and cook until a thermometer

STEP-BY-STEP

MAKE THE CAJUN SEASONING BUTTER Infuse butter with lemon zest, Cajun seasoning or Old Bay, garlic, hot sauce, and salt. Cover to keep warm until ready to toss with finished boil.

BOIL THE COOKING LIQUOR Bring water, wine, clam juice, onion, garlic heads, quartered lemons, bay leaves, thyme, and salt to a boil. Stir in crab boil packets.

BOIL VEGETABLES, SAUSAGE & SHRIMP Place a fitted strainer inside the stockpot with cooking liquor. Cook in stages: first potatoes, then corn and sausage, then shrimp.

LIFT THE STRAINER Carefully lift strainer from pot, letting liquid drain back into pot. Discard the cooking liquor, aromatics, and crab boil packets.

inserted in thickest portion of sausage registers 155°F (or until heated through if using smoked sausages), about 10 minutes. Stir in shrimp; cook, uncovered, until shrimp are pink, opaque, and cooked through, 2 to 4 minutes.

4. Lift strainer from pot, letting liquid strain back into pot, and transfer shrimp boil mixture (potatoes, corn, sausage, and shrimp) to a large heatproof bowl; discard onion, garlic, bay leaves, thyme, lemons, crab boil packets, and strained liquid inside pot. Add reserved butter mixture to shrimp boil mixture; toss to coat. (If you don't have a large enough bowl, you can do this step in batches, tossing half of the shrimp boil with half of the butter mixture at a time.) Arrange coated shrimp boil on a platter or a covered table. Season with additional Cajun seasoning or Old Bay, if desired. Serve with cocktail sauce and mustard, if desired.
—HUNTER LEWIS

DRINK Light-bodied Provençal rosé: 2021 Commanderie de Peyrassol Les Commandeurs, or crisp, lemony pilsner: Firestone Walker Pivo

NOTE For a classic Cajun flavor, choose an andouille sausage, such as North Country Smokehouse, available at Whole Foods.

POUR SEASONED BUTTER OVER BOIL Transfer shrimp boil (potatoes, corn, sausage, and shrimp) to a large heatproof bowl, and add reserved Cajun seasoning butter.

TOSS THE BOIL TO COAT Toss the butter and shrimp boil to thoroughly coat and season. Arrange buttered shrimp boil on a platter or covered table. Garnish and serve.

GAMBERI IN BAGNETTO VERDE

Gamberi in Bagnetto Verde

ACTIVE 35 MIN; TOTAL 45 MIN;
SERVES 1 TO 2

This simple, tapas-inspired plate from Los Angeles chef Evan Funke highlights sweet head-on prawns in a bright green sauce that comes together in the blender.

BAGNETTO VERDE

- 1 cup chopped green garlic (from 3 [2-oz.] green garlic stalks, rinsed and trimmed) or 1 garlic clove
- ¾ cup loosely packed fresh basil leaves
- ¾ cup loosely packed fresh flat-leaf parsley leaves
- ¾ cup loosely packed arugula
- 1 cup extra-virgin olive oil
- ½ tsp. kosher salt

PRAWNS

- 6 (1½-oz.) head-on, tail-on raw prawns or jumbo shrimp
- ½ tsp. kosher salt
- ¼ tsp. black pepper
- 1 Tbsp. extra-virgin olive oil
- 1 Tbsp. canola oil
- 2 Tbsp. unsalted butter
  Lemon wedges, for serving

1. Make the bagnetto verde: Bring a large pot of salted water to a boil over medium-high. Fill a large bowl with ice water; set aside. Add green garlic, basil, parsley, and arugula to boiling water; cook, stirring occasionally, until garlic, herbs, and arugula are very tender and bright green, about 1 minute and 30 seconds. Using a slotted spoon, transfer garlic, herbs, and arugula to prepared ice water; gently stir until completely chilled, 1 to 2 minutes. Remove blanched garlic, herbs, and arugula from ice water; gently wrap with paper towels, and wring out as much water as possible. Repeat drying process as needed with fresh paper towels until blanched garlic, herbs, and arugula are as dry as possible. Reserve ice water in bowl, adding more ice as needed to keep cold.

2. Process olive oil and blanched garlic, herbs, and arugula in a blender until mixture is completely smooth and bright green, about 1 minute. Stir in salt. Transfer bagnetto verde to a medium bowl, and set inside bowl of ice water to cool and preserve the color, being careful to not let ice water overflow into bagnetto verde. Let stand until mixture has cooled, about 5 minutes. Transfer cooled bagnetto verde to an airtight container. Store in refrigerator until ready to use or up to 1 week.

3. Make the prawns: Preheat oven to 250°F. Peel and devein prawns, leaving heads and tails on. Arrange prawns on a rimmed baking sheet or a plate; sprinkle evenly with salt and pepper. Pour olive oil and canola oil into a large skillet, and swirl to combine. Heat over high until oil mixture begins to smoke, 3 to 5 minutes. Using tongs or long tweezers, carefully add prawns to hot oil; cook, undisturbed, 30 seconds. Add butter to skillet, and gently swirl until it begins to brown and coats the prawns, about 15 seconds. Carefully flip prawns. Cook until prawns are just cooked through, about 30 seconds. Carefully add ½ cup bagnetto verde to skillet, and gently swirl to combine; reserve remaining bagnetto verde for another use. Remove skillet from heat. Place an ovenproof platter in preheated oven, and let preheat until platter is warm, 2 to 3 minutes. (The warmth will help keep the sauce from seizing when plated.)

4. Remove cooked prawns from skillet, and arrange on warmed platter. As prawns are removed from skillet, drag them through bagnetto verde mixture in skillet. Generously spoon bagnetto verde mixture from skillet over prawns. Serve immediately with lemon wedges for squeezing over prawns. —EVAN FUNKE, FELIX TRATTORIA, LOS ANGELES

MAKE AHEAD Bagnetto verde can be made up to 1 week in advance and stored in an airtight container in refrigerator.

WINE Citrusy coastal Italian white: 2021 Santa Maria La Palma Aragosta Vermentino di Sardegna

NOTE Source head-on shrimp or prawns from your local fishmonger—the fresher, the better. Substitute green garlic with fresh garlic if green garlic cannot be sourced.

Scallop Grenobloise

TOTAL 20 MIN; SERVES 4

Grenobloise means in the style of the southeastern French city of Grenoble, and refers to a classic French sauce of lemon and capers. Here, beautifully seared scallops with a golden crust are served in a sauce popping with acidity from lemon, brininess from capers, and slight warmth from mildly piquant jalapeños. Toss them with a favorite pasta for a quick, simple meal. For the best results, seek out Massachusetts dayboat scallops. They are harvested daily and are dry-packed, which yields the best flavor and sear.

- 1 large lemon
- 16 jumbo sea scallops
- 1 tsp. kosher salt, divided
- ½ tsp. black pepper, divided
- 2 Tbsp. extra-virgin olive oil
- ¼ cup unsalted butter, cut into cubes
- 2 Tbsp. capers, drained
- 1 medium jalapeño chile, stemmed, seeded, and minced (about 1½ Tbsp.)
- 2 Tbsp. finely chopped fresh flat-leaf parsley

1. Using a paring knife, remove outer peel and bitter white pith from lemon; discard. Cut in between membranes to remove lemon segments, and discard membranes. Cut segments into ¼-inch pieces; remove and discard seeds. Set lemon segments aside.

2. Sprinkle scallops evenly with ½ teaspoon salt and ¼ teaspoon black pepper. Heat oil in a large nonstick skillet over medium-high. Add scallops; cook until well seared and golden brown on bottoms, about 3 minutes. Flip scallops; cook until just opaque throughout, 2 to 3 minutes. Transfer scallops to a platter, and cover with aluminum foil to keep warm. Wipe skillet clean.

3. Add butter to skillet, and melt over medium-high. Add capers and jalapeño; cook, stirring often, until sizzling and fragrant, about 1 minute. Stir in lemon segments, parsley, remaining ½ teaspoon salt, and remaining ¼ teaspoon black pepper. Spoon mixture over scallops. Serve immediately. —JUSTIN CHAPPLE

WINE Bright, grapefruity Sauvignon Blanc: 2020 Dry Creek Vineyard

Shrimp, Coconut, and Avocado Aguachile

ACTIVE 1 HR 15 MIN; TOTAL 2 HR 5 MIN; SERVES 4

Coconut water, celery, ginger, and chiles come together to flavor the base of this delicate aguachile, while pineapple, cucumber, and avocado garnishes help cool it down. Timing is the key to this recipe, as the shrimp is "cooked" in lemon juice.

- 1 whole fresh pineapple (about 28 oz.)
- ¾ tsp. fine sea salt, divided
- ¼ cup unsweetened coconut milk (from 1 [13.6-oz.] can, well shaken and stirred)
- 1 medium (1-oz.) lemongrass stalk, trimmed and roughly chopped (about 2 Tbsp.)
- 1 Tbsp. chopped peeled fresh ginger
- 1 small serrano chile, halved (and seeded, if desired)
- ¾ cup bottled coconut water (such as Vita Coco Pure Coconut Water) (from 1 [11.1-oz.] bottle)
- 5 medium (2-oz.) celery stalks, divided
- 12 peeled and deveined tail-on raw large shrimp (about 8 oz.)
- ⅔ cup fresh lemon juice (from 4 lemons), divided
- 4 dried chiltepin or pequin chiles (unseeded), crushed
- ¼ cup shaved coconut chips (such as Mavuno Harvest Dried Organic Coconut)
- 1 medium (6-oz.) avocado, quartered lengthwise and thinly sliced crosswise
- ½ cup loosely packed fresh cilantro leaves
- ¼ cup thinly sliced red onion (from 1 small [5-oz.] red onion)
- 1 small (2-oz.) Persian cucumber, thinly sliced into half-moons (about ½ cup)
- ¼ tsp. flaky sea salt (such as Maldon)
- Tortilla chips, for serving (optional)

1. Using a sharp knife, remove top and bottom of pineapple; remove and discard outer peel. Quarter peeled pineapple lengthwise; remove core by cutting it out at an angle. Thinly slice 1 pineapple quarter crosswise into ⅛-inch-thick slices to measure ½ cup. Reserve remaining pineapple for another use.

2. Spread pineapple slices in a single layer on a baking sheet or a large plate. Sprinkle evenly with ¼ teaspoon fine sea salt. Let stand 1 hour. Transfer pineapple slices to a small bowl. Cover and refrigerate until ready to use.

3. While pineapple stands, stir together coconut milk, lemongrass, ginger, and serrano chile in a small saucepan; bring to a simmer over medium-low. Simmer, stirring occasionally, until solids have softened slightly, about 5 minutes. Remove from heat; let steep, uncovered, 15 minutes. Transfer to a blender; add coconut water. Roughly chop 4 celery stalks; add to mixture in blender. Process mixture until completely smooth, about 1 minute. Pour mixture through a fine wire-mesh strainer into an airtight container; discard solids. Cover and refrigerate until chilled, at least 1 hour or up to 12 hours.

4. Arrange shrimp in an even layer in a glass baking dish. Sprinkle evenly with ¼ teaspoon fine sea salt, and pour ⅓ cup lemon juice over shrimp. Place in refrigerator; let marinate until shrimp just start to turn opaque, 35 to 40 minutes, flipping shrimp after about 20 minutes.

5. Remove chilled coconut milk mixture from refrigerator; stir in crushed chiltepin chiles, remaining ¼ teaspoon fine sea salt, and remaining ⅓ cup lemon juice.

6. Remove shrimp mixture from refrigerator. Remove shrimp from baking dish; arrange evenly in 4 shallow bowls. Pour chilled coconut mixture evenly over shrimp in bowls. Sprinkle shrimp evenly with shaved coconut chips. Thinly slice remaining celery stalk on a sharp diagonal, and arrange evenly over shrimp. Top evenly with avocado, cilantro, onion, cucumber, and pineapple. Sprinkle evenly with flaky sea salt, and serve with tortilla chips, if desired. —CLAUDETTE ZEPEDA

MAKE AHEAD Pineapple and coconut water mixture can be prepared up to 12 hours in advance and stored in separate airtight containers in refrigerator.

WINE Citrusy French white: 2020 Chéreau Carré Château l'Oiselinière de la Ramée Muscadet Sèvre-et-Maine

SHRIMP, COCONUT, AND
AVOCADO AGUACHILE

FREGULA CUN COCCIULA
(SARDINIAN FREGOLA
WITH CLAMS)

Fregula cun Cocciula (Sardinian Fregola with Clams)

ACTIVE 30 MIN; TOTAL 50 MIN; SERVES 4

This dish spotlights perfectly steamed clams and chewy fregola, a small round pasta from Sardinia, in a golden, spicy, briny broth. Place the clams in a colander and scrub them well under cold running water to remove any grit before steaming. The recipe, which Goodnight Hospitality culinary director Amber Burling developed for March restaurant in Houston, is especially delicious when matched with a Sardinian Vermentino. Sommeliers June Rodil and Mark Sayre, also of March, love it with the 2019 Vigne Rada Stria Vermentino di Sardegna. "Sardinian Vermentino is round, fleshy, and lemon curd–like, and you need that body to go with the heat of the clams," they say. "The salty, briny, orchard-fruit notes combat the richness of the fregola and heat from the red pepper flakes in the Fregula cun Cocciula."

- ¼ cup dry white wine (such as Vermentino)
- 2 lb. littleneck clams (about 30 clams), rinsed and scrubbed
- 4 cups fish stock, plus up to 1½ cups stock if needed, divided
- 1¼ cups thinly sliced fennel bulb (from 1 small fennel head), fronds reserved for garnish
- 5 garlic cloves, thinly sliced (about 1½ Tbsp.)
- 1 Tbsp. olive oil
- 2 Tbsp. tomato paste
- 1 tsp. crushed red pepper
- 2 tsp. kosher salt
- 20 saffron threads (about ¼ tsp.)
- 1⅓ cups uncooked fregola
- 2 tsp. grated lemon zest, plus 3 Tbsp. fresh lemon juice (from 1 lemon), divided
- 1 Tbsp. chopped fresh flat-leaf parsley

1. Bring wine to a simmer in a large saucepan over medium. Add clams; cover and cook, undisturbed, until clam shells have opened, 6 to 8 minutes. Discard any clams that did not open. Gently pour clam mixture through a fine wire-mesh strainer lined with cheesecloth into a heatproof bowl. Reserve opened clams and clam cooking liquid (liquor) separately. Measure clam liquor, and add fish stock as needed to equal 2 cups liquid. Set aside. Rinse saucepan clean, and wipe dry.

2. Return saucepan to heat over medium-high. Add sliced fennel, garlic, and oil; cook, stirring often, until fennel just begins to lightly brown, 4 to 6 minutes. Add tomato paste and crushed red pepper, and cook, stirring constantly, until tomato paste darkens slightly, about 1 minute. Stir in reserved 2 cups clam liquor, scraping browned bits from bottom of pan. Add remaining 4 cups fish stock, salt, and saffron, and bring to a simmer over medium-high. Stir in fregola, and cook, stirring occasionally, until fregola is al dente, 14 to 16 minutes. Remove from heat. Stir in lemon juice and clams. Sprinkle with parsley, fennel fronds, and lemon zest.

—AMBER BURLING, CULINARY DIRECTOR, GOODNIGHT HOSPITALITY, HOUSTON

NOTE Find fregola at specialty grocery stores and online at markethallfoods.com.

Stuffed Clams with Linguiça and Arugula

ACTIVE 45 MIN; TOTAL 1 HR 15 MIN
SERVES 4 TO 6

Littleneck clams are blended with breadcrumbs, jalapeño, celery, arugula, and linguiça—a Portuguese smoke-cured pork sausage—before they are stuffed back into their shells and baked until piping hot and lightly browned. Portuguese rolls are light and airy with a crisp crust, making them ideal for this stuffing: the crumb readily absorbs flavor. Save time by stuffing the clams in advance and then refrigerating them overnight. Bring the stuffed clams to room temperature before baking.

- 1 cup dry white wine
- 1 cup clam juice
- 24 littleneck clams, scrubbed
- 1 (3-oz.) Portuguese roll or piece of bread (such as baguette or crusty bread), torn into chunks
- 2 oz. linguiça, cut into ½-inch cubes
- ¼ cup unsalted butter
- 1 small yellow onion (about 5 oz.), very finely chopped (about ½ cup)
- 1 medium celery stalk, very finely chopped (about 3 Tbsp.)
- 1 medium jalapeño chile, seeded and minced (about 2 Tbsp.)
- ⅓ cup very finely chopped arugula (about 1¼ oz.)
- ½ tsp. kosher salt
- ¼ tsp. black pepper
- Lemon wedges, for serving

1. Combine wine and clam juice in a large saucepan; bring to a boil over high. Add clams; cover and cook until clams begin to open, 5 to 7 minutes. Uncover; using tongs, transfer clams to a large rimmed baking sheet. Let cool 5 minutes. Discard any clams that did not open. Pour cooking liquid through a fine wire-mesh strainer into a heatproof bowl.

2. Working over reserved cooking liquid to catch the juices, remove and discard top shells from clams. Remove clams from bottom shells. Transfer clams to a cutting board, and finely chop. Set aside. Set reserved cooking liquid aside. Wipe baking sheet clean. Arrange bottom shells on cleaned baking sheet. Set aside.

3. Place bread chunks in a food processor; pulse until coarse breadcrumbs form, 7 to 9 pulses. Transfer breadcrumbs to a large bowl. Add linguiça to food processor; pulse until very finely chopped, 5 to 6 pulses. Set aside.

4. Preheat oven to 350°F. Melt butter in a large skillet over medium. Add onion, celery, and jalapeño; cook, stirring occasionally, until vegetables are just softened, about 5 minutes. Add chopped linguiça; cook, stirring occasionally, until fat is rendered, 3 to 5 minutes. Stir in chopped clams, arugula, and ½ cup reserved clam cooking liquid; discard remaining cooking liquid. Remove from heat. Add linguiça mixture, salt, and black pepper to breadcrumbs in bowl; stir well to combine.

5. Lightly pack linguiça stuffing evenly into bottom clam shells on baking sheet; cover with aluminum foil. Bake in preheated oven until hot, about 20 minutes. Remove foil; continue baking until tops are very lightly browned, about 5 minutes. Serve stuffed clams alongside lemon wedges.

—JUSTIN CHAPPLE

MAKE AHEAD Clam shells can be stuffed with filling and refrigerated overnight. Bring to room temperature before baking.

WINE Tart, minerally Vinho Verde: 2021 Anselmo Mendes Pássaros Alvarinho

POULTRY
& GAME

SHEET-PAN TURKEY WITH BROWN
SUGAR AND CORIANDER (P. 136)
OPPOSITE: PEPPER JELLY–
GLAZED CHICKEN THIGHS WITH
GRILLED PEPPERS (P. 124)

CITRUS-AND-FENNEL
CHICKEN WITH OLIVES AND
CALABRIAN CHILES

Citrus-and-Fennel Chicken with Olives and Calabrian Chiles

ACTIVE 30 MIN; TOTAL 1 HR 20 MIN; SERVES 4

A mix of citrus, buttery olives, and spicy, oil-packed chiles punches up the flavor of braised chicken leg quarters. Toasted fennel seeds and dry sherry add a pleasant warmth to the sauce, which begs to be served with a baguette for sopping.

- 2 Tbsp. extra-virgin olive oil
- 4 (12-oz.) chicken leg quarters, patted dry
- 3½ tsp. kosher salt, divided
- 1¼ tsp. black pepper, divided
- 1 garlic head, halved crosswise
- 1 Tbsp. fennel seeds
- ½ cup lower-sodium chicken broth
- ¼ cup (2 oz.) dry sherry
- 1 cup jarred pitted Castelvetrano olives plus 2 Tbsp. brine, divided
- 6 jarred whole Calabrian chiles plus ½ Tbsp. oil from jar, divided
- 1 small fennel head (about 14 oz.), bulb cut through core into ¾-inch-thick wedges, fronds reserved for garnish
- 4 (½-inch-thick) Cara Cara or navel orange slices
- 4 (½-inch-thick) lemon slices
- 2 tsp. finely chopped preserved lemon peel
- Baguette, for serving

1. Preheat oven to 375°F. Heat oil in a 12-inch skillet over medium-high. Sprinkle chicken with 2¾ teaspoons salt and 1 teaspoon black pepper. Working in batches if needed, cook chicken in oil, turning occasionally, until golden brown on both sides, 8 to 12 minutes; transfer to a large plate. Add garlic head halves, cut sides down, to skillet; cook, undisturbed, until lightly browned, about 30 seconds. Transfer to plate with chicken.

2. Remove skillet from heat, and immediately add fennel seeds to drippings. Off heat, stir constantly until fragrant, about 30 seconds. Add broth, sherry, olive brine, chile oil, remaining ¾ teaspoon salt, and remaining ¼ teaspoon black pepper. Using a wooden spoon, scrape up any browned

bits from bottom of skillet. Arrange chicken leg quarters, skin sides up, in skillet. Tuck browned garlic halves, fennel wedges, and orange and lemon slices in skillet around chicken. Sprinkle with olives and chiles.

3. Bring liquid in skillet to a boil over medium-high. Cover skillet tightly with aluminum foil, and transfer to preheated oven. Roast until a thermometer inserted in thickest portion of chicken registers 130°F, 35 to 40 minutes. Remove foil, and roast until chicken registers 165°F and fennel is tender, 15 to 20 minutes. Remove from oven. Sprinkle with preserved lemon peel, and garnish with fennel fronds. Serve with torn baguette. —JUSTIN CHAPPLE

WINE Spicy Calabrian red: 2018 Librandi Duca Sanfelice Cirò Rosso Riserva

NOTE Find Calabrian chiles at specialty grocery stores or online at gustiamo.com.

Chicken, Potatoes, and Leeks with Pine Nut Gremolata

ACTIVE 20 MIN; TOTAL 1 HR 15 MIN; SERVES 6

For the crispiest skin and most flavorful meat, roast bone-in, skin-on chicken thighs and legs over a bed of leeks and potatoes, where they render fat and absorb flavor. A quick turn under the broiler imparts a golden finish to the chicken before it's basted in pan juices and dressed with a zippy gremolata made from toasted pine nuts, garlic, and parsley. Cookbook author Leah Koenig loves to serve these during the Passover holiday, but they're a special dinner any night of the year.

GREMOLATA

- 1 small bunch fresh flat-leaf parsley leaves and tender stems, tough stem ends removed
- ⅓ cup pine nuts, toasted
- 1 Tbsp. grated lemon zest (from 1 large lemon)
- 1 large garlic clove, finely chopped (about 1 tsp.)
- ¼ tsp. kosher salt

CHICKEN

- 1½ lb. Yukon Gold potatoes (about 4 medium potatoes), peeled, quartered lengthwise, and cut into ½-inch-thick wedges
- 3 medium leeks, cut crosswise into ¾-inch-thick pieces (about 4 cups)
- 1 garlic head, cloves separated and peeled (10 to 12 cloves)
- ¼ cup extra-virgin olive oil, divided
- 1½ tsp. kosher salt, divided
- ½ tsp. black pepper, divided
- ½ cup chicken broth
- 4 lb. bone-in, skin-on chicken thighs and legs (about 12 pieces), trimmed

1. Make the gremolata: Combine parsley, pine nuts, lemon zest, and garlic on a cutting board. Sprinkle with salt, and finely chop mixture together. Transfer gremolata to a bowl, and set aside.

2. Make the chicken: Preheat oven to 400°F with rack 8 inches from heat. Arrange potatoes, leeks, and garlic cloves in bottom of a large broiler-safe roasting pan. Drizzle with 2 tablespoons oil; sprinkle with 1 teaspoon salt and ¼ teaspoon pepper. Toss to coat. Pour broth into roasting pan.

3. Arrange chicken pieces, skin side up, on top of vegetable mixture in roasting pan. Brush chicken evenly with remaining 2 tablespoons oil; sprinkle evenly with remaining ½ teaspoon salt and remaining ¼ teaspoon pepper.

4. Roast in preheated oven on rack 8 inches from heat until vegetables are tender and a thermometer inserted in thickest portion of chicken registers 165°F, 40 to 45 minutes, spooning pan juices over chicken after about 20 minutes.

5. Increase oven temperature to broil. (Do not remove roasting pan from oven.) Broil until chicken skin is golden brown, about 5 minutes. Remove from oven, and let cool 10 minutes.

6. Transfer chicken pieces and vegetables to a platter. Spoon sauce from roasting pan over chicken; scatter generously with gremolata (about ¾ cup). Serve hot alongside any remaining gremolata for sprinkling. —LEAH KOENIG

WINE Robust, stone-fruity California Chardonnay: 2019 J. Lohr Riverstone

Pollo Guisado

TOTAL 2 HR 45 MIN, PLUS 12 HR
MARINATING; SERVES 4

"The soup all abuelitas make their grandchildren, cooking a ojo, or by feel, with a million variations," says 2019 F&W Best New Chef Kwame Onwuachi of this comforting recipe. "I didn't have a Puerto Rican grandmother, so this version is a re-creation of the flavors I remember from places like Caridad and Louie's on Gun Hill Road, 188 Cuchifritos, and all the other lechonerias, cuchifritos, lunch counters, full-on restaurants, and street food vendors that nourish and restore the Bronx's massive Nuyorican population. The soup is a festival of comfort. At its base are the annatto and sofrito that define much of Puerto Rican cuisine, plus a touch of cumin and, because it's me who's making it, a bit of house spice to give just the merest hint of heat."

SOFRITO

- ½ cup extra-virgin olive oil
- 3 cups diced (½-inch cubes) yellow onion (from 2 medium [10-oz.] onions)
- 5 Tbsp. Ginger-Garlic Puree (recipe p. 306)
- 1 Tbsp. plus ½ tsp. tomato paste
- 1 Tbsp. ají amarillo paste
- 2 tsp. coriander-annatto seasoning (such as Goya Sazón con Culantro y Achiote) (from 2 [5-gram] pkg.)
- 3½ cups diced (½-inch cubes) plum tomatoes (from about 7 medium [3½-oz.] tomatoes)
- ⅓ cup diced (½-inch cubes) red bell pepper (from 1 small [about 7-oz.] bell pepper)
- 1 medium (¾-oz.) jalapeño, stemmed, seeded, and thinly sliced into rounds
- ¼ cup packed roughly chopped fresh culantro (may substitute with cilantro, if needed), leaves and tender stems only
- ¾ tsp. kosher salt

MARINATED CHICKEN

- 1 Tbsp. annatto powder
- 1 Tbsp. dried oregano
- 2 (5-gram) pkg. coriander-annatto seasoning (such as Goya Sazón con Culantro y Achiote) (about 2½ tsp.)
- 1½ tsp. House Spice (recipe p. 306)
- 1 tsp. ground cumin
- 1 tsp. kosher salt
- 1 medium-size (10-oz.) yellow onion, cut into ⅛-inch slices (about 2¼ cups)
- 1 medium-size (3½-oz.) plum tomato, chopped (about ½ cup)
- 10 medium garlic cloves, minced (about 3½ Tbsp.)
- 4 (12-oz.) chicken leg quarters

ADDITIONAL INGREDIENTS

- 2 Tbsp. canola oil
- 3 large (8-oz.) Yukon Gold potatoes, peeled and diced (½-inch cubes) (about 4 cups)
- 2 medium (3-oz.) carrots, peeled and diced (½-inch cubes) (about 1 cup)
- 3 cups chicken stock
- 2 fresh or dried bay leaves
- 1 (6-gram) chicken bouillon cube (such as Knorr), crushed (about 1½ tsp.)
- 1 tsp. kosher salt
- Perfectly Steamed Rice (recipe p. 216)

1. Make the sofrito: Heat oil in a large pot over medium until shimmering. Add onions; cook, stirring occasionally, until starting to turn translucent, about 5 minutes. Add ginger-garlic puree, tomato paste, ají amarillo paste, and coriander-annatto seasoning; cook, stirring often, until mixture has darkened somewhat and oil has separated, about 5 minutes. Add tomatoes; cook, stirring occasionally, until some liquid from tomatoes has released and evaporated, about 5 minutes. Add bell pepper and jalapeño; cook, stirring occasionally, until softened, 8 to 10 minutes. Add culantro; cook, stirring constantly, until softened and wilted, about 1 minute.

Reduce heat to medium-low, and let come to a simmer; simmer, stirring often, until mixture is thick, glossy, and deep red and oil has risen to the surface, about 1 hour. Stir in salt. Remove from heat. Transfer sofrito to an airtight container, and store in refrigerator up to 1 week or in freezer up to 6 months.

2. Make the marinated chicken: Stir together annatto powder, dried oregano, coriander-annatto seasoning, house spice, cumin, and salt in a large bowl. Add onion, tomato, and garlic; stir to combine. Add chicken leg quarters, and toss to coat thoroughly. Cover and refrigerate 12 hours.

3. Remove marinated chicken from refrigerator; scrape excess marinade from chicken, reserving marinade in bowl. Heat canola oil in a large, high-sided skillet over medium-high until shimmering. Add chicken, skin side down, to skillet; cook until golden brown on both sides, about 4 minutes per side. Transfer chicken to a plate; set aside. Do not wipe skillet clean.

4. Reduce heat under skillet to medium. Add reserved marinade and 1 cup sofrito. (Reserve remaining sofrito for another use.) Cook, stirring often, until caramelized and thick, about 10 minutes. Stir in potatoes, carrots, stock, bay leaves, and bouillon. Return chicken to pot, nestling chicken, skin side up, in vegetable mixture. Bring to a gentle simmer over medium; simmer, uncovered and stirring occasionally, until sauce is thick and deep reddish-brown, potatoes and carrots are tender, and a thermometer inserted in thickest portion of chicken registers 165°F, 40 to 45 minutes.

5. Remove and discard bay leaves from chicken mixture. Stir in salt, and serve alongside perfectly steamed rice.
—KWAME ONWUACHI

MAKE AHEAD Pollo guisado can be stored in an airtight container in refrigerator up to 4 days. Sofrito can be stored in an airtight container in refrigerator up to 1 week or in freezer up to 6 months.

WINE Medium-bodied, lightly earthy Pinot Noir: 2020 Grochau Cellars GC Commuter Cuvée

POLLO GUISADO

TAMARIND CHICKEN

Tamarind Chicken

ACTIVE 15 MIN; TOTAL 1 HR 15 MIN; SERVES 4

A potent tamarind-and-chipotle marinade renders a richly flavored, juicy, and tender chicken in mere minutes, making it equally suited for a weeknight meal or a dinner party. The tamarind concentrate in the marinade adds a sour funk that complements the freshness of the cilantro leaves and smoky heat of the chipotle chile paste. The marinade gives the chicken a dark, lacquered appearance and will char a little as it cooks, becoming caramelized, chewy, and ultimately, mouthwateringly delicious.

1 (3- to 3½-lb.) whole chicken

½ cup packed fresh cilantro leaves, finely chopped, plus more for garnish

¼ cup olive oil

¼ cup tamarind concentrate (such as Tamicon)

2 Tbsp. jarred chipotle chile paste (such as Gran Luchito)

1 Tbsp. plus 2 tsp. paprika

2½ tsp. fine sea salt

2 medium garlic cloves, grated (about 1 tsp.)

½ tsp. black pepper

1. Place chicken on a cutting board, and pat dry. Using kitchen shears, cut on either side of backbone to remove; reserve backbone for another use, if desired. Using a sharp chef's knife, cut through breastbone to separate chicken into halves. Cut each half to separate into 2 pieces, leaving thigh and drumstick attached and breast and wing attached. Set chicken pieces aside.

2. Stir together cilantro, oil, tamarind, chipotle paste, paprika, salt, garlic, and black pepper in a large bowl. Add chicken pieces, and toss to coat, massaging tamarind mixture into skin. Let marinate 5 minutes, or cover and refrigerate up to overnight (about 12 hours).

3. Open bottom vent of a charcoal grill completely. Light charcoal chimney starter filled with briquettes. When briquettes are covered with gray ash, pour them onto bottom grate of grill. Adjust vents as needed to maintain an internal temperature of 350°F to 400°F. (If using a gas grill, preheat to medium [350°F to 400°F].) Coat top grate with oil; place on grill. Transfer chicken pieces to a baking sheet lined with aluminum foil. Brush remaining tamarind mixture in bowl onto chicken skin. Using tongs, place chicken pieces, skin side down, on oiled grates. Cover and grill, flipping chicken every 5 minutes, until a thermometer inserted in thickest portion of meat registers 155°F, 35 to 45 minutes. Transfer chicken to a large plate or clean baking sheet. Let rest 10 minutes. (Internal temperature will continue to rise to 165°F as chicken rests.) Transfer to a platter. Garnish with additional cilantro. —LARA LEE

WINE Light-bodied, spicy red: 2020 Niepoort Drink Me Nat Cool Bairrada

NOTE To make recipe in the oven, at step 3, instead of preparing a charcoal grill, preheat oven to 350°F. Transfer chicken pieces, skin side up, to a baking sheet lined with aluminum foil. Brush remaining tamarind mixture in bowl onto chicken skin. Roast in preheated oven until a thermometer inserted in thickest portion of meat registers 155°F, 35 to 45 minutes. Remove from oven. Let rest 10 minutes. (Internal temperature will continue to rise to 165°F as chicken rests.)

Chicken Thighs with Maple and Grainy Mustard Sauce and Green Salad

ACTIVE 40 MIN; TOTAL 1 HR 40 MIN; SERVES 4

A pinch of ground allspice adds interest to a not-too-sweet maple and mustard concoction inspired by chef Brendan Collins. The simple sauce does double duty as a dressing for salad and as a marinade for chicken thighs—just reserve a little bit of the sauce for adding effortless pizzazz to a quick salad, and use the rest of it as a marinade to give chicken thighs a lacquered shine and deep flavor.

½ cup pure maple syrup

¼ cup olive oil

¼ cup Dijon mustard (such as Maille)

2 Tbsp. whole-grain mustard

½ tsp. kosher salt

¼ tsp. ground allspice

3 lb. bone-in, skin-on chicken thighs (about 8 thighs)

Green salad, for serving

1. Whisk together maple syrup, oil, mustards, salt, and allspice in a small bowl. Measure ½ cup sauce into a large ziplock plastic bag. Cover and store remaining sauce in bowl (about ½ cup) in refrigerator until ready to use or up to 5 days. Add chicken to sauce in ziplock bag; seal bag, and turn to coat chicken in sauce. Let marinate in refrigerator at least 1 hour or up to 24 hours.

2. Preheat a gas grill to high (450°F to 500°F) on one side. Remove chicken thighs from marinade; discard marinade. Place chicken on oiled grates over unlit side of grill. Grill, covered, turning occasionally, until chicken is browned and a thermometer inserted in thickest portion of meat registers 165°F, about 30 minutes. Transfer chicken to a platter. Serve alongside reserved ½ cup sauce and a green salad. —KELSEY YOUNGMAN

MAKE AHEAD Sauce may be stored in an airtight container in refrigerator up to 5 days.

WINE Full-bodied Washington Chardonnay: 2020 Chateau Ste. Michelle Indian Wells

NOTE Alternatively, to bake the chicken: Line a baking sheet with aluminum foil, and grease with oil. Arrange marinated chicken thighs, skin side up, on prepared baking sheet. Bake at 400°F until chicken is browned and a thermometer inserted in thickest portion of meat registers 165°F, 20 to 25 minutes.

Pepper Jelly–Glazed Chicken Thighs with Grilled Peppers
PHOTO P. 116

⏱ TOTAL 35 MIN; SERVES 4

Sweet, spicy, and sticky pepper jelly–glazed chicken thighs pair perfectly with grilled shishito peppers, Anaheim chiles, and scallions. Grilled limes squeezed over the cooked chicken add smoky acidity to the dish.

- 3 limes
- 8 boneless, skinless chicken thighs (about 2 lb. 5 oz.)
- 1 Tbsp. ground coriander
- 2½ tsp. kosher salt, divided
- ½ tsp. mellow red pepper flakes
- ¼ cup olive oil, divided
- 4 Anaheim chiles (10 to 12 oz.)
- 1 (8-oz.) pkg. shishito peppers (10 to 12 peppers)
- 1 bunch scallions, trimmed
- ½ cup hot pepper jelly

1. Preheat a grill to medium-high (400°F to 450°F). Cut limes in half. Squeeze 1 lime into a small bowl to equal 2 tablespoons juice; set juice aside, and discard juiced lime halves. Sprinkle chicken all over with coriander, 1½ teaspoons salt, and mellow red pepper flakes; rub evenly with 2 tablespoons oil. Set aside. Brush Anaheim chiles, shishito peppers, scallions, and cut sides of remaining 4 lime halves evenly with remaining 2 tablespoons oil. Sprinkle chiles, peppers, scallions, and lime halves evenly with remaining 1 teaspoon salt. Whisk together pepper jelly and reserved 2 tablespoons lime juice in a small bowl.

2. Arrange Anaheim chiles, shishito peppers, scallions, and limes, cut side down, on unoiled grill grates. Grill, uncovered, turning scallions often, chiles and peppers occasionally, and leaving limes undisturbed, until gently charred, 3 to 4 minutes for scallions and limes, 4 to 5 minutes for shishito peppers, and 6 to 8 minutes for Anaheim chiles. Transfer charred chiles, peppers, scallions, and limes to a baking sheet, and cover with aluminum foil to keep warm.

3. Arrange chicken thighs on unoiled grates; grill, covered, until nicely browned and a thermometer inserted in thickest portion of meat registers 165°F, 4 to 5 minutes per side. Brush tops of chicken thighs generously with some of the pepper jelly glaze, and grill, uncovered, until glaze is sizzling, about 1 minute. Flip chicken, and repeat with second side. Remove chicken from grill. Squeeze grilled lime halves over chicken; serve alongside chiles, peppers, and scallions. —MOLLY STEVENS

WINE Peppery Rhône-style red: 2020 Bonny Doon Le Cigare Volant

NOTE Any mild to medium-heat fresh chile, such as poblano or Hatch, can be substituted for Anaheim chiles. Padrón peppers, the earthier and slightly spicier cousin to the shishito, would also make a nice substitute. Marash mellow red pepper flakes are available at zingermans.com.

Chicken Cacciatore

ACTIVE 45 MIN; TOTAL 1 HR 35 MIN; SERVES 4

In her version of the classic Italian dish, Karen Akunowicz builds sautéed vegetables, mushrooms, red wine, chicken, and tomatoes into a hearty braise that's delicious served alongside slow-cooked greens, rice, or polenta.

- 2 Tbsp. canola oil
- 4 (4-oz.) bone-in, skin-on chicken thighs
- 1½ tsp. kosher salt, divided, plus more to taste
- 1 tsp. black pepper, divided
- ½ cup chopped bacon or prosciutto (about 4 bacon slices)
- 1 medium garlic clove, thinly sliced (about 1 tsp.)
- 1 small (5-oz.) yellow onion, thinly sliced (about 1 cup)
- 2 large celery stalks (about 4 oz.), cut into small cubes (about ½ cup)
- 1 medium (3-oz.) carrot, cut into small cubes (about ½ cup)
- 1 cup thinly sliced fresh shiitake mushroom caps (about 2 oz.)
- 1 cup dry red wine
- Pinch of crushed red pepper
- 1¾ cups canned whole peeled San Marzano tomatoes (from 1 [28-oz.] can), hand crushed
- 4 (3-inch) thyme sprigs
- 2 cups chicken broth
- Braised greens, rice, polenta, or potatoes, for serving

1. Heat oil in a large Dutch oven over medium-high until oil shimmers. Meanwhile, arrange chicken thighs in a single layer on a baking sheet or plate; sprinkle tops with ½ teaspoon salt and ½ teaspoon pepper. Flip thighs; sprinkle bottoms with ½ teaspoon salt and remaining ½ teaspoon pepper.

2. Reduce heat under shimmering oil to medium. Using a pair of metal tongs, carefully add chicken, skin side down, to Dutch oven. Sear chicken, resisting the temptation to move or turn the pieces until they have browned on the first side, 5 to 8 minutes. Turn chicken over, and cook until browned on other side, 5 to 8 minutes. Transfer chicken to a plate, and set aside. Do not wipe Dutch oven clean.

3. Reduce heat under Dutch oven to medium-low, and add bacon and garlic; cook, stirring constantly, until aromatic and bacon is slightly crispy, about 2 minutes. Increase heat to medium-high. Add onion, celery, carrot, mushroom caps, and ¼ teaspoon salt; cook, stirring occasionally, until onion is translucent, 3 to 5 minutes. Add wine; cook, stirring occasionally, until liquid reduces by half, about 5 minutes. Sprinkle with crushed red pepper and remaining ¼ teaspoon salt; stir in crushed tomatoes and their juices. Bring to a simmer over medium. Reduce heat to low; simmer, stirring occasionally, until sauce starts to get jammy, 5 to 8 minutes. Stir in thyme sprigs.

4. Arrange chicken thighs in a single layer in mixture in Dutch oven, and add broth. Bring to a simmer over medium. Cover and simmer over low, undisturbed, until chicken and vegetables are very tender and a thermometer inserted in thickest portion of chicken registers at least 165°F (temperature will likely be around 190°F), 40 to 50 minutes. Using a wooden spoon, break up some of the tomatoes.

5. Remove Dutch oven from heat. Let chicken mixture rest, covered, about 10 minutes. Remove and discard thyme sprigs. Taste tomato sauce, and add additional salt to taste. Serve with braised greens, rice, polenta, or potatoes, if desired. —KAREN AKUNOWICZ, FOX & THE KNIFE, BOSTON

MAKE AHEAD Cacciatore may be chilled in an airtight container up to 3 days.

WINE Herbal, medium-bodied Chianti: 2019 Fontodi Chianti Classico

CHICKEN LULE KEBAB

CHARRED JALAPEÑOS AND
TOMATOES (RECIPE P. 128)

SHAVED ONIONS WITH SUMAC
AND PARSLEY (RECIPE P. 312)

Chicken Lule Kebab

ACTIVE 1 HR 30 MIN; TOTAL 3 HR 15 MIN;
MAKES ABOUT 8 SKEWERS

*The ground beef lule kebab recipe at
Mini Kabob in Glendale, California, is a
Martirosyan family secret, but they were
willing to share their equally delicious
chicken version. Freshly grinding chicken
thighs with lamb fat gives these kebabs a
rich, savory flavor and juicy, tender texture.
The restaurant grinds all the meat in-house,
and you can, too, with a grinder. (We like
the KitchenAid meat grinder attachment.)
Or ask your butcher. If you don't have a
meat grinder, no problem: The F&W test
kitchen developed an alternative (and
less rich) version you can make using pre-
ground meat (see Note).*

- 2 lb. boneless, skinless chicken
  thighs, cut into 1-inch pieces
- 1 lb. lamb fat, cut into 1-inch pieces
- 1 medium-size (8-oz.) yellow onion,
  cut into ½-inch wedges (about
  2 cups)
- 3½ tsp. kosher salt
- 1½ tsp. black pepper
- 10 large metal skewers (1 inch
  wide×23½ inches long)
  Ghee, at room temperature, for
  brushing
  Charred Jalapeños and Tomatoes
  (recipe p. 128), for serving
  Shaved Onions with Sumac and
  Parsley (recipe p. 312), for serving
  Toum (recipe p. 309), for serving

1. Place chicken and lamb fat on a
baking sheet lined with parchment
paper; spread into a single layer. Freeze,
uncovered, until partially frozen, about
30 minutes. Meanwhile, place meat
grinding attachments, an 8-millimeter
(coarse) grinding plate, and a 4½-millimeter
(medium) grinding plate in freezer until well
chilled, 15 to 30 minutes.

2. Fit meat grinder with chilled grinder
attachments and 8-millimeter grinding
plate. Position a large bowl under grinder.
Grind alternating pieces of chicken, lamb
fat, and onion wedges through feed tube
into bowl for even distribution according
to manufacturer's instructions. Remove
8-millimeter grinding plate, and insert
4½-millimeter grinding plate. Pass chicken
mixture through grinder once more.

3. Spread chicken mixture into a ½-inch-
thick layer on a baking sheet. Sprinkle
evenly with salt and pepper. Loosely
cover with plastic wrap; let stand at room
temperature 20 minutes. Uncover and,
using your hands, fold mixture together
to evenly incorporate seasonings. Spread
into a ½-inch-thick layer on baking sheet.
Loosely cover with plastic wrap; let stand
at room temperature 20 minutes. If using
right away, freeze mixture, covered, until
very cold but not icy, about 30 minutes. Or
transfer mixture to an airtight container,
and store in refrigerator until ready to shape
kebabs, up to 3 days.

4. Open bottom vent of a kettle grill
completely. Light charcoal chimney starter
heaping full of briquettes. When briquettes
are covered with gray ash, pour them onto
the bottom grate, and arrange charcoal
in an even layer into an 8-inch-wide strip
down middle of bottom grate. Do not place
top grate on grill. Arrange 2 skewers in
an "L" shape, resting on rim of grill, with
1 skewer parallel to coal strip and 1 skewer
perpendicular to coals. These will be used
as a rack to suspend the kebabs.

5. While charcoal chimney is heating,
shape the kebabs. Fill a medium bowl
with water. Scoop 7 ounces (about 1 cup)
chicken mixture from bowl; shape into a
meatball, gently compacting it with your
hands. Holding 1 dry skewer in one hand
and meatball in the other hand, press
meat onto skewer about 6 inches down
from the pointed skewer tip. Wet your
hand with water in bowl, and squeeze
meat on skewer to shape into an even tube
around the skewer, about 9 inches long
and 2½ inches down from pointed skewer
tip, rewetting hand as needed to prevent
sticking. Using your thumb and pointer
finger on either side of the skewer, pinch
to remove and straighten the top and
bottom ends of the meat tube, removing
about ½ ounce (¾ inch) from each end. Put
excess meat in bowl with remaining chicken
mixture. Using a wet hand, press meat to
flatten into a 7-inch-long rectangular tube
(about 1½ inches wide) that begins about
3¼ inches down from pointed skewer tip.

Using your thumb and pointer finger on
either side of skewer, starting from pointed
skewer tip end, make 7 divots on 1 side of
meat tube with your thumb, about ½ inch
deep, running down length of meat. Divots
should go about three-fourths of the way
through meat to skewer. Place kebab on a
rimmed baking sheet, resting outer ends of
skewer on rim of baking sheet to suspend
kebab so meat doesn't get smashed. Chill
prepared skewer until ready to grill. Repeat
shaping and skewering procedure with
remaining chicken mixture and remaining
7 skewers.

6. Working in batches if needed, rest
pointed ends of skewers on prepared
"L"-shaped rack with handles overhanging
the edge of grill and meat perpendicular
to the charcoal strip. Grill, uncovered,
turning often, until lightly browned on
both sides, 3 to 5 minutes, repositioning
kebabs over coals as needed to avoid large
flare-ups.

7. Rotate skewers 90 degrees so that
they're parallel to charcoal strip. Continue
cooking over indirect heat, uncovered,
flipping and repositioning kebabs as
needed, until kebabs are cooked through
and a thermometer inserted in thickest
portion of meat (without touching
thermometer probe to skewer) registers
165°F, 5 to 8 minutes. Remove kebabs
from grill.

8. Using tongs, slide kebabs off skewers
and onto a rice- or lavash-lined platter,
if desired. Brush hot kebabs generously
with ghee.

9. Serve immediately with Charred
Jalapeños and Tomatoes, Shaved Onions
with Sumac and Parsley, and Toum.
—OVAKIM AND ALVARD MARTIROSYAN

WINE Emphatic, full-flavored rosé:
2021 Castello di Ama Purple Rosé

NOTE You can find lamb fat
at halal butchers or online at
frankiesfreerangemeat.com. To make
a version without a meat grinder, omit
chicken thighs, lamb fat, and onion wedges.
Stir together 1½ lb. ground chicken (white
and dark meat), ¾ lb. ground pork, and ¾ lb.
ground lamb. Grate 1 medium-size yellow
onion on small holes of a box grater, and add
to chicken mixture. Proceed with step 3.

Charred Jalapeños and Tomatoes

PHOTO P. 126

ACTIVE 15 MIN; TOTAL 30 MIN;
MAKES 1 KEBAB

Hot coals impart a smoky flavor and mellow the jalapeños, while tomatoes soften to juicy sweetness. A wide, flat skewer is the key to preventing the tomatoes and jalapeños from rolling when rotating on the grill. This recipe is for one skewer— just enough to provide a side of grilled vegetables as part of a larger meal —but it can easily be multiplied to make more.

- 3 medium-size plum tomatoes (about 9 oz.)
- 3 medium jalapeños (about 3 oz.)
- 2 large metal skewers (1 inch wide×23½ inches long)

1. Open bottom vent of a kettle grill completely. Light charcoal chimney starter heaping full of briquettes. When briquettes are covered with gray ash, pour them onto bottom grate, and arrange evenly in a 10-inch-wide strip down middle of bottom grate. Do not place top grate on grill. Place 1 skewer across edge of grill, parallel to coal strip, resting on rim of the grill. This will be used as a rack to suspend the kebab.

2. While charcoal chimney is heating, skewer the kebab. Thread tomatoes and jalapeños crosswise onto remaining skewer, starting about 3½ inches down from pointed skewer tip. Set aside at room temperature until ready to grill.

3. Arrange kebab, with pointed end of skewer resting on prepared rack and handle overhanging the edge of the grill, with vegetables perpendicular to the charcoal strip. Grill, uncovered, turning occasionally, until well charred on all sides, 6 to 8 minutes. Serve immediately. —OVAKIM AND ALVARD MARTIROSYAN

NOTE Select firm-ripe plum tomatoes.

Adobo Chicken Wings

ACTIVE 50 MIN; TOTAL 1 HR 10 MIN; PLUS 8 HR MARINATING; SERVES 4

"This dish is fully inspired by my dad," says chef Anna Swann. "His family's chicken adobo is the first Filipino dish he taught me how to make when I first started getting into cooking." At her pop-up, Ulam, in Dallas, Swann combines the flavors of chicken adobo with another childhood favorite, fried chicken wings. The resulting Adobo Chicken Wings are flavored to the bone thanks to a stint in an umami-rich soy sauce and vinegar marinade. While they bake, the marinade is cooked down to concentrate its flavors — the better for tossing the cooked wings in — adding a final, sticky, finger-licking layer of deliciousness. "This dish was a natural blend of the two dishes, an ode to some of my favorite meals he cooked for us," Swann says. "I also think this dish shows the beauty of Filipino food. How it can take simple ingredients and the end result is a rich complex layering of flavors. So simple, but so good!" Serve the Adobo Chicken Wings as Swann does, with steamed rice and a bright and acidic Filipino Pico, which combines chopped fresh tomatoes with herbs, fish sauce, and thin slices of serrano chile.

CHICKEN WINGS

- 2 lb. chicken wing drumettes and flats, patted dry
- 1¼ tsp. kosher salt
- ½ tsp. black pepper
- 1 small (6-oz.) white onion, thinly sliced (about ¾ cup)
- 1 (2-oz.) garlic head, cloves separated, peeled, and smashed (about 14 garlic cloves)
- ⅓ cup soy sauce (such as Silver Swan)
- ⅓ cup white vinegar (such as Datu Puti)
- 2 Tbsp. neutral cooking oil (such as grapeseed oil)
- 2 to 3 dried bay leaves
- Cooking spray

FILIPINO PICO

- 4 medium scallions (about 1¾ oz.), thinly sliced (about ½ cup), divided
- ¼ cup chopped fresh cilantro, divided
- 1 medium (⅜-oz.) serrano chile (unseeded), thinly sliced (about ¼ cup), divided

- 2 medium tomatoes (about 10 oz.), cored and chopped (about 1½ cups)
- 1½ tsp. fish sauce (such as Red Boat or Rufina)
- Kosher salt, to taste

ADDITIONAL INGREDIENTS

- 2 tsp. fried garlic (such as Maesri)
- Hot cooked white rice, for serving

1. Make the chicken wings: Sprinkle chicken all over with salt and pepper. Transfer chicken to a large ziplock plastic bag; add onion, garlic, soy sauce, vinegar, oil, and bay leaves. Seal bag, and toss mixture to evenly combine. Marinate chicken mixture in refrigerator at least 8 hours or up to 1 day.

2. Preheat oven to 425°F. Line a rimmed baking sheet with aluminum foil. Lightly coat an oven-safe wire rack with cooking spray, and set in baking sheet. Remove chicken wings from marinade, scraping off excess, and transfer to a paper towel–lined plate; pat dry. Reserve marinade in bag. Arrange wings at least ¼ inch apart on prepared wire rack. Roast in preheated oven until browned and crisp and a thermometer inserted in thickest portion of meat registers at least 165°F, 45 to 50 minutes, flipping wings after 25 minutes.

3. Meanwhile, bring reserved marinade to a boil in a small saucepan over medium. Boil, stirring occasionally, until liquid is slightly thickened and reduced to about 3 tablespoons, 14 to 16 minutes. Pour mixture through a fine wire-mesh strainer set over a large bowl; discard solids. Set reduced marinade aside.

4. While chicken wings bake, make the Filipino pico: Reserve 1 tablespoon scallions, 1 tablespoon cilantro, and a few slices of serrano for garnish; set aside. Stir together tomatoes and remaining scallions, cilantro, and serrano in a medium bowl. Stir in fish sauce, and season to taste with salt. Set aside.

5. Add chicken wings to bowl with reduced marinade, and toss to coat. Transfer to a platter, and garnish with reserved scallions, cilantro, and serrano. Sprinkle evenly with fried garlic. Serve immediately alongside Filipino pico and white rice. —ANNA SWANN

MAKE AHEAD Chicken wings can be marinated up to 1 day in advance.

ADOBO CHICKEN WINGS

BUTTERMILK FRIED CHICKEN

Buttermilk Fried Chicken

ACTIVE 1 HR 10 MIN; TOTAL 1 HR 20 MIN,
PLUS 12 HR REFRIGERATING; SERVES 6 TO 8

First published in our pages in October 2007, this staff-favorite fried chicken still sets the standard. For the first—and most critical—step in this recipe, Thomas Keller brines chicken for 12 hours in an herb-lemon saltwater mixture, which seasons the meat and helps it stay juicy through frying. After the brining comes a dip in seasoned flour, then in buttermilk, and then back to the seasoned flour. This double-layer crust fries up satisfyingly crisp, crunchy, and craggy, holding up perfectly on the picnic table.

BRINED CHICKEN

- 1 gal. water
- 1 cup Diamond Crystal kosher salt
- ¼ cup clover honey
- 2 lemons, halved
- 12 dried bay leaves
- 1 (2-oz.) bunch fresh flat-leaf parsley
- 1 (½-oz.) pkg. fresh thyme
- 1 head garlic, halved crosswise
- 2 Tbsp. black peppercorns
- 2 (2½- to 3-lb.) whole chickens, giblets removed (see Note)

ADDITIONAL INGREDIENTS

- Peanut oil or canola oil, for deep-frying
- 3 cups all-purpose flour (about 12¾ oz.)
- 2 Tbsp. garlic powder
- 2 Tbsp. onion powder
- 2 tsp. paprika
- 2 tsp. cayenne pepper
- 2 tsp. kosher salt, divided
- 1 tsp. black pepper, divided
- 2 cups whole buttermilk
- Fine sea salt or ground fleur de sel
- Rosemary and thyme sprigs, for garnish (optional)

1. Make the brined chicken: Place 1 gallon water, kosher salt, honey, lemons, bay leaves, parsley, thyme, garlic, and peppercorns in a container large enough to hold brine and chickens, such as a stockpot. Stir brine until salt dissolves. Cut each chicken into 10 pieces: 2 drumsticks, 2 thighs, 4 breast quarters, and 2 wings. Place chicken pieces in brine. Cover and refrigerate 12 hours. (Do not refrigerate chicken longer than 12 hours or it may become too salty.)

2. Remove chicken from brine; discard brine. Rinse chicken under cold water, removing any herbs or spices sticking to skin. Pat dry with paper towels. Let chicken stand until it comes to room temperature, 30 to 45 minutes.

3. Fill a large pot with peanut oil to a depth of 2 inches; heat over medium-high to 320°F. (Adjust heat as needed to maintain oil temperature.) Set a wire rack over a baking sheet; reserve for cooked chicken. Line a second baking sheet with parchment paper; reserve for raw chicken.

4. While oil heats, whisk together flour, garlic powder, onion powder, paprika, cayenne, 1 teaspoon kosher salt, and ½ teaspoon black pepper in a large bowl. Transfer half of the flour mixture (about 1½ cups) to a second large bowl. Pour buttermilk into a third bowl, and season with remaining 1 teaspoon kosher salt and remaining ½ teaspoon black pepper.

5. Working with 1 chicken thigh at a time, dip chicken thighs into first bowl of flour mixture; turn to coat, and pat off excess. Dip into buttermilk mixture, letting excess drip back into bowl. Dip into second bowl of flour mixture. Transfer coated chicken thigh to parchment-lined baking sheet.

6. Carefully lower chicken thighs into hot oil, adjusting heat as needed to return oil to 320°F. Cook 2 minutes, and then carefully move chicken pieces around in oil using tongs or a slotted spoon; continue to cook, monitoring oil temperature and turning chicken as needed for even cooking, until chicken is deep golden brown, very crisp,

and a thermometer inserted in thickest portion of meat registers 165°F, 11 to 12 minutes. Meanwhile, repeat coating process with chicken drumsticks. Transfer coated drumsticks to parchment-lined baking sheet.

7. Transfer cooked thighs, skin side up, to prepared wire rack; let rest while you fry remaining chicken. (Putting the pieces skin side up will allow excess fat to drain, whereas leaving them skin side down could trap some of the fat.) Make sure oil is 320°F, and carefully lower chicken drumsticks into hot oil, adjusting heat as needed to return oil to 320°F. Cook 2 minutes, and then carefully move chicken pieces around in oil using tongs. Continue to cook, monitoring oil temperature and turning chicken as needed for even cooking, until chicken is deep golden brown, very crisp, and cooked to 165°F, 11 to 12 minutes. Transfer drumsticks to wire rack; lean them against thighs, meat side up, to drain. Sprinkle thighs and drumsticks with fine sea salt to taste.

8. Increase heat under hot oil to high, and heat oil to 340°F. Meanwhile, repeat coating process with chicken breast pieces and wings. Carefully lower chicken breast pieces into hot oil; cook until golden brown, crisp, and cooked to 165°F, about 7 minutes, turning once using tongs halfway through cook time. Transfer breasts to wire rack; sprinkle with fine sea salt to taste, and turn skin side up. Add wings to hot oil; cook until golden brown and cooked to 165°F, about 6 minutes, turning once halfway through cook time. Transfer wings to wire rack, and sprinkle with fine sea salt to taste. Remove hot oil from heat.

9. Arrange fried chicken on a platter. If desired, add rosemary and thyme sprigs to oil (which will still be hot); let them cook and crisp for a few seconds, and arrange them over chicken. —THOMAS KELLER

NOTE Small organic chickens are available at most farmers markets. Larger 3- to 4-pound chickens will work in this recipe, but the smaller 2½- to 3-pound birds result in the optimal meat-to-crust ratio.

Charred Chile–Marinated Grilled Chicken and Tomatillo Salsa Cruda

ACTIVE 1 HR; TOTAL 2 HR 30 MIN;
SERVES 4 TO 6

To help build deep layers of flavor in these tacos, Fermín Núñez begins his marinade by toasting and charring aromatics: dried chiles, cinnamon, allspice, and onions all hit the heat before soaking with juicy chicken thighs for an hour, imparting smoky flavor before they cook quickly on the grill or in the oven (see Note). Pair them with fresh tomatillo salsa cruda for a next-level taco night.

MARINADE

6 medium garlic cloves, unpeeled

5 medium-size dried guajillo chiles (about 1¼ oz.)

3 medium-size dried chiles de árbol

4 whole allspice

2 small white or yellow onions (about 1 lb.), cut into 1-inch wedges with root ends left intact

1 (1-inch) cinnamon stick

1½ Tbsp. kosher salt

¼ tsp. black pepper

½ cup water

ADDITIONAL INGREDIENTS

6 bone-in, skin-on chicken thighs (about 1 lb. 12 oz.), trimmed

2 tsp. kosher salt

Tomatillo Salsa Cruda (recipe p. 306)

12 (4½-inch) Homemade Corn Tortillas (recipe p. 236) (optional)

1. Make the marinade: Heat a large cast-iron skillet over medium-high. Add garlic and chiles; cook, turning occasionally, until chiles are blackened and garlic is charred in spots, 1 to 3 minutes for chiles and 5 to 7 minutes for garlic. Remove from heat. Remove and discard stems from chiles, leaving seeds in pods; place chiles in a blender. Set garlic aside. Add allspice to skillet; cook over medium-high, stirring often, until fragrant, about 30 seconds. Add to blender; set aside.

2. Return skillet to heat over medium-high. Working in batches if needed, arrange onion wedges, cut side down, in a single layer in skillet; cook until blackened on both sides, 15 to 20 minutes, flipping halfway through cook time. Remove from heat. Transfer onions to blender. Peel garlic; discard skins. Add garlic cloves, cinnamon, salt, and black pepper to blender.

3. Secure lid on blender, and remove center piece to allow steam to escape. Place a clean towel over opening. Pulse chile mixture until roughly chopped, 2 to 4 pulses. Add ½ cup water to blender; process until smooth, about 1 minute. Uncover and let marinade cool to room temperature, about 15 minutes.

4. Make the chicken: Place chicken in a large bowl, and pour marinade over chicken. Using your hands, spread marinade evenly over chicken. Cover and marinate in refrigerator at least 1 hour or up to 5 hours. (For the best flavor, do not marinate chicken overnight, or the bitterness from the charred aromatics will take over.)

5. Remove chicken from marinade; let excess drip off, leaving a thin coating on each piece, and transfer to a baking sheet lined with aluminum foil. Discard remaining marinade in bowl. Sprinkle chicken evenly with salt. Set aside at room temperature until ready to grill.

6. Open bottom vent of a charcoal grill completely. Light charcoal chimney starter filled with briquettes. When briquettes are covered with gray ash, pour them onto bottom grate of grill, and push to one side of grill. Coat top grate with oil; place on grill. Place chicken, skin side down, on oiled grates over side with coals. Grill, uncovered, flipping chicken occasionally, until chicken is charred in spots on both sides, about 6 minutes. Transfer chicken, skin side up, to grates over side without coals; grill, covered, flipping chicken occasionally, until a thermometer inserted in thickest portion of thighs registers 165°F, 18 to 24 minutes. Transfer chicken to a cutting board; let stand until cool enough to handle, 10 to 15 minutes.

7. Remove and discard bones from chicken. Chop meat with skin into about ½-inch pieces. If using, top tortillas evenly with chopped chicken (about ¼ cup each), and serve with tomatillo salsa cruda. —FERMÍN NÚÑEZ, SUERTE, AUSTIN

BEER Crisp lager beer: Stone Brewing Buenaveza Salt & Lime Lager

NOTE To cook the chicken in the oven, follow recipe through step 5. Preheat oven to 375°F. Place chicken, skin side up, on an aluminum foil–lined baking sheet. Roast in preheated oven until a thermometer inserted in thickest portion registers 165°F, 25 to 35 minutes. Flip thighs, and swipe through juices and marinade on pan to give top of thighs a glossy appearance. Proceed with step 7.

CHARRED CHILE–MARINATED
GRILLED CHICKEN AND
TOMATILLO SALSA CRUDA

GANG GAI KHAO MUN (THAI CHICKEN CURRY)

Gang Gai Khao Mun (Thai Chicken Curry)

ACTIVE 1 HR 30 MIN; TOTAL 1 HR 40 MIN; SERVES 6

Sweet, sticky coconut rice colored and flavored with green herbs pairs with this creamy Thai chicken curry from chef Nok Suntaranon. The foundation of the curry is a vibrant from-scratch curry paste — the same one used at Kalaya in Philadelphia (one of F&W's Best New Restaurants in 2020). Making your own curry paste requires a little sourcing, but the resulting flavor is well worth the effort. The curry paste freezes well for future batches.

KALAYA CURRY PASTE

- ⅓ cup trimmed and thinly sliced lemongrass (from 2 large stalks)
- ⅓ cup thinly sliced shallot (from 1 large [1½-oz.] shallot)
- ¼ cup plus 2 Tbsp. crushed red pepper (about 1½ oz.)
- ¼ cup peeled and thinly sliced fresh turmeric root (from ⅓ cup whole turmeric)
- 2 Tbsp. paprika
- 1½ Tbsp. black pepper
- 1½ Tbsp. ground white pepper
- 1 Tbsp. peeled and thinly sliced fresh galangal
- ½ Tbsp. ground turmeric
- 8 garlic cloves
- 5 makrut lime leaves
- 3 to 4 fresh red Thai chiles
- ¾ cup water, divided

COCONUT RICE

- 2 cups packed fresh cilantro leaves and stems (from 1 [2½-oz.] bunch, trimmed)
- ⅔ cup coconut milk (from 1 [14-oz.] can, well shaken and stirred)
- ½ cup chopped pandan leaves (about 1 oz.) or chopped fresh cilantro
- ¼ cup granulated sugar
- 1½ tsp. kosher salt
- 1½ cups uncooked jasmine white rice
- 1½ cups water
- ¼ cup sliced shallot (from 1 large [1½-oz.] shallot)
- 3 garlic cloves, finely chopped (about 1 Tbsp.)

CHICKEN CURRY

- 2 Tbsp. palm sugar
- 1 Tbsp. shrimp paste
- 1 (13½-oz.) can coconut cream, divided
- 2 lb. boneless, skinless chicken thighs (about 8 thighs), cut into 1- to 2-inch pieces
- 1 (14-oz.) can coconut milk, well shaken and stirred
- ¼ cup fish sauce
- 1 tsp. kosher salt
- 2 cups packed fresh basil leaves, plus more for garnish
- 3 makrut lime leaves, plus more for garnish
- 2 fresh green long hot peppers (about 2½ oz.) (such as cowhorn hot peppers), sliced (about 1 cup)

1. Make the Kalaya curry paste: Combine lemongrass, shallot, crushed red pepper, sliced turmeric, paprika, black pepper, white pepper, galangal, ground turmeric, garlic, lime leaves, and Thai chiles in a food processor, and process until vegetables and herbs are very finely chopped, about 1 minute. Add ½ cup water; process until mixture looks creamy (it will still be coarse), about 2 minutes, stopping to scrape down sides of bowl as needed. Scrape down sides of processor bowl, and stir mixture. With processor running, pour remaining ¼ cup water through food chute, processing until mixture is smooth but slightly gritty and paste-like, about 2 minutes. Set aside ½ cup Kalaya curry paste in a small bowl. Store remaining paste in an airtight container in freezer up to 2 months.

2. Make the coconut rice: Process cilantro, coconut milk, pandan, sugar, and salt in a blender until very smooth, about 1 minute. Set aside. Place rice in a medium bowl, and add water to cover. Agitate rice with your fingers until water turns cloudy. Drain water, holding rice back in bowl with your hands. Repeat process until water runs clear, about 3 times. Stir together rinsed rice, blended cilantro mixture, 1½ cups water, shallot, and garlic in a medium saucepan. Bring to a simmer over medium, stirring occasionally. Cover and reduce heat to low; simmer, stirring bottom and edges of pan occasionally to prevent sticking, until liquid is absorbed, 10 to 12 minutes. Remove from heat; cover and let steam until rice is tender, 10 to 12 minutes. Uncover; gently fluff rice using a fork. (Rice will be sticky.)

3. Make the chicken curry: While coconut rice cooks, heat a medium-size heavy-bottomed pot or a Dutch oven over medium-low. Add palm sugar, shrimp paste, reserved ½ cup Kalaya curry paste, and half of the coconut cream (about ¾ cup), and cook, stirring often, until curry sauce is fragrant and bubbly and palm sugar is dissolved, 3 to 5 minutes. Stir in chicken pieces and coconut milk. Increase heat to medium, and bring to a boil. Gently boil, stirring occasionally, until chicken is tender and a thermometer inserted in thickest portion of chicken registers at least 165°F, 7 to 10 minutes. Stir in fish sauce and salt. Stir in remaining half of coconut cream (about ¾ cup). Remove pan from heat. Stir in basil and makrut lime leaves.

4. Top chicken curry evenly with long hot peppers; garnish with additional basil and lime leaves. Serve alongside coconut rice. —NOK SUNTARANON, KALAYA THAI KITCHEN, PHILADELPHIA, PA

MAKE AHEAD Kalaya curry paste can be stored in an airtight container in freezer up to 2 months.

WINE Citrusy, bright dry Riesling: 2020 Marietta Old Vine Riesling

Sheet-Pan Turkey with Brown Sugar and Coriander

PHOTO P. 117

ACTIVE 30 MIN; TOTAL 3 HR 45 MIN, PLUS 24 HR REFRIGERATING; SERVES 10 TO 12

Spatchcocking turkey speeds up its cooking time, while dry-brining the bird a day ahead of time is the key to the most juicy, flavorful meat.

- ½ cup packed light brown sugar
- 3 Tbsp. kosher salt
- 3 Tbsp. chopped fresh thyme
- 2 Tbsp. crushed coriander seeds
- 1 Tbsp. black pepper
- 2 tsp. grated lemon zest (from 1 lemon)
- 1 (12- to 14-lb.) whole fresh natural turkey or thawed frozen natural turkey, patted dry and spatchcocked (see Note)
- 2 Tbsp. extra-virgin olive oil

1. Stir together sugar, salt, thyme, coriander seeds, pepper, and lemon zest in a small bowl until well combined. Rub all over skin of turkey and underside of turkey cavity, rubbing more where meat is thickest. Set a wire rack inside a large rimmed baking sheet. Place turkey on wire rack. Tuck wing tips under turkey. Refrigerate, uncovered, 24 hours.

2. Remove turkey from refrigerator. Let stand at room temperature 1 hour. Line a large rimmed baking sheet with aluminum foil. Transfer turkey on wire rack to foil-lined baking sheet. Drizzle turkey evenly with oil.

3. Preheat oven to 350°F with rack in lower third position. Roast turkey in preheated oven until an instant-read thermometer inserted in thickest part of breast registers 150°F, 1 hour and 45 minutes to 2 hours and 15 minutes, rotating baking sheet from front to back halfway through roasting time. Tent turkey with aluminum foil during final 30 minutes of roasting time if skin is turning too dark. Remove turkey from oven, and place on a wire rack. Let rest 30 minutes before serving. —JUSTIN CHAPPLE

WINE Appley, earthy Spanish Cava: Segura Viudas Brut Reserva Heredad

NOTE To spatchcock a turkey, place turkey, breast side down, on a work surface. Using sturdy shears, cut along each side of backbone, separating from turkey; reserve for stock, or discard. Flip turkey breast side up. Using heels of your hands, firmly press against breastbone until it cracks and turkey flattens.

Turkey "Carnitas" with Green Mojo

ACTIVE 50 MIN; TOTAL 1 HR 5 MIN; SERVES 4

Shredded cooked turkey replaces the more traditional shredded pork in this riff on carnitas tacos, served with a sauce inspired by Cuban mojo.

MOJO

- 1½ cups loosely packed fresh cilantro leaves
- 6 Tbsp. fresh orange juice (from 2 oranges)
- ¼ cup fresh lime juice (from 2 limes)
- 1 small (½-oz.) serrano chile, (unseeded), chopped (1½ Tbsp.)
- 1 medium garlic clove, smashed
- ¼ cup extra-virgin olive oil
- ½ tsp. kosher salt
- ¼ tsp. black pepper

TURKEY "CARNITAS"

- 6 Tbsp. extra-virgin olive oil
- 1 small (6-oz.) white onion, finely chopped (about 1 cup), plus more for serving
- 3 medium garlic cloves, finely chopped (about 1 Tbsp.)
- 2 tsp. ancho chile powder
- ½ tsp. ground cumin
- ½ tsp. ground coriander
- ½ tsp. ground cinnamon
- 1 cup turkey broth or chicken broth
- ½ cup fresh orange juice (from 2 oranges)
- ¼ cup fresh lime juice (from 2 limes)
- 2 (4-inch) oregano sprigs
- 2 fresh or dried bay leaves
- 4 cups shredded cooked turkey (dark meat and white meat separated) (about 1¼ lb.), divided
- ½ tsp. kosher salt, plus more to taste
- 8 (6-inch) corn tortillas, warmed

1. Make the mojo: Process cilantro, orange juice, lime juice, chile, and garlic in a blender until very smooth, about 45 seconds. Remove center piece of blender lid; with blender running, slowly stream in oil until emulsified and creamy, about 20 seconds. Transfer to a small bowl; stir in salt and pepper. Cover and store in refrigerator until ready to serve.

2. Make the turkey "carnitas": Heat oil in a large cast-iron skillet over medium-high. Add onion and garlic; cook, stirring often, until softened and lightly browned, 6 to 8 minutes. Add ancho chile powder, cumin, coriander, and cinnamon; cook, stirring constantly, until spice mixture is toasted and fragrant, about 1 minute. Add broth, orange juice, lime juice, oregano, and bay leaves; bring to a boil over medium-high. Boil, undisturbed, until orange juice mixture is reduced and just covers onion, about 15 minutes.

3. Add dark turkey meat to mixture in skillet, and cook, stirring occasionally, 3 minutes. Stir in white meat; cook, stirring occasionally, until orange juice mixture is absorbed into turkey meat, 5 to 8 minutes. Stir in salt, plus more to taste. Remove from heat. Serve turkey mixture on tortillas; top with mojo and additional chopped onion. —JUSTIN CHAPPLE

MAKE AHEAD Mojo can be made up to 8 hours in advance and stored in an airtight container in refrigerator.

WINE Citrusy California white blend: 2020 Inglenook Blancaneaux

**TURKEY "CARNITAS"
WITH GREEN MOJO**

THAI-INSPIRED TURKEY
GREEN CURRY

Thai-Inspired Turkey Green Curry

TOTAL 50 MIN; SERVES 4

Leftover turkey breast is easily infused with lots of flavor when reheated in this quick Thai-inspired Turkey Green Curry.

- 1 small (10-oz.) sweet potato, peeled and cut into ¾-inch pieces (about 1¾ cups)
- 1 small (8-oz.) turnip, peeled and cut into ¾-inch pieces (about 1¼ cups)
- 3 Tbsp. canola oil, divided
- ¾ tsp. kosher salt, divided
- ½ tsp. black pepper, divided
- 1 large (1½-oz.) shallot, finely chopped (about ¼ cup)
- 3 Tbsp. minced peeled fresh ginger (from 1 [3-inch] piece ginger)
- 4 medium garlic cloves, finely chopped (about 1½ Tbsp.)
- 1 lemongrass stalk (pale core only), finely chopped (about 1½ Tbsp.)
- 2 fresh red Thai chiles (unseeded), finely chopped (about 1 tsp.)
- ¼ cup green curry paste (such as Maesri or Thai Kitchen)
- 2 cups turkey broth or chicken broth
- 1 (13.66-oz.) can unsweetened coconut milk
- 2 Tbsp. fresh lime juice (from 1 large lime), plus more to taste
- 2 tsp. fish sauce
- 2 cups firmly packed fresh curly leaf spinach, torn, or stemmed Swiss chard, torn
- 1⅓ cups shredded cooked turkey breast (about 8 oz.)
- Fresh basil leaves, for garnish

1. Preheat oven to 425°F. Toss together sweet potato, turnip, 1 tablespoon oil, ¼ teaspoon salt, and ¼ teaspoon black pepper on a rimmed baking sheet. Roast in preheated oven until bottom sides of sweet potato and turnip are browned in spots and just tender, 15 to 20 minutes.

2. Meanwhile, heat remaining 2 tablespoons oil in a large, deep skillet over medium-high. Add shallot, ginger, garlic, lemongrass, chiles, and ¼ teaspoon salt. Cook, stirring often, until shallot mixture

is very fragrant and lightly browned, 3 to 5 minutes. Reduce heat to medium. Add curry paste, stirring to coat shallot mixture. Cook, stirring constantly, until fragrant, about 1 minute. Whisk in broth and coconut milk until combined and smooth. Bring to a simmer over medium, stirring occasionally. Stir in lime juice, fish sauce, remaining ¼ teaspoon salt, and remaining ¼ teaspoon black pepper.

3. Stir sweet potato mixture, spinach, and turkey into coconut milk mixture in skillet. Cook over medium, stirring gently, until spinach is wilted and turkey is heated through, about 2 minutes. Remove from heat. Season with additional lime juice to taste. Ladle curry evenly into 4 shallow bowls, and garnish with basil leaves.

—JUSTIN CHAPPLE

MAKE AHEAD Sweet potato mixture can be stored in an airtight container in refrigerator up to 1 day.

WINE Bright, lime-zesty Australian Riesling: 2021 Best's Great Western

Buffalo Turkey Hand Pies

ACTIVE 45 MIN; TOTAL 2 HR 10 MIN SERVES 6

These delicious, savory hand pies are made by filling store-bought puff pastry with diced leftover turkey that's been tossed with a buffalo-style hot sauce.

- ½ cup buffalo-style hot sauce (such as Frank's RedHot)
- 2 Tbsp. unsalted butter
- 2 cups chopped cooked turkey (white meat) (about 12 oz.)
- 1 medium (2-oz.) celery stalk, finely chopped (about ⅓ cup)
- ¼ cup finely chopped scallions (from 2 large scallions [about 2 oz.])
- ¼ tsp. kosher salt
- ¼ tsp. black pepper, plus more to taste
- 1 large egg
- 1 Tbsp. water
- All-purpose flour, for dusting
- 1 (14-oz.) pkg. all-butter frozen puff pastry (such as Dufour), thawed and chilled
- 3 oz. low-moisture part-skim mozzarella cheese, shredded (about ¾ cup)
- Flaky sea salt, for garnish

1. Line an 18- × 13-inch rimmed baking sheet with parchment paper; set aside.

2. Cook hot sauce and butter in a small saucepan over medium, stirring occasionally, until butter melts, about 2 minutes. Pour into a medium-size heatproof bowl, and let cool slightly, about 10 minutes. Stir in turkey, celery, scallions, kosher salt, and pepper. Refrigerate, uncovered, until ready to use.

3. Stir together egg and 1 tablespoon water in a small bowl; set aside. Working quickly, roll out puff pastry to a 20- × 12-inch rectangle on a lightly floured work surface with short edge facing you; dust puff pastry with flour as needed to prevent sticking. Slice in half crosswise. Slice each half into 3 (10- × 4-inch) rectangles.

4. Spoon ⅓ cup turkey mixture onto bottom half of each rectangle, leaving a ¾-inch border along bottom and sides. Top each with 2 tablespoons cheese. Working with 1 rectangle at a time, lightly brush bottom and side border of puff pastry with egg mixture. Fold top half of puff pastry over filling, and gently press edges together to seal. Crimp edges using a fork. Gently transfer hand pies to prepared baking sheet, spacing evenly apart. Brush hand pies with egg mixture. Cut 2 (¾-inch) slits on top of each hand pie using a paring knife. Sprinkle hand pies with additional pepper to taste, and garnish with flaky sea salt. Freeze 30 minutes. Meanwhile, preheat oven to 425°F.

5. Remove hand pies from freezer, and bake in preheated oven until hand pies are slightly puffed and lightly browned on top, about 15 minutes. Reduce oven temperature to 375°F, and bake until pies are puffed, browned, and crisp, 20 to 25 minutes. Let stand 10 minutes.

—JUSTIN CHAPPLE

MAKE AHEAD Turkey filling can be stored in an airtight container in refrigerator up to 2 days.

BEER Lightly bitter IPA: Port Brewing Wipeout

Stuffat Tal-Fenek (Maltese Braised Rabbit)

ACTIVE 1 HR 30 MIN; TOTAL 3 HR 50 MIN;
SERVES 4 TO 6

This cozy and rustic Maltese stew is studded with carrots, potatoes, sweet garlic confit, and perfectly cooked rabbit. A combination of fresh thyme and rosemary add complexity and stand up to the robust red-wine-and-tomato-based braise. Serve this saucy stew with a large piece of crusty bread for optimal sopping. The recipe is from chef Matthew Hamilton, the executive sous chef of March in Houston. June Rodil and Mark Sayre, who lead the wine program at March, suggest pairing this recipe with a 2019 Ca'n Verdura Negre, from Binissalem-Mallorca, Spain. "The rich tomato-based sauce for the Stuffat Tal-Fenek is begging for a red with rich flavor and dark fruit, but with lift," they say. "Dominated by Mantonegro (an indigenous Mallorcan grape), this crunchy wine provides enough depth for a high-tone braise."

GARLIC CONFIT

- 2 cups peeled garlic cloves (from 6 garlic heads)
- 2 cups grapeseed oil

BRAISED RABBIT

- 1 (about 3-lb.) whole rabbit with offal (kidneys and heart)
- 4 tsp. kosher salt, divided, plus more to taste
- 1 tsp. black pepper
- 2 cups chopped yellow onions (from 2 medium [8-oz.] onions), divided
- 3 Tbsp. garlic confit oil, divided
- 1¾ cups peeled and chopped carrots (from 4 medium [3-oz.] carrots)
- 3 Tbsp. garlic confit cloves (about 15 cloves)
- 2½ Tbsp. tomato paste
- 1¼ cups dry red wine (such as Garnacha)
- 6 cups chicken stock or rabbit stock
- 1½ cups tomato puree (from 1 [28-oz.] can)
- 1 Tbsp. honey
- 2 dried bay leaves
- 1 lb. Yukon Gold potatoes, peeled and cut into 1-inch cubes (about 2½ cups)
- 3 Tbsp. chopped fresh rosemary
- 3 Tbsp. chopped fresh thyme

ADDITIONAL INGREDIENTS

- Extra-virgin olive oil
- Roughly chopped fresh flat-leaf parsley and roughly chopped fresh oregano, for garnish
- Crusty bread, for serving

1. Make the garlic confit: Place garlic cloves and oil in a small saucepan, making sure garlic is completely covered with oil and no cloves float to the surface. Heat over medium until tiny bubbles start to form. Reduce heat to very low, and cook, undisturbed, until garlic is tender and light golden, about 45 minutes. Remove from heat. Let cool slightly, about 30 minutes. Transfer garlic confit to a sterilized lidded jar, ensuring that garlic cloves are completely submerged in oil. Seal jar, and store in refrigerator up to 1 week.

2. Make the braised rabbit: Remove kidneys and heart from cavity of rabbit, and set aside. Cut front and hind legs from body. Cut behind the rib cage to isolate the saddle, and cut off the tail. (The rib cage, tail bone, and pelvic bones can be reserved and used to make stock.) Cut the saddle in half crosswise, cutting in between the vertebrae. Dry rabbit legs and saddle pieces with paper towels; sprinkle with 2 teaspoons salt and pepper. Transfer to a plate, and set aside.

3. Place rabbit kidneys and heart and ⅔ cup chopped onions in a food processor. Process until a smooth paste forms, 2 to 3 minutes, stopping to scrape down sides as needed. Set aside.

4. Heat 2 tablespoons garlic confit oil in a large Dutch oven or heavy-bottomed pot over high. Add half of the rabbit pieces, and cook, turning occasionally, until golden brown on all sides, 5 to 6 minutes. Remove rabbit pieces, and set aside. Add remaining 1 tablespoon garlic confit oil to Dutch oven, and repeat browning process with remaining rabbit pieces. (Do not wipe Dutch oven clean.)

5. Reduce heat under Dutch oven to medium, and add remaining 1⅓ cups chopped onions; cook, stirring often, until translucent and starting to caramelize, 6 to 8 minutes. Stir in carrots and 3 tablespoons garlic confit cloves, and reduce heat to medium-low; cook, stirring occasionally, until carrots are softened, about 10 minutes. Stir in tomato paste and onion-offal puree; cook, stirring constantly, 1 minute. Increase heat to medium-high, and stir in wine. Cook, stirring often and scraping up browned bits from bottom of Dutch oven, until bottom of Dutch oven is nearly dry, about 5 minutes. Stir in stock, tomato puree, honey, and bay leaves.

6. Return rabbit to Dutch oven; bring to a boil over medium-high. Cover and reduce heat to medium-low to maintain a low simmer; simmer 30 minutes. Stir in potatoes, rosemary, thyme, and remaining 2 teaspoons salt. Cover and cook until rabbit is easily pulled apart with a fork and potatoes are tender, 30 to 40 minutes.

7. Taste braised rabbit, and add additional salt if desired. Remove and discard bay leaves. Remove Dutch oven from heat. Drizzle with olive oil. Garnish with parsley and oregano, and serve with crusty bread.
—MATTHEW HAMILTON, EXECUTIVE SOUS CHEF, MARCH, HOUSTON

MAKE AHEAD Garlic confit can be made up to 1 week in advance and stored in an airtight container in refrigerator.

NOTE Rabbit with offal is available online at dartagnan.com.

STUFFAT TAL-FENEK (MALTESE BRAISED RABBIT)

PORK

PORK CHEEKS WITH PICKLED
ONIONS, MUSTARD SEEDS, AND
DAIKON (P. 151)
OPPOSITE: PORK CHOPS WITH
SHERRY PAN SAUCE (P. 148)

KATSU CURRY (JAPANESE
CURRY WITH TONKATSU
NUGGETS AND FRIED EGG)

Katsu Curry (Japanese Curry with Tonkatsu Nuggets and Fried Egg)

ACTIVE 1 HR 15 MIN; TOTAL 1 HR 25 MIN; SERVES 4

Sonoko Sakai's Japanese curry recipe is an ode to two popular Japanese dishes: curry and katsu. The secret to getting the brittle, crispy skin on tonkatsu (Japanese crispy breaded pork cutlets) is to use panko breadcrumbs, which are much larger and coarser than Western-style breadcrumbs. The tonkatsu is served on a bed of rice flavored with curry sauce and topped with cabbage, cilantro, and a fried egg, with pickled cucumber on the side for a delicious blend of textures and flavors.

CURRY POWDER

- 2 to 3 cardamom pods
- 1 (2-inch) cinnamon stick, broken into small pieces
- 1 dried bay leaf
- 1 Tbsp. brown or black mustard seeds
- 1 Tbsp. coriander seeds
- 1 Tbsp. fennel seeds
- 1 Tbsp. cumin seeds
- 1 tsp. fenugreek seeds
- ½ tsp. whole cloves
- 1½ tsp. black peppercorns
- 1 Tbsp. ground ginger
- 1 Tbsp. ground turmeric
- 1 Tbsp. fine sea salt
- 1 tsp. sweet paprika
- 1 tsp. cayenne pepper, plus more to taste

CURRY

- 3 Tbsp. mochiko (sweet glutinous rice flour) (such as Koda Farms)
- 3 cups chicken broth or vegetable broth, divided
- 3 Tbsp. sesame oil, unsalted butter, or canola oil
- 1 medium-size (9-oz.) yellow onion, thinly sliced (1½ cups)
- 2 Tbsp. finely chopped peeled fresh ginger (from 1 [2-inch] piece ginger)
- 3 garlic cloves, minced (about 1 Tbsp.)
- 2 Tbsp. soy sauce
- 4 tsp. ketchup (preferably Japanese Kagome)
- 2 tsp. honey or mirin
- 1 tsp. fresh lemon juice (from 1 lemon) or rice vinegar (optional)
- ½ tsp. fine sea salt, plus more to taste

QUICK CUCUMBER PICKLE

- 3 medium-size Kirby cucumbers (about 12 oz.), sliced into ⅛-inch-thick rounds (about 2¼ cups)
- ½ tsp. cane sugar
- ½ tsp. fine sea salt
- 1 tsp. fresh lemon juice or lime juice (from 1 lemon or 1 lime)

TONKATSU NUGGETS

- Rice bran oil, sesame oil, or grapeseed oil, for frying
- 4 (4- to 5-oz.) boneless pork loin chops (about ¾ inch thick)
- 1 tsp. fine sea salt
- ½ tsp. black pepper
- ⅓ cup all-purpose flour (about 1½ oz.)
- 1 large egg, beaten
- 2 cups panko

ADDITIONAL INGREDIENTS

- 4 cups cooked white rice
- 3 cups finely shredded red or green cabbage (about 8 oz.) (from 1 small head cabbage)
- 4 lemon wedges
- 2 Tbsp. fresh cilantro leaves
- 4 fried eggs

1. Make the curry powder: Cook cardamom pods, cinnamon pieces, bay leaf, mustard seeds, coriander seeds, fennel seeds, cumin seeds, fenugreek seeds, and whole cloves in a medium skillet over medium, tossing or stirring often, until toasted and fragrant, 2 to 4 minutes. Remove from heat; let cool 2 minutes. Transfer toasted cardamom mixture and black peppercorns to a spice grinder; process, stopping to shake grinder a couple of times to make sure cinnamon stick is pulverized, until a powder forms, about 15 seconds. Continue processing until a fine powder forms, about 15 seconds. Pour ground spices through a fine wire-mesh strainer set over a medium bowl. If any coarse pieces remain in strainer, return to spice grinder, and process until they form a fine powder; sift again. Discard any remaining coarse pieces. Add ground ginger, turmeric, salt, paprika, and cayenne to ground cardamom mixture in bowl, and whisk to combine. Add additional cayenne

to taste. Reserve 1 tablespoon curry powder; store remaining curry powder for another use.

2. Make the curry: Whisk together mochiko and ½ cup broth in a small bowl to form a slurry. Set aside. Heat oil in a medium saucepan over medium. Add onion; cook, stirring occasionally, until softened, about 6 minutes. Add chopped ginger and garlic; cook, stirring often, until fragrant, about 1 minute. Pour in remaining 2½ cups broth. Bring mixture to a simmer over medium. Stir in soy sauce, ketchup, honey, lemon juice (if using), salt, and reserved 1 tablespoon curry powder. Stir mochiko slurry in bowl; drizzle slurry into onion mixture, stirring constantly to combine. Cook mixture over medium, stirring bottom of pan often to prevent sticking, until flavors marry, mixture thickens, and onion breaks down further, about 15 minutes. Remove from heat. Using an immersion blender, process mixture in pan until creamy and smooth, about 1 minute. Taste and season with additional salt if needed. Return pan to heat, and bring to a simmer. Simmer, stirring often, 5 minutes. Remove from heat. Cover and set aside until ready to serve.

3. Make the quick cucumber pickle: Place cucumbers in a medium bowl. Sprinkle with sugar and salt; gently massage with your hands for 10 seconds. Let cucumbers stand in brine 5 minutes. Holding cucumbers in bowl using your hands or a slotted spoon, pour out and discard excess brine in bowl. Add lemon juice to cucumbers in bowl; toss to combine. Set aside.

4. Make the tonkatsu nuggets: Pour oil into a medium-size Dutch oven to a depth of 1½ inches; heat over medium until oil reaches 350°F. Trim fat around edges of pork chops; discard. If necessary, pound pork chops using flat side of a meat mallet to slightly flatten them so that all pieces are ¾ inch thick. Cut each chop in half crosswise to make 8 nuggets total. Rub nuggets evenly with salt and pepper. Place flour, egg, and panko in 3 separate shallow bowls. Dredge 1 pork nugget in flour; shake off excess. Dip in egg; let excess drip off. Coat generously with panko, pressing gently to adhere. Transfer coated nugget to a plate. Repeat process with remaining nuggets.

5. Add half of the tonkatsu nuggets to hot oil in Dutch oven; fry until lightly browned

continued on page 146

continued from page 145

on bottom sides, 2 to 3 minutes. Flip and fry until golden brown all over, 2 to 3 minutes. Transfer fried tonkatsu nuggets to a large paper towel–lined plate. Repeat process with remaining tonkatsu nuggets.

6. Reheat curry in pan over medium, stirring occasionally, until warmed through, about 3 minutes. Divide rice evenly among 4 shallow bowls. Spoon curry evenly over half of each bowl. Slice tonkatsu nuggets, and arrange evenly divided pieces on the other half of bowls, using rice as a pillow. Top evenly with shredded cabbage, lemon wedges, and cilantro. Place 1 fried egg on each bowl. Serve alongside quick cucumber pickle. —SONOKO SAKAI

MAKE AHEAD Curry powder can be stored in an airtight container at room temperature up to 1 month. Curry can be prepared through step 2 up to 2 days in advance and stored in an airtight container in the refrigerator.

BEER Malty Japanese beer: Hitachino Nest Red Rice Ale

NOTE Sonoko Sakai's Curry Brick Kits may be substituted for homemade curry powder; find them at sonokosakai.com.

Emperor's Pork

ACTIVE 30 MIN; TOTAL 3 HR 45 MIN; SERVES 4

The late Aussie restaurateur Tony Lo taught his son Buddha how to braise and glaze pork belly in a sweet and savory soy-rich sauce laced with warm notes of cinnamon, rock sugar, and super-savory MSG. Serve the glazed cubes of pork with steamed greens and white rice to soak up the sauce.

- 3 lb. pork belly with skin, cut into 2-inch cubes
- 1 cup chopped (2-inch pieces) scallions (from 1 bunch)
- ½ cup dark soy sauce
- ½ cup sweet soy sauce (such as Kecap Manis)
- ½ cup Shaoxing cooking wine
- ½ cup granulated sugar
- ½ cup rock sugar
- ¼ cup Maggi Seasoning Sauce
- 2 Tbsp. kosher salt
- 2 tsp. monosodium glutamate seasoning (MSG)
- 1 tsp. white pepper
- 4 whole star anise
- 2 (3-inch) cinnamon sticks
- 4 dried bay leaves
- 4 dried red chiles
- 1 (3-inch) piece fresh ginger, peeled and sliced
- 5 large garlic cloves, smashed
- 8 cups plus 2 Tbsp. water, divided
- 3 Tbsp. cornstarch
- Steamed greens (such as Chinese mustard, bok choy, or Asian greens) and cooked white rice, for serving

1. Bring a large pot of water to a boil over high. Add pork belly; boil, undisturbed, 3 minutes. (This will remove blood and impurities from the meat.) Drain and rinse pork belly clean. Set aside. Wash and dry pot.

2. Combine pork, scallions, dark soy sauce, sweet soy sauce, Shaoxing wine, granulated sugar, rock sugar, Maggi Seasoning Sauce, salt, MSG, white pepper, star anise, cinnamon sticks, bay leaves, dried red chiles, ginger, garlic, and 8 cups water in cleaned large pot. Stir to ensure everything is submerged. Bring mixture to a simmer over medium-high. Reduce heat to medium or medium-low to maintain a gentle simmer, and simmer, stirring occasionally, until pork is tender when pierced with a fork but not falling apart, about 2 hours. Remove from heat. Let pork rest in cooking liquid in pot at room temperature, uncovered, 1 hour.

3. Remove pork from cooking liquid in pot, and set aside. Pour cooking liquid through a fine wire-mesh strainer into a large bowl; discard solids. Measure 4 cups strained cooking liquid into a medium pot; bring to a boil over high. (Reserve remaining strained cooking liquid.) Meanwhile, whisk together cornstarch and remaining 2 tablespoons water in a small bowl until well combined.

4. Gradually add cornstarch slurry to boiling cooking liquid, whisking continuously. Continue to boil on high, whisking constantly, until sauce forms a glaze consistency and coats the back of a spoon, about 3 minutes. You might need to add more reserved cooking liquid if glaze becomes too thick. Reduce heat to medium; add pork to mixture, and toss to coat. Cook, stirring occasionally, until warmed through, 5 to 10 minutes. Serve alongside steamed greens and white rice. —BUDDHA LO, HUSO, NEW YORK CITY

MAKE AHEAD Pork can be prepared through step 2 up to 12 hours in advance and stored in an airtight container in refrigerator.

NOTE MSG and Maggi Seasoning Sauce can be found at most grocery stores or online at walmart.com.

EMPEROR'S PORK

Pork Chops with Sherry Pan Sauce

PHOTO P. 142

ACTIVE 30 MIN; TOTAL 1 HR; SERVES 2 TO 4

Dry sherry lends an oxidized, nutty complexity to this pan sauce. Sweetened with fresh orange juice and dried fruit, it's perfect with pork chops or seared duck breasts. The technique here relies on rendering fat from the meat, setting it aside, and using that fat to bloom beautifully complex ras al hanout in the pan, before deglazing it with sherry to incorporate every bit of flavor into the final sauce. This recipe is written for pork chops, but you can make the sherry pan sauce from other proteins; start from step 2, working with 1 tablespoon of reserved drippings, and proceed as written.

- 2 (1-lb.) bone-in, center-cut pork chops (about 1¼ inches thick)
- 1¾ tsp. kosher salt, plus more to taste
- 1 tsp. black pepper, plus more to taste
- 1 Tbsp. neutral oil (such as grapeseed)
- 1 large shallot, finely chopped (about ¼ cup)
- 1½ tsp. ras el hanout
- ⅓ cup dry sherry (such as oloroso)
- 1 tsp. grated orange zest plus 1 cup fresh orange juice (from 4 oranges)
- 3 Tbsp. chopped prunes or dried figs
- 1 Tbsp. chopped fresh flat-leaf parsley or cilantro

1. Season pork with salt and pepper. Heat oil in a large skillet over medium-high. Add pork chops; cook, flipping often, until well browned and a thermometer inserted in thickest portion of meat near the bone registers 130°F, about 15 minutes. Transfer pork to a plate, and pour off all but 1 tablespoon drippings, taking care to preserve browned bits in skillet.

2. Add shallot to skillet over medium-high; cook, stirring often, until softened, about 1 minute. Add ras el hanout; cook, stirring constantly, until fragrant, about 10 seconds. Add sherry; simmer, stirring to loosen browned bits, until liquid has reduced by about half, 1 to 2 minutes. Add orange zest and juice and prunes; cook, stirring occasionally, until mixture has thickened slightly and reduced to about 1 cup, 3 to 5 minutes. Remove from heat; stir in parsley. Season with salt and pepper to taste. Serve with pork chops.
—ANDREA SLONECKER

Sautéed Italian Sausage with Onions and Peppers

ACTIVE 40 MIN; TOTAL 55 MIN; SERVES 4

Searing sweet Italian sausage in a dry skillet renders the fat, resulting in a deliciously crispy sausage. Tender bell peppers add a welcome vegetal sweetness to this one-pan dinner while they cook down in a blend of savory chicken broth and tangy vinegar perfect for sopping up with crusty bread. Sausage, peppers, and onions is a great dinner to pair with a red wine, says sommelier Theo Lieberman of Pasquale Jones in New York City, who provided the inspiration for this recipe. To go with the sausage, peppers, and onions, he says, "I've been digging Forlorn Hope's Queen of the Sierra red—I like it chilled. It's easy to drink and lends itself to all kinds of food."

- 4 (6- to 7-oz.) sweet Italian pork sausages
- 3 medium bell peppers (mix of yellow, red, and green), sliced (about 5 loosely packed cups)
- 1 large red onion, halved lengthwise and thinly sliced crosswise (about 3 cups)
- 2 Tbsp. tomato paste
- 3 large garlic cloves, thinly sliced (about 1½ Tbsp.)
- ½ tsp. kosher salt
- ¼ tsp. crushed red pepper
- 1 cup lower-sodium chicken broth
- 1 Tbsp. red wine vinegar

1. Preheat oven to 400°F. Prick Italian sausages all over using a knife. Place sausages in a cold large ovenproof skillet. Cook over medium-high, flipping occasionally, until browned on all sides, about 14 minutes. Transfer to a plate. Do not wipe skillet clean.

2. Add bell peppers and onion to skillet; cook over medium-high, stirring often, until softened, about 6 minutes. Add tomato paste, garlic, salt, and crushed red pepper; cook, stirring often, until vegetables are well coated in tomato paste and garlic is tender and aromatic, about 2 minutes. Stir in broth and vinegar. Bring to a boil over medium-high. Boil, stirring often, until liquid has almost completely reduced, about 6 minutes. Return sausages to skillet.

3. Transfer skillet to preheated oven, and roast until vegetables are tender and a thermometer inserted in thickest portion of sausages registers 160°F, about 15 minutes. Remove from oven; let stand until cool enough to handle, 3 to 5 minutes. Serve with crusty bread. —ANNA THEOKTISTO

WINE 2018 Forlorn Hope Queen of the Sierra red

SAUTÉED ITALIAN SAUSAGE
WITH ONIONS AND PEPPERS

PORK CHEEKS WITH
PICKLED ONIONS, MUSTARD
SEEDS, AND DAIKON

Pork Cheeks with Pickled Onions, Mustard Seeds, and Daikon

PHOTO P. 143

ACTIVE 1 HR 15 MIN; TOTAL 4 HR 15 MIN, PLUS 2 DAYS BRINING AND 4 HR REFRIGERATION; SERVES 5

This dish spotlights pork cheeks, an unsung but delicious cut that is just one of the ways winemaker and restaurateur André Mack showcases American wine and pork at his Brooklyn ham bar, & Sons. The unctuous and hearty meat is balanced by the fresh tang and pleasant crunch from the pickled onions and mustard seeds. The recipe makes more pickles than you will need immediately; keep the extra in the refrigerator to garnish hard-boiled or deviled eggs, or to add a punch of flavor to a ham or turkey sandwich. This is a good recipe project for a special weekend dinner. Be sure to start planning a few days ahead of time, to allow the pork cheeks their full two days of brining time. And take your time while cooking, especially to keep an eye on the jus as it cooks to ensure it doesn't over-reduce; as it thickens, the bubbling will slow down.

- **7 cups water, divided**
- **2½ tsp. kosher salt, divided**
- **¼ tsp. coarse Himalayan pink salt**
- **10 (3½-oz.) pork cheeks**
- **2 Tbsp. canola oil**
- **1 medium-size (9-oz.) yellow onion, roughly chopped (about 2 cups)**
- **1 large (5-oz.) carrot, cut into 1-inch pieces (about 1 cup)**
- **1 large (2½-oz.) celery stalk, cut into 1-inch pieces (about ⅔ cup)**
- **2 cup dry red wine**
- **2 cups thinly sliced daikon (from 1 small daikon)**
- **Pickled Onion and Mustard Seeds (recipe follows)**

1. Combine 2 cups water, 2 teaspoons kosher salt, and pink salt in a small saucepan; bring to a boil over medium-high. Stir until salt is fully dissolved. Remove from heat. Let cool about 30 minutes.

2. Place pork cheeks in a large ziplock plastic bag; carefully pour salt water into bag. Seal bag, and place on a plate or rimmed baking sheet. Place in refrigerator, and let brine 2 days.

3. Remove pork cheeks from brine; pat with paper towels until fully dry; discard brine. Heat oil in a large skillet over medium-high. Working in 2 batches, add 5 cheeks to skillet; cook until dark brown on both sides, 8 to 10 minutes per batch. Transfer cheeks to a pressure multicooker (such as Instant Pot). Do not wipe skillet clean.

4. Add onion, carrot, and celery to skillet; cook, stirring occasionally, until vegetables start to soften, about 5 minutes. Add wine; cook, stirring often and scraping up browned bits on bottom of skillet, until liquid is completely reduced and skillet is almost dry, about 5 minutes. Arrange vegetables over pork cheeks in multicooker. Pour remaining 5 cups water over cheeks and vegetables to submerge. Cover cooker with lid, and lock in place. Turn steam release handle to SEALING position. Select MANUAL/PRESSURE COOK setting. (Times, instructions, and settings may vary according to cooker brand or model.) Select HIGH pressure for 1 hour. (It will take 15 to 18 minutes for cooker to come up to pressure before cooking begins.) When cooking has finished, let the pressure release naturally. (Float valve will drop.) (This will take 35 to 45 minutes.) Remove lid from cooker, and let pork cheeks cool in liquid 30 minutes. Remove cooker bowl from machine; cover bowl with plastic wrap. Refrigerate until mixture has completely chilled, at least 4 hours or up to 12 hours.

5. Preheat oven to 180°F. Remove plastic wrap from cooker bowl. Scrape off any solidified fat from top of pork cheek mixture, and discard. Transfer cheeks to a large saucepan, reserving liquid in cooker bowl. Pour liquid in cooker bowl through a fine wire-mesh strainer over cheeks in saucepan; discard strained solids. Place saucepan on stovetop, and bring to a simmer over medium. Simmer, stirring occasionally, until cheeks are heated through, about 10 minutes. Remove cheeks from liquid, and place in a baking dish. Ladle about ⅔ cup hot liquid over cheeks in baking dish. Cover with aluminum foil, and place in preheated oven to keep warm.

6. Increase heat under saucepan to medium-high; cook liquid, undisturbed, until thickened, saucy, and reduced to ⅔ cup to ¾ cup, about 20 minutes. Remove from heat. Pour through a fine wire-mesh strainer set over a medium-size heatproof bowl; set aside. Discard solids.

7. Place daikon in a medium bowl. Using a slotted spoon, remove pickled onion and mustard seeds from pickling liquid, and spoon over daikon. Pour ½ cup pickling liquid over daikon mixture; discard remaining pickling liquid. Stir in remaining ½ teaspoon kosher salt.

8. Spoon strained sauce evenly into 5 shallow bowls. Remove pork cheeks from oven; place 2 cheeks on sauce in each bowl. Using a slotted spoon, garnish each bowl with desired amount of pickled onion-daikon mixture. Serve immediately.
—ANDRÉ MACK

WINE 2020 Turley Bechthold Vineyard Cinsault

NOTE Source pork cheeks from your local butcher.

Pickled Onion and Mustard Seeds

ACTIVE 10 MIN; TOTAL 25 MIN, PLUS 4 HR REFRIGERATION; MAKES 2 CUPS

After hot pickling, the onions retain a crisp-tender bite while the mustard seeds burst with juicy brine. The condiment brings a vinegary bite to rich and fatty pork.

- **2⅔ cups water, divided**
- **1 medium-size (6-oz.) yellow onion, finely chopped (about 1 cup)**
- **1 tsp. kosher salt**
- **1 cup plus 1 Tbsp. granulated sugar**
- **1 cup Chardonnay vinegar**
- **1 Tbsp. plus 2 tsp. yellow mustard seeds**

1. Fill a small saucepan with 2 cups water; bring to a boil over medium-high. Add onion and salt; cook, stirring occasionally, until onion has softened, 2 to 3 minutes. Drain through a fine wire-mesh strainer. Transfer drained onion to a medium-size heatproof bowl; set aside. Do not wipe saucepan clean.

2. Add sugar, vinegar, and remaining ⅔ cup water to saucepan; bring to a boil over medium-high. Add mustard seeds; cook, stirring occasionally, until sugar has dissolved, about 2 minutes. Pour mixture over onion in bowl; let cool slightly, about 15 minutes. Cover bowl with plastic wrap. Refrigerate until onion expands slightly in liquid, at least 4 hours or up to 4 days.
—ANDRÉ MACK

BEEF, LAMB & GOAT

BEEF-AND-CHEESE RED CHILE
ENCHILADAS (P. 161)
OPPOSITE: BURNT ENDS (P. 156)

Entrecôte with Green Olive Tapenade Butter

ACTIVE 20 MIN; TOTAL 35 MIN; SERVES 2 TO 4

This recipe offers a simple technique for both a perfectly cooked rib eye and a flavorful compound butter packed with pungent anchovies, piquant Dijon mustard and salty capers that packs a briny punch when melted onto the juicy grilled steaks. Look for small and nutty picholine olives, sweet and buttery Castelvetrano olives, or large and tart Cerignola olives in the olive bar or at specialty grocery stores. For a classic bistro-inspired meal, serve the steak alongside a pile of french fries and a mesclun salad. You can keep the butter in the freezer for up to three months to quickly upgrade grilled steaks, pork chops, or fish fillets.

- ¾ cup pitted green olives (such as picholine, Castelvetrano, or Cerignola)
- ½ cup loosely packed fresh flat-leaf parsley leaves
- 2 Tbsp. capers, drained
- 1 tsp. Dijon mustard
- 2 drained anchovy fillets (from 1 [2-oz.] can)
- 1 large garlic clove, smashed
- 4 oz. unsalted butter, at room temperature
- 2¼ tsp. kosher salt, divided
- 1¼ tsp. black pepper, divided
- 2 (12-oz.) rib eye steaks (1 inch thick)
- 2 tsp. olive oil

1. Pulse olives, parsley, capers, mustard, anchovies, and garlic in a food processor until a coarse paste forms, 7 to 9 pulses. Transfer mixture to a medium bowl. Add butter, ¼ teaspoon salt, and ¼ teaspoon pepper; stir together using a fork or spatula until well combined. Set aside at room temperature until ready to use.

2. Preheat grill to medium-high (400°F to 450°F). Brush steaks evenly with oil; sprinkle evenly with remaining 2 teaspoons salt and remaining 1 teaspoon pepper. Place steaks on oiled grates; grill, uncovered, until steaks are well seared and lightly charred and a thermometer inserted in thickest portion of meat registers 130°F (for medium-rare), 4 to 5 minutes per side. Transfer steaks to a carving board, and generously spread each with 2 tablespoons tapenade butter. Reserve remaining ¾ cup tapenade butter for another use. Let steaks rest 5 minutes. (Butter will melt and coat steaks.) Cut steaks against the grain into ½-inch-thick slices, and serve.
—JUSTIN CHAPPLE

WINE Earthy, spicy Rhône red: 2019 Château de Rouanne Vinsobres

Beef Shish Kebab

ACTIVE 1 HR 5 MIN; TOTAL 1 HR 35 MIN, PLUS 24 HR MARINATING; MAKES ABOUT 8 KEBABS

The inexpensive, tough beef cut called flap meat is full of flavor, with a coarse grain that absorbs marinades well. Marinate it 24 hours and pound it with a meat mallet for the juiciest, most tender kebabs.

- 4 lb. beef flap meat, silver skin removed
- 3 cups vegetable oil
- 2 small yellow onions (about 1 lb.), halved lengthwise and thinly sliced (about 3½ cups)
- 1 cup chopped (1-inch pieces) fresh flat-leaf parsley stems (from 2 bunches fresh parsley)
- 2 Tbsp. kosher salt
- 2 Tbsp. cayenne pepper
- 1 Tbsp. black pepper
- 10 large metal skewers (1 inch wide x 23½ inches long)
  Ghee, at room temperature, for brushing

1. If flap meat is thicker than ½ inch, butterfly horizontally. Cut meat into 2-inch square pieces. Place meat, oil, onions, parsley stems, salt, cayenne, and black pepper in a large bowl. Toss together using your hands to evenly combine. Cover and marinate in refrigerator at least 24 hours or up to 3 days.

2. Open bottom vent of a kettle grill completely. Light charcoal chimney starter heaping full of briquettes. When briquettes are covered with gray ash, pour onto bottom grate; arrange evenly in a 10-inch-wide strip down middle of bottom grate. Do not place top grate on grill. Arrange 2 skewers in an "L" shape, resting on rim of grill, with 1 skewer parallel to coal strip and 1 skewer perpendicular to coals. These will be used as a rack to suspend kebabs.

3. While charcoal chimney is heating, skewer kebabs. Starting about 3½ inches down from pointed skewer tip, thread about 5 meat pieces (6 to 7 ounces) against the grain onto each of remaining 8 skewers, inserting skewer crosswise into cut side of meat, scraping off onion and parsley pieces and spacing meat pieces about ¼ inch apart. Discard marinade. Place 1 meat kebab on a cutting board, and cover with plastic wrap. Using smooth side of a meat mallet, pound meat to tenderize and flatten slightly to about ⅓-inch thickness. Total meat length along skewer should be no longer than 10 inches; if needed, push meat pieces together on skewer. Transfer kebab to a rimmed baking sheet. Repeat procedure with remaining kebabs.

4. Working in batches if needed, rest pointed ends of skewers on prepared "L"-shaped rack with handles overhanging edge of grill and meat perpendicular to charcoal strip. Grill, uncovered, turning often, until charred in spots and cooked to desired degree of doneness, 4 to 6 minutes for medium-rare (125°F), repositioning kebabs over coals as needed to avoid large flare-ups. If kebabs are browning before reaching desired degree of doneness, rotate kebabs 90 degrees so that they're parallel to charcoal strip.

5. Using tongs, slide meat off skewers and onto a rice- or lavash-lined platter, if desired. Brush hot kebabs generously with ghee. Serve immediately. —OVAKIM AND ALVARD MARTIROSYAN

WINE Darkly fruity, earthy red: 2019 Villa Creek Avenger

CHARRED JALAPEÑOS
AND TOMATOES
(RECIPE P. 128)

MINI KABOB POTATOES
(RECIPE P. 215)

SHAVED ONIONS WITH SUMAC
AND PARSLEY (RECIPE P. 312)

BEEF SHISH KEBAB

CHICKEN LULE KEBAB
(RECIPE P. 127)

BURNT ENDS

The crispy, caramelized "burnt" pieces of a smoked brisket are often the best part because the flavor is concentrated and the texture is pleasingly chewy. This recipe creates an entire baking tray of crispy pieces, so there are plenty to go around. Chef Matt Horn likes to serve these with slices of white bread; he shared his step-by-step process for making Burnt Ends with us, from seasoning the brisket to caramelizing the sauce on the cubed meat. If you spend a lot of time barbecuing, you will try out literally hundreds of rubs, not to mention cooking sauces, table sauces, mops, binders, and pastes. Eventually, you will settle on an all-purpose rub that adds loads of flavor to just about anything you put in the smoker. Horn Rub is chef Matt Horn's go-to rub; he keeps it close at hand at all time, and uses it to generously season these savory burnt ends. Instead of vinegar, Horn's thick, sticky Bourbon Sauce gets its kick from its namesake: bourbon. For a classic sauce with Kentucky roots, use dark molasses in place of the honey. This recipe works well with any type of barbecue, and Horn loves it in baked beans, too.

ACTIVE 15 MIN; TOTAL 30 MIN, PLUS 8 HR SMOKING; SERVES 6 TO 8

- 1 (4-lb.) beef brisket point, fat cap trimmed to ¼ inch thick
- 1 Tbsp. plus 1 tsp. kosher salt
- ¼ cup Horn Rub (recipe p. 306)
- 1½ cups Bourbon Sauce (recipe p. 312)
- 2 Tbsp. honey

1. Sprinkle brisket evenly with salt. Sprinkle evenly with Horn rub, gently massaging into brisket to adhere. Let stand at room temperature until ready to use.

2. Prepare a charcoal fire in smoker according to manufacturer's instructions. Place oak chunks on coals. Maintain internal temperature at 250°F for 15 to 20 minutes. Smoke brisket, covered with smoker lid, until a thermometer inserted in center of brisket registers 150°F, about 4 hours. Remove brisket, and wrap tightly in aluminum foil. Return brisket to smoker, and smoke, covered, until a thermometer inserted in brisket registers 185°F, about 2 hours. Remove brisket from smoker; unwrap and cut into ¾-inch cubes, discarding any large seams of fat. Place brisket cubes in a deep 13- x 9-inch aluminum foil baking pan; add bourbon sauce, and stir to coat. Drizzle brisket evenly with honey.

3. Increase smoker temperature to 275°F, adding more hot coals and wood chunks as needed. Place baking pan with brisket in smoker, and smoke, covered, until liquid has reduced and caramelized, 2 to 3 hours. Remove brisket from smoker, and serve immediately, or cover and keep warm up to 30 minutes. —MATT HORN

MAKE AHEAD Burnt ends may be kept warm up to 30 minutes before serving.

BEER Rich, hoppy ale: Dogfish Head 60 Minute IPA

STEP-BY-STEP

SEASON BRISKET Sprinkle brisket point evenly with salt and Horn rub, gently massaging seasonings into the meat. Let brisket stand, and preheat smoker.

SMOKE BRISKET Smoke brisket over charcoal and oak chunks at 250°F until a meat thermometer inserted in center registers 150°F.

WRAP AND COOK TO TARGET TEMP Remove brisket from smoker, and wrap tightly in aluminum foil. Continue smoking until a meat thermometer registers 185°F, about 2 hours.

CHOP AND TRIM Remove brisket from smoker, and unwrap. Cut meat into ¾-inch cubes, discarding any large pieces of fat.

TOSS WITH SAUCE Stir together brisket cubes and bourbon sauce until well coated. Transfer to a 13-×9-inch aluminum baking pan, and drizzle evenly with honey.

SMOKE AND CARAMELIZE Add hot coals to smoker to increase temperature to 275°F. Smoke cubed brisket in baking pan until caramelized and glazed, 2 to 3 hours.

Grilled Rib Eye and Ponzu Aguachile

ACTIVE 1 HR 15 MIN; TOTAL 2 HR 20 MIN; SERVES 4

Claudette Zepeda uses a reverse-sear technique for this steak served with a salty, umami ponzu sauce. She tops the steak with a fresh tomatillo, onion, cucumber, and cilantro salad that balances the richness of the meat. If you can't find a pre-cut 28-ounce ribeye, ask your butcher to cut one. Be sure to stock up on charcoal and have three (3-inch) hardwood oak wood chunks on hand to make the most of this recipe. The flavors of this dish are inspired by the pantry of northern Mexico, where Chinese, Japanese, and Korean ingredients are common because people from those countries were in Tijuana. "Mexico is a complex melting pot of people, where the story stops being about why we're so different and starts being about why we're so similar," Zepeda notes. "Chinese laborers built the city of Tijuana; Japanese immigrants established the entire seafood industry in Ensenada. These are the stories that inspire me."

- 1 cup lower-sodium soy sauce
- 1 cup fresh orange juice (from 3 medium oranges)
- 1 cup packed fresh cilantro leaves, divided
- 7 Tbsp. water, divided
- ¼ cup rice vinegar
- 1 (1-oz.) lemongrass stalk, trimmed and roughly chopped (about 2 Tbsp.)
- 1 Tbsp. mirin
- 1 (½-inch) piece ginger, peeled and chopped (about ½ Tbsp.)
- 2 fresh red Thai chiles, seeded (if desired) and chopped (about 1 tsp.)
- 1 Tbsp. cornstarch
- 5 small (about 1-oz.) tomatillos, husked and thinly sliced crosswise
- 1 tsp. kosher salt, divided
- 3 (3-inch) oak wood chunks, for grilling
- 1 (28-oz.) bone-in rib eye steak
- ½ tsp. black pepper
- ⅓ cup thinly sliced red onion rings (from 1 small [5-oz.] onion)
- 2 medium (2½-oz.) Persian cucumbers, thinly sliced (about ⅛ inch thick) crosswise using a mandoline
- ¼ tsp. flaky sea salt (such as Maldon)

1. Combine soy sauce, orange juice, ½ cup cilantro leaves, 5 tablespoons water, rice vinegar, lemongrass, mirin, ginger, and Thai chiles in a blender; process until smooth, about 1 minute. Transfer mixture to a medium saucepan; bring to a simmer over medium. Simmer, undisturbed, until flavors meld, about 10 minutes. Remove from heat; let steep, uncovered, 10 minutes. Pour through a fine wire-mesh strainer into a medium bowl; discard solids. Rinse pan, and wipe dry. Return soy sauce mixture to pan, and return to a simmer over medium. Whisk together cornstarch and remaining 2 tablespoons water in a small bowl to form a slurry. Add cornstarch slurry to simmering soy sauce mixture; simmer, stirring constantly, until mixture is just thick enough to coat the back of a spoon, about 5 minutes. Remove from heat; let ponzu cool completely, about 20 minutes. Refrigerate, covered, until ready to use or up to 3 days.

2. Place tomatillos on a large plate or baking sheet, and sprinkle evenly with ½ teaspoon kosher salt. Set tomatillos aside until ready to use.

3. Light a charcoal chimney starter filled with briquettes. When briquettes are covered with gray ash, pour them onto bottom grate of grill, and push to one side of grill. Place oak wood chunks over hot coals. Adjust vents as needed to maintain an internal temperature of 250°F to 300°F. Coat top grate with oil; place on grill. Sprinkle steak evenly with pepper and remaining ½ teaspoon kosher salt. Place steak on oiled grate over side of grill without coals. Grill, covered, until a thermometer inserted in thickest portion of meat registers 85°F, about 20 minutes. Flip steak; grill, covered, until thermometer registers 100°F, about 10 minutes. Move steak to side of grill with coals. Grill, uncovered, flipping often, until thermometer inserted in thickest portion of meat registers between 115°F and 120°F for rare, about 5 minutes, or to desired degree of doneness. Transfer to a cutting board. Tent with aluminum foil, and let rest 12 to 15 minutes to allow juices to redistribute in steak. Using a sharp knife, cut meat away from bone in 1 piece. Cut meat against the grain into ½-inch-thick slices.

4. Combine onion, cucumbers, tomatillos, and remaining ½ cup cilantro leaves in a medium bowl; toss to combine. Spoon ponzu onto a rimmed 12-inch plate; top with steak. Arrange tomatillo mixture on and around steak. Sprinkle with flaky sea salt, and serve. —CLAUDETTE ZEPEDA

MAKE AHEAD Ponzu can be made up to 3 days in advance and stored in an airtight container in refrigerator.

WINE Tangy, light-bodied red: 2020 Louis Jadot Beaujolais-Villages

NOTE Select firm tomatillos with tightly wrapped husks.

**STIR-FRIED FLANK STEAK
WITH YELLOW ONIONS**

Stir-Fried Flank Steak with Yellow Onions

⏱ ACTIVE 30 MIN; TOTAL 40 MIN; SERVES 2 TO 4

A simple marinade of Shaoxing wine, soy sauce, and a little flour helps tenderize the generous slices of flank steak and their browning when cooked, while sweet yellow onions cook just enough to soften and gently brown without losing their bite.

- 1 (1-inch-thick) flank steak (12 oz.), sliced diagonally into ¼-inch strips
- 3 Tbsp. soy sauce, divided
- 1 Tbsp. Shaoxing wine
- 1 tsp. all-purpose flour or cornstarch
- 2 Tbsp. canola oil, divided
- 2 medium-size (9-oz.) yellow onions, cut into ½-inch slices (about 3½ cups)
- Cooked white rice, for serving

1. Toss together steak, 2 tablespoons soy sauce, Shaoxing wine, and flour in a medium bowl until coated. Let marinate at room temperature 20 minutes.

2. Meanwhile, heat 1 tablespoon oil in a large wok over medium-high until hot but not smoking. Add onions; cook, stirring often, until translucent and just starting to brown, about 8 minutes. Add remaining 1 tablespoon soy sauce; cook, stirring constantly, until onions absorb soy sauce, about 20 seconds. Transfer to a medium bowl. Carefully wipe wok clean.

3. Heat remaining 1 tablespoon oil in wok over high until smoking. Add beef, leaving marinade in bowl, and spread in an even layer; discard marinade in bowl. Cook steak, undisturbed, until steak is lightly browned around edges but still pink on top, 2 to 3 minutes. Return onions to wok, and toss to combine. Serve immediately with rice.

—LAN SAMANTHA CHANG

WINE Lush, dark-fruited Merlot: 2018 L'Ecole No. 41 Columbia Valley

Beef-and-Cheese Red Chile Enchiladas

PHOTO P. 153

ACTIVE 25 MIN; TOTAL 55 MIN; SERVES 6

Dipping warm corn tortillas in freshly made red chile sauce infuses each rolled enchilada with the smoky-sweet flavor of New Mexico chiles. The hearty cumin scented beef-and-cheese filling stands up well to the bold sauce; for a quicker vegetarian version, fill the tortillas with 1 ounce of melty cheese, like queso Oaxaca or Monterey Jack. Sommelier Liz Martinez of the Daxton Hotel in Detroit, who provided the inspiration for this dish, suggests pairing red chile enchiladas with a Syrah, such as Cattleya The Initiation Syrah. "A super fruity red wine with darker flavors works as a cooling agent for the red spice," she says. "With its brooding fruit and floral aromatics, Syrah is a great match."

SAUCE

- 2 cups boiling water
- 1 oz. New Mexico chiles (about 5 chiles), stemmed and seeded
- 2 medium plum tomatoes, halved
- 1 small yellow onion, quartered
- 3 unpeeled garlic cloves
- 1 Tbsp. apple cider vinegar
- 2 tsp. kosher salt
- ½ tsp. ground cumin
- ¼ tsp. garlic powder

ENCHILADAS

- 1 Tbsp. canola oil, plus more for greasing baking dish
- 1 lb. 90% lean ground beef
- 1 tsp. kosher salt
- 1 tsp. ground cumin
- 12 (5½-inch) corn tortillas, warmed
- 12 oz. queso fresco, crumbled (about 3 cups)

ADDITIONAL INGREDIENTS

- Fresh cilantro leaves, sliced scallions, and thinly sliced red onion rings, for garnish
- Lime wedges and sour cream, for serving

1. Make the sauce: Preheat oven to broil with rack about 6 inches from heat. Line a rimmed baking sheet with aluminum foil. Combine 2 cups boiling water and chiles in a small heatproof bowl; let soak until chiles are softened, about 20 minutes. Drain, reserving 1 cup soaking liquid.

2. While chiles soak, place tomatoes and onion, cut sides down, and garlic cloves on prepared baking sheet. Broil in preheated oven until vegetables begin to char and soften, 8 to 10 minutes. Remove from oven. Remove and discard garlic skin.

3. Transfer roasted tomatoes, onion, and garlic to a blender. Add drained chiles, reserved 1 cup soaking liquid, vinegar, salt, cumin, and garlic powder. Secure lid on blender, and remove center piece to allow steam to escape. Place a clean towel over opening. Process until smooth, about 1 minute. Transfer sauce to a shallow bowl; set aside until ready to use.

4. Make the enchiladas: Preheat oven to 350°F. Heat oil in a large skillet over medium-high. Add beef; cook, stirring often, until browned and just cooked through, about 6 minutes. Stir in salt and cumin; remove from heat.

5. Lightly grease a 13- x 9-inch baking dish with oil; set aside. Dip 1 tortilla into sauce, letting excess drain back into bowl; lay tortilla flat on a clean work surface. Spoon about ¼ cup beef mixture down middle of tortilla, and top with 2 rounded tablespoons queso fresco. Roll up tortilla, and place, seam side down, in prepared baking dish. Repeat process with remaining 11 tortillas. Spoon ½ cup sauce over rolled tortillas. Sprinkle evenly with ½ cup queso fresco.

6. Bake enchiladas in preheated oven until browned and bubbly, 18 to 20 minutes. Transfer enchiladas to a large platter, if desired. Garnish with cilantro, scallions, and red onion. Serve with lime wedges, sour cream, remaining 1 cup sauce, and remaining ½ cup queso fresco.

—ANNA THEOKTISTO

WINE 2019 Cattleya The Initiation Syrah

Steak, Potatoes, and Tomatoes with Quick Chimichurri

ACTIVE 25 MIN; TOTAL 35 MIN; SERVES 4

Juicy late-summer tomatoes, verdant fresh herbs, and golden potatoes pair with simply seared and sliced steaks. This dish is inspired by Matthew Conway, sommelier and owner of The Tippling House in Charleston, who encourages you to level-up this easy steak dinner with a chilled bottle of red wine. "The most overlooked aspect of food and wine pairing is temperature," he notes. "Steak and Syrah isn't revolutionary, but try that red wine cold with hot, fatty steak. The combination of flavor and temperature variation will leave you wanting another bite."

- 1 cup loosely packed fresh flat-leaf parsley leaves, roughly chopped (about ½ cup)
- ½ cup plus 3 Tbsp. extra-virgin olive oil, divided
- 3 Tbsp. fresh oregano leaves, roughly chopped (about 2 Tbsp.)
- 2 Tbsp. red wine vinegar
- 4 tsp. kosher salt, divided
- 2 large garlic cloves, grated with a Microplane grater (about ½ tsp.)
- ¼ tsp. crushed red pepper
- 1½ lb. small golden potatoes, halved lengthwise (about 4 cups)
- ¾ tsp. black pepper, divided
- 2 (1-lb.) boneless strip steaks or 2 lb. hanger steaks
- 3 Tbsp. canola oil
- 2 large (11-oz.) heirloom tomatoes or beefsteak tomatoes, cut into ½-inch-thick slices
  Flaky sea salt, for garnish

1. Preheat oven to 450°F. Stir together parsley, ½ cup olive oil, oregano, vinegar, 1 teaspoon salt, garlic, and crushed red pepper in a small bowl until combined; set chimichurri aside.

2. Toss together potatoes, ¼ teaspoon black pepper, 1 teaspoon salt, and remaining 3 tablespoons olive oil on a large rimmed baking sheet until evenly coated. Roast potatoes in preheated oven until crispy and fork tender, about 20 minutes, stirring once during final 5 minutes of roasting time. Remove from oven.

3. While potatoes roast, sprinkle steaks evenly with remaining 2 teaspoons salt and remaining ½ teaspoon black pepper. Heat canola oil in a large cast-iron skillet over high until oil smokes. Add steaks to skillet; reduce heat to medium-high, and cook, undisturbed, until steaks are evenly browned on bottoms, about 5 minutes. Flip steaks, and cook, undisturbed, until browned on other side, about 5 minutes. Place steaks upright on their sides in skillet; cook, rotating occasionally on their sides and holding upright, until a thermometer inserted in thickest portion of steak registers 130°F for medium-rare, or to desired degree of doneness, 5 to 10 minutes for strip steaks or about 2 minutes for hanger steaks. Transfer to a cutting board, and let rest 5 minutes.

4. Cut steaks into ½-inch-thick slices, and divide evenly among 4 plates. Arrange potatoes and tomatoes evenly on plates. Drizzle evenly with reserved chimichurri, and garnish with flaky sea salt. —ANNA THEOKTISTO

MAKE AHEAD Chimichurri can be made up to 2 days in advance and stored in an airtight container in refrigerator.

WINE 2019 Pax North Coast Syrah

Mini Potato, Steak, and Chorizo Pies

ACTIVE 40 MIN; TOTAL 1 HR 5 MIN; SERVES 6

The remarkable butcher and grass-fed-beef evangelist Pat Whelan is the author of The Irish Beef Book. Coauthored with the restaurant critic Katy McGuinness, the cookbook contains a simple-yet-divine dinner idea: these smallish "pies" filled with a smart combination of fresh chorizo and lean grass-fed ground beef. Seasoned with onion and Worcestershire—we've amped up the filling with extra spices in Senior Food Editor Mary Frances Heck's adaptation of the dish here—they come together in a snap and can easily be made ahead. The topping of thinly sliced starchy russet potatoes form a crispy, potato chip–like topping atop each meaty pie.

- ½ cup unsalted butter (4 oz.), divided, plus more for greasing dishes
- 1 medium-size yellow onion (about 8 oz.), finely chopped (about 1¾ cups)
- 1 medium carrot (about 3 oz.), finely chopped (about ½ cup)
- 2 tsp. kosher salt, divided
- ½ tsp. black pepper, divided
- 1 lb. grass-fed 93% extra-lean ground beef
- 1 (5½-oz.) link fresh Mexican chorizo, casing removed
- 6 Tbsp. all-purpose flour
- 2 cups beef stock
- 2 Tbsp. Worcestershire sauce
- ¾ tsp. smoked paprika
- ½ tsp. dried oregano
- 2 Tbsp. Dijon mustard
- 1 lb. 4 oz. medium-size russet potatoes, peeled and thinly sliced
  Finely chopped fresh flat-leaf parsley, for garnish

1. Preheat oven to 450°F. Grease 6 (12- to 16-ounce) individual pie dishes with butter; set aside. Melt ¼ cup butter in a large skillet over medium-high. Add onion, carrot, 1 teaspoon salt, and ¼ teaspoon pepper, and cook, stirring often, until onion is soft but not browned, about 5 minutes. Add ground beef and chorizo; cook, stirring often, until meat is browned and cooked through, about 5 minutes. Sprinkle flour over mixture, and cook, stirring constantly, 2 minutes. Stir in stock, Worcestershire sauce, paprika, and oregano; bring to a boil over medium-high. Reduce heat to low; simmer, stirring often, until flavors meld and vegetables soften, about 10 minutes. Remove from heat; stir in mustard and ½ teaspoon salt.

2. Spoon filling evenly into prepared dishes (a heaping ⅔ cup filling each). Top evenly with sliced potatoes. Sprinkle potatoes with remaining ½ teaspoon salt and remaining ¼ teaspoon pepper. Microwave remaining ¼ cup butter in a small microwavable bowl on high until melted, about 1 minute. Brush melted butter evenly over potatoes. Transfer dishes to preheated oven. Bake until pies are golden brown, 25 to 35 minutes. Remove from oven; garnish with parsley. —MARY-FRANCES HECK

MAKE AHEAD Filling can be prepared through step 1 up to 2 days ahead. Let cool, and then cover and refrigerate.

WINE Robust, peppery Zinfandel: 2019 Foxglove Paso Robles

MINI POTATO, STEAK, AND CHORIZO PIES

RIB EYE WITH CHARRED SPRING ONIONS AND SALSA VERDE

Stracotto di Fassona Piemontese (Piedmont Braised Beef)

ACTIVE 1 HR 20 MIN; TOTAL 3 HR 20 MIN, PLUS 12 HR CHILLING; SERVES 8

Chef Otto Lucà considers this rustic top blade roast, slow-braised in red wine until it's falling-apart tender, the most important main course of classical Piedmontese cuisine. Marinating the roast overnight jump-starts tenderizing and helps season the meat all the way through. Mashed potatoes make an excellent side for this dish, providing a delicious way to mop up the sauce.

- 2 (750-ml.) bottles Piedmontese red wine (such as Barolo)
- 2 lb. yellow onions (about 4 medium onions), finely chopped (about 6 cups)
- 12 oz. carrots (about 4 medium carrots), peeled and finely chopped (about 2 cups)
- 1 medium (about 1-oz.) celery stalk, finely chopped (about ¼ cup)
- 3 medium garlic cloves, finely chopped (about 1 Tbsp.)
- 1 (5-inch) rosemary sprig
- 2 fresh bay leaves
- ¼ tsp. ground cloves
- 1 (4- to 4½-lb.) boneless top blade roast
- 4 tsp. kosher salt, divided, plus more to taste
- 2 tsp. black pepper, divided, plus more to taste
- 5 Tbsp. extra-virgin olive oil

1. Stir together wine, onions, carrots, celery, garlic, rosemary, bay leaves, and cloves in a large enameled Dutch oven. Rub meat all over with 2 teaspoons salt and 1 teaspoon pepper, and place in wine mixture. Cover with lid, and refrigerate overnight (about 12 hours).

2. Remove meat from wine mixture. Scrape off any vegetables stuck to meat, and transfer meat to a large plate. Pat dry with paper towels. Pour wine mixture through a colander set over a large bowl; reserve vegetables and liquid separately at room temperature. Wash and dry Dutch oven.

3. Add oil to cleaned Dutch oven; heat over medium-high. Sprinkle meat all over with remaining 2 teaspoons salt and remaining 1 teaspoon pepper. Add meat to Dutch oven; cook, turning occasionally, until browned on all sides, 16 to 20 minutes. Transfer meat to a large plate. Add reserved vegetable mixture to drippings in Dutch oven; cook over medium-high, stirring often, until softened, 12 to 16 minutes. Return meat to Dutch oven, and pour in reserved strained wine. Bring to a boil over medium-high. Reduce heat to medium-low; cover and simmer, turning meat occasionally, until meat is fork-tender, 2 hours to 2 hours and 30 minutes.

4. Transfer meat to a cutting board, and tent with foil; let rest while reducing sauce. Remove and discard rosemary sprig and bay leaves from mixture in Dutch oven. Using a fine wire-mesh strainer, scoop and remove vegetable mixture from Dutch oven, and transfer to a medium bowl; set aside. Increase heat under Dutch oven to medium; cook, stirring occasionally, until wine mixture reaches the consistency of jus and has reduced to about 2½ cups, 30 to 35 minutes. Season to taste with salt and pepper, if desired.

5. Slice meat crosswise into ⅓-inch-thick pieces. Arrange on a platter. Ladle about ½ cup sauce over meat on platter. Serve alongside mashed potatoes and reserved vegetables. Serve remaining sauce on the side. —OTTO LUCÀ, LANGOTTO RISTORANTE, PIEDMONT, ITALY

MAKE AHEAD Recipe can be prepared through step 3 up to 1 day in advance. Let cool completely, and chill overnight. Reheat over medium, and proceed with step 4.

WINE Structured, cherry-scented Barolo: 2017 Elvio Cogno Cascina Nuova

Rib Eye with Charred Spring Onions and Salsa Verde

ACTIVE 30 MIN; TOTAL 1 HR 30 MIN; SERVES 2

"This is a great weeknight steak recipe that uses easy-to-find herbs and a few kitchen essentials to really maximize flavor," says chef Hillary Sterling of Ci Siamo in New York City, who shared her recipe with Food & Wine. *"Vincotto — literally 'cooked wine' in Italian — is an ingredient I always have on hand for quick marinades and sauces. If you can't find it at your local specialty store, a combination of equal parts balsamic vinegar and honey works well as a substitute. Sweet and tangy, it will impart a ton of flavor on the rib eye in a short time." Sterling's marinade tenderizes the meat and also adds intense flavor to the skillet-seared steak. The sugar in the marinade mixture, which comes from the tangy-sweet vincotto, caramelizes while the steak cooks, adding delicious char. A drizzle of fresh lemon juice just before serving brightens up the smoky, umami-rich steak alongside an herb-packed salsa verde and juicy spring onions.*

- 1 (1-lb.) boneless rib eye steak (about 1 inch thick)
- 2 Tbsp. plus ⅜ tsp. kosher salt, divided
- 1 (4-inch) rosemary sprig
- 2 Tbsp. vincotto or 1 Tbsp. balsamic vinegar plus 1 Tbsp. honey
- ⅔ cup plus 2 Tbsp. olive oil, divided
- 1 cup packed fresh flat-leaf parsley leaves
- ½ cup packed fresh tarragon leaves
- 6 Tbsp. chopped fresh chives
- 1½ Tbsp. Dijon mustard
- 1 Tbsp. drained capers
- 2 to 3 oil-packed anchovy fillets (to taste) (from 1 [2-oz.] can), drained
- 1 (9-oz.) bunch spring onions (about 4 onions), trimmed and halved lengthwise
- 1 Tbsp. fresh lemon juice (from 1 lemon)

continued on page 166

continued from page 165

1. Sprinkle steak evenly with 2 tablespoons salt. Place steak and rosemary sprig in a large ziplock plastic bag; pour vincotto and 1 tablespoon oil into bag. Seal bag, and place on a plate. Refrigerate at least 1 hour or up to 6 hours.

2. Combine parsley, tarragon, chives, mustard, capers, and anchovies in a food processor. Pulse until roughly chopped, about 10 pulses. With processor running, pour ⅔ cup oil through food chute, and process until mixture is smooth, about 20 seconds. Transfer mixture to a bowl; stir in ⅛ teaspoon salt. Set salsa verde aside until ready to use.

3. Heat remaining 1 tablespoon oil in a 12-inch cast-iron skillet over medium-high until shimmering. Remove steak from marinade, letting excess marinade drip off. Discard marinade in bag. Cook steak in skillet until lightly charred in spots and a thermometer inserted in thickest portion of meat registers 120°F for medium-rare, about 8 minutes (or to desired degree of doneness), flipping halfway through cook time. Transfer steak to a cutting board; let rest 5 minutes. Do not wipe skillet clean.

4. Arrange spring onion pieces in a single layer in skillet; sprinkle evenly with remaining ¼ teaspoon salt. Cook over medium-high, turning occasionally, until charred in spots and bulbs are tender, 3 to 4 minutes. Remove from heat.

5. Slice steak against the grain into ¼-inch-thick pieces, and transfer to a platter. Drizzle fresh lemon juice over steaks; serve alongside spring onions and salsa verde.
—HILLARY STERLING, CI SIAMO, NEW YORK CITY

MAKE AHEAD Steak can be marinated up to 6 hours in advance.

WINE Robust, tannic Napa Cabernet: 2018 Buehler Estate Papa's Knoll

NOTE Vincotto is a thick, sweet syrup made from reduced unfermented grape must. Find it at Italian grocery stores or online at caputos.com.

Grilled Rib Eye Steaks with Okra Suya and Cucumber-Yogurt Sauce

ACTIVE 1 HR 10 MIN; TOTAL 2 HR 10 MIN; SERVES 4 TO 6

Inspired by his West African heritage, Carlton McCoy seasons thick and juicy rib eye steaks and skewered vegetables with suya spice, a spicy, nutty, and smoky peanut-based spice blend. Reverse-searing the steaks ensures a charred crust while the centers stay perfectly tender and medium-rare.

CUCUMBER-YOGURT SAUCE

   1 cup plain whole-milk strained Greek-style yogurt

  ¼ cup fresh lemon juice (from 2 lemons)

  ½ tsp. kosher salt

   1 medium (12-oz.) English cucumber, peeled, seeded, and thinly sliced crosswise (about 2 cups)

STEAK AND VEGETABLES

   2 (2-lb.) bone-in rib eye steaks (2 inches thick)

  12 oz. fresh okra, trimmed

  14 oz. cipollini onions (about 18 small onions)

  ½ cup unsalted butter (4 oz.), softened

   3 Tbsp. suya spice mix (such as Kovafood or Asiko), divided, plus more to taste

4¾ tsp. kosher salt, divided

   1 Tbsp. neutral cooking oil (such as canola oil or grapeseed oil), plus more for brushing

    Applewood chunks

1. Make the cucumber-yogurt sauce: Stir together yogurt, lemon juice, and salt in a medium bowl until well combined. Add cucumber, stirring to dress cucumber in yogurt mixture.

2. Make the steak and vegetables: Wrap steaks in paper towels, and let stand at room temperature 1 hour. Meanwhile, bring a large pot of water to a boil over medium-high. Fill a large bowl with ice water; set aside. Add okra to boiling water, and cook until bright green and barely tender, 2 to 3 minutes. Using a spider or slotted spoon, transfer okra to ice water, and let cool 2 minutes; remove from ice water, and pat dry using paper towels. Add onions to

boiling water, and cook until skins begin to loosen, about 1 minute. Transfer onions to ice water, and let cool 2 minutes. Remove onions from ice water, and carefully trim stem and root ends; use fingers to rub and peel off skins.

3. Stir together butter and 2½ tablespoons suya spice mix in a small bowl; set suya butter aside.

4. Unwrap steaks, and sprinkle all sides evenly with 4 teaspoons salt; let stand 20 minutes. Meanwhile, skewer okra and onions separately, spaced ½ inch apart, on ¼-inch-wide flat metal skewers. Brush okra and onions all over with oil, and sprinkle evenly with remaining ¾ teaspoon salt.

5. Open bottom vent of a charcoal grill completely. Light charcoal chimney starter filled with briquettes. When briquettes are covered with gray ash, pour them onto bottom grate of grill, and push to one side of grill. Scatter applewood chunks over hot coals. Coat top grate with oil; place on grill. Place steaks on oiled grate over side without coals. Grill, uncovered, flipping steaks every 5 minutes, until a thermometer inserted in thickest portion registers 105°F, 25 to 30 minutes. Transfer steaks to grate directly over coals; grill, uncovered, until a thermometer inserted in thickest portion registers 120°F (for medium-rare), about 2 minutes per side, or to desired degree of doneness, smearing top side of each steak with 1 tablespoon suya butter during final 1 minute of grilling time. Transfer steaks to a cutting board, and let rest 10 minutes. Meanwhile, place okra and onion skewers on grates directly over coals; grill, uncovered, until tender and charred in spots, about 2 minutes per side. Remove from grill.

6. Remove okra and onions from skewers, and transfer to a platter. Remove bones from steaks; thinly slice steaks against the grain into ¼-inch-thick slices. Arrange steak slices and bones on a platter with okra and onions. Sprinkle okra and onions evenly with remaining ½ tablespoon suya spice mix (or more to taste). Serve steak and vegetables with remaining suya butter and cucumber-yogurt sauce. —CARLTON MCCOY

MAKE AHEAD Yogurt sauce can be chilled in an airtight container up to 3 days.

WINE Powerful, structured Napa Valley red: 2015 Burgess Cellars Alpinist

NOTE Look for suya spice mix at specialty spice shops or at africanshop.online.

GRILLED RIB EYE STEAKS
WITH OKRA SUYA AND
CUCUMBER-YOGURT SAUCE

LEG OF LAMB COOKED
OVER NEW POTATOES WITH
SPICY MINT-RUM SAUCE

Grilled Lamb Chops with Herby Yogurt Sauce and Cucumber-Couscous Salad

ACTIVE 15 MIN; TOTAL 2 HR 30 MIN;
SERVES 4

Plain yogurt is an excellent base for a marinade. It slowly tenderizes meat, rendering it juicy but never mealy or tough, and leaves a pleasantly tangy flavor behind. This recipe cleverly sets aside a portion of the seasoned yogurt to puree with tender green herbs and lemon juice for a quick finishing sauce after the lamb is done.

1½ cups plain whole-milk yogurt

1 Tbsp. minced shallot (from 1 shallot)

2 tsp. kosher salt, plus more to taste

1 tsp. grated lemon zest, plus 1 Tbsp. fresh lemon juice (from 1 lemon), divided

24 baby rib lamb chops (about 3 oz. each)

Black pepper, to taste

1 cup packed mixed fresh tender herbs (such as parsley, dill, and mint leaves), plus more for serving

Cooked couscous and sliced cucumbers, for serving

1. Stir together yogurt, shallot, salt, and lemon zest in a medium bowl. Measure 1 cup of the mixture into a large ziplock plastic bag. Cover and refrigerate remaining ½ cup yogurt mixture. Add lamb chops to ziplock bag; seal bag, and turn to coat lamb in sauce. Marinate in refrigerator at least 2 hours or up to 24 hours.

2. Preheat grill to high (450°F to 500°F). Scrape off excess marinade from lamb, and discard remaining marinade in bag. Sprinkle chops evenly with salt and pepper to taste. Arrange chops on oiled grill grates; grill, covered, turning once or twice, until browned and a thermometer inserted in thickest portion of meat registers 135°F for medium-rare, about 6 minutes, or to desired degree of doneness. Transfer chops to a platter; let rest 5 minutes.

3. Transfer reserved yogurt mixture to a food processor. Add fresh herbs and lemon juice; pulse until smooth, about 20 pulses. Serve chops alongside sauce, cooked couscous, cucumbers, and additional herbs. —KELSEY YOUNGMAN

MAKE AHEAD Sauce may be kept in an airtight container in refrigerator up to 3 days.

WINE Savory Rhône-style red: 2019 Hahn GSM

NOTE Alternatively, to broil the lamb: Arrange marinated lamb on a greased baking sheet. Broil 4½ inches from heat source until browned and no longer pink on the inside, about 6 minutes, flipping chops halfway through broiling time.

Leg of Lamb Cooked Over New Potatoes with Spicy Mint-Rum Sauce

ACTIVE 30 MIN; TOTAL 1 HR 55 MIN;
SERVES 6 TO 8

Cookbook author and scholar Jessica B. Harris serves this roast leg of lamb cooked over a bed of new potatoes as the centerpiece of her Bastille Day dinner party, which she has traditionally hosted to open up her summers on Martha's Vineyard.

LAMB AND POTATOES

6 large garlic cloves, peeled

1 Tbsp. fresh thyme leaves, finely chopped

1 to 1½ tsp. dried culinary lavender buds, finely chopped

1 (4- to 5-lb.) shank-end lamb leg, trimmed (see Note)

3 lb. small (about 1½- to 2-inch round) Yukon Gold potatoes, halved

¼ cup olive oil

2 Tbsp. plus ½ tsp. flaky sea salt, divided

2 Tbsp. mixed peppercorns

1 Tbsp. dried rosemary

1 Tbsp. herbes de Provence (preferably Simply Organic, see Note)

SPICY MINT-RUM SAUCE

¾ cup mint jelly (such as Stonewall Kitchen)

2 Tbsp. (1 oz.) dark Barbados rum

1 small (⅝-oz.) jalapeño, seeded and finely chopped

1. Make the lamb and potatoes: Preheat oven to 450°F. Finely chop garlic on a cutting board; sprinkle with thyme and lavender. Using the flat side of a chef's knife, smash garlic mixture until a coarse paste forms. Using the tip of a sharp paring knife,

make about 15 (½-inch-wide, ¾-inch-deep) incisions all over lamb leg. Stuff garlic mixture evenly into holes (about ¼ teaspoon mixture each). Set aside.

2. Toss together potatoes, oil, and ½ teaspoon salt in a large roasting pan; spread in an even layer. Roast in preheated oven until potatoes have just started to brown, about 10 minutes.

3. Meanwhile, combine peppercorns, rosemary, herbes de Provence, and remaining 2 tablespoons salt in a spice grinder. Pulse until coarsely ground, about 8 pulses. Rub mixture all over lamb.

4. Remove potatoes from oven; stir mixture in pan. Place lamb, fat side up, on potatoes. Return to oven, and roast at 450°F until lamb just begins to brown, about 15 minutes. Remove from oven. Stir potatoes in pan, lifting lamb to stir potatoes under it. Reduce oven temperature to 350°F. Continue roasting to desired degree of doneness or until a thermometer inserted in thickest portion of meat registers 120°F for medium-rare, 1 hour to 1 hour and 25 minutes. Remove from oven. Let rest 15 minutes.

5. Make the spicy mint-rum sauce: Cook mint jelly, rum, and jalapeño in a small saucepan over medium, stirring often, until jelly liquefies and sauce is warmed through, about 5 minutes.

6. Transfer lamb to a cutting board; carve into long, thin slices. Toss potatoes with pan drippings. Serve lamb alongside potatoes and spicy mint-rum sauce. —JESSICA B. HARRIS

MAKE AHEAD Leftover spicy mint-rum sauce can be stored in an airtight container up to 2 days. Reheat over warm before serving.

WINE Peppery, dark-fruited Sonoma Zinfandel: 2019 Valravn Sonoma County

NOTE The shank-end lamb leg is not a standard cut; it refers to a lamb leg with the butt of the leg removed. It cooks faster than a whole leg and still offers a beautiful presentation. A butcher can prepare this cut upon request, or you can substitute a 3- to 4-pound whole leg of lamb or bone-in shoulder. Herbes de Provence blends have different ratios of herbs and textures. We recommend Simply Organic for this recipe.

Lamb, Sweet Potato, and Coconut Mafé Curry

ACTIVE 1 HR 20 MIN; TOTAL 2 HR 30 MIN; SERVES 6

Perfectly tender lamb shoulder and creamy sweet potatoes balanced by floral coriander, warming turmeric and cumin, and piquant ginger and ground mustard make this West African curry a cozy delight. Fonio is a tiny grain that packs a nutritional punch and provides the perfect base for soaking up the flavorful curry sauce.

CURRY POWDER

- 2 Tbsp. ground coriander
- 2 Tbsp. ground cumin
- 1½ Tbsp. ground turmeric
- 2 tsp. ground ginger
- 1 tsp. dry mustard
- 1 tsp. ground cinnamon
- ½ tsp. black pepper
- ½ tsp. ground cardamom
- ½ tsp. cayenne pepper

CURRY

- 3 Tbsp. peanut oil or vegetable oil, divided
- 2 lb. boneless lamb shoulder, cut into 1- to 2-inch pieces
- 2 tsp. fine sea salt, divided
- 1 cup chopped yellow onion (from 1 medium [8-oz.] onion)
- ½ cup chopped green bell pepper (from 1 small [7-oz.] bell pepper)
- 1 Tbsp. chopped peeled fresh ginger (from 1 [2-inch] piece ginger)
- 1 medium garlic clove, chopped (about 1 tsp.)
- 3 Tbsp. creamy peanut butter (preferably natural and unsweetened)
- 1 Tbsp. tomato paste
- 1 cup chopped tomato (from 1 small [7-oz.] tomato)
- 3 cups vegetable broth
- 1 large (16-oz.) sweet potato, peeled and cut into 1½-inch cubes (about 2½ cups)
- 1 (14-oz.) can coconut milk
- 1 to 2 habanero chiles (about ¾ oz.) (to taste), stemmed, seeded, and finely chopped
- 2 Tbsp. fresh lime juice (from 1 lime)

ADDITIONAL INGREDIENTS

- Cooked fonio (see Note)
- 2 Tbsp. coarsely chopped fresh flat-leaf parsley

1. Make the curry powder: Combine coriander, cumin, turmeric, ginger, mustard, cinnamon, black pepper, cardamom, and cayenne in a small bowl; whisk to combine. Set aside 2 tablespoons curry powder; store remaining curry powder for another use in an airtight container at room temperature up to 2 months.

2. Make the curry: Heat 2 tablespoons oil in a large heavy-bottomed pot or Dutch oven over medium-high. Toss together lamb and 1 teaspoon salt in a medium bowl. Working in 2 batches, add lamb to pot, and cook, turning occasionally, until browned on all sides, 8 to 10 minutes per batch. Using tongs or a slotted spoon, transfer browned lamb to a separate medium bowl; loosely tent with aluminum foil to keep warm.

3. Do not wipe pot clean. Reduce heat under pot to medium. Add onion, bell pepper, ginger, garlic, and remaining 1 tablespoon oil. Cook, stirring often and scraping up browned bits from bottom of pot, until vegetables are softened and lightly browned, about 8 minutes. Add reserved 2 tablespoons curry powder; cook, stirring constantly, until fragrant, about 30 seconds. Add peanut butter and tomato paste; cook, stirring constantly, until tomato paste mixture turns a dark red-mahogany color, about 2 minutes. Return lamb to pot, along with any juices that may have accumulated in bowl. Add chopped tomato; stir until lamb pieces are coated in tomato paste mixture. Slowly stir in broth, scraping up browned bits from bottom of pot. Bring to a boil over medium-high. Cover pot; reduce heat to low, and simmer until lamb is tender, 1 hour and 15 minutes to 1 hour and 30 minutes, stirring bottom of pot once or twice toward end of cook time. Stir in sweet potato, coconut milk, habanero, and remaining 1 teaspoon salt. Increase heat to medium-high, and return to a boil. Reduce heat to medium; simmer, uncovered, stirring occasionally with a wooden spoon to prevent sticking, until sweet potato is tender, 15 to 20 minutes. Remove from heat; stir in lime juice. Spoon curry over cooked fonio, and sprinkle with parsley. —PIERRE THIAM

MAKE AHEAD Curry powder can be stored in an airtight container at room temperature up to 2 months.

WINE Generous, plummy red: 2018 Toad Hollow Sonoma County Merlot

NOTE Boneless lamb shoulder can be found at most grocery stores or butchers. Fonio can be found at Whole Foods or at hivebrands.com.

LAMB, SWEET POTATO, AND
COCONUT MAFÉ CURRY

ROSÉ-MARINATED GRILLED LEG OF
LAMB WITH WALNUT SALSA FRESCA

Rosé-Marinated Grilled Leg of Lamb with Walnut Salsa Fresca

ACTIVE 1 HR 45 MIN; TOTAL 4 HR, PLUS 8 HR MARINATING; SERVES 8 TO 10

Studding a leg of lamb with anchovies adds savory depth to this beautiful cut of meat flavored with a garlicky, herbal rosé-based marinade. The flavors in the walnut salsa fresca served alongside mirror those of the marinade, bringing a final dose of richness and flavor to this standout dish.

GRILLED LAMB

- 1 cup rosé wine (such as Commanderie de Peyrassol Cuvée des Commandeurs)
- 1 Tbsp. kosher salt
- 1 cup fresh rosemary leaves (about 1 oz.) (from 2 bunches), plus rosemary sprigs, for garnish
- 2 garlic heads, cloves separated and peeled (about ¾ cup)
- ½ cup extra-virgin olive oil
- 1½ tsp. black pepper
- 1 (6- to 7-lb.) bone-in leg of lamb with shank attached, trimmed
- 1 (2-oz.) can anchovy fillets in oil (such as Cento), drained

WALNUT SALSA FRESCA

- 2 cups walnuts, toasted and finely chopped (about 1¾ cups)
- 1 (2-oz.) can anchovy fillets in oil (such as Cento), drained and finely chopped
- 2 tsp. grated lemon zest (from 1 lemon)
- 1 tsp. finely chopped fresh rosemary
- ½ tsp. kosher salt
- ½ tsp. black pepper
- 1 cup extra-virgin olive oil

1. Make the grilled lamb: Bring wine to a boil in a small saucepan over high. Boil, undisturbed, until flavors are concentrated, most of the alcohol has cooked off, and liquid is reduced to about ¼ cup, 12 to 14 minutes. Remove from heat; add salt, and stir until dissolved. Let cool to room temperature, about 30 minutes.

2. Combine cooled wine mixture, rosemary leaves, garlic, oil, and pepper in a blender. Process until a thick paste forms, about 1 minute. Set aside. Using a sharp paring knife, puncture lamb leg every 1½ to 2 inches, creating about 1-inch-deep slits (about ½ inch wide). Tear anchovies into small pieces (halves or thirds), and stuff into lamb slits. Smear lamb exterior with rosé mixture, rubbing it into the slits. Wrap lamb tightly in plastic wrap, and refrigerate at least 8 hours or up to 24 hours.

3. Uncover lamb, and let stand at room temperature about 1 hour. Open bottom vent of a charcoal grill completely. Light charcoal chimney starter filled with briquettes. When briquettes are covered with gray ash, pour them onto bottom grate of grill, and push to one side of the grill. Adjust vents as needed to maintain an internal temperature of 400°F. Coat top grate with oil; place grate on grill, and preheat 5 minutes. Place lamb, fat side up, on oiled grates over side with coals. Grill, uncovered, turning occasionally, until lamb is charred with a deep brown crust on all sides, about 15 minutes. A flare-up might occur from the fat rendering; if so, close the lid, or transfer lamb to side of grill without coals until flare-up goes down, and then uncover, or transfer lamb back to grates over coals.

4. Transfer lamb, fat side up, to side of grill without coals. Insert a leave-in thermometer in thickest portion of lamb. Grill, covered, adjusting vents as needed to maintain internal grill temperature of 400°F, until leave-in thermometer in lamb registers 115°F to 120°F for medium-rare, 1 hour and 15 minutes to 1 hour and 45 minutes, rotating lamb 90 degrees on grates every 30 minutes (being mindful of the thermometer probe). If grill temperature drops below 350°F, prepare more briquettes, and replenish as needed. Transfer lamb to a cutting board. Loosely tent with aluminum foil, and let rest 15 minutes.

5. Make the walnut salsa fresca: Stir together walnuts, anchovies, lemon zest, chopped rosemary, salt, and pepper in a medium bowl. Add oil, and stir to combine. Set aside at room temperature until ready to serve.

6. Hold lamb shank in one hand while you cut the meat away from the bone in large slices, rotating the leg as needed. Arrange lamb slices, crust side up, on a platter. Garnish grilled lamb with rosemary sprigs, and serve with walnut salsa fresca.
—ANDREA SLONECKER

WINE Red-fruited, fragrant rosé: 2020 Commanderie de Peyrassol Cuvée des Commandeurs

Grilled Lamb Sliders with Romaine Salad and Yogurt-Tahini Sauce

⏱ TOTAL 35 MIN; SERVES 4

A symphony of herbs—in the form of za'atar—and little bits of toasted pine nuts boost the ground lamb patties that accompany this fresh summer salad.

SAUCE

- ½ cup plain whole-milk strained Greek-style yogurt
- 2 Tbsp. tahini
- 1 Tbsp. fresh lemon juice (from 1 lemon)
- 1 garlic clove, grated (about ½ tsp.)
- ¼ tsp. kosher salt

LAMB PATTIES

- 1½ lb. ground lamb
- ¾ cup finely chopped toasted pine nuts (from 1 cup pine nuts) (see Note)
- 2 Tbsp. za'atar
- 1 tsp. kosher salt
- 2 garlic cloves, grated (about 1 tsp.)
- ½ tsp. black pepper
- 2 Tbsp. pomegranate molasses

SALAD

- 4 cups torn romaine lettuce leaves (from 1 head lettuce)
- 1½ cups sliced Persian cucumbers (from 2 small [3-oz.] cucumbers)
- ⅓ cup thinly sliced red onion
- 1½ Tbsp. extra-virgin olive oil
- 1 Tbsp. fresh lemon juice (from 1 lemon)
- ½ tsp. kosher salt
- ¼ tsp. black pepper

1. Make the sauce: Whisk together yogurt, tahini, lemon juice, garlic, and salt in a medium bowl until combined; set aside.

2. Make the lamb patties: Preheat grill to medium-high (400°F to 450°F). Place lamb in a large bowl. Add pine nuts, za'atar, salt, garlic, and pepper; mix with your hands until well combined. Divide mixture evenly into 8 (3½-ounce) portions; shape each portion into a ½-inch-thick patty. Arrange patties on oiled grates; grill, covered, until well marked and a thermometer inserted in thickest portion of meat registers 125°F, 3 to 4 minutes per side, brushing patties evenly with pomegranate molasses during final 1 to 2 minutes of grill time. Transfer cooked patties to a large platter.

3. Make the salad: Toss together lettuce, cucumbers, and onion in a medium bowl until combined. Drizzle with oil and lemon juice, and sprinkle with salt and pepper; toss gently to coat. Serve salad with lamb patties and sauce. —ANN TAYLOR PITTMAN

MAKE AHEAD Sauce can be refrigerated in an airtight container up to 2 days.

WINE Spicy Mediterranean red: 2017 Cantele Salice Salentino Riserva

NOTE To toast pine nuts: Spread pine nuts on a parchment paper–lined baking sheet. Bake at 300°F for 13 to 15 minutes, stirring or shaking pan occasionally.

Curried Goat

TOTAL 3 HR 30 MIN, PLUS 24 HR MARINATING; SERVES 4

"Goat is at the center of many of Jamaica's best dishes, from mannish water (goat head soup) to this curry, which clearly exhibits the influences of the Indian subcontinent," says 2019 F&W Best New Chef Kwame Onwuachi. "The same can be said in Trinidad, where goat doesn't just make a cameo but has a starring role. This curried goat is actually a hybrid of the Trini and Jamaican versions I remember. I've used Jamaican curry powder along with Trinidad's heavily aromatic green seasoning."

- 1½ lb. goat stew meat or goat shoulder, cut into 1-inch cubes
- 1 medium-size (9-oz.) yellow onion, finely chopped (about 1½ cups)
- 1½ cups Jamaican Green Seasoning (recipe p. 305)
- ¼ cup Caribbean-Style Curry Powder (recipe p. 305)
- 2 tsp. kosher salt, plus more to taste
- 1½ tsp. House Spice (recipe p. 306)
- 2 Tbsp. canola oil
- 4½ cups chicken stock, divided
- 2 tsp. Peppa Sauce (recipe p. 305)
- 3 large Yukon Gold potatoes (about 1½ lb.), peeled and cut into ½-inch cubes (about 4 cups)
- Perfectly Steamed Rice (recipe p. 216)
- Lime wedges, for serving

1. Combine goat, onion, green seasoning, curry powder, salt, and house spice in a medium bowl, and toss to evenly coat. Cover bowl, and let marinate in refrigerator 24 hours.

2. Remove goat mixture from refrigerator. Heat oil in a large pot or a deep-sided skillet over high until shimmering. Working in batches as needed (do not crowd skillet), remove goat from marinade, tapping off excess marinade; add to pot. Cook, turning occasionally, until deeply browned on all sides, 8 to 10 minutes per batch. Transfer goat to a heatproof bowl. Do not wipe pot clean. Discard remaining marinade in bowl.

3. Add ¼ cup stock to pot; cook over medium-high, stirring constantly and scraping bottom of pot, until browned bits have released from bottom of pot, about 1 minute. Return goat to pot; stir in peppa sauce and 3¾ cups chicken stock.

4. Bring mixture to a boil over medium-high. Reduce heat to medium-low; simmer, partially covered and stirring occasionally, until goat is tender and sauce starts to thicken, about 2 hours and 45 minutes, adding potatoes to mixture during final 30 minutes of cook time, plus remaining ½ cup chicken stock if pot seems dry.

5. Season with additional salt to taste. Serve alongside perfectly steamed rice and lime wedges. —KWAME ONWUACHI

MAKE AHEAD Curried goat can be stored in an airtight container in refrigerator up to 4 days or in freezer up to 2 months.

WINE Bright, aromatic rosé: 2021 Maison Noir Wines Love Drunk

CURRIED GOAT

VEGETABLES
& TOFU

MADEIRA-BRAISED SWISS CHARD
WITH GARAM MASALA, SULTANAS,
AND TOASTED ALMONDS (P. 185)
OPPOSITE: RED WINE–ROASTED
BEETS WITH TAHINI YOGURT (P. 182)

PALAK "PANEER" WITH
PRESSED FRESH RICOTTA

Palak "Paneer" with Pressed Fresh Ricotta

ACTIVE 45 MIN; TOTAL 2 HR 45 MIN; SERVES 4

A little extra hands-off pressing time firms up fresh ricotta into a block that can be cut into paneer-like cheese. Fried in ghee, the crispy, cheesy cubes transform into cheese croutons and are a perfect pair for the warm puree of chile-and-ginger-spiked spinach and cilantro.

- 1 lb. Homemade Fresh Ricotta (recipe p. 180) or store-bought fresh ricotta, drained
- 2 Tbsp. ghee
- 1 small yellow onion, finely chopped
- 3 garlic cloves, chopped
- 1 Tbsp. finely chopped peeled fresh ginger
- 1 medium-size fresh serrano chile, stemmed and chopped
- 1 tsp. garam masala
- ¼ tsp. cayenne pepper
- 1 lb. baby spinach, roughly chopped
- 1 cup firmly packed fresh cilantro leaves and stems (about 2 oz.), plus additional cilantro leaves for garnish
- ½ cup water
- ¼ cup heavy cream or plain yogurt
- 1 tsp. kosher salt, plus more to taste
- ½ tsp. kasoori methi (dried fenugreek leaves), optional
- Basmati rice or flatbread, for serving

1. Place a 10-inch square of damp double-lined cheesecloth on a clean work surface. Spoon ricotta into center of square. Using your hands, press to shape ricotta into a 5-inch square. Wrap cheesecloth tightly around ricotta, and press to form a 5½-inch square (about ¾ inch thick). Place wrapped ricotta on a double layer of paper towels. Top with a double layer of paper towels, and weight with a large cast-iron skillet (6 to 8 pounds). Let stand until paneer is firm and set, 1 hour and 30 minutes to 2 hours, changing out paper towels after 45 minutes.

2. Unwrap ricotta, and cut into ¾-inch squares, wiping knife clean after each slice. Heat a large nonstick skillet over medium; add ghee. Fry ricotta cubes, flipping once, until lightly browned on 2 opposite sides, 3 to 5 minutes total. Transfer to a plate; set aside.

3. Return same skillet with ghee to heat over medium. Add onion, and cook, stirring occasionally, until lightly browned, 6 to 8 minutes. Stir in garlic, ginger, serrano, garam masala, and cayenne. Cook, stirring constantly, until fragrant, about 1 minute. Gradually add spinach. Cook, stirring often, until wilted, 3 to 4 minutes. Remove from heat.

4. Transfer spinach mixture to a blender; add cilantro leaves and stems and ½ cup water. Remove insert from blender lid, and cover with a kitchen towel. Process until mixture forms a coarse paste, 5 to 10 seconds. Return mixture to skillet over low. Cook, stirring occasionally, until thickened to desired consistency, 5 to 10 minutes. Stir in cream, salt, and kasoori methi, if using. Add ricotta cubes. Cover and cook until ricotta is heated through, about 2 minutes. Season with salt to taste. Garnish with cilantro leaves, and serve with basmati rice or flatbread. —PAIGE GRANDJEAN

MAKE AHEAD Ricotta can be prepared through step 1, removed from cheesecloth, wrapped tightly in plastic wrap, and refrigerated up to 2 days.

WINE Earthy French red: 2019 Bernard Baudry Le Domaine Chinon

NOTE Find kasoori methi at South Asian markets or online at desiclik.com.

Vegan Collards

ACTIVE 25 MIN; TOTAL 1 HR 55 MIN; SERVES 8 TO 10

Collards are often cooked with a smoked ham hock to add a meaty, smoky flavor; this mildly spicy vegan collard greens recipe from Boricua Soul, a Puerto Rican–Southern restaurant in Durham, North Carolina, achieves the same depth of flavor with quality vegetable broth, adobo seasoning, and a hint of liquid smoke. Soak up the juices (potlikker) with cornbread, or drizzle over steamed rice.

- ¼ cup olive oil
- 1 small yellow onion, chopped (about 1 cup)
- 3 medium garlic cloves, finely chopped (about 1 Tbsp.)
- ¼ cup plus 1 Tbsp. white vinegar
- 6 medium bunches collard greens (about 10 oz. each), washed, stemmed, and cut into ½-inch-thick ribbons (18 to 20 packed cups)
- 12 cups vegetable broth (such as Zoup! or Brodo)
- 2 Tbsp. hot sauce (such as Frank's RedHot)
- 1 Tbsp. adobo all-purpose seasoning powder with pepper
- 1 Tbsp. seasoned salt (such as Lawry's)
- 1 tsp. coarse kosher salt (such as Morton's), plus more to taste
- 1 tsp. black pepper
- ¼ tsp. liquid smoke

1. Heat oil in a large Dutch oven or other large, heavy pot over medium-high until shimmering, about 3 minutes. Add onion and garlic; cook, stirring often, until slightly softened, about 2 minutes. Add vinegar; cook, stirring occasionally, until onion and garlic are translucent, about 6 minutes. Working in batches, add collards, stirring constantly after each addition, until wilted and all greens fit in pot, 1 to 2 minutes. Pour in broth, and bring to a boil over medium-high. Add hot sauce, adobo seasoning, seasoned salt, kosher salt, black pepper, and liquid smoke.

2. Reduce heat to low; cover and simmer until collards are tender but not mushy, about 1 hour and 30 minutes. Season with additional salt to taste. Using a slotted spoon, transfer greens to a large bowl to serve, adding potlikker as desired. —TORIANO FREDERICKS

MAKE AHEAD Collard greens can be made up to 3 days ahead and refrigerated in an airtight container.

HOMEMADE FRESH RICOTTA

This easy homemade fresh ricotta cheese recipe only requires three ingredients—milk, buttermilk, and salt—and yields a light, fluffy ricotta that's a delicious blank canvas for sweet or savory recipes, or you can enjoy it as a decadent toast topper. Source high-quality local dairy if possible for the richest flavor and best results.

ACTIVE 45 MIN; TOTAL 3 HR 10 MIN; MAKES ABOUT 2¼ LB. (ABOUT 5 CUPS)

- 1 gal. organic and/or grass-fed pasteurized whole milk
- 1 qt. organic and/or grass-fed buttermilk
- ½ tsp. kosher salt

1. Stir together milk, buttermilk, and salt in a large, heavy-bottomed stockpot. Cook over medium, stirring occasionally, until mixture reaches 180°F on an instant-read thermometer, 30 to 40 minutes. Remove from heat; let stand, uncovered, at room temperature, until curds have formed and floated to the surface and are surrounded by clear whey, 2 to 3 hours.

2. Line a colander with a double layer of damp cheesecloth, leaving at least 6 inches of overhang on all sides. Set colander over a large bowl. Using a fine wire-mesh strainer, gently scoop ricotta curds from stockpot, and place in colander. Keep curd pieces as large as possible to avoid overworking, which can toughen the ricotta. Let ricotta drain at room temperature 30 minutes for a creamy texture or up to 2 hours for a drier texture. Reserve whey in stockpot for another use.

3. Bring corners of cheesecloth together, and lift ricotta. Gently twist over colander to squeeze out any remaining clear whey from ricotta. Continue twisting until whey draining out becomes opaque and milky. Reserve drained whey for another use. Use ricotta immediately, or store in an airtight container in refrigerator up to 1 week.

—PAIGE GRANDJEAN

MAKE AHEAD Ricotta can be made up to 1 week ahead and stored in an airtight container in refrigerator.

STEP-BY-STEP

HEAT MILK Slowly heat milk, buttermilk, and kosher salt to 180°F, stirring occasionally to prevent bottom from scorching.

COOL CURD LAYER Let stand, undisturbed, to let curds form and float to the surface, 2 to 3 hours. Curds will float in translucent yellow whey.

SET UP COLANDER Set a colander over a large, deep bowl; line with a double layer of damp cheesecloth, leaving a 6-inch overhang.

SCOOP CURDS Using a fine wire-mesh strainer, gently scoop curds in large pieces, and transfer to prepared colander.

BETTER WITH BUTTERMILK

While pro cheese-makers rely on rennet, an enzyme used in commercial cheesemaking, most homemade ricotta recipes call for acidic lemon juice to help form the curds, which can turn tight and rubbery. Here, buttermilk gently transforms the milk into curds and whey—and yields more than double the ricotta as compared to recipes that use lemon juice.

DRAIN RICOTTA Drain ricotta at room temperature; reserve whey for another use, if desired.

TWIST RICOTTA Gather corners of cheesecloth, and lift ricotta. Gently twist to squeeze out remaining clear whey.

Red Wine–Roasted Beets with Tahini Yogurt

PHOTO P. 176

ACTIVE 25 MIN; TOTAL 1 HR 55 MIN; SERVES 6 TO 8

Tart sumac, piquant peppercorns, and herbal yet lightly sweet green cardamom combine to season these wine-cooked beets, infusing them with fresh flavor that complements the fruity red wine in the recipe without overpowering it. After roasting, the sweet and tender beets are served atop a whipped, creamy turmeric- and tahini- seasoned yogurt spread and finished with chopped pistachios, lots of herbs, and a dusting of more sumac.

- 2 tsp. green cardamom pods, smashed
- 2 tsp. whole black peppercorns
- 2 cups fruity red wine (such as Gamay or Grenache)
- 2 Tbsp. plus ½ tsp. ground sumac, divided
- 1 Tbsp. plus ½ tsp. kosher salt, divided
- 2 lb. red beets (about 6 medium beets), trimmed, peeled, and cut into 1-inch pieces
- ¾ cup plain whole-milk strained yogurt
- 3 Tbsp. tahini
- 1 tsp. ground turmeric
- 1 to 2 Tbsp. water, divided
- 2 Tbsp. extra-virgin olive oil
- 1 tsp. red wine vinegar
- ⅓ cup salted roasted pistachios (about 1½ oz.), roughly chopped
- ¼ cup roughly chopped mixed fresh tender herbs (such as mint, cilantro, and dill)
- Flaky sea salt, to taste

1. Preheat oven to 375°F. Place cardamom pods and peppercorns on a 4-inch square of cheesecloth; secure pouch using kitchen twine. Combine wine, cheesecloth pouch, 2 tablespoons sumac, and 1 tablespoon kosher salt in a medium-size Dutch oven. Cook over medium-high, stirring occasionally, until reduced by about half, 6 to 10 minutes. Stir in beets. Cover Dutch oven tightly with aluminum foil, and place lid on top. Transfer to preheated oven, and roast until beets are just tender when pierced with a knife, 45 minutes to 1 hour.

Remove from oven. Remove foil and lid. Let beets cool to room temperature in roasting liquid, about 1 hour.

2. Meanwhile, whisk together yogurt, tahini, turmeric, 1 tablespoon water, and ¼ teaspoon kosher salt in a medium bowl. If needed, whisk in remaining 1 tablespoon water, 1 teaspoon at a time, to thin mixture to a spreadable consistency. Let stand at room temperature for flavor and color to bloom, about 1 hour.

3. Pour beet mixture through a colander; discard liquid and cheesecloth pouch. Toss together drained beets, oil, vinegar, and remaining ¼ teaspoon salt in a medium bowl.

4. Whisk yogurt mixture well; spread on a platter. Top with beets. Sprinkle beets with pistachios, chopped mixed tender herbs, and remaining ½ teaspoon sumac. Season with flaky sea salt to taste. —ANDREA SLONECKER

MAKE AHEAD Yogurt mixture may be stored in an airtight container in refrigerator up to 3 days. Let come to room temperature before serving. Beets can be roasted up to 1 day in advance. Refrigerate them in the roasting liquid, and then strain.

WINE Fruity, peppery Gamay: 2021 Division-Villages Les Petits Fers

Stir-Fried Iceberg Lettuce

TOTAL 20 MIN; SERVES 2 TO 4

Crisp iceberg lettuce becomes tender and slightly sweet after cooking with soy sauce, a touch of sugar, and plenty of fresh ginger. The leftover cooking liquid is perfect for spooning over a bowl of white rice.

- 1 small (20-oz.) head iceberg lettuce, outer leaves discarded, head cored, and leaves separated
- 2 Tbsp. vegetable oil
- 1 Tbsp. soy sauce, plus more to taste
- ½ tsp. granulated sugar
- 12 very thin (about 1-mm.-thick) 1- x ¾-inch slices peeled fresh ginger (about 1½ tsp.)

1. Soak lettuce leaves in a bowl filled with cold water 5 minutes. Drain and spin in a salad spinner until dry. Alternatively, pat lettuce leaves dry using clean kitchen towels. Tear leaves into 1½- to 2-inch pieces; spin again, or pat dry with paper towels.

2. Heat oil in a wok over medium-high until shimmering and fragrant. Add lettuce pieces; cook, stirring constantly, until lettuce just begins to soften, about 45 seconds. Add soy sauce and sugar, stirring to coat lettuce in soy sauce mixture. Add additional soy sauce to taste. Add ginger; cook, stirring constantly, until inner lettuce leaves are translucent in spots and lettuce loses about one-third of its original volume, about 30 seconds. Remove from heat. Serve immediately, leaving liquid in wok. —LAN SAMANTHA CHANG

Roasted Carrots

ACTIVE 10 MIN; TOTAL 20 MIN, MAKES ABOUT 2 CUPS

F&W Best New Chef Gaby Maeda's method for making these flavorful, buttery roasted carrots starts with briefly cooking whole carrots in an ovenproof skillet over medium-high heat and sautéing them in a little olive oil until they are browned in spots. She then tosses them with butter, thyme sprigs, and garlic, and seasons them with salt. The carrots are finally briefly roasted in a hot oven, where the high heat creates caramelized edges that add texture to their outsides, while their interior turns soft and creamy, but not mushy. The entire process takes just 20 minutes, and yields fork-tender carrots with satisfying flavor.

- 1 Tbsp. extra-virgin olive oil
- 6 oz. small carrots, trimmed and scrubbed
- 1 Tbsp. unsalted butter
- 2 (6-inch) thyme sprigs
- 1 medium garlic clove, smashed
- ½ tsp. kosher salt

Preheat oven to 400°F. Heat oil in a large stainless steel skillet over medium-high until wisps of smoke form, 2 to 3 minutes. Carefully add carrots in a single layer; cook, tossing occasionally, until golden brown in spots, 3 to 5 minutes. Add butter, thyme, and garlic; cook, tossing constantly, until butter melts, about 30 seconds. Sprinkle carrots with salt, and toss. Transfer skillet to preheated oven. Roast until carrots are fork-tender, 8 to 10 minutes. If desired, turn oven off, and crack oven door open; keep carrots warm in oven up to 15 minutes. —GABY MAEDA

PICKLED CARROTS
(RECIPE P. 303)

PISTACHIO DUKKAH
(RECIPE P. 303)

ROASTED CARROTS

ROASTED BROCCOLI WITH
PICKLED PEPPER VINAIGRETTE

Roasted Broccoli with Pickled Pepper Vinaigrette

⏱ ACTIVE 15 MIN; TOTAL 35 MIN; SERVES 4

Tossing broccoli pieces with oil, salt, and pimentón (Spanish paprika), then roasting them on a preheated baking sheet in a super-hot oven coaxes out the vegetable's sweet side as the florets crisp and the stems turn meaty and tender. A punchy pickled pepper vinaigrette and shavings of Parmesan cheese transform the roasted broccoli into a satisfying and substantial side dish.

- 1½ lb. fresh broccoli, trimmed and cut into long florets (about 8 cups)
- ¼ cup olive oil, divided
- 1½ tsp. kosher salt, divided
- ¾ tsp. sweet pimentón or paprika
- 3 Tbsp. chopped pickled peppers (from ⅓ cup sliced Refrigerator Pickled Peppers (recipe p. 312)
- 2 Tbsp. pickled pepper brine (from Refrigerator Pickled Peppers (recipe p. 312)
- 1 Tbsp. finely chopped shallot
- 1 tsp. Dijon mustard
- 1 large garlic clove, grated on a Microplane grater (about ½ tsp.)
- Shaved Parmesan cheese, for garnish

1. Place a rimmed baking sheet on middle oven rack. Preheat oven to 450°F. (Do not remove baking sheet while oven heats.)

2. Toss together broccoli, 2 tablespoons oil, 1 teaspoon salt, and pimentón in a large bowl until combined. Carefully remove hot baking sheet from preheated oven; spread broccoli in an even layer on baking sheet. Roast in preheated oven until broccoli is crisp-tender and browned on edges, 15 to 18 minutes, stirring once halfway through cook time. Remove from oven; return broccoli to large bowl.

3. While broccoli roasts, whisk together pickled peppers, pickled pepper brine, shallot, mustard, garlic, and remaining ½ teaspoon salt in a small bowl until combined. Gradually add remaining 2 tablespoons oil to mixture, whisking constantly until combined. Set aside at room temperature until ready to use.

4. Add vinaigrette to broccoli in bowl; toss to combine. Arrange on a serving platter, and garnish with cheese. —MOLLY STEVENS

WINE Herbal Austrian white: 2020 Domäne Wachau Grüner Veltliner Federspiel Terrassen

NOTE Sweet pimentón is available at specialty spice shops or online at burlapandbarrel.com.

Madeira-Braised Swiss Chard with Garam Masala, Sultanas, and Toasted Almonds

PHOTO P. 177

⏱ TOTAL 30 MIN; SERVES 6 TO 8

Swiss chard cooks down into tender, silky ribbons when braised with fruity Madeira and complex, tangy, earthy garam masala in this recipe.

- 2 medium bunches red Swiss chard (about 1½ lb.)
- 3 Tbsp. unsalted butter
- 1 medium-size (8-oz.) red onion, halved and thinly sliced (about 2 cups)
- 1¾ tsp. kosher salt, plus more to taste
- 4 garlic cloves, finely chopped (about 4 tsp.)
- 1 Tbsp. finely chopped peeled fresh ginger (from 1 [½-inch] piece)
- 1½ tsp. garam masala
- 1 cup Madeira
- ¾ cup sultanas (golden raisins)
- ⅓ cup sliced almonds, lightly toasted

1. Remove chard stems and thick veins from chard leaves, and cut stems crosswise into ½-inch pieces. Cut leaves crosswise into ¾-inch-wide ribbons.

2. Melt butter in a 12-inch stainless steel skillet over medium-high. Add onion and 1 teaspoon salt; cook, stirring often, until onion is lightly browned, 5 to 7 minutes. Add chard stems, garlic, ginger, and garam masala; cook, stirring constantly, until fragrant and well combined. Add Madeira; cook, stirring occasionally, until liquid reduces to about ¼ cup, 8 to 10 minutes.

3. Gradually add chard leaves to onion mixture in large handfuls, tossing and stirring until leaves begin to wilt before adding another handful, about 2 minutes total. Stir in sultanas and remaining ¾ teaspoon salt. Reduce heat to medium-low; cook, stirring occasionally, until chard leaves and stems are tender, 2 to 3 minutes. Season with additional salt to taste.

4. Using a slotted spoon, transfer chard mixture to a platter. If desired, reserve cooking liquid in skillet for serving separately. Sprinkle chard mixture with sliced almonds, and serve immediately. —ANDREA SLONECKER

WINE Nutty, dry Madeira: Blandy's 5 Year Old Verdelho

Jamaican Callaloo

TOTAL 1 HR 30 MIN; SERVES 4

This Jamaican Callaloo recipe from Kwame Onwuachi's book, My America, *is filled with protein-rich leaves cooked until tender and given spice and fulsome flavor with the addition of peppers and tomatoes.*

- 2 Tbsp. canola oil
- 1 medium-size (10-oz.) yellow onion, cut into small cubes (about 1¾ cups)
- 1 medium-size (7-oz.) red bell pepper, cut into small cubes (about 1 cup)
- 5 medium garlic cloves, minced (about 5 tsp.)
- 1 tsp. Peppa Sauce (recipe p. 305)
- 1 lb. fresh callaloo, thick stems removed, leaves and tender stems roughly chopped (about 7 packed cups)
- 2 cups vegetable stock
- 2 medium-size (3½-oz.) plum tomatoes, cut into small cubes (about 1 cup)
- 2 tsp. House Spice (recipe p. 306)
- ¾ tsp. kosher salt

1. Heat oil in a large pot over medium until shimmering. Add onion, bell pepper, garlic, and peppa sauce; cook, stirring occasionally, until softened, about 10 minutes. Add callaloo, stock, tomatoes, and house spice; cook, stirring occasionally, until callaloo starts to wilt, 4 to 5 minutes. Increase heat to medium-high, and bring to a simmer. Reduce heat to medium-low, and cover. Cook, stirring occasionally, until callaloo is tender, about 50 minutes.

2. Increase heat to medium, and bring to a boil. Boil, stirring occasionally, until liquid is reduced by two-thirds, 10 to 15 minutes. Stir in salt, and serve. —KWAME ONWUACHI

MAKE AHEAD Callaloo can be refrigerated in an airtight container up to 4 days.

LILLIAN'S WHOLE STUFFED CABBAGE

Basting the whole cabbage with butter as it roasts not only elevates the flavor but also encourages the outer leaves to crisp and brown.

ACTIVE 1 HR; TOTAL 2 HR 30 MIN; SERVES 6

- 2 small heads Savoy cabbage (about 1½ lb. each)
- 2 Tbsp. plus 1 tsp. kosher salt, divided
- ¾ cup unsalted butter (12 oz.), divided
- 1 medium-size (9-oz.) yellow onion, halved lengthwise and thinly sliced crosswise (about 1¾ cups)
- 1 Tbsp. fresh thyme leaves
- 1 Tbsp. chopped fresh flat-leaf parsley
- ½ tsp. cracked black pepper
- ¼ tsp. ground allspice
- 1 (4-oz.) sleeve saltine crackers, coarsely crushed (about 2 cups)
- 2 large eggs
- ½ cup plus 2 Tbsp. freshly grated Parmigiano-Reggiano cheese (about 2½ oz.), divided
- 2 (3-inch) rosemary sprigs
- 2 Tbsp. aged balsamic vinegar

1. Bring a large pot of water to a boil. Meanwhile, using a sharp knife, remove and discard bottom core and stem of each cabbage. Gently peel away outer leaves from each cabbage, using a paring knife to separate the leaves from the core, until you have 10 to 12 leaves total; reserve cabbage hearts. Quickly rinse if there is dirt in the leaves.

2. Fill a large bowl with ice water; set aside. Add cabbage leaves and 2 tablespoons salt to boiling water in pot; cook until softened and pliable, 2 to 3 minutes. Turn off heat. Using tongs, remove leaves from boiling water, and submerge in ice bath to stop the cooking process. (Don't empty the pot of water.) Drain leaves, and transfer to a platter or baking sheet lined with a clean towel to dry.

3. Thinly shred reserved cabbage hearts to equal about 6 cups; reserve remaining cabbage for another use. Melt ½ cup butter in a large saucepan over medium-high. Add onion; cook, stirring often, until translucent, about 2 minutes. Add shredded cabbage and remaining 1 teaspoon salt; cook, stirring occasionally, until cabbage softens, about

10 minutes. Stir in thyme, parsley, cracked pepper, and allspice. Transfer mixture to a large bowl; let cool slightly, about 5 minutes. Add crushed crackers, eggs, and ½ cup Parmigiano-Reggiano; stir gently until combined. To keep cracker crumbs differently sized, do not overmix.

4. Line a medium (cabbage-size) bowl with a lint-free linen towel or 2 layers of cheesecloth with several inches draping over edges of bowl. Begin layering the cabbage leaves in bottom of bowl with tops of leaves pointing toward bottom of bowl, layering them so bottom stem ends drape over rim of bowl. (They will hang halfway over the side.) Start with darker green leaves on the bottom, as this will be the presentation side of the cabbage. Continue layering the leaves until all of the leaves have been used.

5. Place shredded cabbage–cracker filling in center of layered cabbage leaves in bowl, pressing down and shaping filling into a ball, and then begin folding the leaves over the top of the filling, working up and around the filling to cover. (It should begin to look like a

STEP-BY-STEP

COOK THE FILLING Sauté the shredded cabbage, onion, thyme, parsley, pepper, and allspice in butter. Stir in crackers, eggs, and cheese.

ARRANGE THE CABBAGE LEAVES Layer the blanched cabbage leaves in a cheesecloth-lined medium bowl, allowing the stem ends to drape over the edge of the bowl.

STUFF THE CABBAGE Place shredded cabbage–cracker filling in center of layered cabbage, pressing down and shaping filling into a ball. Fold leaves over top.

BOIL THE STUFFED CABBAGE Tie cheesecloth securely around stuffed cabbage, forming a tight ball. Boil the stuffed cabbage in salted water 15 minutes.

whole cabbage.) Lift the sides of the towel or cheesecloth up and twist, squeezing to form a tight ball. Use excess towel or cheesecloth to tie into a knot. Alternatively, secure and tie using kitchen twine.

6. Return the pot of cabbage cooking liquid to a boil. Place tied cabbage in boiling water, and boil 15 minutes. Using tongs, transfer cabbage from water to a colander or kitchen towel; let cool 5 minutes.

7. Preheat oven to 375°F. Cut remaining ¼ cup butter into small cubes, and place in a round or oval baking dish, a cast-iron skillet, or a high-sided 9- × 13-inch baking dish. Untie cabbage, and remove from towel; place cabbage, seam side down, in baking dish. Roast in preheated oven until cabbage has started to turn brown and crispy, about 40 minutes, basting with butter in baking dish every 10 minutes. Remove from oven. Place rosemary sprigs on top of cabbage, and baste again to coat rosemary in butter. Return to oven, and roast at 375°F until rosemary has started to brown and crisp, about 10 minutes. Remove from oven; spoon browned butter from baking dish over top. Sprinkle cabbage with remaining 2 tablespoons Parmigiano-Reggiano. Let cool 5 minutes. Slice cabbage into wedges (similar to a pie). Drizzle evenly with balsamic vinegar, and serve. —SARAH GRUENEBERG

MAKE AHEAD Prepare cabbage through step 5; cover and refrigerate up to 8 hours or overnight.

WINE Umami-rich "natural" white: 2020 Milan Nestarec Bel

ROAST AND BASTE THE CABBAGE Roast boiled stuffed cabbage, seam side down, at 375°F for 40 minutes, basting with butter every 10 minutes.

BROWN WITH HERBS, AND SERVE Top with rosemary, baste with butter, and continue roasting until brown and crispy. Sprinkle with Parmigiano-Reggiano cheese, and serve.

Citrus and Beet Aguachile

ACTIVE 30 MIN; TOTAL 2 HR 20 MIN;
SERVES 4

Chef Claudette Zepeda loves to experiment with different ingredients in her aguachiles, while still showcasing the dish's fundamental flavors of salt, acid, heat, and a little bit of sugar. For this gorgeous beet aguachile (which the chef nicknames "Vampiro" aguachile, for its deep purple-red color and for its inclusion of black garlic), Zepeda makes a bright, spicy broth out of beet juice. The unique, funky flavor from the black garlic and sweetness from the orange juice help balance the acidity of the lime juice. The beets and the broth can both be made a day ahead.

- 8 small red and orange beets (about 1 lb.), scrubbed
- 2 cups kosher salt
- ¾ cup olive oil
- ½ cup store-bought beet juice
- ⅓ cup fresh lime juice (from 2 medium limes)
- 2 medium bunches fresh cilantro (about 2 oz. each), divided
- 1 medium (2-oz.) shallot, roughly chopped (about ⅓ cup)
- ¼ cup rice vinegar
- 1 Tbsp. grated orange zest plus ⅓ cup fresh orange juice (from 1 orange)
- 1 small serrano chile (about ½ oz.), seeded (if desired) and roughly chopped (about 1 Tbsp.)
- 3 medium garlic cloves, roughly chopped (about 2 tsp.)
- 4 dried chiltepin or pequin chiles (unseeded), crushed
- 3 medium-size black garlic cloves, roughly chopped (optional)
- ½ tsp. fine sea salt
- 6 small radishes (about 3 oz.), thinly sliced (about ¹⁄₁₆ inch thick) on a mandoline
- 2 small Persian cucumbers (about 5 oz.), thinly diagonally sliced (about ¹⁄₁₆ to ⅛ inch thick)
- ½ cup thinly sliced red onion (from 1 small [5-oz.] onion)
- 8 (6-inch) tostada shells

1. Preheat oven to 400°F. Place beets in a rimmed baking dish; cover with kosher salt. Roast in preheated oven until beets are tender when poked with a skewer,

50 minutes to 1 hour. Remove from oven; let cool slightly, about 20 minutes. Uncover beets; using a paring knife or a paper towel, remove and discard skin. Cover beets; refrigerate until ready to use or up to 2 days.

2. While beets cook, combine oil, beet juice, lime juice, 1 cilantro bunch, shallot, vinegar, orange zest and juice, serrano chile, garlic, crushed chiltepin chiles, black garlic (if desired), and fine sea salt in a blender. Process until smooth, about 1 minute. Let stand, covered, in refrigerator 1 hour to allow flavors to meld. Pour through a fine wire-mesh strainer into a bowl, pressing on solids to extract all liquid; discard solids. Cover and refrigerate until completely chilled, at least 1 hour or up to 12 hours.

3. Remove beets from refrigerator. Cut lengthwise into quarters or sixths. Remove leaves from remaining cilantro bunch; discard stems. Ladle chilled beet broth onto a large plate, or ladle evenly into 4 shallow bowls. Arrange beet slices evenly among bowls. Top evenly with radishes, cucumbers, onion, and cilantro leaves. Serve with tostada shells. —CLAUDETTE ZEPEDA

MAKE AHEAD Beets can be prepared through step 1 up to 2 days in advance and stored in an airtight container in refrigerator.

WINE Earthy, skin-contact orange wine: 2020 COS Ramí

NOTE Black garlic is fermented garlic that adds an earthy, sweet, umami punch to dishes and is available at nuts.com. Chiltepin or pequin chiles can be found at Latin groceries and mexgrocer.com.

Aloo Matar (Indian Potato and Green Pea Curry)

TOTAL 55 MIN; SERVES 8

A blend of fresh ginger, garlic, and jalapeño chile forms the aromatic base for this vegetarian curry from chef Chintan Pandya of New York's Dhamaka. Studded with russet potatoes and sweet green peas, this Aloo Matar is rich and satisfying, with a touch of warm ghee stirred in just before serving.

- 2 Tbsp. neutral cooking oil (such as grapeseed oil or vegetable oil)
- 1 tsp. cumin seeds
- 1 large (12-oz.) red onion, finely chopped (about 1⅓ cups)

- 1½ Tbsp. finely chopped (and seeded, if desired) jalapeño chile (from 1 chile)
- 1 Tbsp. finely chopped peeled fresh ginger (from 1 [2-inch] piece ginger)
- 1 Tbsp. finely chopped garlic (from 3 garlic cloves)
- 1 Tbsp. ground coriander
- 2 tsp. ground turmeric
- 1½ tsp. red chile powder (preferably Deggi)
- 3 large (4-oz.) plum tomatoes, finely chopped (about 1½ cups)
- 2 Tbsp. kosher salt
- 2½ lb. russet potatoes, peeled and chopped into 1-inch pieces (about 6 cups)
- 4 cups hot water
- 1½ cups thawed frozen green peas
- ¼ cup chopped fresh cilantro
- 3 Tbsp. ghee

1. Heat oil in a large Dutch oven over medium-high. Stir in cumin seeds; cook, stirring constantly, until lightly toasted and aromatic, about 1 minute. Stir in onion; cook, stirring occasionally, until beginning to caramelize, about 8 minutes. Stir in jalapeño, ginger, and garlic; cook, stirring constantly, until fragrant, about 1 minute. Stir in coriander, turmeric, and chile powder; cook, stirring constantly, until mixture is fragrant and spices are lightly toasted, about 30 seconds. Stir in tomatoes and salt until fully combined and mixture forms a paste.

2. Stir potatoes into mixture in Dutch oven; cook, stirring often, 5 minutes. Stir in 4 cups hot water, ensuring potatoes are fully covered. Bring to a boil over medium-high. Reduce heat to medium; cook, stirring occasionally, until potatoes are almost fork-tender, about 12 minutes. Stir in green peas and cilantro; cook, stirring occasionally, until peas are heated through and potatoes are fork-tender, about 2 minutes. Stir in ghee until melted and combined, about 1 minute. Serve hot. —CHINTAN PANDYA, DHAMAKA, NEW YORK CITY

MAKE AHEAD Aloo matar may be kept covered and chilled for 3 days.

WINE Light-bodied cru Beaujolais: 2020 Clos de la Roilette Fleurie

NOTE Buy Deggi red chile powder at Indian grocery stores or at foodsofnations.com.

ALOO MATAR (INDIAN POTATO AND GREEN PEA CURRY)

STRAWBERRY AND
RADISH AGUACHILE

Strawberry and Radish Aguachile

ACTIVE 50 MIN; TOTAL 3 HR; SERVES 4

Aguachile, in literal translation, is 'chile water.' The dish originally comes from the Sonoran Sierras in Mexico, where ranching was the local trade, and was made with machaca (dried beef floss) that was rehydrated in water that got its kick from tiny, round, potent wild Chiltepin chiles. According to chef Claudette Zepeda, "anything can be an aguachile if you take creative freedom with it." For her colorful Strawberry Aguachile, Zepeda cooks strawberries in a double boiler to gently release their sweetness, creating a juice with vibrant color and flavor. When mixed with scallions, cucumber, anise-scented hoja santa, and citrus juices, the juice creates the perfect, punchy base for a strawberry and radish aguachile.

2½ lb. fresh strawberries, hulled and quartered lengthwise (about 7½ cups), divided

1 tsp. granulated sugar

1 tsp. fine sea salt, divided

1 small (5-oz.) red bell pepper

3 medium scallions (about 2 oz.), trimmed

1 small (1¼-oz.) bunch fresh cilantro

¼ cup chopped peeled Persian cucumber (from 1 small [2-oz.] cucumber)

¼ cup fresh lime juice (from 2 medium limes)

2 Tbsp. fresh lemon juice (from 1 medium lemon)

1 Tbsp. chopped fresh hoja santa (from 1 leaf) (optional)

5 dried chiltepin or pequin chiles (unseeded), crushed

1 bunch radishes (such as French breakfast or purple), thinly sliced lengthwise

Radish microgreens, for garnish

¼ tsp. flaky sea salt (such as Maldon)

1. Stir together 6 cups strawberries, sugar, and ½ teaspoon fine sea salt in a heatproof bowl set over a pan of simmering water. Cover and cook, undisturbed, until berries release their juices, about 1 hour. Pour through a fine wire-mesh strainer into a large bowl; let drain, stirring occasionally but not pressing down on berries, until no more liquid drips, about 30 minutes. Discard solids. (You should have 1½ cups strawberry juice.) Store juice, covered, in refrigerator until ready to use or up to 1 day.

2. While strawberries cook, preheat oven to broil with rack 6 inches from heat. Line a baking sheet with aluminum foil; place bell pepper on prepared baking sheet. Broil in preheated oven, turning occasionally, until charred on all sides, about 20 minutes. Remove from oven; transfer bell pepper to a medium bowl. Cover with plastic wrap; let stand 10 minutes. Uncover and place bell pepper on a clean cutting board. Peel off charred skin, and remove and discard stem and seeds. Roughly chop bell pepper. Set aside ⅓ cup chopped bell pepper; reserve remaining bell pepper for another use.

3. Using a knife, separate white and light green parts of scallion from dark green parts. Thinly slice dark green parts on a sharp diagonal, and set aside. Separate cilantro leaves from stems; reserve 4 or 5 stems (⅛ ounce), and discard remaining stems. Set cilantro leaves aside. Combine cucumber, lime juice, lemon juice, hoja santa (if using), chiltepin chiles, strawberry juice, chopped bell pepper, white and light green scallion parts, and reserved cilantro stems in a blender; process until smooth, about 1 minute. Pour through a fine wire-mesh strainer into a large bowl or a liquid measuring cup; discard solids. Stir in remaining ½ teaspoon fine sea salt. Cover with plastic wrap, and refrigerate until chilled, at least 1 hour or up to 12 hours.

4. Fill a bowl with ice water. Add dark green scallion parts, and let stand 30 seconds. Remove from water; drain and pat dry. Divide strawberry broth evenly among 4 bowls. Arrange remaining 1½ cups strawberries over broth. Arrange dark green scallion parts, radishes, and cilantro leaves or radish microgreens, as desired, around strawberries. Top evenly with flaky sea salt; serve immediately. —CLAUDETTE ZEPEDA

MAKE AHEAD Strawberry juice can be prepared up to 1 day in advance and stored in an airtight container in refrigerator. Strawberry broth can be prepared through step 3 up to 12 hours in advance and stored in an airtight container in refrigerator.

WINE Light, berry-scented rosé: 2021 Gérard Bertrand Source of Joy

NOTE Hoja santa is an herb, common in Central American cooking, with an anise-like flavor. It is available at most Latin grocery stores. Chiltepin or pequin chiles can be found online at mexgrocer.com.

SUMMER VEGETABLE BIBIMBAP

Chef Ji Hye Kim's bibimbap technique centers on cooking vegetables simply to showcase and preserve their natural colors and flavors. A 2021 F&W Best New Chef, Kim prepares each separately: salting and sautéing sturdy vegetables like squash and eggplant and blanching leafy greens. A robust yak gochujang, a sauce made with ground beef and Korean chile paste, gives the dish a sensational level of umami. For a quick and satisfying weeknight dinner, make the bibimbap toppings ahead of time, and then add them—and, if you like, a sunny-side-up egg—to freshly cooked rice, then stir them all together, and enjoy.

ACTIVE 1 HR 20 MIN; TOTAL 1 HR 40 MIN; SERVES 4

RICE

- 1½ cups uncooked premium short-grain white rice (such as Tamanishiki) (about 10¾ oz.)
- 1⅔ cups water
- ½ tsp. kosher salt
- ¼ tsp. toasted sesame oil

LEAFY GREENS

- 1 medium bunch young leafy greens (such as Swiss chard, kale, or mustard greens) (about 6 oz.)
- 2 qt. water
- 1¼ tsp. kosher salt, divided
- 1 tsp. toasted sesame oil
- Black pepper, to taste

HARDY VEGETABLES

- 3 medium-size (about 8-oz.) hardy summer vegetables (use a mix of 3 different types, such as cucumber, zucchini, yellow squash, or Japanese eggplant)

- 1½ tsp. kosher salt, divided, plus more to taste
- 3 to 4 Tbsp. neutral cooking oil (such as canola oil), divided
- 1½ tsp. finely chopped garlic (from 2 garlic cloves), divided
- 1 tsp. soy sauce (if using eggplant)

CHILES

- 1 small poblano chile (about 2¾ oz.)
- 2 to 3 small red Fresno chiles (about 2 oz.)
- 1 Tbsp. neutral cooking oil (such as canola oil)
- Kosher salt, to taste

YAK GOCHUJANG

- 2 oz. 97% lean ground beef
- 1 medium scallion (about ¼ oz.), thinly sliced (about 2 Tbsp.)
- 2 medium garlic cloves, finely chopped (about 1 tsp.)
- 3 Tbsp. toasted sesame oil, divided
- ⅔ cup gochujang (such as Assi)
- 2 Tbsp. cane sugar

- 1½ tsp. honey
- ¾ cup water

ADDITIONAL INGREDIENT

- 4 sunny-side-up eggs (optional)

1. Make the rice: Place rice in a medium bowl; rinse under cool water, using your fingers to gently stir. Drain. Repeat rinsing and draining until water runs clear, 5 to 6 times. If cooking on the stove, stir together rinsed rice, 1⅔ cups water, salt, and sesame oil in a large saucepan; let stand 30 minutes. Bring to a boil, uncovered, over medium-high. Boil, undisturbed, 4 minutes. Reduce heat to low; cover and cook until rice starts to smell faintly toasty, 10 to 15 minutes. Remove from heat; let rest, covered, 10 minutes. Gently fluff rice using a rice paddle or fork. Cover to keep warm until ready to serve. Alternatively, if using a rice cooker, combine rinsed rice, 1⅔ cups water, salt, and sesame oil in rice cooker; let stand 30 minutes. Close lid, and cook rice according to manufacturer's instructions. Once timer

STEP-BY-STEP

STEAM AND FLUFF RICE Rinse and steam short-grain white rice until tender and fragrant. Let rest, covered, 10 minutes before fluffing with a rice paddle or fork.

BLANCH AND SHOCK GREENS Cook leafy greens in boiling salted water until bright green, 15 to 30 seconds. Shock in ice water, drain well, and pat dry with paper towels.

SLICE AND SALT VEGETABLES Arrange sliced hardy vegetables on paper towel–lined baking sheets, keeping each type of vegetable separate, and sprinkle with salt.

SAUTÉ VEGETABLES AND CHILES Sauté prepared hardy vegetables and chiles in separate batches until softened, tender, and blistered.

signals rice is done, do not open lid; let rest 10 minutes. Gently fluff rice using a rice paddle or fork. Cover to keep warm until ready to serve.

2. While uncooked rice soaks, prepare the leafy greens: Remove thick stems from leaves; discard. Fill a large bowl with ice water; set aside. Bring 2 quarts water to a boil in a large pot over medium-high. Stir in 1 teaspoon salt. Add greens; cook, stirring occasionally, until bright green but not completely soft, 15 to 30 seconds. Using a spider or tongs, transfer greens to prepared ice water; let cool 2 minutes. Drain and squeeze out excess water. Pat greens dry with paper towels. If leaves are large, cut into 2-inch pieces. Combine greens, sesame oil, and remaining ¼ teaspoon salt in a medium bowl; toss well. Add black pepper to taste. Set aside.

3. While rice cooks, prepare the hardy vegetables: Cut each vegetable in half lengthwise; using a mandoline, thinly slice into half-moons (about ⅛ inch thick). Line a baking sheet with paper towels. Arrange about 1 cup of the vegetable slices in a single layer on paper towels. (Keep each type of vegetable separate.) Sprinkle slices on paper towel with ¼ teaspoon salt. Top with a layer of paper towels. Repeat process on separate baking sheets with remaining vegetables and salt. Alternatively, stack layers of salted vegetables on a single baking sheet with paper towels between layers. Let stand 10 minutes. Press firmly to remove excess moisture.

4. Working in 3 batches, heat 1 tablespoon neutral oil (or 2 tablespoons oil, if using eggplant) in a large nonstick skillet over medium-high. Add 1 type of vegetable slices; cook, stirring constantly, until just beginning to soften, 10 to 15 seconds. Add ½ teaspoon garlic, and sprinkle with salt to taste (or add 1 teaspoon soy sauce for eggplant). Cook, stirring constantly, until garlic is fragrant and vegetables are crisp-tender, 10 to 15 seconds. Immediately spread sautéed vegetables in a thin layer on a baking sheet to cool quickly. Set aside. Repeat cooking process with remaining neutral oil, vegetables, garlic, and salt, keeping each type of vegetable separate and wiping skillet clean after each batch.

5. Make the chiles: Remove stems from poblano and Fresno chiles. Cut chiles in half lengthwise, remove seeds, and cut crosswise into thin slices. Heat neutral oil in a large nonstick skillet over medium-high. Add poblano and Fresno slices, and sprinkle with salt to taste. Cook, stirring constantly, until chile skins are lightly blistered and chiles are crisp-tender, 20 to 30 seconds. Spread in a thin layer on a baking sheet to cool quickly. Set aside.

6. Make the yak gochujang: Combine ground beef, scallion, garlic, and 1½ tablespoons sesame oil in a small bowl. Using your hands, mix until well combined. Heat a large nonstick skillet over medium. Add beef mixture; cook, stirring often, until mostly browned, 1 to 2 minutes. Stir in gochujang, sugar, honey, and remaining 1½ tablespoons sesame oil. Cook, stirring often, until slightly thickened, about 5 minutes. Stir in ¾ cup water. Cook, stirring often, until mixture has reduced to about 1½ cups and is thicker than gravy but thinner than peanut butter, 3 to 5 minutes. Set aside, and let cool 10 minutes. Yak gochujang can be stored in an airtight container in refrigerator up to 3 days.

7. Divide rice evenly among the centers of 4 large serving bowls (about 1 cup each). Arrange about ¼ cup leafy greens, ¼ cup hardy vegetables, and ¼ cup chiles in a circle around rice in each bowl. Spoon about ¼ cup yak gochujang in center of each bowl. (Reserve remaining yak gochujang for another use.) If desired, top each bowl with 1 sunny-side-up egg. Gently stir contents of each bowl with chopsticks, and serve with a spoon. —JI HYE KIM, MISS KIM, ANN ARBOR, MICHIGAN

ARRANGE BOWL Arrange prepared vegetables in a circle around rice in shallow serving bowls. Top rice with yak gochujang and, if desired, a sunny-side-up egg.

MIX AND SERVE Using chopsticks, gently stir to combine the contents of the serving bowl. Serve bibimbap with a spoon.

VAGHARELI CORN FLAUTAS
WITH CHUTNEY CREMA

Vaghareli Corn Flautas with Chutney Crema

TOTAL 1 HR 15 MIN; SERVES 4

The corn in this recipe gets a punch of flavor by being sautéed in oil that has had spices bloomed in it. "Vaghar in Gujarati means to sauté, and is used to refer to oil that has had spices tempered in it," explains Hetal Vasavada. "This technique is also called chhonk, tadka, and poron, and has many other names in other Indian languages. Typically, vaghar is added to a dish after it's been done cooking (as with a dal). However, when you reverse the method and temper the oil and spices first and then add ingredients into it, it's referred to as vaghareli." For her inspired twist on Mexican flautas, Vasavada makes vaghareli makai (corn). The spiced kernels are combined with mild cheese, rolled up in tortillas, and deep-fried. Serve the flautas piled high with colorful garnishes alongside a ginger-lime avocado crema for a vibrant summer entertaining staple.

CHUTNEY CREMA

- 1 (6-oz.) avocado, halved, pitted, and peeled
- 2 cups packed fresh cilantro leaves (about 2 oz.)
- ½ cup packed fresh mint leaves
- ½ cup crema or sour cream
- ½ cup water
- 3 Tbsp. fresh lime juice (from 2 limes)
- 1 (½-inch) piece fresh ginger, peeled
- 1 small (1-oz.) fresh jalapeño, stemmed and, if desired, seeded
- 1 tsp. kosher salt

VAGHARELI MAKAI

- ½ cup plus 2 Tbsp. canola oil, divided
- ½ tsp. black mustard seeds (see Note)
- 10 fresh curry leaves (see Note)
- ¾ tsp. ground cumin
- ¾ tsp. ground coriander
- ¾ tsp. cayenne pepper
- ½ tsp. ground turmeric
- 1½ cups fresh corn kernels (about 8 oz.) (from 2 [7-oz.] ears)
- 3 garlic cloves, minced (about 1 Tbsp.)
- 1 Tbsp. minced fresh ginger (from 1 [2-inch] piece peeled ginger)
- 1 Tbsp. plus 1 tsp. fresh lime juice (from 2 limes)
- ½ tsp. kosher salt
- ¼ tsp. black pepper
- 8 oz. queso Oaxaca or mozzarella cheese, shredded (about 2 cups)
- 12 (5- to 6-inch) corn tortillas
   Optional toppings: Shredded iceberg lettuce, chopped red onions, chopped tomatoes, chopped fresh cilantro, Cotija cheese, and lime wedges

1. **Make the chutney crema:** Reserve 1 avocado half for another use. Combine cilantro, mint, crema, ½ cup water, lime juice, ginger, jalapeño, salt, and remaining avocado half in a blender. Process until completely smooth, about 2 minutes. Cover and chill until ready to serve, up to 2 hours.

2. **Make the vaghareli makai:** Heat 2 tablespoons oil in a large skillet over medium-high. Add black mustard seeds. Once they start to sputter, reduce heat to low; add curry leaves, cumin, coriander, cayenne, and turmeric; cook, stirring constantly, 10 seconds. Add corn; increase heat to medium, and cook, stirring often, until corn is tender, about 6 minutes. Add garlic and ginger; cook, stirring constantly, until fragrant, 1 to 2 minutes. Stir in lime juice, salt, and black pepper. Remove from heat. Transfer mixture to a large bowl; let cool 3 minutes. Stir in shredded cheese until combined. Set aside.

3. Place tortillas on a microwavable plate, and cover with a damp paper towel. Microwave on high until tortillas are warm and pliable, about 45 seconds. Working with 1 tortilla at a time and keeping remaining tortillas covered with damp paper towel, place 3 tablespoons corn-cheese mixture on center of 1 tortilla. Tightly roll into a cigar shape, and secure with a wooden toothpick. Repeat process with remaining tortillas and corn-cheese mixture.

4. Heat remaining ½ cup oil in a 12-inch nonstick skillet over medium-high. Working in about 3 batches, gently place filled tortillas, seam side down, in skillet. (Be sure not to crowd the skillet.) Reduce heat to medium, and fry until golden brown, 5 to 6 minutes per batch, using tongs to turn flautas often so they cook evenly. Transfer flautas to a wire rack to drain. Remove and discard any solids from oil in skillet. Repeat process with remaining filled tortillas.

5. Remove wooden picks from flautas. Arrange on a platter; drizzle with chutney crema, and top with desired toppings.

—HETAL VASAVADA, MILK & CARDAMOM

MAKE AHEAD Chutney crema can be stored in an airtight container in refrigerator up to 2 hours.

WINE Lightly oaky California Chardonnay: 2021 Fess Parker Santa Barbara County

NOTE Find black mustard seeds and curry leaves at foodsofnations.com.

Watermelon Curry

ACTIVE 30 MIN; TOTAL 45 MIN; SERVES 4

Wow guests by bringing this sweet and savory side to your next summer picnic. Sharp, pungent ajwain seeds permeate the curry with a thyme-like earthiness and complexity. Nigella seeds impart a slight bitterness and toasty onion flavor to play off the sweet melon.

1 small (4-lb.) seedless watermelon

2 Tbsp. canola oil

1 tsp. cumin seeds

½ tsp. ajwain seeds

½ tsp. nigella seeds

2 chiles de árbol

2 tsp. finely chopped peeled fresh ginger

1½ tsp. finely chopped garlic

1½ tsp. kosher salt, plus more to taste

½ tsp. ground turmeric

1 cup water

1½ Tbsp. chopped fresh cilantro

1. Using a sharp knife or a vegetable peeler, remove outer dark green skin from watermelon, and discard. Cut away pale green rind from red flesh, and chop rind into 1- to 2-inch pieces to measure about 4 cups (about 1 pound); place in a medium bowl, and set aside. Chop red flesh into 1- to 2-inch cubes to measure about 7 cups (about 1 pound, 6 ounces); set aside in a separate medium bowl.

2. Heat oil in a Dutch oven over medium-high until shimmering. Add cumin seeds, ajwain seeds, and nigella seeds; cook, stirring constantly, until fragrant, about 15 seconds. Add chiles, ginger, and garlic; cook, stirring constantly, until fragrant and garlic just picks up a little color, 20 to 30 seconds. Add pale green rind, salt, and turmeric. Reduce heat to medium; cook, stirring occasionally, until rind starts to deepen in color, about 5 minutes. Add 1 cup water; cover and reduce heat to medium-low. Cook, undisturbed, 15 minutes. If rind has not softened, cook up to 5 additional minutes, stirring and checking for softness occasionally. Uncover and gently stir in red flesh. Bring to a boil over high. Boil, stirring occasionally, until flesh has absorbed some liquid and rind has completely softened,

about 5 minutes. Remove from heat. Let stand, stirring occasionally, 5 to 10 minutes to allow watermelon to marinate. Add additional salt to taste. Stir in cilantro, and serve. —VISHWESH BHATT

WINE Fragrant, floral rosé: 2020 Bonny Doon Vin Gris de Cigare

NOTE You can find ajwain and nigella seeds online at spicewallabrand.com or at your neighborhood Indian grocery store.

Ratatouille

ACTIVE 1 HR 35 MIN; TOTAL 2 HR 5 MIN; SERVES 6

Rebekah Peppler's ratatouille relies on a simple technique for creating a richly flavorful dish: cooking each vegetable separately. After just a few minutes in the pan, the vegetables release water, deepen in flavor, and become just tender enough to begin to break down. Finishing the stew with a generous portion of rosé melds the flavors together.

2 medium (1-lb.) eggplants, cut into ½-inch pieces (about 11 cups)

2½ tsp. fine sea salt (such as La Baleine), divided, plus more to taste

¾ cup mild extra-virgin olive oil, divided, plus more as needed

2 medium (8-oz.) zucchini, cut into ½-inch pieces (about 3½ cups)

2 medium-size (8-oz.) yellow onions, cut into ½-inch pieces (about 2⅔ cups)

2 medium-size (8-oz.) red bell peppers, cut into ½-inch pieces (about 2½ cups)

4 medium garlic cloves, finely chopped (about 1 Tbsp. plus 1 tsp.)

3 small beefsteak tomatoes or heirloom tomatoes (about 1 lb.), cut into ½-inch pieces (about 2½ cups)

6 to 8 (4-inch) basil sprigs, to taste

Pinch of crushed red pepper (optional)

¼ cup rosé

3 Tbsp. premium extra-virgin olive oil (such as Laudemio), plus more if desired

1. Place eggplant pieces in a colander. Sprinkle eggplant with 2 teaspoons salt, and toss to combine. Let stand 20 minutes.

Working in batches, pat eggplant dry with paper towels. Heat ¼ cup mild olive oil in a large, deep skillet over medium. Add eggplant, and cook, stirring often, until eggplant is tender but not falling apart, 12 to 15 minutes, adding 1 to 2 tablespoons additional oil as needed if eggplant sticks to bottom of skillet. Remove from heat. Transfer eggplant to a large bowl. Do not wipe skillet clean.

2. Return skillet to heat over medium, and add 2 tablespoons mild olive oil. Add zucchini, and cook, stirring often, until zucchini is very tender and just turns translucent, about 10 minutes. Stir in ⅛ teaspoon salt. Remove from heat, and transfer zucchini to bowl with eggplant. Do not wipe skillet clean. Return skillet to heat over medium, and add 2 tablespoons mild olive oil. Add onions, and cook, stirring occasionally, until softened, 6 to 8 minutes. Add bell peppers, 2 tablespoons mild olive oil, and ⅛ teaspoon salt, and cook, stirring occasionally, until bell peppers are very tender, 10 to 15 minutes. Stir in garlic, and cook, stirring often, 2 minutes. Remove from heat. Transfer bell pepper mixture to bowl with eggplant mixture. Do not wipe skillet clean.

3. Return skillet to heat over medium. Add tomatoes, basil sprigs, crushed red pepper (if using), remaining ¼ teaspoon salt, and remaining 2 tablespoons mild olive oil. Cook, stirring occasionally, until tomatoes break down and most tomato juices evaporate, 10 to 15 minutes. Stir in rosé; cook, stirring often, until rosé is absorbed, about 2 minutes. Return reserved eggplant mixture to skillet; cook over medium, stirring often to prevent sticking, until flavors meld and mixture is creamy but textured, 12 to 15 minutes. Remove from heat. Drizzle ratatouille with premium olive oil. Let cool to room temperature, about 30 minutes. Season with additional salt to taste. Remove and discard basil sprigs. Serve warm or at room temperature with a drizzle of premium olive oil over each serving, if desired. —REBEKAH PEPPLER

MAKE AHEAD Ratatouille may be stored in an airtight container in refrigerator up to 3 days.

WINE Lively Languedoc rosé: 2021 Gérard Bertrand Côte des Roses

RATATOUILLE

SAGANAKI HALLOUMI
(CYPRIOT FRIED HALLOUMI)

Saganaki Halloumi (Cypriot Fried Halloumi)

⏱ TOTAL 45 MIN; SERVES 2

Halloumi cheese is fried in clarified butter, then brushed in a spiced honey and served with lemon yogurt, brandy-basted nectarines, and fresh tomatoes in this sweet and savory appetizer from Christian Hernandez, chef de cuisine of March in Houston. Sommeliers June Rodil and Mark Sayre pair a bottle of 2020 Benanti Etna Bianco, from Sicily, with this vibrant dish. "Carricante inherently has peachy stone-fruit and melon notes and a texture that goes really well with the squeaky Saganaki Halloumi," they say. "It's bright and fresh, with a lovely coastal salinity."

SPICED HONEY

- ½ cup honey
- 6 rosemary sprigs
- 2 whole coriander seeds
- ½ tsp. kosher salt
- ½ tsp. black pepper

LEMON YOGURT

- ⅓ cup plain whole-milk yogurt
- 2 tsp. grated lemon zest plus 1 Tbsp. fresh lemon juice (from 1 lemon)
- ¼ tsp. kosher salt

NECTARINE

- 2 tsp. clarified butter or neutral cooking oil (such as canola, grapeseed, or vegetable oil)
- 1 medium (6-oz.) nectarine, halved and pitted
- 2 Tbsp. (1 oz.) brandy

HALLOUMI

- ¾ cup clarified butter (from 1 [7½-oz.] jar) or neutral cooking oil (such as canola, grapeseed, or vegetable oil)
- 1 (4-oz.) Halloumi cheese block (2-×2-×3-inch) (such as Alambra), drained
- ¼ cup finely chopped fresh mint
- 1 Tbsp. finely chopped fresh oregano

ADDITIONAL INGREDIENTS

- ¼ cup Sun Gold or multicolored cherry tomatoes, halved lengthwise (about ⅓ cup)
- 2 Tbsp. extra-virgin olive oil
- Flaky sea salt, for garnish

1. Make the spiced honey: Combine honey, rosemary sprigs, coriander seeds, salt, and pepper in a small saucepan; cook over low, stirring occasionally, 15 minutes. Pour through a fine wire-mesh strainer into a small heatproof bowl. Discard solids. Let spiced honey cool 15 minutes.

2. Make the lemon yogurt: While spiced honey cooks, whisk together yogurt, lemon zest and juice, and salt in a small bowl. Cover and refrigerate until ready to serve.

3. Make the nectarine: Heat clarified butter in a medium-size nonstick skillet over medium-high. Brush cut sides of nectarine halves evenly with some of the brandy. Place nectarine halves, cut side down, in skillet, and brush tops evenly with some of the brandy. Cook, undisturbed, until cut sides are golden, 2 to 3 minutes. Flip nectarine halves, and cook until golden, 1 to

2 minutes, brushing liberally with brandy every 10 to 15 seconds. Remove from heat. Transfer nectarine halves to a cutting board. Cut into bite-size oblique pieces, and set aside.

4. Make the Halloumi: Wipe skillet clean, and add clarified butter. Heat over medium until butter shimmers. Cut Halloumi evenly into 2 (1-×1-×3-inch) pieces, and pat dry with paper towels. Add cheese pieces to skillet, and cook, turning occasionally, until golden brown on all sides, 3 to 5 minutes. Remove from heat. Transfer cheese to a plate. Stir together mint and oregano in a shallow dish. Spread 2 tablespoons spiced honey on all sides of cheese. (Reserve remaining spiced honey for another use.) Dip cheese in mint mixture until evenly coated, pressing gently to adhere. Cut each cheese piece in half lengthwise to create 4 (1-×½-×3-inch) pieces.

5. Divide lemon yogurt evenly among 2 shallow bowls. Top evenly with cheese pieces. Arrange nectarine halves evenly on and around cheese. Arrange tomato halves evenly on and around cheese. Drizzle evenly with extra-virgin olive oil, and garnish with flaky sea salt. Serve immediately. —CHRISTIAN HERNANDEZ, CHEF DE CUISINE, MARCH, HOUSTON

MAKE AHEAD Spiced honey can be stored in an airtight container at room temperature up to 6 months.

NOTE Halloumi can be found at most Middle Eastern markets and online at parthenonfoods.com.

Carrot Aguachile with Trout Roe

TOTAL 20 MIN; SERVES 4

Claudette Zepeda uses fresh carrot juice as the base for this aguachile, which is complemented by fresh ginger, spicy habanero, and scallions to amp up the flavor of the juice. Thin strips of carrot and cucumber are mixed and topped with salty smoked roe, thinly sliced red onion, and roasted cashews for a dish with deep layers of flavor and complex textures. For a vegan alternative, replace the trout roe with 1 bunch of roasted or grilled carrots.

- 1 (½-oz.) habanero chile, stemmed
- 3 medium scallions (about 2 oz.), trimmed
- 1 cup store-bought carrot juice
- 1 (1-inch) piece fresh ginger, peeled and chopped (about 1½ Tbsp.)
- ½ tsp. fine sea salt
- 3 Tbsp. fresh lemon juice (from 1 medium lemon)
- 2 Tbsp. fresh lime juice (from 1 medium lime)
- 2 small multicolored carrots (about 2 oz.), scrubbed
- 2 medium (about 4-oz.) Persian cucumbers
- ½ cup smoked trout roe
- ¼ cup thinly sliced red onion (from 1 small [5-oz.] onion)
- 3 Tbsp. roasted cashews, roughly crushed

1. Cut habanero in half lengthwise. If desired, remove seeds. Set aside 1 habanero half. Reserve remaining habanero half for another use. Using a knife, separate white and light green parts of scallions from dark green parts. Thinly slice dark green parts on a sharp diagonal, and set aside. Combine carrot juice, ginger, salt, habanero half, and white and light green scallion parts in a blender; process until completely smooth, about 30 seconds. Pour through a fine wire-mesh strainer into an airtight container, pressing solids in strainer to extract liquid; discard solids. Add lemon and lime juices, and stir to combine. Cover carrot broth, and refrigerate until ready to use or up to 12 hours.

2. Fill a large bowl with ice water, and set aside. Using a mandoline or vegetable peeler, thinly slice carrots lengthwise. (You'll have about ½ cup loosely packed slices.) Transfer carrot slices to ice water to shock. Thinly slice cucumbers lengthwise using mandoline. (You'll have about ½ cup loosely packed slices.) Transfer to bowl with carrots in ice water to shock. Let carrots and cucumbers stand 30 seconds. Remove from ice water, and transfer to a large bowl. Add refrigerated carrot broth, and toss lightly to coat. Place reserved dark green scallion parts in ice water, and let stand 30 seconds. Remove from water.

3. Divide carrot broth mixture evenly among 4 shallow bowls, or spoon into 1 large bowl. Dollop roe evenly around carrot and cucumber slices. Sprinkle evenly with dark green scallion parts, onion, and cashews. Serve immediately.
—CLAUDETTE ZEPEDA

MAKE AHEAD Carrot broth can be made up to 12 hours in advance and stored in an airtight container in refrigerator.

WINE Juicy, tart Sauvignon Blanc: 2021 Craggy Range Marlborough

NOTE Smoked trout roe is available online at paramountcaviar.com.

Halloumi-and-Vegetable Skewers with Pomegranate-Tahini Sauce

ACTIVE 25 MIN; TOTAL 1 HR 5 MIN; SERVES 4

Pomegranate molasses is the secret ingredient in this simple marinade. Its punchy, sweet, earthy notes add long-cooked depth of flavor to cheese and vegetable skewers in just 30 minutes of marination, with pleasantly bitter tahini rounding things out. The pomegranate-tahini marinade goes the extra mile as a final drizzle for the skewers; thinned with fresh orange juice, it supplies the perfect, sweet-savory finish to the dish. Be sure to soak wooden skewers in water before threading on the cheese and vegetables to prevent flare-ups while grilling or broiling.

- ½ cup tahini, well stirred
- 6 Tbsp. extra-virgin olive oil
- 10 Tbsp. fresh orange juice (from 2 oranges), as needed, divided
- 2 Tbsp. pomegranate molasses
- 1½ tsp. kosher salt
- ½ tsp. black pepper
- 1 medium (8-oz.) bell pepper, cut into 1-inch pieces (about 1½ cups)
- 1 small (7-oz.) red onion, cut into 10 (½-inch-thick) wedges
- 1 cup cherry tomatoes
- 1 lb. halloumi cheese, cut into 1-inch cubes
  Cooked white rice and chopped fresh cilantro, for serving

1. Place 10 (8-inch) wooden skewers in a large bowl or sealed bag with water, and let soak 20 minutes; remove from water.

2. Whisk together tahini, oil, 5 tablespoons orange juice, pomegranate molasses, salt, and black pepper in a medium bowl until emulsified and smooth. Measure ½ cup sauce into a small bowl; cover and store in refrigerator until ready to use or up to 5 days. Thread bell pepper, onion, tomatoes, and halloumi evenly onto wooden skewers. Place skewers on a large baking sheet, and brush evenly with remaining sauce (about ½ cup) in medium bowl. Let stand at room temperature at least 30 minutes or up to 1 hour.

3. Preheat grill to medium-high (400°F to 450°F). Place skewers on lightly oiled grates; grill, covered, turning occasionally, until tender and lightly charred, 8 to 10 minutes. Transfer to a platter with rice.

4. Stir up to remaining 5 tablespoons orange juice into reserved ½ cup sauce as needed to reach desired consistency. Drizzle over vegetable skewers and rice; sprinkle with cilantro. Serve immediately.
—KELSEY YOUNGMAN

MAKE AHEAD Sauce can be refrigerated in an airtight container up to 3 days.

WINE Tart, minerally Greek white: 2020 Gai'a Monograph Assyrtiko

NOTE Alternatively, to broil the skewers: Cover ends of skewers with aluminum foil to prevent burning. Arrange skewers on a greased baking sheet. Broil 4½ inches from heat source until browned, about 8 minutes, flipping skewers halfway through broiling time.

NOTE Pomegranate molasses can be found at foodsofnations.com.

HALLOUMI-AND-VEGETABLE
SKEWERS WITH POMEGRANATE-
TAHINI SAUCE

CURRIED PUMPKIN AND BUSS
UP SHUT (PARATHA ROTI)

Curried Pumpkin and Buss Up Shut (Paratha Roti)

ACTIVE 2 HR 20 MIN; TOTAL 2 HR 45 MIN, PLUS 2 HR RESTING; SERVES 6

Chef Nina Compton's Curried Pumpkin is packed with warm spices, aromatic ginger and rich coconut milk. Buss up shut gets its name from "busted-up shirt," which describes the flatbread's torn, crinkled texture, perfect for sopping up flavorful curry. Drizzle the curry with pumpkin seed salsa for crunch and punch of garlic.

BUSS UP SHUT

- 3 cups (about 12¾ oz.) plus 4 Tbsp. all-purpose flour, divided, plus more for dusting
- 2 tsp. baking powder
- 1½ tsp. kosher salt, plus more to taste
- 1 tsp. granulated sugar
- 1¼ cups warm water (95°F to 110°F)
- 3 Tbsp. ghee, divided, plus more for brushing
- 6 Tbsp. unsalted butter (3 oz.), softened, divided

CURRIED PUMPKIN

- ½ cup loosely packed fresh curry leaves (about ⅜ oz.) (from 3 curry sprigs)
- 2 (3-inch) cinnamon sticks
- 10 whole star anise (about 2 Tbsp.)
- 2 Tbsp. coriander seeds
- 1 Tbsp. cardamom pods
- ½ Tbsp. whole cloves
- ¼ cup canola oil
- 1 medium-size (8-oz.) yellow onion, thinly sliced lengthwise (about 1½ cups)
- ¼ cup finely chopped peeled fresh ginger (from 1 [1½-oz.] piece ginger)
- ¼ cup peeled and grated fresh turmeric root
- 2 fresh habanero chiles (about 1 oz.)
- 2 Tbsp. garam masala (preferably Spicewalla)
- 8 cups chopped peeled pumpkin (1- to 2-inch chunks) (from 1 small [4- to 5-lb.] pumpkin)
- 2 cups fresh callaloo leaves (about 2 oz.), trimmed and cut into 1-inch pieces
- 1 Tbsp. kosher salt, plus more to taste
- 4 cups vegetable stock
- 1 (14-oz.) can coconut milk, well shaken and stirred

PUMPKIN SEED SALSA

- ½ cup finely chopped garlic (from 20 garlic cloves)
- ½ cup olive oil
- ¼ cup toasted pepitas
- 2 tsp. grated lemon zest plus 1 tsp. fresh lemon juice (from 1 lemon)
- 2 garlic cloves, grated using a Microplane (about 1 tsp.)
- ¼ tsp. kosher salt

1. Make the buss up shut: Whisk together 3 cups flour, baking powder, salt, and sugar in a large bowl. Make a well in center; add 1¼ cups warm water and 1 tablespoon ghee. Stir using a wooden spoon to bring dough together. Knead dough using your hands until a soft, sticky dough forms, about 1 minute. Using floured hands, divide dough evenly into 6 pieces (about 4 ounces each). Cover with a clean towel; let rest until dough is easy to use and stretch, 15 to 30 minutes.

2. Lightly brush a rimmed baking sheet with remaining 2 tablespoons ghee. Place 1 dough piece on a heavily floured work surface, and roll out to an 8- to 9-inch round. (They do not need to be perfect circles.) Using your fingers or a small offset palette knife, rub 1 tablespoon butter on surface of dough; lightly sprinkle with 2 teaspoons flour. Using a knife, cut a straight line starting from outer edge to center of circle to make a radius. Pick up dough at lower outer edge of where you made the cut, and roll dough clockwise, using your hands, into a tight cone shape. (The cone will be somewhat flat in shape.) Pinch the ends into the bottom (wider part) of the cone. Place the bottom (wider part) of the cone on the work surface, and push cone tip down into cone to create a volcano-like shape, folding the cone tip into the center until the dough is pushed down to an about 2-inch mound. Press down lightly to flatten the dough. Transfer to prepared greased baking sheet, and brush surface with ghee to prevent dough from drying out. Repeat process with remaining 5 pieces of dough, butter, and flour. Cover baking sheet with plastic wrap. Let dough rest in a cool (about 70°F) place for 2 hours.

3. Heat a griddle, nonstick skillet, or tawa over medium. Lightly flour a work surface. Uncover dough. Gently flatten each dough mound, and roll each out into a 10-inch round, starting from center of each mound and working outward, rotating the dough each time you roll it to help form a perfect circle. (The dough rounds should be thin at the edges.)

4. Working with 1 dough round at a time, gently transfer rolled dough to heated griddle. Cook until bubbles or air pockets appear on top of dough, about 4 minutes. Heavily brush top of dough, including edges, with ghee, oil, or melted butter. Flip and cook until golden, puffed, and flaky in parts, about 3 minutes. To create a torn texture, use 2 spatulas to crush paratha inward from outer edges while still on the griddle. Alternatively, wrap paratha in a clean cloth, and shake it. Sprinkle buss up shut with additional salt to taste, if desired. Place buss up shut in a bowl or on a platter. Cover with a clean towel to keep warm until ready to serve. Repeat process with remaining dough.

5. Make the curried pumpkin: Cut a square of cheesecloth about 8 inches wide. Place curry leaves, cinnamon sticks, star anise, coriander, cardamom, and whole cloves in center of cheesecloth. Tie sachet closed with kitchen twine. Heat oil in a large pot over medium. Add onion, ginger, turmeric, and habaneros; cook, stirring often, until onion starts to soften, about 5 minutes. Add garam masala and spice sachet; cook, stirring often, 5 minutes. Stir in pumpkin, callaloo, and salt. Stir in stock and coconut milk. Increase heat to medium-high, and bring to a simmer. Cover and reduce heat to low. Cook until pumpkin and callaloo are tender, about 20 minutes. Remove and discard spice sachet. Taste for seasoning, and add additional salt if desired.

6. Make the pumpkin seed salsa: While curried pumpkin simmers, place chopped garlic and oil in a small saucepan. Bring to a simmer over low. Simmer, undisturbed, until garlic just starts to turn golden, about 10 minutes. Remove from heat. Let cool to room temperature, about 20 minutes. Fold in pepitas, lemon zest and juice, grated garlic, and salt. Serve pumpkin seed salsa alongside curried pumpkin and buss up shut. —NINA COMPTON

MAKE AHEAD Buss up shut dough can be rolled into spirals up to 2 hours in advance.

WINE Earthy, spicy natural red: 2020 Matassa Tattouine Rouge

NOTE Callaloo, popular in Caribbean cooking, is a leafy green with a strong, spinach-like flavor. Look for it at Caribbean grocery stores.

Enmoladas de Calabaza

ACTIVE 1 HR 25 MIN; TOTAL 2 HR 30 MIN;
SERVES 6

To make these Enmoladas de Calabaza, lightly fried tortillas are generously stuffed with tender strands of spaghetti squash and then covered in a concentrated kabocha squash mole. The kabocha mole is seasoned with dried chiles and five-spice powder, which lend a delicate smokiness to the savory sauce. "The inspiration for these enmoladas was spaghetti squash, which I love using in the fall," says chef T.J. Steele of Claro in Brooklyn, who shared his recipe with Food & Wine. "I don't find that a lot of dishes highlight it, especially as an entrée. It felt like the perfect ingredient to use for a filling for enmoladas, since the individual strands offer a lot of texture. Kabocha squash also comes into play in the mole, which has spices that are a great complement and also remind me of fall — they give the dish a warming quality. There are also unusual flavors and textures in the garnishes to keep every bite exciting. This recipe is also completely vegetarian, and if you want to make it vegan, you can swap out the crema for coconut yogurt."

- 3 medium-size fresh tomatillos (about 8 oz.), husks removed
- 1 medium spaghetti squash (about 3½ lb.)
- ¼ cup plus 1 Tbsp. kosher salt, divided, plus more to taste
- ½ cup plus 2 Tbsp. refined coconut oil, divided
- 1 medium-size dried guajillo chile (about ⅛ oz.), stemmed and seeded
- 1 small dried ancho chile (about ¼ oz.), stemmed and seeded
- 3 cups plus 2 tsp. warm water, divided
- ½ cup thinly sliced yellow onion (from 1 [6-oz.] onion)
- 2 medium garlic cloves
- 1 Tbsp. golden raisins
- 1 fresh bay leaf
- 1 tsp. five-spice powder
- ½ tsp. dried Mexican oregano
- 2½ cups cubed (about 1-inch pieces) peeled kabocha squash (about 12 oz.) (from 1 small [2-lb.] squash)
- 1 Tbsp. masa harina (such as Masienda)
- ¾ tsp. demerara sugar
- ¾ tsp. white vinegar
- 12 (5½-inch) yellow corn tortillas
- Mexican crema or sour cream
- Fresh cilantro leaves
- Salted roasted pepitas

1. Preheat oven to broil with 1 rack in middle position and 1 rack 6 inches from heat. Place tomatillos on a rimmed baking sheet lined with aluminum foil. Broil in preheated oven 6 inches from heat, turning occasionally, until blackened in spots, 10 to 15 minutes. Set aside.

2. Reduce oven temperature to 350°F. Prick spaghetti squash all over with a fork. Spread ¼ cup salt in a small mound on a rimmed baking sheet. Place spaghetti squash on salt mound to prevent it from rolling. Roast on center rack at 350°F until squash is softened and a thermometer inserted in thickest portion of squash flesh registers 160°F, 1 hour to 1 hour and 15 minutes. Set aside; let cool 30 minutes. Do not turn oven off.

3. While squash roasts, heat 2 tablespoons coconut oil in a large saucepan over medium. Add guajillo and ancho chiles; cook, turning often, until fragrant and puffed, 2 to 3 minutes. Remove from heat. Transfer chiles to a small bowl; add 1 cup warm water, and set aside. Reserve oil in pan.

4. Heat reserved oil in saucepan over medium-high. Add onion; cook, stirring often, until softened and just beginning to brown, 3 to 5 minutes. Add garlic, raisins, bay leaf, five-spice powder, and oregano; cook, stirring constantly, until mixture is fragrant and raisins are puffed, about 30 seconds. Stir in kabocha squash, broiled tomatillos, 2 teaspoons salt, and 2 cups warm water. Drain soaked chiles, and add to squash mixture in pan; discard chile soaking liquid. Bring mixture in pan to a boil over medium-high. Reduce heat to low; simmer, uncovered, stirring occasionally, until squash is very tender, 20 to 25 minutes.

5. Using your fingers, knead together masa harina and remaining 2 teaspoons warm water in a small bowl until smooth and well combined, about 1 minute. Crumble mixture into kabocha squash mixture in saucepan. Stir in sugar. Remove from heat. Using an immersion blender, process mixture in pan until smooth, about 2 minutes. Stir in vinegar, and season with salt to taste. Set kabocha mole aside.

6. Cut cooled spaghetti squash in half lengthwise. Remove and discard seeds. Using a fork, scrape flesh into separate strands, and release from skin. Transfer 4 cups squash flesh to a medium bowl; add remaining 1 teaspoon salt, and toss to combine. Set aside. Discard squash skins; reserve any remaining squash flesh for another use.

7. Heat remaining ½ cup coconut oil in a small skillet over medium until melted. Working with 1 tortilla at a time, fry tortillas until softened, 5 to 10 seconds per side. Drain tortillas on paper towels.

8. Working with 1 fried tortilla at a time, top each tortilla with ⅓ cup spaghetti squash flesh; roll up tortilla, and place, seam side down, in a 9- × 13-inch baking dish. Pour 2 cups kabocha mole evenly over rolled enmoladas in baking dish; reserve remaining kabocha mole. Bake, uncovered, at 350°F until heated through, about 20 minutes.

9. Spoon about ¼ cup reserved kabocha mole onto each of 6 plates, and top each with 2 enmoladas. Drizzle enmoladas with crema, and garnish with cilantro and pepitas. Serve immediately. —T.J. STEELE, CLARO, BROOKLYN

MAKE AHEAD Kabocha mole can be made up to 3 days in advance and stored in an airtight container in refrigerator. Let stand at room temperature 30 minutes before assembling enmoladas.

BEER Toasty Mexican lager: Dos Equis Ambar Especial

KING TRUMPET SCHNITZEL
WITH MIXED HERB PESTO

King Trumpet Schnitzel with Mixed Herb Pesto

⏱ TOTAL 40 MIN; SERVES 4

King trumpet mushrooms get the schnitzel treatment in this recipe, and a bright, herb-packed pesto complements the crispy, juicy mushrooms.

MUSHROOM SCHNITZEL

- 5 large fresh king trumpet mushrooms (about 1 lb.), trimmed and cut lengthwise into ½-inch-thick slices
- 4 cups panko, divided
- 4½ tsp. ground turmeric, divided
- 2 tsp. Himalayan pink salt, divided
- 7 large eggs
- ½ tsp. black pepper, divided
- 2½ cups neutral cooking oil (such as safflower oil)

MIXED HERB PESTO

- 4 cups packed mixed fresh herb leaves (such as basil, oregano, mint, and parsley)
- 3 medium garlic cloves, smashed
- ¾ cup extra-virgin olive oil
- 4 oz. pecorino cheese or Parmesan cheese, grated (about ½ cup)

- 1 Tbsp. grated Meyer lemon zest plus 2 Tbsp. fresh Meyer lemon juice (from 2 lemons)
- ¼ tsp. crumbled dried chile de árbol
- ¼ tsp. Himalayan pink salt, plus more to taste

ADDITIONAL INGREDIENTS

- Flaky sea salt, for garnish
- Meyer lemon wedges, for serving

1. **Make the mushroom schnitzel:** Preheat oven to 200°F. Using a rolling pin, gently roll mushroom caps to flatten to same thickness as stems.

2. Combine 2 cups panko, 2¼ teaspoons turmeric, and 1 teaspoon pink salt in a wide, shallow bowl, and toss to combine. Whisk together 3 eggs and ¼ teaspoon pepper in a separate wide, shallow bowl.

3. Working with 1 mushroom slice at a time, dip into egg mixture, letting excess drip off; dip into panko mixture, turning to coat completely. Place coated mushrooms on a wire rack.

4. Stir together remaining 2 cups panko, remaining 2¼ teaspoons turmeric, and remaining 1 teaspoon pink salt in a third wide, shallow bowl. Stir together remaining 4 eggs and remaining ¼ teaspoon pepper in a fourth wide, shallow bowl. Dip breaded mushroom slices into egg mixture, letting excess drip off; dip into panko mixture, turning to coat completely. Set aside on wire rack until ready to fry.

5. Place a heatproof wire rack inside a rimmed baking sheet. Heat neutral oil in a 12-inch cast-iron skillet over medium until shimmering but not smoking. Working in 3 batches, fry mushrooms until golden, 3 to 5 minutes per side. Transfer to wire rack; place in preheated oven to keep warm.

6. **Make the mixed herb pesto:** Pulse herbs and garlic in a food processor until finely chopped, about 10 pulses. With processor running, pour olive oil through food chute, processing until just combined, about 10 seconds. Add cheese, and pulse until just combined, about 3 pulses. (Do not overprocess.)

7. Transfer herb mixture to a medium bowl; stir in lemon zest and juice, chile, and pink salt. Season with additional pink salt to taste.

8. Transfer mushroom schnitzel to a platter, and garnish with flaky sea salt. Serve with lemon wedges and mixed herb pesto.

—EXCERPTED FROM *COOKING WITH MUSHROOMS* BY ANDREA GENTL. ARTISAN BOOKS © 2022

MAKE AHEAD Mixed herb pesto can be made up to 8 hours in advance. Drizzle 2 teaspoons oil over the pesto, press plastic wrap directly onto the surface, and refrigerate until ready to use.

WINE Full-bodied Rhône-style white: 2021 Joey Tensley Fundamental White

NOTE Use a rolling pin to gently flatten the mushrooms; using a mallet can cause the mushrooms to break.

Mushroom Parmesan

ACTIVE 35 MIN; TOTAL 2 HR 5 MIN; SERVES 8

This crunchy and flavorful Mushroom Parmesan recipe pairs briny olives and capers with tomato sauce and hen-of-the-woods mushrooms.

MUSHROOMS

- 2 lb. fresh hen-of-the-woods mushrooms (about 6 mushrooms)
- ⅓ cup extra-virgin olive oil
- ¾ tsp. Himalayan pink salt (see Note)
- ¼ tsp. black pepper
- 2 cups panko

SAUCE

- 1 (28-oz.) can whole peeled San Marzano plum tomatoes
- 1 (14-oz.) can whole peeled plum tomatoes
- ¼ cup extra-virgin olive oil
- 8 medium garlic cloves, smashed
- 20 pitted Castelvetrano olives, roughly chopped (about ½ cup)
- 2 Tbsp. chopped fresh oregano or 1 Tbsp. dried oregano (such as Sicilian oregano)
- 1 Tbsp. drained capers, roughly chopped
- ¾ tsp. Himalayan pink salt, plus more

ADDITIONAL INGREDIENTS

- 1 lb. fresh mozzarella cheese, thinly sliced
- 4 oz. Parmesan cheese, grated (about 1 cup)
- 1 Tbsp. fresh oregano leaves or 1½ tsp. dried oregano (such as Sicilian oregano)

1. Make the mushrooms: Preheat oven to 400°F. Cut mushrooms into 2- × 1- × 1-inch rectangles. Arrange in an even layer on a large baking sheet. Drizzle evenly with oil, and sprinkle evenly with salt and pepper. Toss mushrooms using your hands to evenly coat with oil; top evenly with panko, and toss again. Spread mushroom mixture in a single layer on baking sheet.

2. Roast mushrooms in preheated oven until mushrooms are soft and caramel-colored but not crispy and panko is golden brown, about 25 minutes, flipping mushrooms halfway through roasting time. Remove from oven, and set aside. Reduce oven temperature to 350°F.

3. Make the sauce: Pour both cans of tomatoes with juices into a large bowl; crush tomatoes using your hands. (Alternatively, use an immersion blender; process about 1 minute for a smoother puree.) Set aside.

4. Heat oil in a large skillet over medium until oil starts to shimmer. Add garlic, and cook until just beginning to brown, about 1 minute, flipping halfway through cooking time. Remove from heat; let oil cool 1 minute (to prevent tomatoes from splattering when added to oil).

5. Add reserved tomatoes with juices to oil in skillet, and return to heat over medium. Cook, stirring occasionally, until tomato sauce is thickened and you can just see the bottom of skillet when stirred, about 12 minutes. Stir in olives, oregano, capers, and salt. Add additional salt to taste. Remove from heat, and set aside.

6. Spread a thin layer of sauce on bottom of a 13- × 9-inch baking dish. Arrange one-third of mushroom-panko mixture evenly over sauce; top with one-third of remaining sauce. Sprinkle evenly with one-third of mozzarella; sprinkle evenly with ⅓ cup Parmesan. Repeat layering process 2 more times, ending with remaining ⅓ cup Parmesan. Bake at 350°F until bubbling and browned, about 45 minutes. Let cool 15 minutes. Sprinkle evenly with oregano, and serve.

—EXCERPTED FROM *COOKING WITH MUSHROOMS* BY ANDREA GENTL. ARTISAN BOOKS © 2022

MAKE AHEAD Sauce can be made up to 1 day in advance and stored in an airtight container in refrigerator.

WINE Earthy, berry-inflected Italian red: 2019 Poliziano Vino Nobile di Montepulciano

NOTE Himalayan pink salt adds a faintly floral, sweet flavor. Find it at most specialty grocery stores. Substitute with kosher salt, if desired.

MUSHROOM PARMESAN

SHEET-PAN TOFU WITH
BROCCOLINI, MUSHROOMS,
AND SWEET POTATOES

Sheet-Pan Tofu with Broccolini, Mushrooms, and Sweet Potatoes

ACTIVE 20 MIN; TOTAL 50 MIN; SERVES 4

A citrus-soy marinade adds zing to crisp roasted tofu in this easy sheet-pan dinner. Spreading the tofu and vegetables across two baking sheets ensures that they roast, rather than steam, in the oven. For the crispiest tofu and tender vegetables, space the ingredients evenly so hot air can circulate among them. This recipe is inspired by a favorite weeknight dish of Arthur Hon, the Beverage Director at The Modern in New York City, who recommends enjoying the tofu alongside a bottle of The Eyrie Vineyards' Chasselas Doré. "Simple sesame-and-soy-marinated tofu and seasonal veggies are balanced by its fresh and savory notes," he says.

Cooking spray

1 (16-oz.) pkg. extra-firm tofu, drained and cut crosswise into ½-inch-thick slices (see Note)

⅓ cup lower-sodium soy sauce

¼ cup fresh orange juice (from 1 orange)

1½ Tbsp. rice vinegar

2 tsp. toasted sesame oil

1 garlic clove, grated with a Microplane grater (about ¼ tsp.)

3 Tbsp. cornstarch

2 medium-size (12-oz.) sweet potatoes (unpeeled), cut into ½-inch rounds

1 lb. fresh Broccolini, ends trimmed and larger stalks halved lengthwise

8 oz. fresh shiitake mushrooms, stemmed and cut into ½-inch-thick slices (about 3 cups)

6 scallions (about 6 oz.), cut into 2-inch pieces (about 2 cups)

¼ cup olive oil

2 tsp. kosher salt

¼ tsp. black pepper

Fresh cilantro leaves, for garnish

1. Preheat oven to 400°F with racks in middle and lower third positions. Coat a large rimmed baking sheet with cooking spray. Cut tofu slices in half crosswise; place on a paper towel–lined plate, and firmly pat dry.

2. Whisk together soy sauce, orange juice, vinegar, sesame oil, and garlic in a medium bowl. Reserve ½ cup soy sauce mixture in a small bowl. Add tofu to remaining soy sauce mixture in medium bowl, and toss gently until evenly coated. Transfer tofu to a large bowl; sprinkle with cornstarch, and stir gently to evenly coat. Arrange in an even layer on one half of prepared baking sheet.

3. Combine sweet potatoes, Broccolini, mushrooms, and scallions in a large bowl; add olive oil, salt, and pepper, and toss until evenly coated. Place two-thirds of the vegetable mixture on a second large rimmed baking sheet. Place remaining one-third of vegetable mixture on opposite side of tofu on baking sheet. Place baking sheet with tofu on middle oven rack, and place baking sheet with vegetables on bottom rack. Bake in preheated oven until browned, about 30 minutes, flipping tofu and vegetables halfway through baking time. Garnish with cilantro. Serve alongside reserved soy sauce mixture. —ANNA THEOKTISTO

WINE 2020 The Eyrie Vineyards Chasselas Doré

NOTE To drain tofu, place tofu slices in a single layer on a paper towel–lined baking sheet. Top with a double layer of paper towels. Place a second baking sheet on the tofu, and weight with heavy cans or a large cast-iron skillet. Let stand 10 minutes.

POTATOES, GRAINS & BEANS

CHANA DAAL WITH SQUASH (P. 215)
OPPOSITE: ITALIAN WEDDING RISOTTO (P. 221)

Mini Kabob Potatoes

⏱ TOTAL 30 MIN; SERVES 4 TO 6

A crispy exterior with a soft, fluffy center makes these quick-cooking fried potatoes a fun addition to a kebab feast. At Mini Kabob in Los Angeles, these popular potatoes are served alongside skewers such as a Beef Shish Kabob (recipe p. 154), Ikra (Eggplant Caviar) (recipe p. 313), Toum (recipe p. 309), and Shaved Onions with Parsley and Sumac (recipe p. 312).

    Neutral cooking oil, for frying

2 lb. medium-size russet potatoes (about 4 medium potatoes), peeled

1½ tsp. kosher salt, divided, plus more to taste

¾ tsp. black pepper, divided, plus more to taste

¾ tsp. Aleppo pepper, divided, plus more to taste

    Ketchup, hummus, or Ikra (Eggplant Caviar) (recipe p. 313), for dipping

1. Pour oil to a depth of 1½ inches into a large Dutch oven; heat over medium-high to 375°F.

2. Using mandoline with crinkle-cut blade, cut potatoes crosswise into ¼-inch-thick slices. Working in 3 batches, add potato slices to hot oil; fry, stirring occasionally, until golden brown and lightly crisped, 4 to 6 minutes. Using a spider, transfer fried potatoes to a large heatproof bowl lined with a paper towel. Gently toss once in bowl. Remove and discard paper towel. Sprinkle potatoes with ½ teaspoon salt, ¼ teaspoon black pepper, and ¼ teaspoon Aleppo pepper; toss to evenly coat. Season with additional salt, black pepper, and Aleppo pepper to taste.

3. Repeat frying process with remaining potatoes, salt, black pepper, and Aleppo pepper. Oil temperature will drop to about 350°F while frying potatoes; let oil reheat to 375°F between batches. Serve immediately.
—OVAKIM AND ALVARD MARTIROSYAN

Chana Daal with Squash
PHOTO P. 213

ACTIVE 35 MIN; TOTAL 2 HR 35 MIN; SERVES 4

Chana daal adds texture, heft, and density to this stew of tender summer squash. Adding the squash at the very end ensures it doesn't completely disintegrate before the daal is softened. "The inspiration for this recipe is doodhi chana, a stew of bottle gourd and dried split chickpeas that I grew up eating in Gujarat," chef Vishwesh Bhatt says. "I always thought it lacked the oomph of other preparations my mother made. Then I discovered ras el hanout, preserved lemons, and pomegranate molasses, which elevated the previously boring gourd to new heights." Here, they do the same for yellow squash. Added at the very end of cooking, ras el hanout, preserved lemon rind, pomegranate molasses, and fresh dill and parsley add beautiful color and flavor to the finished dish.

1 cup dried chana daal (split chickpeas)

9 cups water, divided

2 Tbsp. olive oil

1 cup chopped scallion whites (from 3 medium [4-oz.] scallion bunches)

1 Tbsp. finely chopped garlic (from 3 medium garlic cloves)

1 Tbsp. finely chopped peeled fresh ginger

2 cups chopped tomatoes (from 2 [7-oz.] tomatoes)

8 cups chopped yellow squash (from 12 small [3-oz.] squash)

1½ Tbsp. ras el hanout

1½ Tbsp. chopped preserved lemon rind

2 tsp. Urfa or Aleppo pepper flakes

2 Tbsp. chopped fresh flat-leaf parsley

1 Tbsp. chopped fresh dill

2 tsp. kosher salt, plus more to taste

2 tsp. pomegranate molasses

    Warm pita rounds, for serving

1. Place daal in a large bowl; add 3 cups water, and let stand at room temperature 2 hours. Drain and set aside.

2. Heat oil in a Dutch oven over medium until shimmering. Add scallions, garlic, and ginger; cook, stirring constantly, until scallions are soft and garlic and ginger are fragrant, about 4 minutes. Add tomatoes; cook, stirring occasionally, until they start to release their juices, about 2 minutes.

3. Add drained daal and remaining 6 cups water to tomato mixture, and stir to combine. Increase heat to high; cook, stirring occasionally, until mixture comes to a simmer. Reduce heat to medium; cover and simmer until daal is just soft, 10 to 15 minutes. Stir in squash, ras el hanout, preserved lemon rind, and pepper flakes. Cover and cook over medium until squash is soft but not mushy, 10 to 12 minutes. Remove from heat. Stir in parsley, dill, salt, and molasses. Season with additional salt to taste. Serve hot with pita. —VISHWESH BHATT

WINE Tangy, light-bodied white: 2020 McPrice Myers Beautiful Earth White

NOTE Chana daal and ras el hanout can be found at Indian and Middle Eastern grocery stores or online. Preserved lemons can be found at Middle Eastern or specialty grocery stores. In a pinch, substitute 2 tablespoons fresh lemon zest

Perfectly Steamed Rice

ACTIVE 20 MIN; TOTAL 50 MIN;
MAKES ABOUT 4 CUPS

Here, Kwame Onwuachi shares his top tip for making the best steamed rice. "The secret to perfectly steamed rice lies in toasting the grains before they go into the water," he says. "This gives them a wonderful nutty flavor that carries through and is augmented by stock and aromatics. It isn't strictly necessary, of course, but once you start toasting, you'll never go back to straight steaming again."

- 1½ cups uncooked long-grain white rice (about 10 oz.)
- 2 Tbsp. canola oil
- 1½ cups chicken stock
- 1½ tsp. kosher salt, plus more to taste
- 3 (4-inch) thyme sprigs
- 1 fresh or dried bay leaf

1. Preheat oven to 350°F. Rinse rice until water runs clear; set aside. Heat oil in a small ovenproof saucepan (with a tight-fitting lid) over medium-high until shimmering.

2. Add rice; cook, stirring often, until toasted and shiny with a light golden hue, about 8 minutes. Add stock, salt, thyme, and bay leaf. Bring mixture to a boil over medium-high, stirring often. Remove from heat, and cover with lid. Transfer pot to preheated oven, and cook 20 minutes.

3. Remove pan from oven; let stand, covered, 5 minutes. Uncover and fluff rice gently using a fork; let it steam out, uncovered, 5 minutes. Remove and discard thyme and bay leaf. If desired, add additional salt to taste. —KWAME ONWUACHI

MAKE AHEAD Perfectly steamed rice can be stored in an airtight container in refrigerator up to 4 days.

Owamni Sweet Potatoes with Maple-Chile Crisp

ACTIVE 40 MIN; TOTAL 2 HR 40 MIN;
SERVES 8

Maple sugar lends complex sweetness to chef Sean Sherman's mouthwatering chile crisp, which he drizzles over roasted sweet potatoes.

OWAMNI MAPLE-CHILE CRISP

- 30 medium-size chiles de árbol (about ½ oz.), stemmed
- 4 medium chipotle or morita chiles (about ½ oz.), stemmed and cut into 2 pieces each
- 3 medium guajillo chiles (about ½ oz.), stemmed and cut into 3 pieces each
- 1 small ancho chile (about ½ oz.), stemmed and cut into 3 pieces
- 4 medium scallions (about 2 oz.)
- 2½ Tbsp. maple sugar
- 4 medium garlic cloves, minced (about 1 Tbsp.)
- 2 tsp. kosher salt, plus more to taste
- 2 cups sunflower oil

SWEET POTATOES

- 4 medium-size (8-oz.) sweet potatoes, scrubbed
- Kosher salt

1. Make the Owamni maple-chile crisp: Spread half of the chile pieces in a single layer with minimal overlap on a microwavable plate. Microwave on high 45 seconds. (Many of the chiles will puff up; steam usually appears.) Repeat process with remaining half of chiles. Let cool about 5 minutes.

2. Wearing a pair of disposable gloves, gently press open brittle chiles, shaking out and discarding seeds. Cut seeded chiles into pieces no larger than ¾ inch using scissors.

3. Working in 4 batches, place one-fourth of the chile pieces in a spice grinder or coffee grinder. Process until chopped, about 4 pulses. (Aim for most pieces to be no larger than ¼ inch.) Transfer chiles to a 9-×13-inch baking pan.

4. Finely chop white and light green scallion parts to measure about 1 tablespoon. Thinly slice dark green scallion parts to measure about ¼ cup; reserve for sweet potatoes. Add chopped white and light green scallion parts, maple sugar, garlic, and salt to chiles in baking pan; stir until well combined. Season with additional salt to taste for a balanced spicy, sweet, savory finish. (Keep baking pan on the stove or a heatproof surface.)

5. Pour sunflower oil into a small, heavy saucepan with a lip for easy pouring. Heat oil over medium to 400°F. Remove from heat, and carefully pour hot oil over chile mixture in baking pan; gently shake baking pan to evenly coat chiles. Let cool completely, about 1 hour.

6. Make the sweet potatoes: Preheat oven to 350°F. Place sweet potatoes on a parchment paper–lined baking sheet. Roast in preheated oven until just tender in center, 45 minutes to 1 hour. (Test doneness by inserting a skewer or knife in thickest part of sweet potato; you should have slight resistance at the center.) Let cool slightly, about 15 minutes.

7. Heat a cast-iron grill pan over medium-high. Cut each sweet potato in half lengthwise. Sear sweet potatoes, cut side down, until grill marks appear, 3 to 5 minutes, rotating halfway through cooking time using a metal spatula and tongs to create crosshatch grill marks. Transfer to 8 individual plates or a platter, and drizzle with Owamni maple-chile crisp (solids plus oil) as desired. Sprinkle evenly with reserved dark green scallion slices, and garnish lightly with salt. —SEAN SHERMAN

MAKE AHEAD Sweet potatoes can be roasted up to 3 days in advance and stored in an airtight container in refrigerator. Bring to room temperature before searing. Cooled Owamni maple-chile crisp can be stored in a lidded 24-ounce jar in refrigerator up to 3 months.

OWAMNI SWEET POTATOES
WITH MAPLE-CHILE CRISP

GATEWAY CASSOULET

By cooking several recipe components separately in the same pot before combining them all to meld in the oven, Sylvie Bigar, author of Cassoulet Confessions: Food, France, Family, and the Stew That Saved My Soul, *reduces the active cooking time for cassoulet to a little over an hour, while retaining the long-cooked, richly developed flavor of the traditional recipe.*

ACTIVE 1 HR 10 MIN; TOTAL 4 HR 35 MIN, PLUS 12 HR SOAKING; SERVES 4 TO 6

- 2 cups dried cannellini beans (preferably Rancho Gordo Marcella Beans)
- 1 medium-size (10-oz.) yellow onion, coarsely chopped (about 2 cups)
- 8 medium garlic cloves
- ¼ cup water
- 1 Tbsp. torn fresh flat-leaf parsley leaves
- 1¾ tsp. kosher salt
- ½ tsp. fresh thyme leaves
- 1 (12-oz.) skin-on pork belly
- 1 Tbsp. duck fat
- 8 oz. fresh pork sausage (such as French garlic sausage), cut into about 2-inch-long pieces
- 1 medium (3-oz.) carrot, peeled and finely chopped (about ½ cup)
- 1 small (14-oz.) fresh ham hock
- 2 fully cooked confit duck legs (about 7 oz. each)
- ¼ tsp. ground nutmeg
- Freshly ground pepper, to taste
- 5 cups chicken stock, as needed

1. Rinse beans thoroughly. Place beans in a large bowl, and add water to cover by at least 2 inches. Soak, uncovered, at room temperature 12 hours.

2. Drain beans; rinse under cold water. Fill a large pot or Dutch oven with water; bring to a boil over high. Add beans; return to a boil over high. Boil 7 minutes. Drain beans; rinse under cold water. Transfer beans to a medium bowl, and set aside.

3. Process onion, garlic, ¼ cup water, parsley, salt, and thyme in a blender until smooth, about 30 seconds; set aside.

4. Trim about 3 tablespoons fat cap with skin from pork belly, and chop into small pieces. Cut remaining pork belly into 1-inch cubes. Add chopped pork belly fat to a Dutch oven or large skillet; cook over medium, stirring occasionally, until fat has rendered, about 4 minutes. Add pork belly cubes; cook, turning occasionally, until browned on all sides, 12 to 15 minutes. Transfer pork belly to a small bowl. Reserve drippings in Dutch oven.

5. Preheat oven to 350°F. Add duck fat to drippings in Dutch oven. Add sausage pieces; cook over medium, turning often,

until browned all over, 3 to 5 minutes. Transfer sausage pieces to a small bowl. Reserve drippings in Dutch oven.

6. Carefully pour pureed onion mixture into drippings in Dutch oven. Reduce heat to low. Cook, stirring often and scraping any pieces of meat stuck to bottom of Dutch oven, until some of the water cooks off and onion mixture thickens and darkens, about 10 minutes. Remove from heat.

7. Scrape onion mixture into blanched beans in bowl. Add carrot to mixture, and stir until well coated.

8. Spread about one-third of the bean mixture (about 1⅔ cups) in a 3½- to 4½-quart oven-safe clay cassole or Dutch oven, enough to cover the bottom. Layer pork belly over beans. Add sausages and ham hock in an even layer. Finally, place duck legs on top, and cover with remaining beans; spread beans in an even layer. Sprinkle with nutmeg and a good grind of pepper. Pour in 3 cups stock, just enough to cover beans, pressing down to submerge, if needed. Reserve remaining 2 cups stock to add during the cooking process.

STEP-BY-STEP

PARCOOK BEANS Bring a large pot of water to a boil, and add soaked beans. Return to a boil, and cook 7 minutes. Drain beans, and rinse under cold water.

PUREE ONIONS AND HERBS Combine chopped onion, garlic, parsley leaves, thyme leaves, salt, and ¼ cup water in a blender, and puree until smooth, about 30 seconds.

BROWN THE PORK BELLY Cook chopped pork belly fat cap until rendered, about 4 minutes. Add cubed pork belly, and cook until browned on all sides, 12 to 15 minutes.

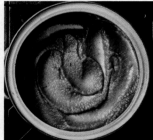

COOK THE ONION PUREE Add onion-herb puree to Dutch oven with reserved drippings. Cook over low until mixture thickens and darkens, about 10 minutes.

9. Bake, uncovered, in preheated oven until cassoulet comes to a simmer, bubbling along sides and in spots in center of cassole, and a crust begins to form (surface of beans will look dry), 1 hour to 1 hour and 15 minutes. Remove cassoulet from oven. Reduce oven temperature to 325°F. Break the cassoulet crust in 1 spot using the back of a spoon, and drizzle ½ cup stock over bean mixture to ensure cassoulet remains moist. Immediately return to oven. Bake at 325°F, uncovered, until beans are tender and a crust forms over top of beans, 2 hours to 2 hours and 15 minutes, breaking the crust in 1 spot with the back of a spoon every 30 minutes to drizzle in about ⅓ cup stock to ensure that cassoulet remains moist. (Cassoulet should be gently bubbling throughout cook time.)

10. Remove cassoulet from oven. Let cool 15 minutes. Place cassole at the center of the table, and serve family-style.
—SYLVIE BIGAR

MAKE AHEAD Cassoulet may be stored in an airtight container in refrigerator up to 3 days.

WINE Robust Southern French red: 2019 Vincent Paris Les Côtes St-Joseph

NOTE Rancho Gordo Marcella Beans, a thin-skinned cannellini bean, may be purchased at ranchogordo.com. Fully cooked confit duck legs and French garlic pork sausage may be purchased at dartagnan.com. Epic Provisions duck fat can be purchased at epicprovisions.com.

LAYER THE CASSOULET Spread one-third of bean mixture in an oven-safe cassole or Dutch oven. Top with sausages, ham hock, duck legs, remaining beans, and stock.

BREAK THE CRUST Throughout bake time, use the back of a spoon to break the thin, film-like crust on top of cassoulet, and drizzle in stock.

Red Beans and Rice

ACTIVE 55 MIN; TOTAL 2 HR 25 MIN, PLUS 12 HR SOAKING; SERVES 6 TO 8

"Everyone with roots in southern Louisiana, where red beans and rice is a staple, thinks that their mom makes the best version," says 2019 F&W Best New Chef Kwame Onwuachi. *"But I'm the only one who's right. Growing up, my mom used this recipe as a base, sometimes adding in smoked turkey necks or smoked, spiced, and cured tasso ham, in addition to the ham hocks and andouille sausage that impart their smoke, fat, and spice to the Holy Trinity (celery, bell peppers, and onions) and, of course, the sturdy red kidney beans."*

- 2 cups dried red kidney beans (12 oz.)
- 2 Tbsp. canola oil
- 1 (14-oz.) andouille sausage, sliced crosswise into 1½-inch-thick pieces
- 1 large (12-oz.) yellow onion, chopped (about 2 cups)
- 2 medium-size (7 oz. each) green bell peppers, chopped (about 1¾ cups)
- 2 medium (3 oz. each) celery stalks, chopped (about 1 cup)
- 6 medium garlic cloves, finely chopped (about 2 Tbsp.)
- 1½ Tbsp. House Spice (recipe p. 306)
- 2 (14-oz.) smoked ham hocks
- 6 cups vegetable stock
- 4 (4-inch) thyme sprigs
- 2 fresh or dried bay leaves
- Kosher salt, to taste
- Perfectly Steamed Rice (recipe p. 216)

1. Place beans in a medium pot or bowl; add water to cover by 2 inches. Cover and refrigerate overnight (up to 12 hours).

2. Heat a Dutch oven over medium-high. Add oil, and heat until shimmering. Add sausage; cook until browned on both sides, about 3 minutes per side. Remove from heat. Transfer sausage to a plate (do not wipe Dutch oven clean); let cool slightly, about 10 minutes. Cover and refrigerate until ready to stir into beans.

3. While sausage cools, drain soaked beans; set aside. Add onion, bell peppers, celery, and garlic to Dutch oven; cook over medium, stirring often, until tender, about 10 minutes. Add house spice; cook, stirring often, until fragrant, about 2 minutes. Add

beans, ham hocks, stock, thyme, and bay leaves; stir to combine. Bring to a simmer over medium-high. Reduce heat to low; cover and cook very gently until beans are completely tender and ham hock is fork-tender, 1 hour and 30 minutes to 2 hours and 30 minutes. Start checking for doneness after about 1 hour. (The beans could take up to 3 hours.)

4. When beans are completely tender, remove from heat. Remove and discard thyme and bay leaves. Transfer ham hocks to a small bowl or a cutting board; remove and discard bones and skin, and shred meat. Transfer 1 cup red beans and ½ cup cooking liquid to a blender. Secure lid on blender, and remove center piece to allow steam to escape. Place a clean towel over opening. Process until mixture is velvety smooth, about 1 minute. Stir pureed mixture back into red beans in Dutch oven. Stir in shredded ham and cooked sausage. Bring to a simmer over medium. Simmer, stirring occasionally, until sausage and ham are heated through, about 5 minutes. Season with salt to taste. Serve red beans alongside perfectly steamed rice.

—KWAME ONWUACHI

WINE Spicy, fruit-driven red: 2020 Bedrock Wine Co. California Syrah

Italian Wedding Risotto

PHOTO P. 212

TOTAL 45 MIN; SERVES 4 TO 6

Inspired by the classic Italian wedding soup, this heartier risotto is filled with just-wilted spinach and topped with crispy, garlicky meatballs. Remove the risotto from the heat while it's still a little soupy—it will thicken slightly as it rests.

- 1 lb. ground pork
- ½ cup panko
- 1½ oz. Parmigiano-Reggiano cheese, finely grated with a Microplane (about ⅔ cup), divided, plus more for garnish
- ¼ cup finely chopped fresh flat-leaf parsley, plus more for garnish
- 1 large egg, lightly beaten
- 4 garlic cloves, finely chopped, divided
- 2 tsp. kosher salt, plus more to taste
- 1 tsp. black pepper, plus more to taste and for garnish

- 4 cups lower-sodium chicken stock or broth
- 2 cups water
- 2 Tbsp. extra-virgin olive oil, plus more for drizzling
- ¼ cup unsalted butter (2 oz.), divided
- 1 medium-size yellow onion, finely chopped (about 2 cups)
- 1 medium celery stalk, finely chopped (about ⅓ cup)
- 1½ cups uncooked arborio rice (about 10½ oz.)
- ¾ cup dry white wine
- 3 cups packed fresh baby spinach (about 3 oz.), torn

1. Preheat oven to broil with rack 9 inches from heat. Combine pork, panko, ⅓ cup of the cheese, parsley, egg, 2 teaspoons chopped garlic, salt, and pepper in a medium bowl. Mix gently until just combined. Roll mixture into 20 meatballs (about 2 tablespoons each). Place 1 inch apart on a broiler-safe baking sheet lined with aluminum foil. Broil until browned and cooked through, 6 to 9 minutes.

2. Combine stock and 2 cups water in a medium saucepan; bring to a simmer over medium. Reduce heat to medium-low.

3. Heat oil and 2 tablespoons butter in a large saucepan over medium. Add onion, celery, and remaining chopped garlic; cook, stirring often, until softened, about 5 minutes. Add rice, and cook, stirring constantly, until translucent, 1 to 2 minutes. Add wine, and cook, stirring often, until almost completely reduced, 1 to 2 minutes. Add 1 cup warm stock mixture, and cook, stirring constantly, until most of the liquid has been absorbed. Add remaining stock mixture, 1 cup at a time, stirring until liquid has been absorbed after each addition, until rice is al dente, about 20 minutes.

4. Remove from heat. Stir in remaining cheese and remaining 2 tablespoons butter. Add spinach. Stir until just wilted, about 30 seconds. Divide risotto and meatballs among bowls. Drizzle with oil; garnish with additional cheese, parsley, and pepper.

—JUSTIN CHAPPLE

MAKE AHEAD Uncooked meatballs can be frozen up to 2 months. Place on a rimmed baking sheet; freeze 2 hours. Transfer to a freezer bag. Let thaw before broiling.

WINE Herbal, red-fruited Chianti Classico: 2017 Ruffino Riserva Ducale

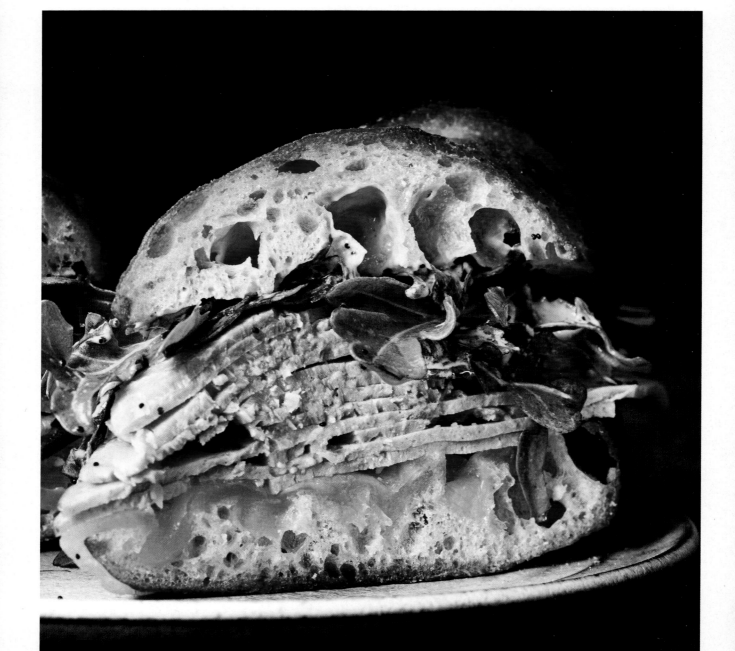

BREADS, PIZZAS & SANDWICHES

WILD MUSHROOM PIZZA (P. 249)
OPPOSITE: THE ORIOLE "HAM
SANDOVAL" (P. 227)

Hawaij-Spiced Fried Chicken Sandwiches

TOTAL 1 HR 15 MIN, PLUS 12 HR MARINATING; SERVES 4

In these decadent fried chicken sandwiches from Hakim Sulaimani, proprietor of Yafa Cafe in Brooklyn, boneless, skinless chicken breasts are infused with golden color and warming flavors from a buttermilk brine seasoned with hawaij, a Yemeni spice mixture usually consisting of cardamom, turmeric, black pepper, cloves, and coriander. Nutmeg in the crunchy panko coating for the fried chicken further spices up the sandwich, as does the slightly smoky adobo chile and plum sauce. Fresh coleslaw and pickles add a crisp bite and a subtle vinegary punch.

BUTTERMILK MARINADE

- 1 cup whole buttermilk
- 2 Tbsp. hawaij spice blend (such as Sahadi)
- 1 Tbsp. kosher salt
- 1 Tbsp. black pepper
- 1½ tsp. paprika
- 4 (7-oz.) boneless, skinless chicken breasts

COLESLAW

- 1 cup shredded brussels sprouts
- 1 cup shredded red cabbage
- ½ cup shredded green cabbage
- ¼ cup plus 2 Tbsp. mayonnaise
- 1 Tbsp. water
- ½ tsp. kosher salt

PANKO BREADING

- 1½ cups panko
- 1 tsp. kosher salt
- 1 tsp. black pepper
- 1 tsp. dried oregano
- 1 tsp. ground nutmeg

SAUCE

- 2 small plums, unpeeled, coarsely chopped (about 1 cup)
- ¼ cup packed fresh cilantro leaves
- 2 tsp. honey
- 1½ tsp. adobo sauce from canned chipotle chiles in adobo sauce (such as La Morena)
- 1 tsp. fresh lemon juice

- ½ tsp. granulated garlic
- ½ tsp. kosher salt
- ¼ tsp. black pepper

ADDITIONAL INGREDIENTS

- Vegetable oil, for frying
- 4 brioche hamburger buns, split
- Dill pickles, for serving

1. Make the buttermilk marinade: Whisk together buttermilk, hawaij, salt, pepper, and paprika in a large bowl. Using tongs, add chicken, and turn to coat in marinade. Cover and refrigerate 12 hours.

2. Make the coleslaw: Stir together brussels sprouts, cabbage, mayonnaise, 1 tablespoon water, and salt in a medium bowl. Cover and refrigerate until ready to use.

3. Make the panko breading: Pulse panko in a food processor until texture resembles grated cheese, about 5 pulses. Transfer panko to a wide, shallow bowl. Stir in salt, pepper, oregano, and nutmeg; set aside.

4. Make the sauce: Process plums, cilantro, honey, adobo sauce, lemon juice, garlic, salt, and pepper in a blender until smooth, about 40 seconds. Set aside.

5. Pour vegetable oil to a depth of ¾ inch in a 12-inch cast-iron skillet; heat oil over medium-high to 325°F. Meanwhile, set a wire rack inside a large rimmed baking sheet; set aside. Remove chicken from refrigerator. Working with 1 chicken breast at a time, scrape excess marinade off chicken. Dredge chicken in panko breading to coat, pressing to adhere. Shake off excess breading. Place chicken on a plate.

6. Working in 2 batches, fry chicken in hot oil until panko is browned and a thermometer inserted in thickest portion of chicken registers 160°F, 11 to 14 minutes, gently turning chicken every 2 to 3 minutes and adjusting heat as needed to maintain oil temperature of 320°F to 325°F. Transfer chicken to prepared rack on baking sheet.

7. Spread 2 tablespoons sauce onto cut sides of each bun bottom. Place 1 chicken breast on each bun bottom; top with heaping ¼ cup coleslaw and desired amount of pickles. Cover with bun tops. —HAKIM SULAIMANI

WINE Bright, light-bodied red: 2019 Tilia Bonarda

NOTE Find hawaij at Middle Eastern markets or online at kalustyans.com.

7-Eleven Egg Salad Sandwich

ACTIVE 20 MIN; TOTAL 1 HR 50 MIN; SERVES 1

Jason Diamond's desire for the famous Japanese 7-Eleven egg salad sandwich inspired him to recreate it at home. Kewpie mayonnaise is key to this recipe—made with only egg yolks and rice or apple cider vinegar—along with a fluffy Japanese milk bread and just the right ratio of whites to yolks.

- 5 large eggs
- ¼ cup Kewpie mayonnaise
- ½ tsp. kosher salt, plus more to taste
- ½ tsp. granulated sugar
- ⅛ tsp. black pepper
- 2 tsp. heavy cream
- 1 Tbsp. unsalted butter, softened
- 2 (1½-oz.) Japanese milk bread slices (½ inch thick)

1. Bring a medium saucepan of water to a boil over medium-high. Using a slotted spoon, carefully lower eggs into boiling water; cook 11 minutes. Remove eggs using a slotted spoon, or carefully drain into a sink. Plunge eggs into a bowl filled with ice water, and let stand until cool, about 15 minutes. Drain well. Carefully peel eggs.

2. Using your hands, split eggs open; separate yolks and whites. Place yolks in a medium bowl, and mash using the back of a fork until broken down and a few chunks remain; set aside. Finely chop egg whites; place in a small bowl, and set aside.

3. Add mayonnaise, salt, sugar, and pepper to mashed yolks in bowl; gently stir until mixture is combined and some chunks remain. (Mixture should not be too chunky or a paste.)

4. Add half of the chopped egg whites to yolk mixture in medium bowl; reserve remaining egg whites for another use. Gently fold whites into yolk mixture until just coated. Chill 1 hour.

5. Stir cream into chilled egg mixture; season with additional salt to taste. Set aside. Spread butter evenly over one side of each bread slice. Top 1 slice, butter side up, with egg salad. Cover with remaining slice, butter side down. Trim off and discard crust; cut sandwich in half diagonally so you have 2 triangles. Serve. —JASON DIAMOND, NEW YORK CITY

7-ELEVEN EGG SALAD SANDWICH

THE BEST CUCUMBER SANDWICH

The Best Cucumber Sandwich

ACTIVE 15 MIN; TOTAL 1 HR; SERVES 4

The only reason you think cucumber sandwiches are boring is because you haven't had one that is made right, says chef Vishwesh Bhatt. Benedictine, a creamy spread of cucumber and herbs; along with a spicy and herbaceous peanut pesto with serrano chile, cilantro, and citrus; and chaat masala add verve to these sandwiches. And after layering in the crisp cucumbers, spicy chile slices, and juicy tomatoes, take a bite. "Once you serve this one, it's going to become a fixture at your summer parties," Bhatt says.

BENEDICTINE SPREAD

- 2 medium cucumbers, peeled, seeded, and finely chopped (about ¾ cup)
- 2 tsp. kosher salt, divided
- 8 oz. cream cheese, softened
- 8 oz. mascarpone cheese
- 2 (4-oz.) bunches fresh flat-leaf parsley, chopped (leaves and tender stems only) (about 2¼ cups)
- ½ cup finely chopped red onion (from 1 small onion)
- 1 medium-size fresh jalapeño (about 1 oz.), seeded and finely chopped
- 2 tsp. chopped fresh dill
- 1 tsp. black pepper

PEANUT PESTO

- 2 (4-oz.) bunches fresh cilantro, chopped (leaves and tender stems only) (about 1¾ cups)
- 1½ cups raw peanuts
- 5 Tbsp. fresh lemon juice (from 2 lemons)
- 4 medium garlic cloves, chopped (about 4 tsp.)
- 3 Tbsp. chopped peeled fresh ginger
- 1 small fresh serrano chile, seeded and chopped (about 1½ Tbsp.)
- 1 tsp. granulated sugar
- 1 tsp. kosher salt
- Water, as needed

ADDITIONAL INGREDIENTS

- 8 (1½-oz.) white bread slices (crusts removed, if desired)
- 24 (¼-inch-thick) cucumber slices (from 2 [3-oz.] cucumbers)
- 2 Tbsp. fresh lime juice (from 1 lime)
- ½ tsp. kosher salt
- 12 (¼-inch-thick) plum tomato slices (from 2 [3-oz.] plum tomatoes)
- 1 tsp. chaat masala (such as MDH)
- 1 small fresh serrano chile (about ½ oz.), seeded and finely chopped (about 1½ Tbsp.)
- Potato chips, for serving (optional)

1. Make the benedictine spread: Place cucumbers in a colander set over a bowl or sink, and sprinkle with 1 teaspoon salt. Toss together using your hands to fully coat cucumbers in salt; let drain 20 minutes. Meanwhile, stir together cream cheese, mascarpone, parsley, onion, jalapeño, and dill in a medium bowl; set aside until ready to use.

2. Fold drained cucumber, black pepper, and remaining 1 teaspoon salt into cream cheese mixture. Refrigerate at least 30 minutes or up 12 hours.

3. Make the peanut pesto: Combine cilantro, peanuts, lemon juice, garlic, ginger, serrano, sugar, and salt in a food processor; pulse until well blended and smooth, about 10 pulses, adding water 2 teaspoons at a time if needed to help process. (Alternatively, place in a mortar, and pound using a pestle, scraping down sides as you go until you have a smooth paste. Once smooth, thin the pesto with a bit of water if you prefer a thinner consistency.)

4. Assemble the sandwiches: Make 2 rows of 4 bread slices each on a clean work surface or cutting board. On the bottom row, spread about ¼ cup benedictine spread on each slice. On the top row, spread about 2 tablespoons peanut pesto on each slice. Toss together cucumber slices, lime juice, and salt in a small bowl; arrange evenly on bread slices on bottom row. Top bread slices on bottom row evenly with tomato slices, and sprinkle evenly with chaat masala and serrano. Sandwich the two topped bread slices together. If desired, cut sandwiches into halves or quarters, and serve with chips. —VISHWESH BHATT

MAKE AHEAD Benedictine spread and peanut pesto can be refrigerated in separate airtight containers up to 3 days.

WINE Fruity, lightly herbal Prosecco: NV Bisol Jeio Prosecco Superiore

NOTE Add fresh radishes and thinly sliced beets to these sandwiches in the springtime.

The Oriole "Ham Sandoval"

PHOTO P. 222

TOTAL 15 MIN; SERVES 1

Nutty raclette cheese melted on toasted baguette gets piled high with rich country ham and silky mortadella studded with cinnamon and black pepper in this exquisite ham sandwich from 2017 F&W Best New Chef Noah Sandoval of Oriole in Chicago. Tangy walnut mustard aïoli, peppery arugula, and poppy-citrus dressing cut through the richness and add fresh flavor to every bite.

- 1 (6-oz.) demi baguette
- 2 oz. thinly sliced Roelli Cheese Haus raclette cheese
- 3 Tbsp. Sur Les Quais Moutarde aux Noix (mustard with walnut)
- 1 Tbsp. Hellmann's mayonnaise
- 3 oz. Smoking Goose mortadella, thinly shaved
- 4 oz. Edwards Virginia Smokehouse country ham, thinly shaved
- 1 Tbsp. fresh lemon juice (from 1 lemon)
- 1 Tbsp. Agrumato Lemon Extra-Virgin Olive Oil & Lemon
- 1 tsp. poppy seeds
- ⅛ tsp. kosher salt
- 1½ cups arugula (about ¾ oz.)

1. Preheat broiler to high with oven rack in middle position. Split baguette in half, and shingle bottom half with raclette cheese. Place baguette halves on a baking sheet, and broil until cheese is melted, 2 to 4 minutes.

2. Stir together mustard and mayonnaise; smear evenly over top half of toasted baguette. Line bottom half of baguette with shaved mortadella. Top with ham.

3. Whisk together lemon juice and oil in a medium bowl. Whisk in poppy seeds and salt. Add arugula, and toss to coat well. Top country ham with dressed arugula, and crown with top half of baguette. Slice in half diagonally, and serve immediately. —NOAH SANDOVAL, ORIOLE, CHICAGO

WINE Juicy, berry-rich Rhône-style blend: 2020 Bonny Doon Le Cigare Volant

NOTE Edwards country ham is available online at edwardsvaham.com. Mortadella is available online at smokinggoose. com. Walnut mustard is available from rareteacellar.com.

Blackened Fish Sandwiches with Horseradish Tartar Sauce

PHOTO P. 348

TOTAL 20 MIN; SERVES 4

Fresh fillets of haddock are coated with smoky paprika, garlic powder, oregano, and thyme before they get a quick sear to develop a delicious crust. They are then sandwiched between toasted brioche buns smeared with a strong, tangy tartar sauce laced with refreshingly piquant horseradish. If your fish fillets are thicker than ¾ inch, butterfly them by carefully cutting through the center of the fillet (parallel to the work surface), leaving ½ inch of the meat attached at the side so it can be opened like a book.

TARTAR SAUCE

- ¼ cup mayonnaise
- ¼ cup sour cream
- 3 Tbsp. minced shallot (from 1 medium shallot)
- 2 Tbsp. minced fresh flat-leaf parsley
- 1½ Tbsp. drained prepared horseradish
- 1½ Tbsp. fresh lemon juice
- 1½ Tbsp. minced cornichons (about 4 small cornichons)
- 1 Tbsp. drained capers, chopped
- ¼ tsp. kosher salt
- ¼ tsp. black pepper

SANDWICHES

- 1 tsp. hot paprika
- 1 tsp. garlic powder
- 1 tsp. minced fresh oregano
- 1 tsp. minced fresh thyme
- 1 tsp. kosher salt
- ½ tsp. black pepper
- 4 (4- to 5-oz.) skinless haddock fillets (about ¾ inch thick)
- ¼ cup plus 2 tsp. unsalted butter, divided
- 4 brioche hamburger buns, split
- 1 Tbsp. canola oil
  Butter lettuce leaves, for serving

1. Make the tartar sauce: Whisk together mayonnaise, sour cream, shallot, parsley, horseradish, lemon juice, cornichons, capers, salt, and pepper in a small bowl. Refrigerate until ready to use.

2. Make the sandwiches: Stir together paprika, garlic powder, oregano, thyme, salt, and pepper in a small bowl. Sprinkle spice mixture evenly over both sides of fish fillets. Set aside.

3. Heat a large cast-iron skillet over high. Spread 1 teaspoon butter over cut side of each bun half. Place buns, buttered side down, in hot skillet; cook until well toasted and browned, about 1 minute. Transfer to a work surface. Do not wipe skillet clean.

4. Add oil and remaining 2 tablespoons butter to skillet; cook over high until butter is melted. Add fish fillets; cook until blackened on bottoms, about 3 minutes. Flip fillets; cook until blackened on other sides and just cooked through, 2 to 3 minutes. Remove from heat, and transfer fish to a plate.

5. Spread 1 tablespoon tartar sauce over toasted side of each bun half. Arrange fish and lettuce evenly on bottom bun halves. Cover with top bun halves, toasted side down. Serve alongside remaining ½ cup tartar sauce at the table. —JUSTIN CHAPPLE

WINE Lightly spicy Rhône-style white: 2020 Tablas Creek Vineyard Côtes de Tablas Blanc

Niçoise Salad Sandwich (Pan Bagnat)

ACTIVE 30 MIN; TOTAL 50 MIN; SERVES 4

Essentially a Niçoise salad in sandwich form, the pan bagnat is sold at nearly every outdoor market in Nice, France, as well as at bakeries and restaurants. For this version, tuna is pureed with red wine vinegar, olive oil, anchovies, and garlic to form a unique sandwich spread inspired by tonnato sauce. Spreading a tangy tuna dressing on the cut sides of the ciabatta allows it to get absorbed into the bread, giving the sandwich plenty of flavor while also making it easier to eat.

- 4 large eggs
- 14 oz. canned tuna in olive oil (from 4 [5-oz.] cans), drained (about 2 cups)
- ½ cup red wine vinegar
- ½ cup extra-virgin olive oil
- 4 anchovy fillets (from 1 [2-oz.] can), drained

- 2 medium garlic cloves, smashed
- 1 tsp. kosher salt, divided
- ½ tsp. black pepper, divided
- 1 (14- to 16-oz.) ciabatta loaf, split horizontally
- 1 cup multicolored pitted olives, halved if large
- 2 medium beefsteak tomatoes (about 10 oz. each), cored and sliced crosswise into ¼-inch-thick slices
- 1 small red onion (about 6 oz.), halved lengthwise and thinly sliced crosswise (about 1¼ cups)
- 4 large radishes, thinly sliced crosswise (about ⅓ cup)
- 4 large or 6 medium Bibb lettuce leaves (from 1 head lettuce)
- 12 large fresh basil leaves

1. Fill a medium saucepan halfway with water; bring to a boil over high. Carefully lower eggs into boiling water; cook, undisturbed, 8 minutes. Pour off water, reserving eggs in saucepan; add ice water to cover eggs. Let eggs cool completely, about 10 minutes. Drain and peel eggs. Cut each egg lengthwise into 3 slices. Set aside.

2. Combine tuna, vinegar, oil, anchovies, garlic, ¾ teaspoon salt, and ¼ teaspoon pepper in a food processor; process just until smooth, 20 to 30 seconds, stopping to scrape down sides using a spatula as needed. Spread tuna mixture evenly onto cut sides of ciabatta halves. Scatter olives on bottom ciabatta half. Top with sliced eggs, tomatoes, onion, and radishes; sprinkle with remaining ¼ teaspoon salt and remaining ¼ teaspoon pepper. Top with lettuce and basil. Cover with top ciabatta half. Cover sandwich with aluminum foil or plastic wrap. Place a baking sheet on top of sandwich, and place a skillet on top of baking sheet to weigh it down. Let sandwich stand 10 to 20 minutes. Cut crosswise into 4 sandwiches, and serve. —JUSTIN CHAPPLE

MAKE AHEAD Eggs may be boiled and chilled up to 2 days in advance. Peel and slice just before assembling sandwich.

WINE Light-bodied French white: 2020 Hugues Beaulieu Picpoul de Pinet

**NIÇOISE SALAD SANDWICH
(PAN BAGNAT)**

TOFU-TEMPEH SLOPPY JOES

Tofu-Tempeh Sloppy Joes

ACTIVE 35 MIN; TOTAL 55 MIN; SERVES 6

With jalapeño for heat and brown sugar for sweetness, these vegan sloppy joes will please meat eaters and vegetarians alike. Made from fermented soybeans, tempeh gives these meatless sloppy joes a heartier texture than firm tofu alone.

- 1 (14- to 16-oz. pkg.) extra-firm tofu, drained
- ¼ cup extra-virgin olive oil
- 1 medium-size yellow onion, finely chopped (about 2 cups)
- 1 jalapeño chile, seeded, stemmed, and finely chopped
- 3 garlic cloves, finely chopped
- ¾ tsp. kosher salt, plus more to taste
- ½ tsp. black pepper, plus more to taste
- 8 oz. tempeh, finely crumbled
- 2 Tbsp. tomato paste
- 2 tsp. ancho chile powder
- 1½ cups strained, canned, diced tomatoes
- ½ cup water
- 2 Tbsp. apple cider vinegar
- 2 Tbsp. light brown sugar
- 1 Tbsp. sriracha
- 2 tsp. liquid aminos or soy sauce
- 6 brioche hamburger buns, toasted
  Bread-and-butter pickle chips, for serving

1. Place tofu on a double layer of paper towels. Top with another double layer of paper towels. Place a plate on top, and weight with a can. Let stand at room temperature to drain at least 20 minutes or up to 1 hour. Discard liquid. Coarsely crumble tofu so it resembles ground meat. (It will break down a bit more during cooking.)

2. Heat oil in a large skillet over medium. Add onion, jalapeño, garlic, salt, and black pepper; cook, stirring occasionally, until onion is lightly browned, about 8 minutes. Add tempeh, tomato paste, and chile powder; cook, stirring constantly, until tempeh is evenly coated and a crust starts to form on bottom of skillet, 1 to 2 minutes.

3. Add tomatoes, ½ cup water, vinegar, brown sugar, sriracha, and liquid aminos to skillet; bring to a simmer over medium-high, stirring occasionally. Gently stir in

tofu. Reduce heat to medium-low; simmer, stirring occasionally, until thickened, 10 to 12 minutes. Season with additional salt and black pepper to taste. Serve on buns with pickle chips. —JUSTIN CHAPPLE

MAKE AHEAD Sloppy joe mixture can be made up to 3 days ahead and refrigerated in an airtight container.

BEER Rich, lightly spicy amber ale: Anderson Valley Brewing Company Boont

Khaliat Al Nahl (Honeycomb Buns)

ACTIVE 30 MIN; TOTAL 1 HR 50 MIN, PLUS 7 DAYS STANDING; SERVES 12

A traditional Yemeni pastry, khaliat al nahl are sweet, cloudlike balls of dough that are filled with cream cheese and drenched in cardamom-infused honey before they are topped with crunchy white sesame seeds and black nigella seeds.

CARDAMOM-INFUSED HONEY

- ⅓ cup clover honey
- 5 green cardamom pods, smashed, or ⅛ tsp. ground cardamom

BUNS

- ¾ cup whole milk, warmed (about 110°F), divided
- 1 tsp. active dry yeast (from 1 [¼-oz.] envelope)
- 1 Tbsp. granulated sugar, divided
- 2 cups all-purpose flour (about 8½ oz.)
- ¼ cup vegetable oil, plus more for work surface, hands, and bench scraper
- 1 tsp. baking powder
- ½ tsp. fine sea salt
  Unsalted butter, softened, for greasing baking pan
- 6 oz. cream cheese (about ½ cup), chilled
- 1 tsp. white sesame seeds
- ½ tsp. nigella seeds

1. Make the cardamom-infused honey: If using cardamom pods, stir together honey and smashed cardamom pods in a small bowl. Cover tightly, and let stand at room temperature until honey has a faint cardamom flavor, at least 7 days or up to 10 days. Remove and discard cardamom pods before using. Alternatively, stir

together honey and ground cardamom in a small bowl. Set aside.

2. Make the buns: Stir together ¼ cup warm milk, yeast, and 1 teaspoon sugar in a small bowl. Let stand until foamy, about 5 minutes.

3. Stir together flour, oil, baking powder, salt, and remaining 2 teaspoons sugar in a large bowl. Stir in yeast mixture until incorporated. Stir in ¼ cup warm milk. Knead dough in bowl until a ball forms, about 30 seconds. Add remaining ¼ cup warm milk, and knead dough in bowl until milk is incorporated, 1 to 2 minutes. Dough will be very sticky. Scrape down sides of bowl using a rubber spatula. Cover bowl with a clean towel, and let dough rest in a warm (75°F to 80°F) place until doubled in volume, 1 hour to 1 hour and 30 minutes. Preheat oven to 400°F during final 15 minutes of dough proofing time, and lightly grease an 8-inch square metal baking pan with butter.

4. Divide and shape cream cheese evenly into 24 (¼-ounce) balls (about 1 teaspoon each). Place cream cheese balls on a parchment paper–lined plate, and chill until ready to use.

5. Turn dough out onto a well-oiled work surface. Using oiled hands and an oiled bench scraper, divide dough evenly into 24 (about ⅝-ounce) pieces (about 2 tablespoons each). Working with 1 dough piece at a time, push 1 cream cheese ball into center of dough piece. Pull dough up and over to fully encase cream cheese. Using oiled hands, gently roll dough on a well-oiled surface to form a ball with cream cheese in center of ball. Place filled dough ball, seam side down, in prepared baking pan. Repeat process with remaining dough pieces and cream cheese balls, arranging filled dough balls side by side and just touching each other in baking pan.

6. Bake in preheated oven until buns are light golden brown, 15 to 18 minutes. Remove from oven, and immediately drizzle buns with ¼ cup warmed cardamom-infused honey. Sprinkle evenly with sesame seeds and nigella seeds. Let buns cool in baking pan 5 minutes. Serve warm or at room temperature, drizzling with remaining cardamom-infused honey, if desired. —HAKIM SULAIMANI, YAFA CAFÉ, BROOKLYN

NOTE Find nigella seeds and whole cardamom pods at Middle Eastern markets or online at kalustyans.com.

Tocino Burgers

ACTIVE 1 HR 30 MIN; TOTAL 1 HR 55 MIN;
SERVES 8

It's no secret why this burger is the signature dish for Paolo Dungca and Tom Cunanan at Pogiboy in Washington, DC Who doesn't want a purple burger bun? Enjoy the ultimate indulgence with a balance of richness from the pork, acidic crunch from the achara, and a creamy secret sauce bringing it all home. Each layer of this showstopping burger is delicious on its own, but once combined, they all come together as one to create a craveable burger with just enough sweet to balance the savory.

GREEN PAPAYA ACHARA

- 1 small (2½-lb.) green papaya, peeled and seeded
- 2 Tbsp. plus 1 tsp. fine sea salt, divided
- 2 cups shaved red cabbage (from 1 small [1-lb.] cabbage)
- 1 small (6-oz.) red onion, thinly sliced (about 1 cup)
- 1 small (5-oz.) red bell pepper, thinly sliced (about ¾ cup)
- 1 medium (3-oz.) carrot, peeled and cut into ⅛- x ⅛- x 2-inch pieces
- 1 (1½-inch) piece fresh ginger, peeled and cut into ⅛- x ⅛- x 1½-inch pieces
- ½ tsp. black pepper
- ¾ cup white vinegar or sugarcane vinegar (such as Datu Puti)
- ¼ cup granulated sugar

SECRET SAUCE

- ¾ cup mayonnaise (such as Duke's)
- ⅓ cup cornichons (about 1½ oz.), finely chopped
- ⅓ cup banana ketchup (such as Jufran)
- 1 Tbsp. chile vinegar (such as Datu Puti)
- 1¼ tsp. Korean chile flakes
- ¾ tsp. black pepper
- ¾ tsp. fine sea salt, plus more to taste

TOCINO BURGER PATTIES

- 1 lb. marinated cured pork tocino (such as Magnolia or Lucia)
- 12 oz. 80% lean ground pork
- 3 Tbsp. light brown sugar
- 1 Tbsp. plus 1 tsp. sugarcane vinegar (such as Datu Puti) or apple cider vinegar
- 2½ tsp. annatto oil (such as La Favorita)
- 4 medium garlic cloves, finely chopped (1 Tbsp. plus 1 tsp.)
- 1 tsp. fine sea salt
- 1 tsp. black pepper

ADDITIONAL INGREDIENTS

- ¼ cup unsalted butter, divided
- 8 Ube Buns (recipe p. 235), split horizontally
- 8 (¼-inch-thick) slices fresh pineapple (from 1 [16-oz.] peeled and cored pineapple)
- 1 Tbsp. canola oil

1. Make the green papaya achara: Cut papaya into ⅛- x ⅛- x 2-inch matchsticks to yield about 6 cups. (Reserve remaining papaya for another use.) Toss together papaya matchsticks and 2 tablespoons salt in a large bowl. Let stand at room temperature 30 minutes.

2. Transfer papaya mixture to a colander, and rinse under cold water. Using a clean dish towel, squeeze papaya mixture to remove as much excess moisture as possible. Toss together papaya, cabbage, onion, bell pepper, carrot, ginger, and black pepper in a large heatproof bowl. Bring white vinegar, granulated sugar, and remaining 1 teaspoon salt to a boil in a small saucepan over medium-high, stirring often to dissolve sugar. Pour hot vinegar mixture over papaya mixture; toss to combine. Cover and refrigerate until mixture is softened and vibrant in color, at least 30 minutes or up to 3 days.

3. Make the secret sauce: While papaya mixture chills, stir together mayonnaise, cornichons, banana ketchup, chile vinegar, Korean chile flakes, black pepper, and salt in a medium bowl. Season with additional salt to taste.

4. Make the tocino burger patties: Process tocino in a food processor until

finely chopped, about 20 seconds. Transfer to a large bowl; add ground pork, brown sugar, sugarcane vinegar, annatto oil, garlic, salt, and black pepper. Using your hands, mix until evenly combined. Divide mixture evenly into 16 balls (about 1¾ ounces or 3 tablespoons each). Flatten each ball to a 3-inch-round, ½-inch-thick patty. Set patties aside.

5. Melt 1 tablespoon butter in a large cast-iron skillet over medium. Place 2 ube buns, cut sides down, in skillet, and cook until golden and lightly crisp, about 2 minutes. Remove from skillet. Repeat process 3 times with remaining 3 tablespoons butter and remaining 6 buns. Set toasted buns aside. Increase heat under skillet to medium-high. Working in batches, cook pineapple slices in skillet until browned and starting to char on both sides, about 4 minutes per batch. Transfer pineapple to a plate. Do not wipe skillet clean.

6. Add canola oil to skillet, and reduce heat to medium. Arrange 4 tocino burger patties in skillet, and press firmly with a spatula to flatten to about ¼-inch thickness. Cook until browned on both sides and a thermometer inserted in thickest portion of meat registers 160°F, about 2 minutes per side. Transfer to a rimmed baking sheet, and tent with aluminum foil to keep warm. Repeat process with remaining 12 tocino burger patties (no need to add more oil in between batches).

7. Spread about 1 tablespoon secret sauce on each top ube bun half. Top each bottom bun half with 1 pineapple slice, 2 tocino burger patties, about ⅓ cup green papaya achara, and top bun half. Reserve remaining green papaya achara for another use. Serve burgers with additional secret sauce, if desired. —PAOLO DUNGCA AND TOM CUNANAN, POGIBOY, WASHINGTON, DC

MAKE AHEAD Green papaya achara and secret sauce can be made up to 3 days in advance and kept in separate airtight containers in the refrigerator. Tocino burger patty mixture can be combined and refrigerated in an airtight container up to 1 day before shaping into patties.

NOTE Datu Puti vinegar, annatto oil, and banana ketchup are available at most Asian markets or on amazon.com.

UBE BUNS

Ube Buns

ACTIVE 40 MIN; TOTAL 2 HR 35 MIN;
MAKES 8 BUNS

These vibrant purple buns — which serve as hamburger buns for the Tocino Burger (recipe p. 232) at PogiBoy in Washington, D.C. — are soft and bouncy with a tight, fluffy crumb, making them a great base for the restaurant's signature sweet-and-spicy burger. The fat from the coconut milk gives the buns a tender mouthfeel, while purple sweet potato powder and ube extract add vivid color. Their mild, subtle flavor makes them the ideal canvas for anything from hamburgers to lobster rolls or pulled pork, but they're especially well-matched for the spicy-sweet pork patties in the Tocino Burger. It's important to keep the steamer closed while the buns steam, and not to peek for at least 5 minutes while they are cooling, or the quick change in temperature can cause them to deflate and wrinkle.

- 1 cup water
- ⅓ cup unsweetened coconut milk (such as Aroy-D) (from 1 [14-oz.] can, well shaken and stirred)
- 1½ tsp. instant yeast
- 1 Tbsp. unsalted butter, melted
- 1 tsp. ube extract
- 3 cups all-purpose flour (about 12¾ oz.) plus 2 Tbsp. if needed
- ½ cup purple sweet potato flour (such as Suncore Foods Supercolor Powder) (about 3 oz.)
- 2 Tbsp. granulated sugar
- 2¼ tsp. baking powder
- ¾ tsp. fine sea salt
- Cooking spray

1. Combine 1 cup water and coconut milk in a medium-size microwavable bowl. Microwave on high until warmed to about 110°F, 30 to 40 seconds. Stir in yeast; let stand until foamy, about 5 minutes. Stir in butter and ube extract. Set aside.

2. Stir together all-purpose flour, purple sweet potato flour, sugar, baking powder, and salt in bowl of a stand mixer fitted with the dough hook. With mixer running on low speed, gradually stream yeast mixture into flour mixture. Beat on low speed until all dry ingredients are incorporated, about 1 minute. Increase mixer speed to medium, and beat until dough is smooth, elastic, and sticky, about 5 minutes. If dough feels too sticky, add up to 2 tablespoons additional flour, starting with 1 tablespoon, and beat until incorporated.

3. Using lightly greased (with cooking spray) hands, shape dough into a ball, and transfer to a lightly greased large bowl. Cover tightly with plastic wrap, and let proof at room temperature until doubled in volume, at least 40 minutes or up to 1 hour.

4. Meanwhile, cut 8 (4-inch) parchment paper squares. Arrange parchment paper squares evenly spaced on each tray of a 12-inch double-tier bamboo steamer, and set aside.

5. Turn dough out onto a lightly greased (with cooking spray) work surface, and divide evenly into 8 pieces (about 3¾ ounces each). Using a lightly greased hand, place 1 dough ball on an ungreased work surface. Make a claw shape with your hand, and, using the tension of the surface, shape dough into a taut ball. Place ball on 1 prepared parchment square in bamboo steamer. Repeat process with remaining dough pieces, regreasing hand as needed.

6. Stack bamboo trays, and place lid on steamer. Let dough proof at room temperature until volume has increased by about 1½ times, about 45 minutes. After about 30 minutes of proofing time, fill a wok or large skillet with water to a depth of 2 inches, and bring to a boil over medium-high.

7. Once buns have proofed, place steamer over boiling water; crack lid slightly to form a ¼-inch gap for steam to release. Cook over medium-high, without opening lid, 25 minutes. Remove from heat; let buns cool, without opening lid, 5 minutes.

8. Remove steamer from wok; remove lid, and unstack trays. Let buns cool slightly, about 15 minutes, or let cool completely, about 30 minutes. Split buns in half horizontally for burgers. Buns may be stored in an airtight container or ziplock plastic bag up to 1 day or in freezer up to 1 month. —PAOLO DUNGCA AND TOM CUNANAN, POGIBOY, WASHINGTON, DC

MAKE AHEAD Frozen buns should be thawed overnight in the refrigerator then cut in half before toasting and serving.

HOMEMADE CORN TORTILLAS

F&W Best New Chef Fermín Núñez of Suerte restaurant in Austin shared this recipe for making fresh tortillas at home using just the highest-quality masa harina, salt, and warm water. Mildly nutty with a little bit of natural sweetness and a deliciously strong corn fragrance, these tortillas are a tasty canvas for tacos. Choose a heavy tortilla press: the weight of the press does all of the work and will help form the most evenly shaped tortillas. Núñez prefers the Doña Rosa x Masienda Tortilla press. "This is the press that will outlive you," he says. "It's like the tortilla press you find in any reputable place that does tortillas in Mexico, from fancy restaurants to markets." Pair the fresh tortillas with Núñez's Charred Chile–Marinated Grilled Chicken and Tomatillo Salsa Cruda (p. 132), or enjoy them with your favorite taco fillings. Follow his step-by-step instructions here.

⏲ TOTAL 30 MIN; MAKES 12 (4½-INCH) TORTILLAS

- 1 cup masa harina (such as Masienda Chef-Grade Masa Harina White) (about 4¼ oz.)
- ¼ tsp. fine sea salt
- ⅔ cup plus 2 Tbsp. warm water (about 100°F), divided

1. Stir together masa harina and salt in a medium bowl. Add ⅓ cup warm water; mix together using your hands until mixture is evenly crumbly. Add ⅓ cup warm water; knead mixture in bowl until water is absorbed and dough is soft and smooth, 5 to 8 minutes, adding remaining 2 tablespoons warm water, 1 teaspoon at a time, as needed if dough feels dry. (Dough should be firm enough to hold an imprint and not stick to your hands but not so dry that it cracks when flattened between your palms.) Divide masa evenly into 12 (about ¾-ounce) pieces. Roll each piece into a ball using your hands, and place on a clean work surface; cover with a damp towel to prevent from drying out.

2. Cut along the side creases of a gallon-size ziplock plastic bag, leaving bottom edge attached. Line a tortilla press with the bag, covering the bottom plate, with attached edge of plastic bag running along hinge side of tortilla press.

3. Heat an ungreased comal or a large cast-iron skillet over medium-high. Open tortilla press, and place 1 masa ball on center of bottom plate in between layers of plastic. Cover with top plate; press down firmly to form a 5-inch tortilla. (Don't press too hard or masa will be too thin, and it will be difficult to lift off the bag.) Open tortilla press; carefully peel off top of bag from flattened tortilla. Lift bag, and flip tortilla onto 1 hand. Carefully peel back bottom of bag. If tortilla breaks or folds over, it's OK; just reroll tortilla into a ball, and repeat flattening process in tortilla press.

4. Gently lay tortilla on preheated comal. Cook until tortilla releases from comal and

STEP-BY-STEP

MIX AND KNEAD DOUGH Stir together masa harina and salt, gradually adding water and kneading, until dough is soft and smooth.

DIVIDE AND ROLL DOUGH Evenly divide dough into 12 portions. Roll each portion into a ball using your hands.

PREPARE THE PRESS Set a plastic bag, cut open along sides, on bottom plate of press. Place 1 masa ball in center of plate between the 2 layers of plastic.

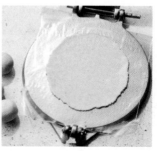

PRESS TORTILLAS Close press, and apply gentle pressure to flatten dough. Open and gently transfer tortilla to a preheated comal or cast-iron skillet.

can slide around and tortilla edges begin to lift, 20 to 30 seconds. Flip tortilla; cook until tortilla is matte white and looks dry on bottom, about 15 seconds. Flip tortilla again; cook until tortilla begins to puff up, 15 to 25 seconds. If tortilla doesn't puff, give it a little nudge by patting it gently with a damp towel to encourage puffing. Transfer puffed tortilla to a basket lined with a clean kitchen towel, and cover with towel to keep warm.

5. Repeat steps 3 and 4 using remaining 11 masa balls. Tortillas are best eaten hot off the comal. —FERMÍN NÚÑEZ

NOTE Masienda masa harina can be ordered from masienda.com

COOK THE TORTILLAS Cook tortillas over medium-high until they release from comal and edges lift, 20 to 30 seconds.

FLIP AND FINISH Flip tortillas, and cook until dry and matte white. Flip again, and cook until tortillas puff, patting with a damp towel to encourage puffing.

Scallion Pancakes

PHOTO P. 341

ACTIVE 1 HR; TOTAL 1 HR 30 MIN; SERVES 4

A generous layer of vegetable shortening not only helps incorporate the fresh scallions into the dough but also creates beautiful and delicious flaky layers in Lan Samantha Chang's scallion pancakes.

- 2 cups (about 8½ oz.) plus 2 Tbsp. all-purpose flour, plus more for dusting
- 1¼ tsp. kosher salt, divided
- ½ cup plus 2 Tbsp. warm water (110°F)
- 2 to 3 Tbsp. vegetable shortening (such as Crisco), divided
- ½ cup thinly sliced scallions, divided
- 6 Tbsp. vegetable oil, divided

1. Using chopsticks, stir together flour and ½ teaspoon salt in a large bowl. Create a small well in center of flour mixture. Add ½ cup plus 2 tablespoons warm water, and stir quickly using chopsticks until clumps of dough form. Knead until a smooth ball forms, 3 to 4 minutes. (Dough should not be sticky.) Cover bowl with plastic wrap; let rest at room temperature 30 minutes.

2. Uncover dough, and divide evenly into 2 portions. Shape 1 dough portion into a ball, keeping remaining dough portion covered with a towel until ready to use. Place dough ball on a lightly floured work surface or rolling board, and flatten slightly. Using a rolling pin, roll dough away from you and back toward you into an oval. Flip dough over, and rotate 90 degrees on work surface. Sprinkle with flour, if needed to prevent sticking, and repeat rolling process. Repeat rolling, flipping, and rotating process until dough forms a 12-inch round.

3. Using the back of a spoon, gently spread 1 to 1½ tablespoons shortening over dough round. The shortening does not need to be evenly spread, but the entire surface of dough should be covered. Sprinkle evenly with ¼ teaspoon plus ⅛ teaspoon salt. Sprinkle evenly with ¼ cup scallions, leaving a 1-inch border. Starting at bottom of dough round, roll dough into a tight log. Slice log in half crosswise. Working with 1 log half at a time, gently squeeze log to an even thickness and width (about 7×1 inch). Gently squeeze cut end of dough to enclose cut side by pressing exterior layer of dough together to seal. Starting with sealed end, coil log to form a tight spiral, tucking loose end under spiraled dough. Lightly dust with flour, and cover with a clean kitchen towel.

4. Repeat rolling and shaping process with remaining covered dough portion to yield 4 dough spirals total. Working with 1 dough spiral at a time, gently flatten and roll each spiral into a 7-inch pancake.

5. Heat 1½ tablespoons oil in a 10-inch cast-iron skillet or a 14-inch wok over medium-high until oil is fragrant and shimmering. Gently place 1 pancake in hot oil. Cook, gently pressing center of pancake to flatten as needed, until deep golden brown and cooked through, 2 to 3 minutes per side. Using tongs or a spatula, remove pancake from skillet, letting oil drip off, and place on a baking sheet lined with paper towels. Repeat cooking process with remaining 3 pancakes, adding 1½ tablespoons oil to skillet per pancake and reducing heat as needed to prevent burning. Cut each pancake into 4 wedges, and serve immediately. —LAN SAMANTHA CHANG

Socca with Zucchini and Olives

ACTIVE 25 MIN; TOTAL 50 MIN; SERVES 2 TO 4

Socca, also called farinata in Liguria, is a tender pancake made from chickpea flour. Unlike the versions in Nice, which are cooked in copper pans, this one is baked in a cast-iron skillet before it is topped with a summery marinated squash salad. Preheating the cast-iron skillet in a 450°F oven yields a socca that is both crisp and tender.

- 1 cup chickpea flour (such as Bob's Red Mill) (about 3¼ oz.)
- 1 cup lukewarm water
- 2½ Tbsp. extra-virgin olive oil, divided
- 1 tsp. kosher salt, divided
- ½ tsp. black pepper, divided
  Canola oil, for brushing
- 1 small zucchini (about 6 oz.), shaved lengthwise with a vegetable peeler
- 1 small yellow squash (about 5 oz.), shaved lengthwise with a vegetable peeler
- ⅓ cup pitted Niçoise or kalamata olives, chopped
- ⅓ cup sliced (¼- to ½-inch pieces) fresh chives
- 1½ Tbsp. fresh lemon juice (from 1 lemon)
- 1 tsp. fresh oregano leaves
  Shredded ricotta salata cheese, for garnish

1. Preheat oven to 450°F. Place a 12-inch cast-iron skillet in preheated oven; let heat 10 minutes. Meanwhile, whisk together flour, 1 cup water, 1 tablespoon olive oil, ¾ teaspoon salt, and ¼ teaspoon pepper in a medium bowl until completely smooth, about 30 seconds. Let stand at room temperature 10 minutes.

2. Carefully remove hot skillet from oven; lightly brush skillet with canola oil. Pour flour mixture into prepared skillet. Return to oven, and bake at 450°F until socca is set and lightly browned around edges, about 12 minutes.

3. Meanwhile, toss together zucchini, yellow squash, olives, chives, lemon juice, remaining 1½ tablespoons olive oil, remaining ¼ teaspoon salt, and remaining ¼ teaspoon pepper in a medium bowl until well combined. Set aside until ready to serve.

4. Invert socca onto a clean work surface. Top with zucchini mixture, leaving a 1-inch border; sprinkle with oregano, and garnish with ricotta salata. Cut into 8 slices. Serve immediately. —JUSTIN CHAPPLE

WINE Coastal French rosé: 2021 Clos Cibonne Cuvée Tradition

SOCCA WITH ZUCCHINI AND OLIVES

CURRY CHICKEN–AND–
SWEET POTATO GALETTE

Curry Chicken–and–Sweet Potato Galette

ACTIVE 30 MIN; TOTAL 2 HR 35 MIN,
SERVES 6

Alexander Hardy infuses flavor into each layer of this golden galette. The crust, seasoned with turmeric and garlic, surrounds a savory blend of green seasoning–spiked chicken thighs, roasted sweet potatoes, and sweet mixed bell peppers. Choose jarred sofrito for a shortcut, or make the piquant, herbal green seasoning from scratch.

CHICKEN

- 1 cup finely chopped yellow onion
- ½ cup thinly sliced scallions
- 2 Tbsp. finely chopped garlic
- 2 Tbsp. curry powder, divided
- 1½ tsp. chopped fresh Scotch bonnet chile (optional), seeded, if desired
- ½ tsp. grated peeled fresh ginger
- 1½ tsp. ground allspice, divided
- ½ tsp. kosher salt
- ¼ tsp. black pepper
- 2 (4-oz.) boneless, skinless chicken thighs, cut into 1-inch chunks
- 2 Tbsp. olive oil
- ¼ cup water

SAVORY PASTRY

- 1½ cups all-purpose flour (about 6⅜ oz.), plus more for work surface
- 10 Tbsp. unsalted butter (5 oz.), cut into 16 cubes and frozen
- 1 tsp. ground turmeric
- 1 tsp. garlic powder
- 1 tsp. fresh thyme leaves
- ½ tsp. kosher salt
- ½ tsp. black pepper
- ½ cup ice water, as needed

GREEN SEASONING

- 1 cup roughly chopped fresh flat-leaf parsley
- ⅔ cup chopped yellow bell pepper
- ⅔ cup chopped green bell pepper
- ⅔ cup chopped red bell pepper
- 1 small red onion, roughly chopped (about ⅔ cup)
- 1 small white onion, roughly chopped (about ⅔ cup)
- 4 medium scallions, roughly chopped (about ½ cup)
- 8 medium garlic cloves, smashed
- 2 Tbsp. grated peeled fresh ginger
- 2 Tbsp. olive oil
- 2 Tbsp. fresh lime juice

- 1½ tsp. chopped fresh Scotch bonnet chile (optional), seeded, if desired
- ¾ tsp. kosher salt
- 6 (3-inch) thyme sprigs

SWEET POTATO FILLING

- 1 medium-size (8-oz.) sweet potato, peeled, cut into ¼-inch-thick rounds, and then cut into quarters
- 2 Tbsp. olive oil
- 1 tsp. garlic powder
- 1 tsp. ground ginger
- 1 tsp. smoked paprika
- ½ tsp. kosher salt

SEASONED SOUR CREAM

- ¼ cup sour cream
- 3 Tbsp. Green Seasoning or sofrito
- 1½ tsp. ground turmeric
- 1½ tsp. garlic powder
- ½ tsp. kosher salt
- ½ tsp. black pepper

ADDITIONAL INGREDIENTS

- 5 yellow bell pepper slices
- 5 green bell pepper slices
- 5 orange or red bell pepper slices
- 1 large egg, lightly beaten

1. Make the chicken: Combine onion, scallions, garlic, 1 tablespoon curry powder, Scotch bonnet chile (if using), ginger, ½ teaspoon allspice, salt, and black pepper in a ziplock plastic bag or an airtight container with a lid. Add chicken; seal and toss to fully coat. Refrigerate at least 1 hour or up to overnight (12 hours).

2. Make the savory pastry: Pulse flour, frozen butter, turmeric, garlic powder, thyme leaves, salt, and black pepper in a food processor until combined, about 6 pulses. Add ice water, 1 tablespoon at a time, as needed, pulsing until mixture begins to come together and resembles coarse sand. Transfer dough mixture to a lightly floured work surface; gather and knead gently until combined. (Chunks of butter should be speckled throughout.) Place dough in center of a sheet of plastic wrap; using a rolling pin or your hand, flatten dough into a 1-inch-thick disk. Wrap tightly in plastic wrap. Refrigerate until firm, at least 1 hour or up to overnight (12 hours).

3. Make the green seasoning: Process parsley, chopped bell peppers, red and white onions, scallions, garlic, ginger, oil, lime juice, Scotch bonnet chile (if using), salt, and thyme in a blender or food processor until smooth, about 30 seconds.

Refrigerate in an airtight container until ready to use or up to 3 days.

4. Make the sweet potato filling: Preheat oven to 375°F. Toss together sweet potato, oil, garlic powder, ginger, smoked paprika, and salt a large bowl until coated. Transfer to a baking sheet lined with parchment paper. Roast in preheated oven until golden brown and tender, about 15 minutes. Let cool about 15 minutes.

5. Meanwhile, cook the chicken: Heat oil in a large skillet over medium. Add remaining 1 tablespoon curry powder and remaining 1 teaspoon allspice to oil, and cook, stirring constantly, until spices begin to toast and darken, about 1 minute. Remove chicken from marinade; brush off and discard excess marinade. Add chicken to skillet, stirring to coat in oil mixture. Cook, stirring occasionally, until chicken begins to brown, 2 to 3 minutes. Add ¼ cup water; cover and cook until chicken is tender and an instant-read thermometer inserted in thickest portion of meat registers 160°F, 6 to 8 minutes. Uncover skillet; cook, uncovered, stirring occasionally, until liquid is reduced, about 1 minute. Remove from heat; let cool slightly, about 10 minutes.

6. Make the seasoned sour cream: Stir together sour cream, green seasoning, turmeric, garlic powder, salt, and black pepper until well combined. Set aside.

7. Assemble the galette: Roll savory pastry dough out into a 12-inch circle on a lightly floured work surface. Transfer pastry to a rimmed baking sheet lined with parchment paper. Spread ¼ cup seasoned sour cream over pastry, leaving a 2-inch border. Arrange sweet potato filling on sour cream within border. Top with cooked chicken. Arrange bell pepper slices on and around chicken.

8. Fold pastry edges up and over the outer 1-inch edge of galette, pleating crust as needed. Brush top of pastry with beaten egg. Bake at 375°F until crust is golden brown and bell peppers are starting to wilt and brown, about 45 minutes. Remove from oven. Let rest 5 to 10 minutes. Serve warm or at room temperature with additional seasoned sour cream and green seasoning.

—ALEXANDER HARDY

MAKE AHEAD Savory pastry can be made and refrigerated up to 2 days ahead or frozen up to 1 month.

NOTE Find store-bought jarred sofrito at loisa.com.

Zucchini, Corn, and Shrimp Flatbread

ACTIVE 30 MIN; TOTAL 40 MIN; SERVES 4

Store-bought naan flatbreads get toasty on the grill, layered with mascarpone cheese, sweet shrimp, juicy corn, and tender ribbons of fresh zucchini. Don't skimp on the garnish of smoked paprika — it adds a dash of vibrant color and enhances the smoky flavor. This recipe was inspired by a favorite combination of Wine Director Mikayla Cohen of Starr Restaurant Group in Philadelphia and New York City, who loves to match toasty flatbreads with a white wine — specifically, with Keplinger Eldorado Sierra Foothills White Rhône Blend. "The creamy mascarpone base pairs perfectly with Keplinger Eldorado's blend of Viognier, Roussanne, and Grenache Blanc," she says.

- 1 (8-oz.) container mascarpone cheese
- 1 garlic clove, grated with a Microplane grater (¼ tsp.)
- 2 tsp. kosher salt, divided
- 3 medium (8-oz.) zucchini, sliced lengthwise into ⅛-inch-thick planks
- 2 (8-oz.) ears fresh yellow corn, husks removed
- ¼ cup extra-virgin olive oil, divided
- ½ tsp. black pepper, divided, plus more for serving
- 1 lb. unpeeled raw medium shrimp (thawed if frozen)
- 4 (3-oz.) naan flatbreads (such as Stonefire)
- ½ tsp. smoked paprika
- Torn fresh basil, for garnish

1. Stir together mascarpone, garlic, and ½ teaspoon salt in a medium bowl; set aside. Toss together zucchini, corn, 1 tablespoon oil, ¼ teaspoon pepper, and 1 teaspoon salt in a large bowl.

2. Peel shrimp, and devein. Using a paring knife, gently cut along back of shrimp, cutting three-fourths of the way through, until you reach the tail. Toss together butterflied shrimp, 1 tablespoon oil, remaining ½ teaspoon salt, and remaining ¼ teaspoon pepper in a medium bowl. Brush both sides of flatbreads evenly with remaining 2 tablespoons oil.

3. Preheat grill to high (450°F to 500°F). Place corn on oiled grates; grill, uncovered, until corn is bright yellow and evenly charred, about 10 minutes, turning occasionally. Add zucchini, shrimp, and flatbreads during final 5 minutes of corn grilling time; grill, uncovered, until shrimp are just pink on each side, about 1 minute and 30 seconds per side; zucchini is charred and just tender, 1 to 2 minutes per side; and flatbreads are lightly toasted on bottoms, 1 to 2 minutes. Transfer corn to a cutting board, and transfer zucchini, shrimp, and flatbreads to a baking sheet. Cut corn kernels from cobs; discard cobs.

4. Reduce grill temperature to medium (350°F to 400°F). Stir corn kernels into mascarpone mixture in medium bowl until combined. Spread about ¼ cup corn-mascarpone mixture over grilled side of each flatbread. Top evenly with zucchini and shrimp. Sprinkle evenly with smoked paprika. Grill flatbreads, covered, until bottoms are lightly toasted, 2 to 3 minutes. Garnish with basil and additional pepper. Cut into planks, and serve. —ANNA THEOKTISTO

MAKE AHEAD Prepared shrimp and vegetables may be grilled up to 1 day ahead and kept covered and chilled before assembling and grilling flatbreads.

WINE 2018 Keplinger Eldorado Sierra Foothills White Rhône Blend

ZUCCHINI, CORN, AND
SHRIMP FLATBREAD

ARTISAN PIZZA DOUGH

Despite its reputation as a convenience food, the most essential element of great pizza is time. A slow fermentation gives our pizza dough its chewy-crispy texture and depth of flavor. It starts with your choice of sourdough starter (aka levain) or a simple mixture of flour, water, and active dry yeast (poolish) left to ferment for 12 hours. Both options start fermentation and build flavor in the dough overnight. Strategic stretching of the dough during the initial fermentation stage develops gluten and makes the dough evenly elastic and forgiving to work with. Each 9-ounce dough ball will make one 10-inch pizza, a personal-size pie that's also easy to maneuver around home countertops and ovens. This overnight dough is easily doubled for pizza parties. Not cooking for a crowd? The raw dough may be frozen.

ACTIVE 20 MIN; TOTAL 3 HR 20 MIN, PLUS 12 HR STANDING; MAKES 6 (9-OZ.) PIZZA DOUGH BALLS

- 2¼ cups (about 18 oz. or 510 grams) warm water (about 80°F)
- Levain or poolish (see sidebar, opposite)
- 7 cups (about 1 lb. 13¾ oz. or 850 grams) organic unbleached bread flour (such as King Arthur), plus more for work surface
- 1 Tbsp. (about ½ oz. or 16 grams) fine sea salt
- 2 Tbsp. (about ¾ oz. or 20 grams) extra-virgin olive oil, plus more for greasing

1. Stir together 2¼ cups warm water and levain in a large bowl until levain is mostly dissolved. Add flour and salt. Stir using a wooden spoon to form a shaggy dough. When dough becomes too stiff to stir with spoon, knead dough in bowl to form a ball. Turn dough onto a clean work surface, and knead until there are no dry patches of flour, about 1 minute. (Dough will be sticky. To easily clean doughy hands, sprinkle hands lightly with flour, and rub together over a trash can to loosen any stuck dough.) Place dough in a clean large bowl, and drizzle with oil. Knead dough in bowl until oil is incorporated, about 1 minute. Cover bowl tightly with plastic wrap, and let rest at room temperature until dough begins to rise, about 1 hour.

2. Uncover dough; starting at edge of bowl farthest from body, use a wet hand to lift edge of dough and stretch until there is tension, approximately 1 foot in the air (see photo, opposite). Press the dough in toward the center; rotate bowl 90 degrees, and repeat motion to fold dough 4 times total. Flip dough seam side down; cover tightly with plastic wrap, and let stand 1 hour. Repeat folding process 1 more time.

3. Cover dough bowl tightly with plastic wrap, and let stand at room temperature until tripled in volume, about 12 hours, or refrigerate until increased in volume 2½ to 3 times, at least 24 hours or up to 48 hours.

4. Line a large rimmed baking sheet with plastic wrap, leaving about 3 inches of overhang on all sides; lightly grease plastic wrap with oil. Alternatively, lightly grease insides of 6 lidded plastic pint containers with oil. Set aside.

5. Uncover dough, and gently press to release air bubbles. Turn dough out onto a heavily floured work surface. Divide dough evenly into 6 portions (about 9 ounces or 255 grams each). Working with 1 dough piece at a time, stretch and fold 4 corners of dough in toward center. Flip dough seam side down. Using a bench scraper and a

---

STEP-BY-STEP

TURN IT OUT Gently press dough to release air bubbles, then turn out onto a heavily floured work surface.

DIVIDE DOUGH Divide the dough evenly into 6 portions (about 9 ounces or 255 grams each).

SHAPE DOUGH Working with 1 dough piece at a time, stretch and fold 4 corners of dough in toward center. Using a bench scraper, rotate gradually until dough forms a taut ball.

REPEAT THE PROCESS Repeat shaping process with remaining dough pieces, placing each one on a rimmed baking sheet lined with oiled plastic wrap (or place in 6 oiled plastic pint containers).

DO THE "POKE" TEST After proofing, poke the dough with your finger. if it bounces back right away, let it rise a bit longer. If an indentation remains, it's ready to go.

lightly floured hand, drag dough across work surface, rotating dough gradually with your hand as you pull it with bench scraper, until dough forms a taut ball. Using bench scraper, transfer dough ball, seam side down, to prepared baking sheet (or to 1 prepared pint container). Repeat process with remaining 5 dough pieces, spacing evenly apart on baking sheet, and pulling plastic wrap up between dough balls to prevent sticking (or place in 6 oiled plastic pint containers). Cover tightly with plastic wrap or lids.

6. For faster dough, let proof at room temperature 1 hour, and then refrigerate at least 1 hour or up to 5 hours. Alternatively, for more flavorful dough, let dough proof more slowly in refrigerator, at least 6 hours or up to 3 days. —MARY- FRANCES HECK AND PAIGE GRANDJEAN

MAKE AHEAD Dough balls can be frozen in lightly greased individual freezer-safe pint containers up to 2 weeks. Let thaw in refrigerator at least 12 hours or up to 2 days.

NOTE If you're new to making pizza, prepare a double batch of dough to get the hang of shaping and baking. Practice makes perfect.

POOLISH

Stir together ¾ cup unbleached bread flour (about 3¼ ounces or 95 grams), ½ cup warm water (about 80°F) (4 ounces or 115 grams), and a pinch of active dry yeast (about 1/16 teaspoon) in a medium bowl. Cover loosely with a clean kitchen towel, and let ferment at cool room temperature (about 65°F) until increased in volume 2½ to 3 times, about 12 hours.

LEVAIN

Stir together ½ cup warm water (about 80°F) (4 ounces or 115 grams) and ¾ ounce mature sourdough starter (about 1½ tablespoons or 25 grams) in a medium bowl until starter is mostly dissolved. Stir in ¾ cup unbleached bread flour (about 3¼ ounces or 95 grams) until well combined and mixture resembles thick batter. Cover loosely with a clean kitchen towel; let stand at room temperature until increased in volume 2½ to 3 times, at least 4 hours or up to 8 hours.

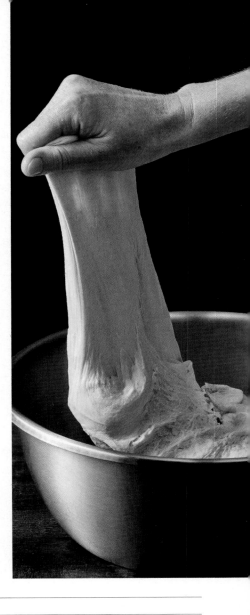

PRESS IT OUT Transfer 1 dough ball to a heavily floured surface. Using floured fingertips, firmly press all over dough, leaving a ½-inch border.

DEFINE THE OUTER CRUST Form a C-shape with the outer edge of your hand, and press firmly inside dough border to define a ½-inch wide ring around edge of dough.

THIN IT OUT Lift the dough onto the knuckles of both hands, and gently stretch.

KEEP IT ROUND Continue gently stretching the dough, rotating after each stretch, allowing gravity to help it expand until, a 10-inch circle of even thickness forms, with a slightly thicker outer ring.

GET READY TO TOP Lay dough round on a semolina-dusted pizza peel, reshaping as needed to form a circle.

Classic Cheese Pizza

ACTIVE 20 MINS; TOTAL 1 HR 40 MINS;
SERVINGS 1

Sometimes all you want at the end of the day is a simple cheese pizza. This recipe turns simple into sublime with the addition of an exceptional pizza dough, low-moisture mozzarella cheese, and an easy to make tomato sauce that hits all of the right sweet and savory notes to marry all of the flavors in this pie. A simple garnish of fresh herbs, and you've got perfection on a plate.

- 1 ball Artisan Pizza Dough (recipe p. 244)
- All-purpose flour, for dusting
- Semolina flour, for dusting
- ¼ cup Basic Pizza Sauce (recipe p. 309)
- 3 ounces shredded low-moisture mozzarella
- Fresh basil or oregano leaves, for garnishing

1. Let chilled covered dough stand at room temperature until dough is cool (not cold) and a fingerprint remains when dough is pressed, 1 to 2 hours. Transfer 1 dough ball to a heavily floured surface. Using floured fingertips, firmly press all over dough, leaving a ½-inch border.

2. If cooking in your home oven, preheat to 500°F with a baking steel or large round cast-iron pizza pan (such as Lodge 15-inch) on middle rack. Let pan preheat in oven for about 30 minutes. If using an outdoor pizza oven, preheat pizza oven and pizza stone according to manufacturer's instructions on high 20 minutes. (Note: Cooking with wood takes more experience to control the heat, so we've only included instructions for gas oven cooking here.)

3. Form a C-shape with the outer edge of your hand, and press firmly inside dough border to define a ½-inch wide ring around edge of dough. Lift dough onto the knuckles of both hands, and gently stretch, rotating dough after each stretch to maintain its round shape. Continue gently stretching dough, allowing gravity to help it expand, until a 10-inch circle of even thickness forms, with a slightly thicker outer ring. Lay dough round on a semolina-dusted pizza peel, reshaping as needed to form a circle. Spread dough round with Basic Pizza Sauce. Top with shredded mozzarella.

4. Gently shake pizza peel with prepared pie to loosen. If pizza feels stuck in any areas, carefully lift pizza edge with a bench scraper, and dust peel with a 1:1 mixture of semolina and bread flour. Unload pizza onto preheated pan in home oven, or onto stone in outdoor pizza oven using quick, decisive movements: Set the peel edge on the pan at about a 20-degree angle, and quickly pull back peel to slide half of the pizza onto the pan. Gently shake the peel side to side while pulling it back to slide the rest of the pizza onto the pan, allowing it to stretch slightly.

5. If baking in a home oven, bake at 500°F until edges of crust have puffed slightly, about 3 minutes. Rotate pan 90 degrees, and increase oven temperature to broil. Broil until pizza is cooked through and crust is browned, 3 to 6 minutes. If baking in an outdoor pizza oven, cook pizza, using peel to rotate pizza 90 degrees every 20 to 30 seconds, until cooked through and crust is risen and charred in spots, 2 to 4 minutes.

6. Using peel, transfer pizza to a cutting board. Garnish with fresh basil or oregano, if desired, and cut into wedges.

CLASSIC CHEESE PIZZA

Potato Pizza with Crème Fraîche and Bacon

ACTIVE 20 MIN; TOTAL 1 HR 40 MIN;
SERVINGS 1

It may seem like a crazy idea, but doubling the carbs on this pizza is one delicious way to serve up a pie. This pizza starts with the flavors of the classic Alsatian pizza, made with crème fraîche, caramelized onion, and bacon, and adds soft confit garlic cloves and thin slices of potatoes. A little greenery from kale and chives, and you've got an exceptional pizza to both look at and eat.

- 1 ball Artisan Pizza Dough (recipe p. 244)
  All-purpose flour, for dusting
  Semolina flour, for dusting
- 3 tablespoons crème fraîche
- 4 smashed cloves of Garlic Confit (recipe p. 303)
- 2 ounces thinly sliced potato
- ¾ ounce caramelized onions
- ¼ ounce cooked crumbled bacon
- 6 baby kale leaves
  Chopped fresh chives, for garnishing

1. Let chilled covered dough stand at room temperature until dough is cool (not cold) and a fingerprint remains when dough is pressed, 1 to 2 hours. Transfer 1 dough ball to a heavily floured surface. Using floured fingertips, firmly press all over dough, leaving a ½-inch border.

2. If cooking in your home oven, preheat to 500°F with a baking steel or large round cast-iron pizza pan (such as Lodge 15-inch) on middle rack. Let pan preheat in oven for about 30 minutes. If using an outdoor pizza oven, preheat pizza oven and pizza stone according to manufacturer's instructions on high 20 minutes. (Note: Cooking with

wood takes more experience to control the heat, so we've only included instructions for gas oven cooking here.)

3. Form a C-shape with the outer edge of your hand, and press firmly inside dough border to define a ½-inch wide ring around edge of dough. Lift dough onto the knuckles of both hands, and gently stretch, rotating dough after each stretch to maintain its round shape. Continue gently stretching dough, allowing gravity to help it expand, until a 10-inch circle of even thickness forms, with a slightly thicker outer ring. Lay dough round on a semolina-dusted pizza peel, reshaping as needed to form a circle. Spread dough round with crème fraîche and 4 smashed garlic confit. Layer with potato, onions, bacon, and baby kale.

4. Gently shake pizza peel with prepared pie to loosen. If pizza feels stuck in any areas, carefully lift pizza edge with a bench scraper, and dust peel with a 1:1 mixture of semolina and bread flour. Unload pizza onto preheated pan in home oven, or into stone in outdoor pizza oven using quick, decisive movements: Set the peel edge on the pan at about a 20-degree angle, and quickly pull back peel to slide half of the pizza onto the pan. Gently shake the peel side to side while pulling it back to slide the rest of the pizza onto the pan, allowing it to stretch slightly.

5. If baking in a home oven, bake at 500°F until edges of crust have puffed slightly, about 3 minutes. Rotate pan 90 degrees, and increase oven temperature to broil. Broil until pizza is cooked through and crust is browned, 3 to 6 minutes. If baking in an outdoor pizza oven, cook pizza, using peel to rotate pizza 90 degrees every 20 to 30 seconds, until cooked through and crust is risen and charred in spots, 2 to 4 minutes.

6. Using peel, transfer pizza to a cutting board. Garnish with chives, and cut into wedges.

Wild Mushroom Pizza
PHOTO P. 223

ACTIVE 20 MIN; TOTAL 1 HR 40 MIN;
SERVINGS 1

It's important not to weigh your pizza down with too many toppings, which can make for a soggy pie, so this pizza only requires a small amount of wild mushrooms. Choose whatever looks best at the market. That said, we love this pizza with a drizzle of Fancy Ranch dressing (which almost makes it a salad, right?) Fancy Ranch is a homemade ranch dressing gussied up with a few chopped briny anchovies. But why stop with just a drizzle when you can also serve the pizza with a small bowl of the dressing alongside for dipping?

- 1 ball Artisan Pizza Dough (recipe p. 244)
  All-purpose flour, for dusting
  Semolina flour, for dusting
- ¼ cup Basic Pizza Sauce (recipe p. 309)
- 2 ounces torn fresh mozzarella
- 1 ounce sliced or torn wild mushrooms
  Olive oil
  Salt
  Fancy Ranch, for drizzling (recipe p. 303)

1. Let chilled covered dough stand at room temperature until dough is cool (not cold) and a fingerprint remains when dough is pressed, 1 to 2 hours. Transfer 1 dough ball to a heavily floured surface. Using floured fingertips, firmly press all over dough, leaving a ½-inch border.

2. If cooking in your home oven, preheat to 500°F with a baking steel or large round cast-iron pizza pan (such as Lodge 15-inch) on middle rack. Let pan preheat in oven for about 30 minutes. If using an outdoor pizza oven, preheat pizza oven and pizza stone according to manufacturer's instructions on high 20 minutes. (Note: Cooking with wood takes more experience to control the heat, so we've only included instructions for gas oven cooking here.)

3. Form a C-shape with the outer edge of your hand, and press firmly inside dough border to define a ½-inch wide ring around edge of dough. Lift dough onto the knuckles of both hands, and gently stretch, rotating

continued on page 250

continued from page 249

dough after each stretch to maintain its round shape. Continue gently stretching dough, allowing gravity to help it expand, until a 10-inch circle of even thickness forms, with a slightly thicker outer ring. Lay dough round on a semolina-dusted pizza peel, reshaping as needed to form a circle. Spread dough round with Basic Pizza Sauce. Top with fresh mozzarella. Place mushrooms in a small bowl, drizzle with olive oil, and season with salt. Scatter over pizza.

4. Gently shake pizza peel with prepared pie to loosen. If pizza feels stuck in any areas, carefully lift pizza edge with a bench scraper, and dust peel with a 1:1 mixture of semolina and bread flour. Unload pizza onto preheated pan in home oven, or into stone in outdoor pizza oven using quick, decisive movements: Set the peel edge on the pan at about a 20-degree angle, and quickly pull back peel to slide half of the pizza onto the pan. Gently shake the peel side to side while pulling it back to slide the rest of the pizza onto the pan, allowing it to stretch slightly.

5. If baking in a home oven, bake at 500°F until edges of crust have puffed slightly, about 3 minutes. Rotate pan 90 degrees, and increase oven temperature to broil. Broil until pizza is cooked through and crust is browned, 3 to 6 minutes. If baking in an outdoor pizza oven, cook pizza, using peel to rotate pizza 90 degrees every 20 to 30 seconds, until cooked through and crust is risen and charred in spots, 2 to 4 minutes.

6. Using peel, transfer pizza to a cutting board. Drizzle with Fancy Ranch, and cut into wedges.

Soppressata Pizza with Calabrian Chilies and Hot Honey

ACTIVE 20 MIN; TOTAL 1 HRS 40 MINS; SERVINGS 1

Take a little soppressata, some chopped calabrian chiles, and a drizzle of hot honey, and you'll end up with the pizza of the moment. Calabrian chiles, fiery chiles from Italy, add heat and a distinctly fruity flavor to this pie. The hot honey mirrors the flavors of the chiles, and adds a touch of sweetness.

- 1 ball Artisan Pizza Dough (recipe p. 244)
- All-purpose flour, for dusting
- Semolina flour, for dusting
- ¼ cup Basic Pizza Sauce (recipe p. 309)
- 1½ ounces torn fresh mozzarella
- 1 ounce thinly sliced soppressata
- ¼ ounce thinly sliced red onion
- ½ ounce jarred Calabrian chiles (optional)
- Fresh oregano leaves
- Hot Honey (recipe p. 303)

1. Let chilled covered dough stand at room temperature until dough is cool (not cold) and a fingerprint remains when dough is pressed, 1 to 2 hours. Transfer 1 dough ball to a heavily floured surface. Using floured fingertips, firmly press all over dough, leaving a ½-inch border.

2. If cooking in your home oven, preheat to 500°F with a baking steel or large round cast-iron pizza pan (such as Lodge 15-inch) on middle rack. Let pan preheat in oven for about 30 minutes. If using an outdoor pizza oven, preheat pizza oven and pizza stone according to manufacturer's instructions on high 20 minutes. (Note: Cooking with wood takes more experience to control the heat, so we've only included instructions for gas oven cooking here.)

3. Form a C-shape with the outer edge of your hand, and press firmly inside dough border to define a ½-inch wide ring around edge of dough. Lift dough onto the knuckles of both hands, and gently stretch, rotating dough after each stretch to maintain its round shape. Continue gently stretching dough, allowing gravity to help it expand, until a 10-inch circle of even thickness forms, with a slightly thicker outer ring. Lay dough round on a semolina-dusted pizza peel, reshaping as needed to form a circle. Spread dough round with Basic Pizza Sauce. Top with torn mozzarella, soppressata, red onion, chiles, if using, and fresh oregano leaves.

4. Gently shake pizza peel with prepared pie to loosen. If pizza feels stuck in any areas, carefully lift pizza edge with a bench scraper, and dust peel with a 1:1 mixture of semolina and bread flour. Unload pizza onto preheated pan in home oven, or into stone in outdoor pizza oven using quick, decisive movements: Set the peel edge on the pan at about a 20-degree angle, and quickly pull back peel to slide half of the pizza onto the pan. Gently shake the peel side to side while pulling it back to slide the rest of the pizza onto the pan, allowing it to stretch slightly.

5. If baking in home oven, bake at 500°F until edges of crust have puffed slightly, about 3 minutes. Rotate pan 90 degrees, and increase oven temperature to broil. Broil until pizza is cooked through and crust is browned, 3 to 6 minutes. If baking in an outdoor pizza oven, cook pizza, using peel to rotate pizza 90 degrees every 20 to 30 seconds, until cooked through and crust is risen and charred in spots, 2 to 4 minutes.

6. Using peel, transfer pizza to a cutting board. Drizzle with Hot Honey, and cut into wedges.

NOTES Find Tutto Calabria chiles online at supermarketitaly.com.

SOPPRESSATA PIZZA
WITH CALABRIAN CHILIES
AND HOT HONEY

VEGAN WILD MUSHROOM PIZZA

Vegan Wild Mushroom Pizza

ACTIVE 55 MIN; TOTAL 2 HR 15 MIN;
MAKES 4 (9-INCH) PIZZAS

Store-bought pizza dough makes these vegan pies a quick weeknight meal. "The Wild Mushroom & Truffle Pizza has all the right moves to achieve ultimate comfort-food status. The garlic crema balances the mushrooms' earthy flavor, while thinly sliced brussels sprouts add an awesome crunch," says chef Mary Dumont of PlantPub in Cambridge, Massachusetts, who shared her recipe with Food & Wine. *"When I was creating the 100% plant-based menu for PlantPub, I wanted to reimagine classic pub fare that everyone knows and loves. It's been the perfect gateway for people to eat food that is better for them and better for the planet." When assembling the pies, keep the toppings sparse in the center as they will slide toward the middle when the dough puffs. For the best results, allow the baking stone to reheat after each pizza to ensure consistently crispy crusts.*

DOUGH

- 2 (1-lb.) balls fresh prepared pizza dough
- All-purpose flour, for dusting

GARLIC RANCH

- 8 oz. silken tofu (about 1 cup) (from 1 [16-oz.] pkg.)
- ½ cup vegan mayonnaise
- 1 Tbsp. chopped fresh dill
- 2 garlic cloves, chopped (about 1 Tbsp.)
- ¾ tsp. garlic powder
- ¾ tsp. rice vinegar
- ¾ tsp. red wine vinegar
- ¾ tsp. kosher salt
- ½ tsp. onion powder

WILD MUSHROOMS

- 1 Tbsp. plant-based salted butter (such as Miyoko's Creamery European Style Cultured Vegan Butter)
- 1 Tbsp. finely chopped shallot
- 1 garlic clove, finely chopped (about 1 tsp.)
- 1 (8-oz.) pkg. mixed fresh wild mushrooms, broken into small clusters or cut lengthwise into ¼-inch-thick slices
- 1 tsp. chopped fresh thyme
- 1 tsp. kosher salt
- ½ tsp. black pepper

ADDITIONAL INGREDIENTS

- 6 oz. vegan mozzarella shreds (such as Numu) (about 1½ cups)
- 3 oz. fresh brussels sprouts (about 5 medium brussels sprouts), trimmed and shaved lengthwise using a chef's knife (about 1⅓ cups)
- White truffle oil

1. Make the dough: Divide pizza dough balls evenly into 4 pieces total (about 8 ounces each). Shape each dough piece into a taut ball, and place, seam side down, on a well-floured surface. Cover loosely with plastic wrap, and let rest until dough is room temperature, 1 hour to 1 hour and 30 minutes. Meanwhile, place a baking stone or steel on middle oven rack, and preheat oven to 450°F for 30 minutes.

2. Make the garlic ranch: Process tofu, vegan mayonnaise, dill, garlic, garlic powder, rice vinegar, red wine vinegar, salt, and onion powder in a blender until smooth, about 30 seconds. Set aside.

3. Make the wild mushrooms: Heat a large skillet over medium-high. Add butter; cook, stirring constantly, until melted, about 5 seconds. Add shallot and garlic;

cook, stirring constantly, until fragrant, about 15 seconds. Add mushrooms, thyme, salt, and pepper; cook, stirring often, until mushrooms are tender, 3 to 4 minutes. Remove from heat; transfer mixture to a medium bowl.

4. Place 1 dough ball on a well-floured work surface. Using your fingers, stretch dough into a 10-inch round. Transfer dough round to a lightly floured pizza peel.

5. Spread 3 tablespoons garlic ranch over dough round, leaving a ½-inch border. Top with 1½ ounces (heaping ¼ cup) wild mushrooms, 1½ ounces (about ½ cup) mozzarella shreds, and ¾ ounce (about ⅓ cup) shaved brussels sprouts.

6. Carefully slide pizza onto preheated baking stone in preheated oven. Bake until pizza is bubbly in the center, brussels sprouts are starting to crisp, and crust is charred in spots, 15 to 18 minutes. If needed to get a nice char on top, increase oven temperature to broil with oven rack 8 inches from heat; broil pizza 2 to 3 minutes. Transfer pizza to a cutting board, and drizzle lightly with white truffle oil. Repeat process with remaining dough balls, garlic ranch, wild mushrooms, mozzarella shreds, and brussels sprouts. Serve pizzas alongside remaining garlic ranch, or reserve for another use. —MARY DUMONT, PLANTPUB, CAMBRIDGE, MASSACHUSETTS

MAKE AHEAD Homemade dough can be chilled up to 24 hours. Garlic ranch can be made up to 3 days in advance and stored in an airtight container in refrigerator.

WINE Earthy Italian white: 2019 Garofoli Podium Verdicchio

NOTE For scratch-made pizza dough, use our Artisan Pizza Dough recipe on page 244.

BREAKFAST & BRUNCH

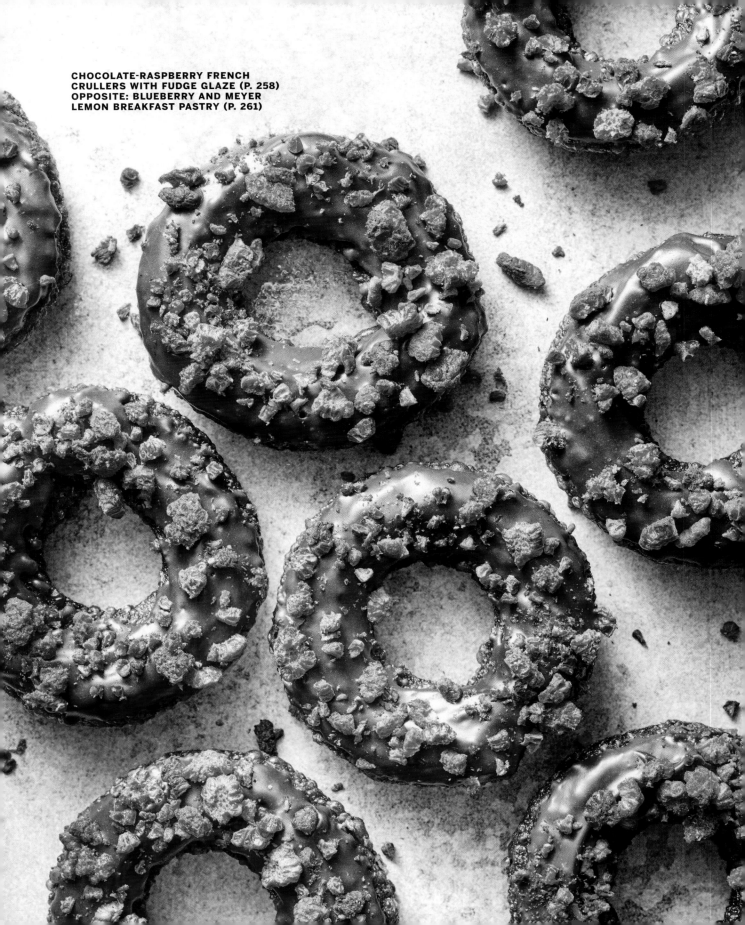

CHOCOLATE-RASPBERRY FRENCH
CRULLERS WITH FUDGE GLAZE (P. 258)
OPPOSITE: BLUEBERRY AND MEYER
LEMON BREAKFAST PASTRY (P. 261)

SWEET PLUM FOCACCIA

Sweet Plum Focaccia

ACTIVE 15 MIN; TOTAL 1 HR 20 MIN, PLUS
3 HR RISING SERVES 8 TO 12

With a delicate and airy crumb, this focaccia is the perfect showcase for ripe plums, which caramelize in the oven as the focaccia bakes. The delicate sweetness from the fruit is contrasted by fragrant rosemary and a sweet-salty crunch from a sprinkle of turbinado sugar and flaky sea salt, yielding a balanced pastry that's perfect for pairing with a dessert wine; Kate Leahy says late-harvest and ice wines are an ideal pairing.

- 3 cups (about 12¾ oz.) plus 2 Tbsp. all-purpose flour, plus more for dusting
- 1 tsp. instant yeast
- 1¼ cups water, at room temperature
- ¼ cup extra-virgin olive oil, divided, plus more as needed
- 2 tsp. kosher salt
- 3 medium-size (8-oz.) red plums (unpeeled), pitted and cut into ½-inch-thick wedges (about 2 cups)
- 3 Tbsp. fresh rosemary leaves
- 1 Tbsp. plus 1 tsp. turbinado sugar
- 1 tsp. flaky sea salt

1. Stir together flour and yeast in a large bowl until combined. Add 1¼ cups water and 1 tablespoon oil to flour mixture; gently stir with your hands until a shaggy dough forms. Cover bowl with a kitchen towel, and let rest at room temperature 20 minutes to allow flour to hydrate. Transfer dough to a lightly floured work surface. Sprinkle dough with kosher salt, and gently rub salt into dough. Knead dough by pressing the heel of your hand into the dough and dragging it back, repeating this motion until the dough feels smooth to the touch, about 5 minutes. Transfer dough to a lightly oiled bowl; cover with plastic wrap, and let rise at room temperature until doubled in size, about 2 hours.

2. Brush a 13- × 18-inch rimmed baking sheet with 1 tablespoon oil. Transfer dough to a lightly floured work surface. Cut dough in half; tuck cut edges under, and pat each dough half into a 9- × 7-inch oval. Transfer dough ovals to prepared baking sheet spaced at least 1 inch apart. Cover dough with a towel; let rest in a warm (about 80°F) area for 30 minutes. (The top of the dough may get a little dry, but that's OK.)

3. Uncover dough. Using your fingers, press down deeply into dough to form dimples spaced about ½ inch apart. Cover dough with a towel, and let rise in a warm area for 30 minutes. Place a pizza stone on middle oven rack, and preheat oven to 450°F.

4. Uncover dough, and lightly press plum slices evenly into dough ovals. Brush dough ovals evenly with remaining 2 tablespoons oil; sprinkle evenly with rosemary, sugar, and flaky salt. Place baking sheet on hot pizza stone in preheated oven, and bake until plum juices have started to caramelize and edges of focaccia are golden brown, 25 to 30 minutes. Remove baking sheet from oven. Let focaccia cool on baking sheet about 15 minutes. Serve warm or at room temperature. —KATE LEAHY

WINE Riesling ice wine with apricot notes: Eroica Ice Wine Horse Heaven Hills

Pear, Honey, and Parmigiano-Reggiano Tart

ACTIVE 35 MIN; TOTAL 2 HR 25 MIN;
SERVES 8

This sweet and savory tart pairs Parmigiano-Reggiano cheese and freshly cracked black pepper with juicy pears and a drizzle of fragrant honey. The addition of Parmigiano-Reggiano to the pastry dough gives Kate Leahy's already flaky crust an extra richness and a subtle nutty flavor. If you're brunching with wine, pair with a Passito or other dessert wine.

PASTRY DOUGH

- 1½ cups all-purpose flour (about 6⅜ oz.), plus more for work surface
- ¼ tsp. kosher salt
- ½ cup unsalted butter (4 oz.), chilled and cut into ½-inch pieces
- 1¼ oz. Parmigiano-Reggiano cheese, finely grated on box grater (about ½ cup)
- 3 Tbsp. ice water
- 1 Tbsp. apple cider vinegar

PEAR FILLING

- 1½ lb. firm-ripe red Anjou pears (unpeeled), cored and cut into ¾-inch-thick wedges
- ¼ cup honey
- 2 Tbsp. unsalted butter, melted
- 1 tsp. grated lemon zest plus 1 Tbsp. fresh lemon juice (from 1 lemon)
- 3 Tbsp. cornstarch

- ½ tsp. black pepper
- ½ tsp. kosher salt

ADDITIONAL INGREDIENTS

- ½ large egg, beaten
- Honey
- Shaved Parmigiano-Reggiano cheese

1. Make the pastry dough: Whisk together flour and salt in a large bowl. Using your fingers, rub butter into flour mixture until butter forms pea-size pieces. Add cheese, and toss to incorporate. Stir together 3 tablespoons ice water and vinegar in a small bowl, and add to flour mixture. Using your hands, gently mix flour mixture until a shaggy dough forms. Gently knead dough by pressing the heel of your hand into the dough so it compacts against the base of the bowl and comes together. Transfer dough to a lightly floured work surface, and shape into a 6-inch disk (about ½ inch thick). Wrap tightly in plastic wrap. Chill at least 1 hour or up to 5 days.

2. Preheat oven to 400°F with rack in lower third position. Unwrap dough, and transfer to a lightly floured work surface. Roll into a 14-inch round, flouring dough as needed to prevent sticking. Transfer to a parchment paper–lined rimmed baking sheet. Place dough in refrigerator until ready to use.

3. Make the pear filling: Toss together pears, honey, butter, and lemon zest and juice in a large bowl. Sprinkle with cornstarch, pepper, and salt; stir until well combined.

4. Arrange pear filling in center of chilled pastry dough, leaving a 2-inch border. Fold uncovered dough edges inward by about 1½ inches, pleating dough to form a crust and gently pressing to adhere. Brush crust lightly with beaten egg.

5. Bake in preheated oven until crust is golden brown and filling is thickened and bubbly, 30 to 35 minutes. Remove from oven; let cool at least 15 minutes or up to 12 hours. Drizzle with additional honey, and garnish with shaved cheese. Slice and serve. —KATE LEAHY

MAKE AHEAD Pastry dough can be made up to 5 days in advance and stored, wrapped tightly in plastic wrap, in refrigerator.

WINE Golden, candied orange peel–scented Passito di Pantelleria: 2020 Donnafugata Ben Ryé

Chocolate-Raspberry French Crullers with Fudge Glaze

PHOTO P. 255

TOTAL 1 HR 15 MIN; SERVES 10

From slinging s'mores at one of her The Baking Bean pop-ups to creating pastries for hot NYC spot Kimika to competing on popular cooking shows, there's never a dull moment for pastry chef Clarice Lam. Made with a classic choux dough, her French crullers feature a crunchy crust, an airy center, and a colorful topping of dried raspberries and fudge. Dip the chocolate crullers in the warmed fudge glaze so the dried raspberries stick for a sweet-tart topping that's as tasty as it is beautiful.

CRULLERS

- 1½ cups water
- ½ cup unsalted butter (4 oz.)
- ¼ cup granulated sugar
- ½ tsp. kosher salt
- 1 cup all-purpose flour (about 4¼ oz.)
- ¼ cup unsweetened cocoa
- 4 large eggs
- Vegetable oil, for frying

FUDGE GLAZE

- ¼ cup unsalted butter (2 oz.)
- 2 Tbsp. plus 1 tsp. whole milk
- 1½ cups unsifted powdered sugar (about 6 oz.)
- ¼ cup unsweetened cocoa
- ¼ tsp. kosher salt

ADDITIONAL INGREDIENT

- ¼ cup freeze-dried raspberries (about ¼ oz.), crushed lightly

1. Make the crullers: Combine 1½ cups water, butter, sugar, and salt in a medium saucepan; bring to a boil over medium. Remove from heat. Vigorously stir in flour and cocoa until mixture comes together and begins to form a ball. Return to heat over medium, and cook, stirring constantly, until dough is tight and pulls away from sides of pan and a thin skin forms on bottom of pan, 2 to 3 minutes.

2. Transfer hot dough to a stand mixer fitted with the paddle attachment. Beat on medium-high speed until no longer steaming, about 1 minute. Reduce mixer speed to medium; beat in eggs, 1 at a time, until dough is smooth and glossy, about 2 minutes. (Dough is ready when you can draw a line in dough using your finger and the dough slowly caves in on itself.) Transfer dough to a piping bag fitted with a large star attachment. Cut 10 (4-inch) squares of parchment paper; pipe a 3½-inch dough circle onto each parchment square.

3. Pour vegetable oil to a depth of 2 inches in a large Dutch oven. Heat over medium until oil reaches 350°F, adjusting heat as needed to maintain a consistent temperature. Working with 1 parchment square at a time, invert square, and gently place in oil, dough side down. Parchment will release within 5 seconds; remove and discard. Fry cruller until slightly puffed and cooked through, 2 to 3 minutes per side. Transfer cooked cruller to a wire rack set inside a baking sheet. Repeat frying process with remaining dough circles.

4. Make the fudge glaze: Microwave butter in a medium-size microwavable bowl on medium (50% power) until melted, 1 to 2 minutes, stirring every 30 seconds. Whisk in milk. Add powdered sugar, cocoa, and salt, and whisk until smooth. Return to microwave, and microwave on medium until warm, about 30 seconds. Remove from microwave; whisk until smooth. Dip top of each cruller into warm fudge glaze, and quickly sprinkle with crushed raspberries. —CLARICE LAM

NOTE Crullers can be fried in batches of 3; start with 1 at a time and increase to your comfort level.

Rhubarb Coffee Cake

ACTIVE 30 MIN; TOTAL 1 HR 55 MIN
SERVES 10 TO 12

This streusel-topped rhubarb coffee cake is a standout celebration of spring. With a tender, springy crumb, the cake is the perfect match for the rosy, tart rhubarb on top. The addition of buttermilk lends tanginess and richness to the cake batter, while the rhubarb is marinated in sugar before baking, softening the fibrous stalks to result in a deliciously jammy texture.

STREUSEL

- ¾ cup all-purpose flour (about 3¼ oz.)
- ¾ cup packed light brown sugar
- 1 tsp. ground cinnamon
- ¾ tsp. kosher salt
- 6 Tbsp. unsalted butter (3 oz.), chilled and cut into ½-inch pieces

CAKE

- 1½ lb. 10- to 12-inch-long rhubarb stalks (about 8 stalks), halved lengthwise if thick
- 1¾ cups granulated sugar, divided
- 2½ cups all-purpose flour (about 10⅝ oz.), plus more for dusting
- 1 tsp. kosher salt
- 1 tsp. baking powder
- ¾ tsp. baking soda
- ½ cup unsalted butter (4 oz.), at room temperature, plus more for greasing
- 2 large eggs
- 1¼ cups buttermilk
- 1 Tbsp. vanilla extract

1. Make the streusel: Stir together flour, brown sugar, cinnamon, and salt in a medium bowl. Add butter; using fingers, work butter into flour mixture until completely incorporated and mixture clumps together. Cover and refrigerate until ready to use or up to overnight (12 hours).

2. Make the cake: Preheat oven to 350°F. Lightly grease a 13- × 9-inch baking pan or dish with butter. Dust pan with flour, and shake out excess. Place rhubarb on a rimmed baking sheet, and sprinkle with ¼ cup granulated sugar; toss to coat. Let stand, tossing occasionally, until sugar is mostly dissolved, 20 to 30 minutes.

3. Whisk together flour, salt, baking powder, and baking soda in a medium bowl; set aside. Beat butter and remaining 1½ cups granulated sugar with a stand mixer fitted with the paddle attachment on medium speed until light and fluffy, about 2 minutes, stopping to scrape down sides of bowl as needed. With mixer running on medium speed, add eggs, 1 at a time, beating well after each addition. Reduce mixer speed to low, and beat in buttermilk and vanilla. With mixer running on low speed, gradually add flour mixture, beating until just incorporated, about 1 minute, stopping to scrape down sides of bowl as needed.

4. Transfer batter to prepared pan, and spread evenly. Arrange rhubarb lengthwise in a single layer on top of batter. Sprinkle with streusel. Bake in preheated oven until a wooden pick inserted in center of cake comes out clean, 55 minutes to 1 hour and 5 minutes. Remove from oven; let cake cool in pan on a wire rack at least 20 minutes or up to 6 hours. Serve warm, or let cool completely. —JUSTIN CHAPPLE

RHUBARB COFFEE CAKE

**CARROT AND SPRING ONION
TOAD-IN-THE-HOLE**

Carrot and Spring Onion Toad-in-the-Hole

⏱ ACTIVE 20 MIN; TOTAL 40 MIN; SERVES 4

The traditional toad-in-the-hole consists of whole sausages cooked in an egg-and-flour batter. This recipe delivers a taste of the British classic but stars tender baby carrots and spring onions for a flavorful, vegetable-forward spring twist.

- 2 Tbsp. extra-virgin olive oil
- 2 Tbsp. unsalted butter
- 6 oz. small multicolored carrots (about 10 carrots), trimmed
- 6 oz. small spring onions (about 4 onions), green parts cut into 3-inch pieces and bulbs halved lengthwise
- 4 (1-oz.) breakfast sausage links
- 1 tsp. finely chopped fresh thyme
- 2 tsp. kosher salt, divided
- 1 tsp. black pepper, divided
- 3 large eggs
- ¾ cup whole milk
- Pinch of freshly grated nutmeg
- ¾ cup all-purpose flour (about 3¼ oz.)
- Finely chopped fresh flat-leaf parsley, for garnish

1. Preheat oven to 425°F. Combine oil and butter in a 12-inch cast-iron skillet, and heat in preheated oven 10 minutes. Carefully remove hot skillet from oven. Add carrots, spring onion greens and bulbs, sausage links, thyme, 1 teaspoon salt, and ½ teaspoon pepper to skillet, and toss to coat. Spread mixture in an even layer. Roast at 425°F until vegetables and sausages are sizzling and just starting to brown, about 8 minutes.

2. Meanwhile, whisk together eggs, milk, nutmeg, remaining 1 teaspoon salt, and remaining ½ teaspoon pepper in a medium bowl until well combined. Add flour, and whisk until batter is very smooth.

3. Remove skillet from oven, and transfer vegetables and sausages to a plate. Do not wipe skillet clean. Immediately pour batter into hot skillet, and quickly arrange vegetables and sausages on top, leaving a ½-inch border. Bake at 425°F until puffed, golden brown on edges, and set in center, 22 to 28 minutes. Remove from oven. Garnish with parsley, and serve immediately. —JUSTIN CHAPPLE

WINE Lively, juicy sparkling wine: NV Mionetto Prosecco Brut

Blueberry and Meyer Lemon Breakfast Pastry
PHOTO P. 254

ACTIVE 20 MIN; TOTAL 1 HR 30 MIN; SERVES 6

Baking up flaky and buttery in a few short minutes, frozen puff pastry is the secret to simple morning pastries. This sweet, easy breakfast pastry comes together without much planning (just thaw some puff pastry the night before). Be sure to leave the 1-inch border around the edges of the filling to prevent the sweet jam and tangy Meyer lemon–flecked cream cheese from escaping during baking. The tart dried blueberries aren't just a pretty topping; they help balance the sweetness of this nostalgic breakfast treat. While the cream cheese filling and assembly are essential, feel free to play with your choice of fruit preserve in place of the blueberry preserves, or try adding a few chocolate chips if the occasion calls for it.

- 1 (14-oz.) pkg. frozen puff pastry (such as Dufour), thawed
- All-purpose flour, for dusting
- 4 oz. cream cheese (such as Philadelphia), at room temperature
- 1 cup unsifted powdered sugar (about 4 oz.)
- 1 tsp. grated Meyer lemon zest plus 1 Tbsp. fresh Meyer lemon juice
- ¼ cup blueberry preserves (such as Bonne Maman)
- ½ tsp. cornstarch
- 1 large egg
- 1 Tbsp. water
- 2 Tbsp. whole milk
- 1 Tbsp. crushed freeze-dried blueberries (from about 1½ Tbsp. whole freeze-dried blueberries)

1. Line a large rimmed baking sheet with parchment paper. Roll out thawed puff pastry on a lightly floured work surface into a 17- x 10-inch rectangle. Cut pastry in half lengthwise; place 1 pastry half on prepared baking sheet.

2. Beat cream cheese, powdered sugar, and lemon zest and juice with an electric mixer fitted with the paddle attachment on low speed, gradually increasing mixer speed to medium-high, until mixture is smooth, about 2 minutes, stopping to scrape down sides of bowl as needed. Measure ⅓ cup cream cheese mixture into a separate medium bowl; set aside for icing in step 5. Spoon remaining cream cheese mixture (about ½ cup) in a 1½-inch-wide strip lengthwise down the middle of pastry half on prepared baking sheet, leaving a 1-inch border along short pastry edges.

3. Stir together preserves and cornstarch in a small bowl. Spoon preserves mixture evenly along long edges of cream cheese strip (about 2 tablespoons per side), leaving a 1-inch border on each long side. Beat together egg and 1 tablespoon water in a small bowl. Brush border of topped pastry lightly with egg mixture; reserve remaining egg mixture. Place remaining pastry half on top of filled pastry, pressing edges firmly to seal. Chill until firm, about 20 minutes. Meanwhile, preheat oven to 350°F.

4. Brush chilled pastry lightly with reserved egg mixture. Using a paring knife, cut 6 small (about ½-inch) slits on top of pastry. Bake in preheated oven until golden brown and evenly puffed, 40 to 45 minutes. Transfer baking sheet to a wire rack; let pastry cool 10 minutes.

5. Whisk milk into reserved ⅓ cup cream cheese mixture until smooth. Drizzle over warm pastry, and sprinkle with crushed freeze-dried blueberries. Serve warm. —ANNA THEOKTISTO

SOFT-COOKED EGGS WITH
HOLLANDAISE AND HAM

Soft-Cooked Eggs with Hollandaise and Ham

ACTIVE 40 MIN; TOTAL 50 MIN; SERVES 4

Winemaker André Mack shared the recipe for this elegant breakfast dish of ham thinly sliced with eggs and hollandaise. The salty ham complements golden, jammy egg yolks and a simple hollandaise, showcasing the excellence of each ingredient in this classic dish. Patience is key with hollandaise; adding only a little butter at a time helps the sauce come together without breaking. At & Sons, his ham and wine bar in Brooklyn, Mack uses Mangalista ham in this recipe, but any thinly sliced ham will do nicely. Mangalista ham is smoked over hardwood, giving it a deliciously savory flavor, but also high in fat, so it stays moist and tender even after smoking.

- 6 **large eggs**
- 1 **cup dry white wine**
- ½ **cup Chardonnay vinegar**
- 1 **tsp. coriander seeds**
- 1 **fresh or dried bay leaf**
- ¾ **cup clarified butter, melted**
- ½ **tsp. kosher salt**
- ½ **tsp. black pepper**
- 4 **ham or prosciutto slices (about 2 oz.)**
- 1 **Tbsp. plus 1 tsp. thinly sliced fresh chives**
- 2 **tsp. extra-virgin olive oil**

1. Bring a large pot of water to a boil over high. Gently place 4 eggs in boiling water; cook 6 minutes and 30 seconds. Quickly remove from water using a spider or slotted spoon, and transfer to a bowl filled with ice water. Let stand until completely cooled, about 10 minutes. Peel eggs, and set aside.

2. Combine wine, vinegar, coriander, and bay leaf in a large saucepan, and bring to a simmer over medium-high. Simmer until reduced by one-third (about ½ cup), 12 to 15 minutes. Remove from heat. Pour through a fine wire-mesh strainer into a large heatproof bowl, and discard solids. Let cool slightly, about 5 minutes. Wipe saucepan clean.

3. Meanwhile, separate whites and yolks from remaining 2 eggs; discard whites, or reserve for another use.

4. Add yolks to slightly cooled wine reduction in bowl, and whisk constantly until foamy, about 15 seconds. Add water to a depth of 1 to 2 inches to cleaned saucepan; bring to a simmer over medium-low. Place bowl with egg yolk mixture on top of saucepan so that bowl is sitting on sides of pan and not touching the water. With water at a constant simmer, slowly and gradually drizzle in melted clarified butter, whisking constantly, until a thick emulsion forms and mixture is thicker than heavy cream, about 10 minutes. Stir in salt, and remove from heat.

5. Fill a separate large saucepan with water; bring to a simmer over medium. Add peeled eggs, and cook until warmed, about 3 minutes. Drain.

6. Spoon about ⅓ cup hollandaise sauce onto each of 4 plates. Halve warmed eggs lengthwise, and arrange evenly on hollandaise. Sprinkle evenly with pepper. Drape ham slices evenly over eggs. Sprinkle each plate with 1 teaspoon chives and ½ teaspoon oil. —ANDRÉ MACK

PIES, TARTS & FRUIT DESSERTS

FIGS 'N' CREAM (P. 277)
OPPOSITE: PIÑA COLADA
PIE (P. 270)

LEMON CHESS PIE

Lemon Chess Pie

ACTIVE 20 MIN; TOTAL 3 HR 50 MIN;
SERVES 8

Scholar and cookbook author Jessica B. Harris's good friend Karen Finley shares her family recipe for buttery, silky, and lusciously tart lemon chess pie. The recipe is modeled on one that Finley remembers from her childhood in Richmond, Virginia, where a lemon chess pie from Thalheimer's — a local department store — was on the cafeteria menu. For years, her family would buy and ship Thalheimer's lemon chess pie across the country every Thanksgiving. Eventually, Thalheimer's went out of business, and the family spent years trying to recreate the beloved dessert. Finally, Finley says, "My sister-in-law, Regina, joyously sent out the proclamation that she had finally found the winner — and she had! She sent this recipe to all of us and we've been enjoying it ever since. We save it for holidays or special occasions. It's always a big hit." Harris is among the many lucky friends of Finley's who have enjoyed this Lemon Chess Pie — she loves to include it on her dinner party menus at her summer home on Martha's Vineyard. It's easy to see why the pie is such a hit: The flavor of the filling is similar to a lemon bar, but a touch sweeter and with some pleasant texture from floral lemon zest.

- 1 (9-inch) unbaked pie shell (see Note)
- 2 cups granulated sugar
- 1 Tbsp. plus 1 tsp. all-purpose flour
- 1 Tbsp. plus 1 tsp. fine yellow cornmeal
- ½ tsp. fine sea salt
- 4 large eggs, lightly beaten
- ½ cup unsalted butter (4 oz.), melted and cooled slightly
- ⅓ cup whole milk
- 2 Tbsp. grated lemon zest plus ¼ cup fresh lemon juice (from 2 lemons)

1. Preheat oven to 375°F. Freeze pie shell until hardened, about 15 minutes. Line frozen pie shell with aluminum foil, and fill completely with pie weights or dried beans. Bake in preheated oven until crust is set and just beginning to brown around edges, 22 to 26 minutes. Remove from oven. Carefully lift foil to remove weights; discard foil. Return pie shell to oven. Bake at 375°F until bottom is set and no longer looks doughy, 5 to 8 minutes. Transfer to a wire rack; let cool completely, about 30 minutes.

2. Reduce oven temperature to 350°F. Using a fork, stir together sugar, flour, cornmeal, and salt in a medium bowl. Using a fork, stir together eggs, butter, milk, and lemon zest and juice in a large bowl. Add sugar mixture to egg mixture; stir until well combined. Pour into cooled pie shell.

3. Bake pie at 350°F until filling is lightly browned, puffed slightly, and barely jiggles in the center, 45 to 55 minutes, tenting crust edges with foil after 15 minutes to prevent overbrowning, if needed. Transfer pie to a wire rack; let cool completely, about 2 hours. —KAREN FINLEY

MAKE AHEAD Pie can be made and kept chilled up to 3 days in advance.

NOTE Check out *Food & Wine*'s Master Pie Dough recipe on foodandwine.com.

Nutty Baklava Pie

ACTIVE 30 MIN; TOTAL 3 HR 30 MIN,
PLUS 6 HR CHILLING; SERVES 8 TO 10

This pie combines the best aspects of pecan pie and baklava. It's topped with crispy phyllo bursts, which add crispy flair.

- 3 cups mixed raw nuts (such as walnuts, pecans, slivered almonds, and pistachios) (about 12 oz.)
- 1½ cups organic cane sugar
- 3 Tbsp. water
- ½ tsp. fresh lemon juice (from 1 lemon)
- 1 cup coconut milk (from 1 [13.66-oz.] can, well shaken), warmed
- 2 Tbsp. orange liqueur (such as Grand Marnier)
- ¾ tsp. ground cardamom
- ½ tsp. kosher salt
- 1 (9-inch) prepared piecrust
- 4 (13- × 9-inch) sheets frozen phyllo dough (from 1 [16-oz.] pkg.), thawed
- 3 Tbsp. salted vegan (plant-based) butter, melted
- Organic powdered sugar

1. Preheat oven to 375°F. Spread nuts evenly on a baking sheet. Bake in preheated oven until toasted and fragrant, 8 to 12 minutes. Remove from oven. Let cool 15 minutes. Finely chop nuts; set aside.

2. Stir together cane sugar, 3 tablespoons water, and lemon juice in a large saucepan; bring to a boil over medium-high. Boil, swirling pan occasionally but not stirring, until caramel is very dark and registers 390°F on an instant-read thermometer, 8 to 12 minutes. Remove from heat. Immediately and carefully stir in warmed coconut milk using a long-handled wooden spoon. (Mixture will boil up and sputter.) Stir in nuts, orange liqueur, cardamom, and salt.

3. Pour nut filling into a large heatproof bowl. Let cool, uncovered, at room temperature 30 minutes. Stir filling, and pour into prepared piecrust. Chill pie, uncovered, until set, at least 6 hours or up to 1 day (24 hours).

4. Preheat oven to 375°F. Unfold thawed phyllo sheets, and place on a work surface; cover with a damp towel to prevent from drying out. Working with 1 phyllo sheet and keeping remaining sheets covered, brush top lightly with some of the melted butter. Using your hands, tear sheet crosswise into 3 strips (about 4×9 inches each). Scrunch each phyllo strip, and place each in 1 cup of a 12-cup muffin tin, with phyllo edges sticking up randomly in all directions like tissue paper. Repeat process with remaining phyllo sheets to form 12 phyllo bursts total.

5. Bake phyllo bursts in preheated oven until golden brown and crispy, 6 to 9 minutes. Let cool completely in tray, about 15 minutes. Arrange phyllo bursts around edge of chilled pie. Garnish with powdered sugar. —PAIGE GRANDJEAN

MAKE AHEAD Pie can be made up to 1 day in advance and stored in refrigerator. Top with phyllo bursts just before serving.

NOTE Warming the coconut milk before adding it to the hot sugar mixture prevents the caramel from seizing.

Roasted Spiced Cranberry Pie

ACTIVE 25 MIN; TOTAL 1 HR 25 MIN, PLUS
4 HR CHILLING; SERVES 8 TO 10

---

*Tart cranberries are roasted with
lemongrass and gochugaru (Korean chile
flakes) to give this vibrant pie its fruity
and fragrant kick.*

- 1¼ lb. fresh or frozen (unthawed) cranberries (about 6 cups)
- 1½ cups granulated sugar, divided
- 1 (5-inch) lemongrass stalk, bruised
- 1 Tbsp. gochugaru
- ½ tsp. kosher salt
- 1 cup unsweetened cranberry juice
- 3 oz. dried unsweetened mango slices, thinly sliced crosswise (about ¾ cup)
- ¼ cup quick-cooking tapioca (such as Kraft Minute)
- 1 tsp. grated lime zest plus 2 Tbsp. fresh lime juice (from 1 lime)
- 2 tsp. grated fresh ginger (from 1 [1-inch] piece peeled ginger)
- 1 (9-inch) prepared piecrust

1. Preheat oven to 425°F. Toss together
cranberries, ½ cup sugar, lemongrass,
gochugaru, and salt on a rimmed baking
sheet. Spread in an even layer. Bake in
preheated oven until cranberries just
begin to burst and release juices, 15 to
20 minutes, stirring once after 10 minutes.
Remove from oven. Remove and discard
lemongrass.

2. Stir together cranberry juice, mango,
tapioca, and remaining 1 cup sugar in a
medium saucepan. Let stand 10 minutes.
Bring to a boil over medium, stirring
occasionally. Boil, stirring constantly, until
mixture thickens and tapioca is softened,
about 4 minutes. Remove from heat; stir in
lime zest and lime juice, ginger, and roasted
cranberries with any juices on baking sheet.

3. Transfer cranberry filling to a large bowl.
Let cool, uncovered, stirring occasionally,
30 minutes. Spoon filling in an even layer
in prepared piecrust. Chill, uncovered, until
cold and set, at least 4 hours or up to 1 day
(24 hours). —PAIGE GRANDJEAN

MAKE AHEAD Pie can be made up to 1 day
in advance and stored in refrigerator.

NOTE Find gochugaru at most
Asian grocery stores or online at
spicewallabrand.com.

Apple Flambé Pie

ACTIVE 50 MIN; TOTAL 1 HR 10 MIN, PLUS
4 HR CHILLING; SERVES 8 TO 10

---

*Apple cider and fresh and dried apples join
forces in this stovetop apple pie filling. The
pie is topped with flaming apple brandy
just before serving.*

- 1½ cups unsweetened apple cider
- 1 cup organic light brown sugar
- 2½ oz. dried soft (not crunchy) apple rings, chopped (about ½ packed cup)
- 1 Tbsp. fennel seeds, toasted
- 1½ tsp. ground cinnamon
- ½ tsp. kosher salt
- ¼ tsp. ground cloves
- 4 medium Honeycrisp apples (about 2¼ lb.)
- 3 Tbsp. cornstarch
- 2 Tbsp. cold water
- 1 tsp. grated orange zest plus 2 Tbsp. fresh orange juice (from 1 orange)
- 1 (9-inch) prepared piecrust
- 1 Tbsp. turbinado sugar
- ¼ cup apple brandy (such as Calvados) or cinnamon whiskey (such as Fireball)
- Vanilla ice cream (dairy or nondairy) (optional)

1. Bring cider, brown sugar, chopped dried
apple rings, fennel seeds, cinnamon, salt,
and cloves to a boil in a large saucepan over
medium-high. Reduce heat to medium-low;
simmer, stirring occasionally, until dried
apples are plump, about 5 minutes. Remove
from heat.

2. Peel and core 3 Honeycrisp apples; cut
into ¼-inch-thick slices, and add to cider
mixture in pan. Cook over medium-low,
stirring often, until Honeycrisp apples are
tender, about 15 minutes. Whisk together
cornstarch and 2 tablespoons water in a
small bowl. Gradually add cornstarch slurry
to apple mixture, stirring constantly. Cook
over medium-low, stirring constantly, until
thickened and bubbly, about 2 minutes.
Remove from heat; stir in orange zest and
juice. Transfer mixture to a large heatproof
bowl. Let cool, uncovered, stirring
occasionally, 20 minutes.

3. Pour apple filling into piecrust, and
spread in an even layer, reserving about
1 tablespoon thickened apple syrup in

bowl. Core and cut remaining Honeycrisp
apple into ⅛-inch-thick slices. Arrange
fanned slices on top of apple filling. Lightly
brush fanned apples evenly with reserved
thickened syrup. Chill, uncovered, until set,
at least 4 hours or up to 1 day.

4. Sprinkle pie evenly with turbinado
sugar. Place apple brandy in a heatproof
measuring cup with a spout; set aside. Heat
a small saucepan over medium until warm,
about 30 seconds. Remove from heat
(making sure to turn off burner); pour in
brandy. Using a utility lighter, carefully ignite
fumes just above surface of brandy. Slowly
and carefully pour flaming liquid over pie.
Let flames extinguish. If desired, serve with
ice cream. —PAIGE GRANDJEAN

MAKE AHEAD Pie can be made up to 1 day
in advance and stored in refrigerator.
Sprinkle with turbinado sugar and flambé
just before serving.

NOTE Look for unsweetened cold-pressed
apple cider in the refrigerated section of the
grocery store. Shelf-stable cider is often
heat-treated and will have a muted flavor.
Any bourbon or brandy with an ABV of 40%
or higher will work for flambéing.

Black Sesame Pumpkin Pie

ACTIVE 30 MIN; TOTAL 1 HR, PLUS 4 HR
CHILLING; SERVES 8 TO 10

---

*A silky stovetop pumpkin custard sits
on top of a layer of nutty black sesame
paste in this delicious twist on a
classic pumpkin pie.*

- 1 cup canned pumpkin (from 1 [15-oz.] can)
- 2 large egg yolks
- 1 large egg
- 1 tsp. vanilla extract
- ¾ cup granulated sugar
- ¼ cup cornstarch
- 1½ tsp. ground cinnamon
- ¼ tsp. ground nutmeg
- 1 cup whole milk
- 1 (8-oz.) container mascarpone cheese
- 1½ Tbsp. jarred black sesame paste (such as Kadoya)
- 1 (9-inch) prepared piecrust
- 2 Tbsp. mixed black and white sesame seeds

1. Whisk together pumpkin, egg yolks, egg, and vanilla in a large heatproof bowl until smooth. Whisk together sugar, cornstarch, cinnamon, and nutmeg in a small bowl; whisk into egg mixture until well combined. Set aside.

2. Bring milk to a boil in a medium saucepan over medium, stirring occasionally. Gradually add hot milk to egg mixture in large bowl, whisking constantly. Pour milk-egg mixture into saucepan. Cook over medium-low, whisking constantly, until thickened and bubbly, 3 to 4 minutes. Remove from heat; whisk in mascarpone.

3. Pour pumpkin mixture into a separate large bowl; press plastic wrap directly onto surface of mixture. Let cool at room temperature 30 minutes.

4. Remove and discard plastic wrap from pumpkin mixture. Transfer ½ cup pumpkin mixture to a small bowl, and stir in black sesame paste. Spread black sesame paste mixture onto bottom of piecrust in an even layer. Top with remaining pumpkin mixture, and spread evenly. Press clean plastic wrap directly onto surface of pie. Chill until set, at least 4 hours or up 1 day (24 hours).

5. Remove plastic wrap from pie. Decorate top of pie with mixed sesame seeds.

—PAIGE GRANDJEAN

MAKE AHEAD Pie can be made up to 1 day in advance. Decorate with sesame seeds just before serving.

NOTE Black sesame paste is available at most Japanese grocery stores or online at yamibuy.com.

Peanut Butter Chai Pie

⏱ TOTAL 20 MIN, PLUS 4 HR CHILLING; SERVES 8 TO 10

This no-bake spiced peanut butter pie comes together in minutes, and delivers big flavors.

- 1½ tsp. ground cinnamon, plus more for garnish
- ¾ tsp. ground cardamom
- ¾ tsp. ground ginger
- ¼ tsp. ground allspice
- ⅛ tsp. ground nutmeg
- 1 (8-oz.) pkg. cream cheese, softened
- 1 cup creamy peanut butter
- ½ cup plus 2 Tbsp. honey, divided
- 2 tsp. vanilla extract

- ½ tsp. kosher salt
- 2½ cups heavy cream, divided
- 1 (9-inch) prepared piecrust
- Chopped salted roasted peanuts
- Chocolate curls

1. Stir together cinnamon, cardamom, ginger, allspice, and nutmeg in a small bowl; set aside. Beat cream cheese, peanut butter, ½ cup honey, vanilla, salt, and 1 tablespoon cinnamon-cardamom mixture with a stand mixer fitted with the whisk attachment on medium-high speed until light and fluffy, about 2 minutes. With mixer running, gradually pour in ½ cup heavy cream. Beat until well combined and fluffy, 10 to 20 seconds. Transfer mixture to a large bowl.

2. Wipe mixer bowl clean. Place remaining cinnamon-cardamom mixture, remaining 2 tablespoons honey, and remaining 2 cups heavy cream in bowl of stand mixer. Beat on medium-high speed until stiff peaks form, 1 to 2 minutes.

3. Fold about 1 cup whipped cream mixture into peanut butter mixture. Transfer mixture to prepared piecrust, and spread in an even layer. Top pie with remaining whipped cream mixture. Chill, uncovered, until filling is cold and set, at least 4 hours or up to 1 day (24 hours). Garnish with peanuts, chocolate curls, and additional cinnamon; serve immediately.

—PAIGE GRANDJEAN

MAKE AHEAD Pie can be made up to 1 day in advance and stored in refrigerator.

NOTE For chocolate curls, microwave a block of chocolate in 10-second increments until chocolate is soft but not melted. Use a Y-shaped peeler to shave curls onto a paper towel or parchment paper.

PEANUT BUTTER CHAI PIE

Piña Colada Pie

ACTIVE 40 MIN; TOTAL 1 HR 30 MIN, PLUS
6 HR CHILLING; SERVES 8

*In this swoon-worthy dessert, the classic
tropical flavors of a piña colada cocktail
are transformed into Piña Colada Pie
featuring layers of silky coconut custard
and a caramelized pineapple jam made
by simmering fresh pineapple with brown
sugar. Adding rum to the hot pineapple
mixture burns off the harsher taste of
the alcohol while leaving a pleasant kick.
Spread across a buttery shortbread
crust, the jam is ultimately layered with a
double-coconut custard and piled high with
cloud-like coconut cream whipped topping.
Served ice-cold, this make-ahead pie is
destined for your next summer gathering.
Rum shooters optional.*

- 7 Tbsp. unsalted butter (3½ oz.), divided
- 2 cups pure butter shortbread cookie crumbs (such as Walker's) (8 oz.) (about 16 cookies)
- ⅔ cup plus ¼ cup packed light brown sugar, divided
- 1 tsp. kosher salt, divided
  Cooking spray
- 1 large fresh pineapple (about 4 lb.)
- 3½ Tbsp. cornstarch, divided
- 3 Tbsp. (1½ oz.) gold rum
- 1 (13.5-oz.) can unsweetened coconut milk (unshaken), chilled
- 2 large egg yolks
- 2 cups heavy cream, divided
- 1 cup sweetened shredded coconut (about 4½ oz.)
- 2 tsp. vanilla extract
  Shaved coconut, brandied or fresh cherries, and fresh mint leaves, for garnish (optional)

1. Preheat oven to 350°F. Microwave 5 tablespoons butter in a medium-size microwavable bowl on high until melted, about 45 seconds. Stir in cookie crumbs, 2 tablespoons brown sugar, and ½ teaspoon salt. Press mixture evenly into bottom and up sides of a lightly greased (with cooking spray) 9-inch pie plate. Bake in preheated oven until golden brown and crisp, 8 to 12 minutes. Transfer to a wire rack, and let cool completely, about 30 minutes.

2. While crust bakes, cut a ¼-inch-thick round of pineapple; cut round into wedges. Place wedges in a ziplock plastic bag; seal bag, and reserve wedges in refrigerator for garnish. Peel remaining pineapple. Working over a medium bowl, grate peeled pineapple using largest holes of a box grater, avoiding the core, to yield 2 cups combined pulp and juice. Stir together grated pineapple pulp and juice, 1½ tablespoons cornstarch, ⅓ cup brown sugar, and ¼ teaspoon salt in a small saucepan. Cook over medium, stirring often, until very thick and light golden, 18 to 22 minutes. Remove from heat; stir in rum. Let cool slightly, about 15 minutes.

Spread cooled pineapple mixture evenly in cooled crust. Refrigerate, uncovered, until ready to use.

3. Open chilled coconut milk can. Spoon off ⅓ cup hardened coconut cream from the top, and transfer to a small bowl; cover and place in refrigerator. Place remaining coconut milk in a medium saucepan; whisk in egg yolks, ½ cup heavy cream, ⅓ cup brown sugar, remaining 2 tablespoons cornstarch, and remaining ¼ teaspoon salt. Cook over medium, whisking constantly, until mixture is very thick and bubbly, 6 to 8 minutes. Remove from heat; stir in shredded coconut, vanilla, and remaining 2 tablespoons butter. Let cool slightly, about 15 minutes, stirring occasionally. Spread evenly over pineapple mixture in piecrust. Press plastic wrap directly onto surface; chill until cold and set, about 6 hours.

4. Beat reserved coconut cream, remaining 2 tablespoons brown sugar, and remaining 1½ cups heavy cream with a stand mixer fitted with the whisk attachment on medium-high speed until stiff peaks form, 1 to 2 minutes. Spread evenly over pie. Garnish with pineapple wedges, shaved coconut, cherries, and mint leaves as desired. —PAIGE GRANDJEAN

MAKE AHEAD Pie can be assembled up to 1 day in advance without the whipped cream topping.

DRINK Serve with a rum shooter, if you like.

PIÑA COLADA PIE

Brown Sugar Shortbread Crust

ACTIVE 15 MIN; TOTAL 1 HR 30 MIN;
MAKES 1 (9-INCH) PIECRUST

Sweet and buttery, this cookie-like gluten-free crust has a sandy texture and deep toffee flavor from the brown sugar.

- 1¼ cups gluten-free flour baking blend (such as King Arthur Measure for Measure) (about 5¾ oz.), plus more for dusting
- 3 Tbsp. light brown sugar
- ½ tsp. kosher salt
- ½ cup cold unsalted butter (4 oz.), cut into ½-inch pieces
- 1 Tbsp. ice water
- Cooking spray

1. Pulse flour, brown sugar, and salt in a food processor until well combined, about 3 pulses. Add butter; pulse until mixture resembles small peas, 10 to 12 pulses. Gradually add 1 tablespoon ice water, pulsing until evenly incorporated, 6 to 8 pulses.

2. Transfer mixture to a lightly greased (with cooking spray) 9-inch pie plate; using your fingers, distribute crust evenly into bottom and up sides of pan. Using the floured bottom of a metal measuring cup, press crust firmly into bottom and up sides of pan. Freeze, uncovered, until hard, at least 20 minutes or up to 1 day (24 hours).

3. Preheat oven to 350°F. Bake crust in preheated oven until golden, 22 to 26 minutes. Remove from oven. Let cool completely on a wire rack, about 30 minutes. —PAIGE GRANDJEAN

MAKE AHEAD Crust can be made up to 2 days in advance and stored, covered, at room temperature.

Walnut and Date Crust

ACTIVE 20 MIN; TOTAL 1 HR 20 MIN;
MAKES 1 (9-INCH) PIECRUST

Walnuts, tahini, and cocoa powder balance out sticky, sweet dates to create an earthy and nutty pie crust.

- 2½ cups walnuts (about 9 oz.)
- 8 pitted Medjool dates (about 3½ oz.), roughly chopped
- ¼ cup uncooked old-fashioned rolled oats
- ¼ cup unsweetened cocoa, plus more for crimping crust, if desired
- 1 Tbsp. tahini
- ½ tsp. kosher salt
- Cooking spray

1. Preheat oven to 350°F. Spread walnuts in a single layer on a baking sheet. Bake in preheated oven until toasted and fragrant, 8 to 12 minutes. Remove from oven; let cool completely, about 15 minutes. Do not turn oven off.

2. Combine toasted walnuts, dates, oats, cocoa, tahini, and salt in a food processor; process until mixture is finely ground and begins to clump, about 30 seconds, stopping to scrape down sides of bowl as needed. Press mixture evenly into bottom and up sides of a lightly greased (with cooking spray) 9-inch pie plate. If desired, crimp edges, dusting fingertips with cocoa if needed to prevent sticking.

3. Bake crust at 350°F until edges are dry and matte, 6 to 8 minutes. Transfer to a wire rack; let cool completely, about 30 minutes. —PAIGE GRANDJEAN

MAKE AHEAD Crust can be made up to 1 day in advance and stored, covered, at room temperature.

Sweet-and-Salty Pretzel and Waffle Cone Crust

ACTIVE 10 MIN; TOTAL 55 MIN; MAKES 1 (9-INCH) PIECRUST

If you love a classic graham cracker crumb crust, this equally versatile version of finely ground pretzels and crushed waffle cones is a must-try.

- 2 cups miniature pretzel twists
- 6 (5½-inch) waffle cones (about 4 oz.), broken into large pieces
- ¼ cup light brown sugar
- ½ cup unsalted butter (4 oz.), melted
- Cooking spray

1. Preheat oven to 350°F. Process pretzels, waffle cones, and brown sugar in a food processor until finely ground and well combined, about 20 seconds. Add butter; pulse until mixture resembles wet sand, 6 to 8 pulses.

2. Press mixture evenly into bottom and up sides of a lightly greased (with cooking spray) 9-inch pie plate. Bake in preheated oven until golden brown and crisp, 8 to 12 minutes. Transfer to a wire rack; let cool completely, about 30 minutes. —PAIGE GRANDJEAN

MAKE AHEAD Crust can be made up to 2 days in advance and stored, covered, at room temperature.

NOTE Waffle cones are available at most grocery stores or can be purchased from your local ice cream shop. To make this piecrust gluten free, look for gluten-free pretzels and cones.

Granola and Marshmallow Crust

ACTIVE 10 MIN; TOTAL 40 MIN;
MAKES 1 (9-INCH) PIECRUST

Granola stays nice and crunchy even once coated in gooey melted marshmallow in this grown-up version of a Rice Krispies Treat in crust form.

Cooking spray

3 cups miniature marshmallows (about 5¼ oz.)

¼ cup unsalted butter (2 oz.)

1 Tbsp. white miso

3 cups gluten-free maple granola (about 11 oz.) (such as Bob's Red Mill Maple Sea Salt Granola), lightly crushed

½ tsp. ground cinnamon

½ tsp. kosher salt

1. Grease a 9-inch pie plate with cooking spray. Combine marshmallows, butter, and miso in a large saucepan. Cook over medium-low, stirring constantly, until melted and smooth, 3 to 4 minutes. Remove from heat. Stir in granola, cinnamon, and salt.

2. Quickly transfer mixture to prepared pie plate. Lightly spray bottom of a measuring cup with cooking spray; using bottom of measuring cup, press granola mixture into bottom and up sides of pie plate, creating a ½-inch-high lip above edge of pie plate. Let stand, uncovered, at room temperature until hardened and set, about 30 minutes. —PAIGE GRANDJEAN

MAKE AHEAD Crust can be made up to 2 days in advance and stored, covered, at room temperature.

NOTE Lightly crush granola in a large zip-lock plastic bag using a rolling pin. The smaller pieces bind together better for easier slicing.

White Chocolate Meringue Crust

ACTIVE 35 MIN; TOTAL 3 HR 5 MIN, PLUS
4 HR COOLING; MAKES 1 (9-INCH) PIECRUST

Marshmallowy Italian meringue is baked and then brushed with melted white chocolate to create a barrier to help prevent this crust from getting soggy once filled and chilled

Cooking spray

Cornstarch

¾ cup granulated sugar

¼ cup water ·

3 large egg whites, at room temperature

¼ tsp. cream of tartar

⅛ tsp. kosher salt

½ tsp. vanilla extract

¾ cup white chocolate chips

1. Preheat oven to 200°F with rack in lower third position. Lightly grease a 9-inch deep-dish pie plate (with at least a ½-inch lip) with cooking spray, and line bottom with parchment paper. Generously dust pie plate with cornstarch; set aside. Combine sugar and ¼ cup water in a small saucepan. Cook over medium-low, swirling pan occasionally, until sugar is dissolved and syrup registers 240°F on an instant-read thermometer, 10 to 14 minutes.

2. Meanwhile, when syrup reaches about 225°F, beat egg whites with a stand mixer fitted with the whisk attachment on medium speed until foamy, about 30 seconds. Add cream of tartar and salt; beat until soft peaks form, 1 to 2 minutes.

3. With mixer running on medium speed, gradually stream hot sugar syrup into whipped egg white mixture. Continue beating until meringue is glossy and forms stiff peaks and outside of mixer bowl has cooled slightly, 3 to 5 minutes. Reduce

mixer speed to low, and beat in vanilla until combined.

4. Measure about 3½ cups meringue into a large (about 18-inch) piping bag fitted with a ½-inch closed star piping tip (such as Ateco 854). Pipe into a tight spiral pattern in bottom and up sides of prepared pie plate, starting in center and working outward and then up sides of pie plate, ensuring there are no gaps. If desired, pipe a decorative edge at the top, resting on the lip of the pie plate. Place remaining meringue (about ¾ cup) in piping bag, and pipe into small kisses on a parchment paper–lined small baking sheet.

5. Bake crust and kisses on lower third rack in preheated oven until dry and no longer sticky, 2 hours to 2 hours and 30 minutes. Turn oven off, and let meringues cool completely in oven until crisp, at least 4 hours or up to 1 day (24 hours). Reserve meringue kisses for garnish or for another use.

6. Place white chocolate chips in a small microwavable bowl. Microwave on high until smooth and melted, 1 to 2 minutes, stopping to stir every 20 seconds. Brush melted chocolate evenly on bottom and sides of piecrust, leaving top edge of crust bare. Let stand at room temperature until chocolate hardens, about 30 minutes. Just before filling pie, use a torch to lightly toast the top edge of the crust. Fill piecrust; chill just until filling is set. —PAIGE GRANDJEAN

MAKE AHEAD Crust and kisses can be made up to 2 days in advance and stored in an airtight container.

NOTE If the temperature of your oven can only go as low as 250°F, bake piecrust for 1 hour, removing meringue kisses when dry and no longer sticky, after 35 to 40 minutes. Turn oven off, and let piecrust cool completely in oven until crisp, at least 4 hours or up to 24 hours.

Sugared Melon with Cardamom and Mint

ACTIVE 25 MIN; TOTAL 1 HR 25 MIN;
SERVES 2 TO 4

Sugar, cardamom, and fresh mint are all you need to transform ripe melon into a memorable dessert. Muskmelons, such as cantaloupe and honeydew, are sometimes treated like an afterthought—that's why chef Vishwesh Bhatt sometimes calls this recipe Don't Forget the Melon. "If you have the right melon that's nice and ripe, it's just so good," he says. "Summer is just the perfect time for melons. If you think they're boring, then jazz them up with this recipe. Just a tiny bit of sugar, cardamom, and fresh mint transform ripe melon into something so special you'll want to eat it over and over again." Ripe, peak-season cantaloupe, honeydew, or other muskmelon will all work beautifully here. Serve it over ice cream for an extra-special treat.

- 4 cups chopped cantaloupe (from 1 small [3½-lb.] peeled and seeded cantaloupe)
- 4 cups chopped honeydew melon (from 1 small [3½-lb.] peeled and seeded honeydew)
- 2 tsp. turbinado sugar
- ½ tsp. kosher salt
- 3 cardamom pods, smashed, husks discarded
- 2 Tbsp. torn fresh mint
  Whipped cream or vanilla ice cream (optional)

1. Toss together cantaloupe, honeydew, sugar, salt, and cardamom in a large bowl. Stir gently until melon is evenly coated. Cover with plastic wrap, and refrigerate until melon has started to release juices and flavors have married, at least 1 hour or up to 3 hours.

2. Sprinkle melon mixture with mint. The melon is great on its own, but feel free to add a dollop of fresh whipped cream or a good-quality vanilla ice cream, if desired. —VISHWESH BHATT

MAKE AHEAD Prepare recipe through step 1 up to 3 hours in advance.

Mango Fluff

TOTAL 20 MIN, PLUS 8 HR CHILLING;
SERVES 8

"My favorite sweets are the ones that embody tropical fruit and summer flavors," says chef Sam Fore, the owner of Tuk Tuk Sri Lankan Bites in Lexington, Kentucky. "Mango Fluff is an old standby—one I would consume by the bowlful when I was younger and one that's always a fixture at Sri Lankan parties. Its fluffy texture makes it a dessert that is light and refreshing, yet still rich with the sweetness of Kesar mangoes. The secret to my recipe is the sweetened canned Kesar mango pulp, which makes the resulting fluff just sweet enough. Airy whipped cream gives each bite a light and decadent mouthfeel." This fruity and delicate chilled mousse, with its silky, cloudlike texture and bold sweetness, is sure to become a regular at your summer table. Gelatin thickens the fluff into a spoonable consistency and gives it a melt-in-your-mouth quality for a dessert that is equally refreshing and rich. Garnish it with slippery fresh mango and spicy candied ginger.

- 1½ cups hot water
- 2 (¼-oz.) envelopes unflavored gelatin
- 2 cups heavy cream
- ½ cup powdered sugar (about 2 oz.)
- 1 (30-oz.) can Kesar mango pulp
- 1 (14-oz.) can condensed milk
- 1 tsp. kosher salt
  Whipped cream, diced fresh mango, and crystallized ginger, for serving (optional)

1. Whisk together 1½ cups hot water and gelatin in a medium bowl until gelatin is dissolved. Let cool slightly, about 10 minutes.

2. Beat cream and powdered sugar in a stand mixer fitted with the whisk attachment on high speed until stiff peaks form, about 1 minute and 30 seconds. Spoon whipped cream into a large bowl.

3. Add mango pulp, condensed milk, salt, and cooled gelatin mixture to mixer bowl; whisk until well combined.

4. Gradually fold one-third of the mango mixture into whipped cream in large bowl until almost combined; gradually fold in remaining mango mixture. Gently transfer mixture to a large glass bowl. Cover and chill until firm, about 8 hours. Serve with desired toppings. —SAM FORE

MAKE AHEAD Fluff can be stored in an airtight container in refrigerator up to 2 days.

NOTE Canned Kesar mango pulp is available at most Indian grocery stores or online at desibasket.com. Other mango pulps may be substituted, if desired.

MANGO FLUFF

TROPICAL JACKFRUIT–GINGER ALE
SORBET WITH CHARRED PINEAPPLE

Tropical Jackfruit–Ginger Ale Sorbet with Charred Pineapple

ACTIVE 15 MIN; TOTAL 1 HR 30 MIN;
SERVES 6

Chef Sam Fore of the pop up Tuk Tuk Sri Lankan Bites in Lexington, Kentucky, created this summer fruit dessert recipe for an icy, quenching sorbet of jackfruit, pineapple, and ginger ale. The sorbet has become an ever-present treat at her summer pop-up dinners, combining pineapple and jackfruit, both popular in Sri Lanka, with the spicy flavors of Ale-8-One, a Kentucky ginger ale.

- 1 cup chopped (¾-inch pieces) fresh pineapple (about 5 oz.)
- 2 tsp. granulated sugar
- 1 cup warm water
- ¼ cup plus ½ tsp. kosher salt, divided
- 1 (20-oz.) can jackfruit in syrup, drained
- 1 (8-oz.) can pineapple juice
- 1 (12-oz.) can Ale-8-One soda or good-quality ginger ale, chilled

1. Preheat oven to broil with oven rack about 6 inches from heat. Spread pineapple pieces evenly on a baking sheet lined with aluminum foil; sprinkle evenly with sugar. Broil in preheated oven until charred in spots, 15 to 17 minutes. Remove from oven; let cool completely, about 30 minutes.

2. Whisk together 1 cup warm water and ¼ cup salt in a medium bowl until salt is dissolved. Add jackfruit, and stir 30 seconds. Drain and discard saltwater.

3. Combine drained jackfruit, pineapple juice, and remaining ½ teaspoon salt in a blender; process until smooth, about 1 minute. Pour mixture though a fine wire-mesh strainer into a medium bowl. Carefully stir soda into mixture.

4. Pour jackfruit mixture into an ice cream maker; process according to manufacturer's instructions. Serve immediately for a soft-serve consistency, or transfer to a shallow container, cover, and freeze until firm, about 3 hours. Garnish with charred pineapple just before serving. —SAM FORE

MAKE AHEAD Sorbet can be stored in an airtight container in freezer up to 2 days. Let stand at room temperature 20 minutes before serving. Charred pineapple can be stored in an airtight container in refrigerator up to 2 days.

Honey-Ricotta Mousse with Strawberries

ACTIVE 15 MIN; TOTAL 1 HR 15 MIN;
SERVES 4 TO 6

This velvety-smooth, berry-topped mousse requires very little time to make – it comes together in just 15 minutes, and then needs just an hour in the refrigerator to firm up. Ricotta cheese, quickly whipped in a food processor with honey and vanilla, forms the base of the mousse. Folding whipped cream into the ricotta yields a luscious, velvety dessert. With a recipe like this one that calls for just a few ingredients, it's important to use the best you can find. Start with homemade ricotta, or the best, freshest ricotta you can find at the store or farmer's market. Then, to complement the subtly milky, pleasantly grassy flavor of that ricotta, use a mild clover honey. The honey-ricotta mousse is a beautiful canvas for all kinds of toppings. Here, it's garnished with crunchy sliced toasted almonds and juicy fresh strawberries and a final drizzle of honey, but it's adaptable to what's in season or what you like best: you can substitute sweet orange segments or jammy figs for the strawberries, change up the honey drizzle with maple syrup, or try another crunchy topping, like your favorite granola or crushed pistachios, in place of the sliced almonds.

- 1 lb. Homemade Fresh Ricotta (recipe p. 180) or store-bought fresh ricotta, drained
- 2 Tbsp. clover honey, plus more for drizzling
- 1½ tsp. vanilla bean paste or extract
  Pinch of kosher salt
- 1 cup heavy cream
  Toasted almond slices, sliced fresh strawberries, and fresh mint leaves, for garnish

1. Process ricotta, honey, vanilla bean paste, and salt in a food processor until very smooth, about 2 minutes, stopping to scrape down sides of bowl as needed.

2. Whip heavy cream in a large bowl until stiff peaks form, 1 to 2 minutes. Add ricotta mixture, and gently whisk to combine. Using a rubber spatula, fold mixture until evenly incorporated, 3 to 5 times. Divide mixture evenly among 4 glasses or bowls. Cover and refrigerate until firm and set, at least 1 hour or up to overnight.

3. Garnish mousse with toasted almond slices, sliced fresh strawberries, mint leaves, and a drizzle of honey. Serve immediately. —PAIGE GRANDJEAN

MAKE AHEAD Prepared mousse can be covered and refrigerated up to 1 day.

Figs 'n' Cream
PHOTO P. 265

TOTAL 15 MIN; SERVES 2

This dessert is a seasonal special at Beit Rima in San Francisco. It's a simple dish, but striking: a geometric bloom of fresh figs laid atop a layer of labneh and topped with carob molasses, olive oil, toasted sesame seeds and hazelnuts, and a shower of black pepper. Carob molasses is a staple Middle Eastern ingredient—it's a dark, thick, sweet syrup with a subtle chocolate flavor. The final dish is an intoxicating combination of olive oil, figs, and carob, all produce that grows on trees in the Levant.

- ⅔ cup labneh (preferably Byblos) (about 6 oz.)
- 4 to 6 fresh figs (about 5 oz.), quartered lengthwise
- ½ tsp. kosher salt, plus more to taste
- ½ tsp. black pepper, plus more to taste
- 2 Tbsp. extra-virgin olive oil
- 2 tsp. carob molasses
- 2 tsp. toasted and crushed hazelnuts
- 1 tsp. white and black sesame seeds, toasted

Spread a bed of labneh on a 7-inch plate, and lay down figs, cut side up. Sprinkle figs evenly with salt and pepper. Drizzle evenly with olive oil and molasses, and sprinkle with hazelnuts and sesame seeds. Serve immediately. —SAMIR MOGANNAM, BEIT RIMA, SAN FRANCISCO

WINE Sweet, brightly tart German Riesling: 2019 Selbach-Oster Zeltinger Sonnenuhr Spätlese

NOTE Find carob molasses at most Middle Eastern grocery stores or online. Putting the carob molasses in a squeeze bottle makes for easy plating. Any brand of labneh may be used if Byblos is unavailable and can be found in most grocery stores.

CAKES, COOKIES & MORE

BLUE CORN–CHERRY–CHOCOLATE
CHIP COOKIES (P. 286)
OPPOSITE: LEMON-RICOTTA
CAKE (P. 281)

Chocolate-Raspberry Icebox Cake

TOTAL 15 MIN, PLUS 4 HR FREEZING;
SERVES 8

This Chocolate-Raspberry Icebox Cake is the answer to summer days when you want to serve a beautiful cake but it's too hot to turn on the oven. It's creamy, it's dreamy, and it's so simple to make. Crushed cookies, fresh raspberries, and layers of tart raspberry sorbet and vanilla ice cream transform into a gorgeous marbled layer cake in about 15 minutes — no frosting required. The raspberries sink into the milky, sweet layers of ice cream, adding a tart flavor and pops of color to the cake, and crunchy chocolate cookie crumble layers are the perfect sweet and salty counterpoint, adding satisfying texture and a hint of bittersweet flavor. Finally, after a deep chill in the freezer, the cake is topped with whipped cream and more raspberries. The finished cake slices beautifully, revealing deep pink, creamy white, and rich dark-chocolate cookie swirls. Bonus: The recipe doubles easily, if you're making cake for a crowd — or if you just want more for yourself. Leave your ice cream at room temperature for about 10 minutes to soften before using.

- Cooking spray
- 2 pt. vanilla ice cream, softened
- 1 pt. raspberry sorbet, softened
- 1 (9-oz.) pkg. chocolate wafer cookies (such as Nabisco Famous Chocolate Wafers), crushed (about 2½ cups)
- 2 cups fresh raspberries (about 9 oz.), plus more for garnish
- 1 cup heavy cream
- 3 Tbsp. powdered sugar

1. Lightly coat a 9- × 5-inch loaf pan with cooking spray. Line with parchment paper, making sure all sides are fully covered and leaving a 2-inch overhang on all sides.

2. Fold softened ice cream and sorbet together in a large bowl until sorbet is just streaked through ice cream but not quite swirled, 2 to 3 folds.

3. Sprinkle ½ cup crushed cookies into bottom of prepared loaf pan. Spread 1½ cups ice cream mixture over crushed cookies. Scatter ½ cup fresh raspberries over top, gently pressing into ice cream mixture. Repeat layers 3 times, ending with remaining ½ cup crushed cookies.

4. Wrap loaf pan tightly with plastic wrap, and freeze until cake is firm, at least 4 hours or up to 24 hours.

5. Remove ice cream cake from freezer; unwrap and let stand at room temperature 5 minutes. Meanwhile, whisk together cream and powdered sugar in a medium bowl until stiff peaks form, about 2 minutes.

6. Lift ice cream cake out of loaf pan using parchment paper overhang as handles, and invert onto a large plate or platter. Dollop whipped cream over top of cake. Garnish with additional fresh raspberries. Slice and serve. —ANNA THEOKTISTO

MAKE AHEAD Cake can be frozen up to 3 weeks. Top with whipped cream just before serving.

NOTE This recipe easily doubles to serve 16. Make the cake in a 9-inch square pan, and double the ingredients.

Lemon-Ricotta Cake
PHOTO P. 278

ACTIVE 25 MIN; TOTAL 1 HR 55 MIN;
SERVES 8

This light and airy cake gets its texture from whole-milk ricotta in the batter. "I first created this cake by accident, substituting the ricotta I had in my refrigerator for the sour cream that my recipe called for," says 2020 F&W Best New Chef Camille Cogswell of Asheville, North Carolina. "The result was, happily, far superior to the original! Now, this super moist and tender ricotta cake with bright lemon flavor is one of my go-tos; it comes together quickly and easily and is still exceptional even after a few days sitting on the counter. By itself, it's a perfect gift to a friend. Dressed up with soft whipped cream and showered in seasonal fresh fruit, it becomes quite an elegant dinner dessert with minimal effort."

- Cooking spray
- 1 cup plus 2 Tbsp. granulated sugar
- 2 Tbsp. grated lemon zest (from 2 lemons)
- 9 Tbsp. unsalted butter (4½ oz.), softened
- 3 large eggs, at room temperature
- ½ tsp. lemon extract (optional)
- 1⅓ cups all-purpose flour (about 5¾ oz.)
- 1½ tsp. baking powder
- ¼ tsp. kosher salt

- ½ cup plus 1 Tbsp. whole-milk ricotta cheese
- Powdered sugar, whipped cream, and fall fruit, for serving (see Note)

1. Preheat oven to 350°F. Coat an 8-inch cake pan with cooking spray. Line bottom of cake pan with a round of parchment paper; coat parchment with cooking spray.

2. Combine sugar and lemon zest in bowl of a stand mixer, and rub them together between your hands, dispersing the zest and infusing the sugar with the lemon oils. Add butter to lemon sugar, and attach paddle attachment to mixer. Beat butter and lemon sugar on medium-high speed until very light and fluffy, about 10 minutes, stopping to scrape down bowl and paddle occasionally.

3. Add eggs to butter mixture, 1 at a time, beating on low speed after each addition to fully incorporate before adding next egg, about 45 seconds total. Beat in lemon extract, if using, until combined, about 10 seconds.

4. Stir together flour, baking powder, and salt in a medium bowl. Add half of the flour mixture to butter mixture in mixer bowl; beat on low speed until just combined, about 15 seconds. Stop mixer, and scrape down sides of bowl. Add ricotta; beat on low speed until just incorporated, about 15 seconds. Add remaining flour mixture; beat on low speed until just combined, about 15 seconds. Scrape the bowl and paddle with a spatula, then beat for 3 more seconds, until homogenous.

5. Pour batter into prepared pan, and smooth top using an offset spatula. Bake in preheated oven until cake top springs back at the touch and has a light golden hue and a wooden pick poked in center of cake comes out without looking wet, 30 to 35 minutes.

6. Remove cake from oven; let cool in pan 15 minutes. Run a knife around edge of pan; turn cake out onto a wire rack. Let cool to room temperature, about 45 minutes. Dust with powdered sugar. Serve with whipped cream and fruit. —CAMILLE COGSWELL

MAKE AHEAD Cake can be made up to 1 day in advance and stored in an airtight container at room temperature.

NOTE Figs, pears, late-season melons, persimmons, and preserved citrus are great options for serving.

Ube Basque Cakes

ACTIVE 1 HR 20 MIN; TOTAL 3 HR 15 MIN,
PLUS 2 HR FREEZING; MAKES 12 CAKES

These tender and flaky mini cakes created by the dynamic duo of Timothy Flores and Genie Kwon at Kasama, a modern Filipino bakery and restaurant in Chicago, highlight the cultural phenomenon of ube, a purple tuber native to the Philippines. To make the cakes, Kwon uses a technique for shaping the batter into rounds rather than piping the batter into a baking vessel as sometimes done for traditional Gâteau Basque, making it easier to make lots of the mini Basque cakes. "[Making] flat discs is more efficient and ergonomic," she notes. "It might not make much of a difference when you are making a dozen, but when you're making hundreds, it is a game changer." The buttery cakes are filled with a creamy and mildly sweet ube pastry cream and tart huckleberries, and are finished with a sprinkling of powdered sugar. (At Kasama, the shape of the powdered sugar is in the shape of the sun design from the flag of the Philippines). If you can't source fresh ube, store-bought ube jam (ube halaya) can be used instead.

BASQUE BATTER

- 2 cups bleached cake flour (such as Swans Down) (about 7½ oz.)
- ½ cup all-purpose flour (about 2⅛ oz.)
- 1¼ tsp. baking powder
- 1 tsp. kosher salt
- 1½ cups granulated sugar
- 1 cup unsalted butter (8 oz.), softened
- 2 large eggs
- 1 tsp. vanilla extract

UBE JAM

- 1 small (about 7-oz.) fresh ube, peeled and cut into ½-inch pieces (about 1⅓ cups)
- ¾ cup heavy cream
- ¾ cup granulated sugar

PASTRY CREAM

- 1 large egg plus 1 egg yolk
- 3 Tbsp. dark brown sugar
- 3 Tbsp. granulated sugar
- 1 Tbsp. bleached cake flour (such as Swans Down)
- 1 cup heavy cream
- ¾ tsp. vanilla extract
- ¼ tsp. kosher salt

ADDITIONAL INGREDIENTS

- Cooking spray
- 1 cup fresh or frozen huckleberries or wild blueberries (about 6 oz.)
- Powdered sugar

1. Make the Basque batter: Whisk together cake flour, all-purpose flour, baking powder, and salt in a medium bowl; set aside. Beat granulated sugar and butter with a stand mixer fitted with the paddle attachment on medium speed until smooth, about 3 minutes. Add eggs; beat on medium speed until mixture is light and fluffy, about 2 minutes, stopping to scrape down sides of bowl as needed. Beat in vanilla until incorporated, about 10 seconds. Add flour mixture all at once. Pulse mixer 3 to 4 times to begin incorporating flour mixture. Beat on medium-low speed until evenly combined, about 45 seconds.

2. Using a 1½-inch scoop, drop 6 balls of batter (about 1¼ ounces or 2½ tablespoons each) on a large piece of parchment paper, spacing balls at least 3 inches apart and away from outer edge of paper. Place a second piece of parchment paper on top of balls. Using bottom of an 8-cup liquid measuring cup, press to flatten each ball into a 4-inch round (about ⅛ inch thick). Repeat process with remaining batter and 6 additional sheets of parchment paper to form 24 dough rounds total. Stack the parchment-sandwiched rounds on a baking sheet. Freeze until very firm and parchment can be peeled off cleanly from batter, at least 2 hours or up to 3 days.

3. Make the ube jam: Stir together ube, cream, and granulated sugar in small saucepan. Bring to a boil over medium-high. Reduce heat to medium-low; cover and simmer, stirring occasionally, until ube is very soft, 25 to 30 minutes. Using an immersion blender, process mixture in pan until very smooth, about 2 minutes. Let ube jam cool to room temperature, about 30 minutes.

4. Make the pastry cream: While ube jam cools, whisk together egg and egg yolk, brown sugar, granulated sugar, and cake flour in a medium-size heatproof bowl; set aside. Bring cream to a simmer in a small saucepan over medium. Reduce heat to medium-low. Whisking egg mixture constantly, gradually ladle about ⅔ cup of the hot cream into egg mixture. Pour egg mixture into remaining hot cream in pan. Cook over medium-low, whisking constantly, until mixture thickens to a pudding-like consistency, 2 to 3 minutes. Press pastry cream through a fine wire-mesh strainer set over a large bowl; discard solids. Stir in vanilla and salt. Press plastic wrap directly onto surface. Let cool to room temperature, about 30 minutes.

5. Whisk together cooled pastry cream and ube jam in a medium bowl. Ube pastry cream can be stored in an airtight container in refrigerator up to 3 days.

6. Preheat oven to 350°F with racks in upper third and lower third positions. Line 2 rimmed baking sheets with parchment paper. Lightly coat 12 (4- × 1-inch) ring molds with cooking spray; arrange 6 molds evenly spaced on each prepared baking sheet. Remove 1 sheet of batter rounds from freezer. Working quickly to avoid batter softening, peel off parchment paper, and carefully press 1 batter round into bottom of 1 mold. Repeat process with 5 additional batter rounds and ring molds. If batter round cracks, press the pieces back together in the mold. Repeat procedure with second sheet of batter rounds and remaining 6 ring molds.

7. Transfer ube pastry cream to a pastry bag with a 1-inch hole cut in the tip. Starting in the center and working outward, pipe about 2 tablespoons ube pastry cream in a spiral on each batter round, leaving a ¾-inch border. Top ube pastry cream spirals evenly with huckleberries (a scant 1 tablespoon each). Remove 1 sheet of batter rounds from freezer. Working quickly, peel off parchment paper. Top each mold with a second batter round, pressing just until it touches the huckleberries. (The layers will fuse together in the oven.) Repeat process with remaining sheet of batter rounds and remaining molds.

continued on page 285

UBE BASQUE CAKES

PINE NUT OLIVE OIL CAKE

continued from page 282

8. Bake cakes in preheated oven until deep golden brown on top, 38 to 46 minutes, rotating baking sheets between top and bottom racks halfway through bake time. Transfer baking sheets to a wire rack; let cakes cool completely, about 30 minutes. Run an offset spatula around the edge of each mold, and remove cakes.

9. Garnish top of each cake with powdered sugar, using a 3-inch stencil of the Filipino sun, if desired. —TIMOTHY FLORES AND GENIE KWON, KASAMA, CHICAGO

MAKE AHEAD Basque batter rounds can be prepared up to 3 days in advance and stored in the freezer between parchment paper. Ube pastry cream can be chilled in an airtight container up to 3 days.

NOTE A 3-inch Filipino sun stencil is available on amazon.com, or you can cut out your own design using the lid of a plastic container as a stencil.

Pine Nut Olive Oil Cake

ACTIVE 1 HR 20 MIN; TOTAL 3 HR; SERVES 12

White wine–glazed persimmons, fruity olive oil, and buttery pine nuts come together with tuiles and vanilla ice cream in this simple yet elegant cake.

CAKE

- 1 cup extra-virgin olive oil, plus more for pan
- 2½ cups all-purpose flour (about 10⅝ oz.), plus more for pan
- 2 tsp. baking powder
- ½ tsp. baking soda
- ½ tsp. fine sea salt
- ½ cup whole milk
- 2 tsp. grated lemon zest plus 3 Tbsp. fresh lemon juice (from 1 lemon), divided
- 1 cup granulated sugar
- 3 large eggs
- ½ cup pine nuts

TUILES

- 2 large egg whites
- ¼ cup granulated sugar
- ⅓ cup all-purpose flour (about 1½ oz.)
- ¼ cup unsalted butter, melted
- ½ tsp. vanilla extract
- ¼ cup pine nuts
- ⅛ tsp. fine sea salt

GLAZED PERSIMMONS

- 2 (750-ml.) bottles unoaked dry white wine (such as Sauvignon Blanc)
- 1 medium-size (11-oz.) orange
- 2 cups granulated sugar
- 6 whole star anise
- 1 (3-inch) piece fresh ginger, peeled and cut into ½-inch pieces (about ¼ cup)
- 1 vanilla bean pod, halved lengthwise
- 2 lb. firm-ripe Fuyu persimmons (about 8 small persimmons), peeled and cut into 1½-inch wedges (about 5 cups)

ADDITIONAL INGREDIENT

- Vanilla ice cream, for serving

1. Make the cake: Preheat oven to 350°F. Lightly grease bottom of a 9-inch springform pan with olive oil. Line bottom with parchment paper. Lightly grease and flour parchment paper and sides of springform pan; set aside.

2. Whisk together flour, baking powder, baking soda, and salt in a medium bowl. Stir together milk and lemon juice in a small bowl; set aside.

3. Combine sugar, eggs, and lemon zest in bowl of a stand mixer fitted with the whisk attachment. Beat on medium-high speed until pale and thick, 3 to 4 minutes. Gradually stream in olive oil, beating on medium-high speed until mixture is well combined and thickened, 2 to 3 minutes. Reduce mixer speed to medium-low, and add flour mixture in 3 additions alternately with milk mixture, beginning and ending with flour mixture; beat until just combined, about 20 seconds. Transfer batter to prepared springform pan, and smooth top using a spatula. Sprinkle with pine nuts.

4. Bake in preheated oven until a wooden pick inserted in center of cake comes out clean, about 45 minutes. Transfer to a wire rack, and let cake cool in springform pan 15 minutes. Remove sides and base of springform pan, and let cake cool completely, about 1 hour. Do not turn off oven.

5. While cake cools, make the tuiles: Whisk egg whites in a medium bowl until foamy, about 1 minute. Add sugar, and whisk until sugar dissolves, about 30 seconds. Whisk in flour, butter, and vanilla until smooth. Cover and chill until batter is cold, about 20 minutes.

6. Line 2 baking sheets with silicone baking mats. Spoon about 1 tablespoon batter for each tuile onto prepared baking sheets, spacing batter at least 1 inch apart (6 tuiles per baking sheet). Using the back of a spoon or a small offset spatula, spread each scoop into a 4-inch round (about ⅛ inch thick). Sprinkle evenly with pine nuts and salt. Bake in 2 batches at 350°F until light golden brown, 8 to 9 minutes. Remove from oven; let cool completely on baking sheets, about 20 minutes. Set aside.

7. Make the glazed persimmons: Bring wine to a boil in a medium saucepan over high. Boil, undisturbed, until wine reduces to about 1½ cups, 45 to 50 minutes. Peel orange rind into large strips (about ¼ cup); reserve orange flesh for another use. Reduce heat to medium, and stir in orange rind strips, sugar, star anise, and ginger. Scrape seeds from vanilla bean, discarding pod; add seeds to sugar mixture. Simmer, stirring occasionally, until sugar dissolves, 1 to 2 minutes. Add persimmons; simmer, stirring occasionally, until persimmons are tender, 20 to 35 minutes, adjusting heat as needed to maintain a low simmer. (The liquid should never come to a boil.) Using a slotted spoon, transfer persimmons to a medium bowl; set aside. Pour poaching liquid through a fine wire-mesh strainer into a medium bowl; discard solids.

8. Return poaching liquid to saucepan, and bring to a boil over medium-high. Boil, undisturbed, until liquid is reduced to about 1¼ cups, is syrupy, and coats the back of a spoon, about 15 minutes. Remove from heat, and stir in reserved persimmons.

9. Cut cake evenly into 12 slices. Top each slice with ⅓ cup glazed persimmons and syrup. Serve with 1 tuile and ice cream. —CARLTON MCCOY

MAKE AHEAD Glazed persimmons can be made up to 1 day in advance and stored in an airtight container in refrigerator. Warm over low until heated through before serving.

Blue Corn–Cherry–Chocolate Chip Cookies

PHOTO P. 279

ACTIVE 20 MIN; TOTAL 1 HR 5 MIN; SERVES 8

With a soft interior that has a hint of almond flavor, these fresh cherry–studded cookies are not only colorful but also incredibly delicious. "After developing dozens of cookie recipes for All Day Baby, I find that the formula for a well-received cookie is to incorporate familiarity with the somewhat unusual," says 2021 F&W Best New Chef Thessa Diadem of All Day Baby in Los Angeles. "These cookies use blue corn flour, which makes them nutty and hearty. Cherry and chocolate is a classic combination that I love and that works well with blue corn. These cookies are best served warm and are absolutely perfect with a cup of coffee or Mexican hot chocolate."

- 1¼ cups packed dark brown sugar
- ¾ cup unsalted butter (6 oz.), at room temperature
- 1 large egg, at room temperature
- 2 tsp. almond extract
- ½ tsp. vanilla extract
- 1½ cups blue corn flour (about 6⅖ oz.)
- ¾ cup all-purpose flour (about 3¼ oz.)
- ¾ tsp. kosher salt
- ½ tsp. baking powder
- ¼ tsp. baking soda
- 1½ cups dark chocolate chips or chopped feves (about 7 oz.)
- 1½ cups fresh red cherries, pitted and halved (about 7 oz.)

1. Preheat oven to 325°F with racks in upper third and lower third positions. Line 2 large rimmed baking sheets with parchment paper; set aside. Beat brown sugar and butter with an electric mixer on high speed until very light, fluffy, and almost tripled in volume, about 4 minutes. Beat in egg, almond extract, and vanilla extract until just combined, about 1 minute.

2. Whisk together corn flour, all-purpose flour, salt, baking powder, and baking soda in a medium bowl. With electric mixer running on low speed, gradually add flour mixture to brown sugar mixture, beating until just combined, about 1 minute. Using a spatula or wooden spoon, fold in chocolate and cherries until combined.

3. Using a 1½-tablespoon cookie scoop, scoop half of the dough onto prepared baking sheets (8 scoops per baking sheet with scoops spaced about 2 inches apart). Bake in preheated oven until cookie edges are browned, 15 to 18 minutes, rotating baking sheets between top and bottom racks halfway through bake time. Remove from oven. Let cookies cool on baking sheets 5 minutes. Transfer cookies to a wire rack, and let cool completely, about 15 minutes. Repeat scooping and baking procedure with remaining dough. —THESSA DIADEM, ALL DAY BABY, LOS ANGELES

MAKE AHEAD Cookies can be stored in an airtight container up to 2 days.

NOTE Blue corn flour is available at Mexican grocery stores or online at masienda.com.

Aperol Spritz Cake with Prosecco-Poached Rhubarb

ACTIVE 40 MIN; TOTAL 1 HR 50 MIN; SERVES 8 TO 10

Choose deep red stalks of rhubarb for the most vibrant color atop this springtime dessert. The poached rhubarb syrup slowly soaks into the sponge, lightly glazing the top while adding delicious moisture to the cake below.

- 2 large eggs
- 1¾ cups granulated sugar, divided
- 1 (750-ml.) bottle Prosecco, divided
- ½ cup unsalted butter (4 oz.), melted
- ¼ cup extra-virgin olive oil, plus more for greasing pan
- 1½ cups all-purpose flour (about 6⅜ oz.)
- 1½ tsp. baking powder
- 1 tsp. kosher salt, divided
- ¼ tsp. baking soda
- ¼ cup Aperol
- 1 lb. fresh red rhubarb stalks (about 3 stalks), cut diagonally into 1-inch pieces
- 1 medium-size (about 9½-oz.) navel orange, cut crosswise into ¼-inch slices

1. Preheat oven to 350°F. Grease a 9-inch round cake pan with oil, and line bottom of pan with parchment paper. Lightly grease parchment with oil. Set aside.

2. Whisk together eggs and ¾ cup sugar in a large bowl until pale and foamy, 1 to 2 minutes. Whisk in 1¼ cups Prosecco, butter, and oil until well combined. Add flour, baking powder, ¾ teaspoon salt, and baking soda; whisk until combined and almost smooth. Pour batter into prepared cake pan, and tap pan on counter to release any trapped bubbles.

3. Bake in preheated oven until a wooden pick inserted in center of cake comes out clean, 22 to 26 minutes. Transfer cake pan to a wire rack, and let cool 15 minutes. Run a small offset spatula around edge of pan, and invert cake onto a wire rack. Let cool completely, about 30 minutes.

4. Meanwhile, stir together Aperol, remaining 1 cup sugar, remaining Prosecco (about 2 cups), and remaining ¼ teaspoon salt in a large saucepan. Bring to a simmer over medium-high, stirring occasionally to dissolve sugar. Add rhubarb to mixture, and fan orange slices over surface to keep rhubarb submerged in liquid. Return mixture to a simmer over medium-high. Reduce heat to medium-low to keep poaching liquid just below a simmer, and cook, gently swirling pan occasionally, until rhubarb is very tender but still holds its shape, 6 to 10 minutes. Remove from heat. Remove orange slices, and spread on a plate; let stand until cool enough to handle, about 5 minutes. Using a slotted spoon, carefully transfer delicate poached rhubarb to a fine wire-mesh strainer set over a medium bowl; set aside.

5. Bring poaching liquid in saucepan to a boil over high. Squeeze cooled orange slices over poaching liquid in pan; discard squeezed orange slices. Boil mixture, stirring occasionally, until liquid thickens to a syrupy consistency, coats the back of a spoon, and reduces to about ¾ cup, 20 to 24 minutes. Remove from heat. Pour into a large heatproof bowl, and let cool to room temperature, about 1 hour.

6. When ready to serve, transfer cake to a rimmed plate or a cake stand. Add drained rhubarb to cooled syrup in saucepan, and toss to coat. Spoon rhubarb mixture over top of cake, piling rhubarb pieces in center. Let syrup soak into cake 10 minutes. Slice and serve. —ANDREA SLONECKER

MAKE AHEAD Cake is best served the day it is baked. Rhubarb mixture can hold at room temperature about 3 hours before topping cake.

WINE NV Fruity, crisp Prosecco: Santa Margherita Superiore Valdobbiadene

APEROL SPRITZ CAKE WITH
PROSECCO-POACHED RHUBARB

SPICED CARROT CAKE WITH
BROWN BUTTER FROSTING

Spiced Carrot Cake with Brown Butter Frosting

ACTIVE 30 MIN; TOTAL 3 HR; SERVES 12

A warming blend of cardamom, ginger, cinnamon, and nutmeg bring festive flavors to Hetal Vasavada's tender, moist spiced carrot cake studded with golden raisins and crunchy pistachios. Brown butter ghee does double duty in this recipe: It enriches and flavors the cake batter, and the caramelized milk fat left over from making it adds a nutty flavor to the cream cheese frosting.

CAKE

- 1 cup plus 6 Tbsp. unsalted butter (11 oz.)
- Cooking spray
- 1 cup packed dark brown sugar
- 1½ Tbsp. grated orange zest
- 4 large eggs
- 1 large egg yolk
- 1 Tbsp. vanilla extract
- 1 Tbsp. ground cinnamon
- 1 Tbsp. ground cardamom
- 2 tsp. ground ginger
- ½ tsp. ground nutmeg
- 4½ cups shredded peeled carrots (from 1 lb. carrots)
- 1¼ cups unsalted roasted pistachios, coarsely chopped
- ½ cup golden raisins
- 2⅔ cups all-purpose flour (about 11⅜ oz.)
- 2½ tsp. baking powder
- ½ tsp. baking soda
- ½ tsp. kosher salt

FROSTING

- 1 cup unsalted butter (8 oz.), at room temperature
- 4 oz. cream cheese, at room temperature
- 1 Tbsp. vanilla extract
- 2½ cups powdered sugar (about 10 oz.)

ADDITIONAL INGREDIENTS

- Finely chopped pistachios and shredded carrots, for garnish

1. Make the cake: Melt butter in a large, heavy-bottomed saucepan over medium-high, stirring often; gently simmer butter until white milk solids separate from butterfat, about 10 minutes. Reduce heat to low, and cook, stirring constantly, until butter is golden brown and spoon is covered in flecks of caramelized milk solids, about 2 minutes. Remove from heat. Line a fine wire-mesh strainer with 3 layers of cheesecloth, and place strainer over a heatproof container. Pour melted butter through strainer and into container. Reserve caramelized milk fat (about 1 teaspoon), and set aside. Let strained ghee cool completely at room temperature, about 1 hour.

2. Preheat oven to 350°F. Coat a 13-×9-inch baking pan with cooking spray; set aside. Combine brown sugar and orange zest in a large bowl. Rub orange zest into sugar using your fingers. Add eggs, egg yolk, vanilla, cinnamon, cardamom, ginger, nutmeg, and cooled brown butter ghee. Beat with an electric mixer on high speed until pale and fluffy, 2 to 3 minutes. Fold in shredded carrots, pistachios, and raisins until well combined. Whisk together flour, baking powder, baking soda, and salt in a medium bowl until combined. Fold flour mixture into carrot mixture, stirring until just combined. Pour batter into prepared pan; spread in an even layer.

3. Bake carrot cake in preheated oven until a wooden pick inserted in center comes out clean, about 35 minutes. Remove from oven. Let cool completely in pan, about 1 hour.

4. Meanwhile, make the frosting: Beat butter, cream cheese, vanilla, and reserved caramelized milk fat with a stand mixer fitted with the paddle attachment on medium-high speed until smooth, about 1 minute. Reduce mixer speed to low; gradually beat in powdered sugar until combined. Increase mixer speed to medium-high, and beat until pale and fluffy, 2 to 3 minutes.

5. Spread frosting onto cooled cake in an even layer. Garnish with finely chopped pistachios and shredded carrots, if desired.
—HETAL VASAVADA

MAKE AHEAD Frosting can be made up to 3 days ahead and stored in an airtight container in refrigerator; let come to room temperature before using.

Fiadone (Corsican Cheesecake) with Chestnut Honey and Figs

ACTIVE 50 MIN; TOTAL 1 HR 30 MIN, PLUS 12 HR DRAINING AND 4 HR CHILLING; SERVES 8

Fiadone, a slightly sweet Corsican cheesecake, is traditionally made with brocciu, a fresh goat or sheep's milk cheese, which gives it a crumbly texture. In this recipe from pastry chef Shawn Gawle of March restaurant in Houston, the cheesecake is topped with chestnut honey, which pairs perfectly with sweet caramelized figs and candied lemon zest. June Rodil and Mark Sayre, who lead the wine program at March, like to pair 2016 Marco de Bartoli Vigna La Miccia Marsala Superiore Oro, Sicily, Italy, with this dish. "Marco de Bartoli's late-harvest wine still has good acidity, and the maple, fig, and baked-plum notes play nicely with the Fiadone," they say.

FIADONE

- 1 lb. brocciu cheese or fresh sheep's milk ricotta cheese
- 1 Tbsp. unsalted butter, softened
- 4 large eggs
- 1 egg yolk
- 1 cup granulated sugar
- 1½ Tbsp. (¾ oz.) brandy
- 1 Tbsp. plus 1 tsp. grated lemon zest (from 2 lemons)
- 1 Tbsp. chestnut honey, plus more for drizzling
- ½ tsp. kosher salt

CANDIED LEMON ZEST

- 1 cup water
- ⅓ cup very thinly sliced lemon peel strips (no wider than ⅛ inch) (from 3 lemons)
- 1 Tbsp. plus 1 tsp. fresh lemon juice (from 1 lemon)
- 2 tsp. glucose syrup or agave syrup
- ½ cup granulated sugar, divided

ADDITIONAL INGREDIENT

- 8 fresh figs (about 1 lb.), halved lengthwise

1. Make the fiadone: Place brocciu cheese in a colander lined with a layer of cheesecloth, and fold cheesecloth over cheese to cover. Place a saucer or small plate directly on top of cheese, and place a weight (such as a 28-ounce can) on plate. Place colander over a large bowl or a drain pan, and let cheese drain in refrigerator overnight (12 hours).

2. Preheat oven to 350°F. Grease a 9-inch springform pan with some of the softened butter. Line bottom of pan with a 9-inch round of parchment paper cut to fit. Lightly butter parchment paper with remaining softened butter. Place pan in refrigerator until ready to use.

3. Beat eggs and egg yolk with a stand mixer fitted with the whisk attachment on medium-high speed until pale and frothy, about 45 seconds. Slowly stream in sugar, beating until thickened, fluffy, and tripled in volume, 3 to 5 minutes.

4. Remove colander from refrigerator. Remove strained cheese from colander, and transfer to a large bowl. Add brandy, lemon zest, chestnut honey, and salt to cheese in bowl, and whisk to combine. Gently fold beaten egg mixture into cheese mixture until smooth and emulsified. Pour mixture into prepared springform pan.

5. Bake in preheated oven until sides of cheesecake pull away from pan slightly and there is a slight jiggle in cake center, 35 to 40 minutes. There should be light browning on the edges and some brown spotting throughout the top. Remove from oven. Let cheesecake cool in pan on a wire rack until slightly cooled, about 30 minutes. Cover cheesecake, and place in refrigerator until completely chilled, at least 4 hours or up to 24 hours.

6. Make the candied lemon zest: Combine 1 cup water, lemon peel strips, lemon juice, glucose syrup, and ¼ cup sugar in a small pot. Bring to a simmer over medium. Simmer, undisturbed, until lemon peels are soft and translucent and liquid is almost evaporated, 25 to 30 minutes. Pour mixture through a fine wire-mesh strainer into a small heatproof bowl; discard strained syrup, and reserve strained peels. Transfer lemon peels to a shallow bowl. Add remaining ¼ cup sugar, and toss until peels are evenly coated. Let dry and cool in sugar 10 minutes. Sift away and discard excess sugar.

7. Heat a cast-iron skillet over medium-high until very hot. Place figs, cut side down, in skillet, and cook until figs are golden on cut sides, 2 to 3 minutes. Remove skillet from heat.

8. Carefully release sides of springform pan. If desired, remove base from pan, and transfer fiadone to a platter. Using a clean knife, cut fiadone evenly into 8 slices, being sure to clean your knife in between slices with a damp cloth. Place 2 grilled fig halves on top of each fiadone slice or on the side of the slice. Drizzle fiadone slices with chestnut honey, and garnish with candied lemon zest. —SHAWN GAWLE, EXECUTIVE PASTRY CHEF, GOODNIGHT HOSPITALITY, HOUSTON

MAKE AHEAD Candied lemon zest can be made up to 3 weeks in advance and stored in an airtight container at room temperature.

NOTE Brocciu cheese, made from a combination of goat or sheep's milk and whey, is a soft, fresh cheese popular on the island of Corsica. Find it at specialty cheese shops, or substitute fresh sheep's milk ricotta cheese, available at Italian grocery stores.

FIADONE (CORSICAN CHEESECAKE)
WITH CHESTNUT HONEY AND FIGS

Sweet Potato Cheesecake Empanadas

ACTIVE 45 MIN; TOTAL 3 HR 15 MIN;
MAKES 16 EMPANADAS

Puerto Rico and the American South intersect deliciously in this unique dessert empanada from Boricua Soul in Durham, North Carolina, which combines the flavors of marshmallow-topped sweet potato casserole with spiced pumpkin cheesecake, encasing it all in caramel-drizzled, crisp pastry. Thanks to the smart use of store-bought shortcuts like empanada wrappers and canned sweet potatoes, the creamy filling comes together in minutes.

- 1 (15-oz.) can cut sweet potatoes in light syrup (such as Princella), drained and mashed
- 1 lb. cream cheese, softened
- ½ cup packed dark brown sugar
- ½ tsp. kosher salt
- ¼ cup marshmallow creme
- 2 tsp. vanilla extract
- 1½ tsp. ground cinnamon
- 16 (5½-inch) frozen empanada wrappers, thawed

  Neutral oil (such as peanut oil or vegetable oil), for frying

  Sweetened whipped cream and caramel sauce (optional)

1. Combine mashed sweet potatoes, cream cheese, brown sugar, and salt in bowl of a stand mixer fitted with the paddle attachment. Beat on medium speed until fluffy and mostly smooth, about 3 minutes, stopping to scrape down sides of bowl as needed. Add marshmallow creme, vanilla, and cinnamon. Beat on medium speed until well combined, about 1 minute. Cover and chill filling until firm, at least 2 hours or up to 1 day.

2. On a clean work surface, roll out 1 empanada wrapper into a 6-inch circle. Spoon about ¼ cup filling onto center of wrapper. Fold wrapper over filling, and press to seal; crimp edges using a fork. Repeat process using remaining wrappers and filling.

3. Fill a large Dutch oven with oil to a depth of 2½ inches; heat over medium to 350°F. Working in about 4 batches, fry empanadas in hot oil, turning occasionally, until golden brown and crisp, about 4 minutes per batch, letting oil return to 350°F between batches.

Using a spider, transfer empanadas to a baking sheet lined with paper towels; let cool 15 minutes. Serve warm with whipped cream and caramel sauce, if desired. —TORIANO FREDERICKS

MAKE AHEAD Empanadas can be prepared through step 2, frozen in an even layer on a parchment paper–lined baking sheet, and transferred to a resealable freezer bag. Freeze up to 2 months. Fry directly from frozen.

NOTE Find empanada wrappers in the freezer section at most Latin markets.

Tamarind Millionaire's Shortbread

ACTIVE 25 MIN; TOTAL 3 HR 45 MIN;
MAKES ABOUT 36 SQUARES

The sourness of tamarind breathes new life into the classic Millionaire's Shortbread (also affectionately known as Caramel Slice), a traybake of layered shortbread, caramel, and chocolate that has been a fixture in home cooks' kitchens since 1970, when the recipe was first published in the Australian Women's Weekly *Magazine. If you are struggling to find room in the fridge to set the final chocolate layer, simply leave the slice to set on the kitchen counter for 2 hours instead. Slices should be served at room temperature for the best chew.*

PASTRY BASE

- 1½ cups all-purpose flour (about 6⅜ oz.), sifted
- ½ cup coconut sugar or packed light brown sugar
- ½ cup unsweetened desiccated coconut
- ¼ tsp. fine sea salt
- ½ cup unsalted butter (4 oz.), melted, plus softened butter, for greasing

TAMARIND CARAMEL

- 1 Tbsp. unsalted butter
- 1 (14-oz.) can sweetened condensed milk
- 2½ Tbsp. coconut sugar or light brown sugar
- 2 Tbsp. tamarind concentrate (such as Tamicon)
- ¼ tsp. fine sea salt

CHOCOLATE TOPPING

- 2 (3½-oz.) dark chocolate bars (70% cacao), roughly chopped
- 3 Tbsp. unsalted butter, cut into ½-inch pieces

1. Make the pastry base: Preheat oven to 350°F. Line a 9-inch square baking pan with parchment paper, leaving at least 2 inches of overhang on all sides. Lightly grease parchment paper with softened butter. Stir together flour, coconut sugar, desiccated coconut, and salt in a medium bowl. Stir in melted butter until well combined. Spoon mixture into prepared pan, and spread evenly. Firmly press mixture into an even layer using bottom of a dry measuring cup. Bake in preheated oven until light golden brown, 12 to 15 minutes. Transfer pan to a wire rack. Do not turn oven off.

2. Make the tamarind caramel: After about 10 minutes of pastry bake time, melt butter in a small saucepan over medium-low. Stir in condensed milk, coconut sugar, tamarind concentrate, and salt; cook, whisking constantly, until mixture is smooth and just begins to bubble, about 5 minutes.

3. Pour hot caramel over pastry base in pan, and spread in an even layer. Return to oven, and bake at 350°F until caramel is bubbly and set in the center and edges are slightly puffed, 8 to 10 minutes. Transfer pan to a wire rack. Let cool completely, about 1 hour and 30 minutes.

4. Make the chocolate topping: Fill a medium saucepan with water to a depth of 1 inch. Bring to a boil over medium-high. Reduce heat to medium-low to maintain a simmer. Combine chocolate and butter in a medium-size heatproof bowl, and set over pan of simmering water, ensuring bottom of bowl doesn't touch water. Cook, stirring often, until mixture is smooth and melted.

5. Pour topping over caramel on cooled pastry, and spread in an even layer; tap pan on counter to smooth surface. Loosely cover pan with plastic wrap, ensuring it doesn't touch topping. Chill until topping is hardened, about 1 hour and 30 minutes.

6. Using parchment paper overhang as handles, lift pastry bar from pan, and transfer to a cutting board. Cut evenly into 36 (1½-inch) squares, wiping knife clean with a damp towel after each cut. Serve at room temperature. —LARA LEE

MAKE AHEAD Store bars in an airtight container in refrigerator up to 1 week.

TAMARIND MILLIONAIRE'S
SHORTBREAD

Bunet (Chocolate Crème Caramel with Amaretti)

PHOTO P. 336

ACTIVE 30 MIN; TOTAL 2 HR 45 MIN, PLUS 4 HR CHILLING; SERVES 8 TO 10

Bunet (also known as bonet) is a creamy, rich custard dessert hailing from Piedmont. The addition of amaretti cookies as a garnish enhances the almond flavor of the pudding while adding a lovely crunch. This version is from Daniel Zeilinga at Fàula Ristorante, whose recipe offers a simple technique for this silky Piedmontese dessert.

- 1½ cups superfine sugar, divided
- 2 Tbsp. water
- 4 large eggs
- 1½ cups whole milk
- 1½ cups heavy cream
- 1½ cups amaretti cookies (such as Asturi) (about 2¾ oz.), crumbled, plus more whole cookies for garnish
- ¾ cup unsweetened cocoa (about 2½ oz.)
- ¼ tsp. fine sea salt
- Hot water, as needed

1. Preheat oven to 350°F. Stir together ½ cup sugar and 2 tablespoons water in a small saucepan over medium. Cook, stirring occasionally, until sugar is dissolved, 2 to 3 minutes. Bring to a boil, undisturbed, brushing sides of pan with a wet pastry brush to prevent crystals from forming. Boil, swirling pan occasionally, until caramel is a medium amber color and registers 400°F on a candy thermometer, 4 to 6 minutes. Immediately pour caramel into an 8-inch round cake pan. Quickly tilt pan to evenly coat bottom of pan with caramel. Set aside.

2. Whisk together eggs and remaining 1 cup sugar in a medium bowl; set aside. Bring milk and cream to a boil in a medium saucepan over medium, stirring occasionally. Remove from heat; whisk in crumbled cookies, cocoa, and salt. Let stand 5 minutes. Whisking constantly, gradually pour milk mixture into egg mixture in bowl. Whisk until well combined.

3. Set a fine wire-mesh strainer over cake pan with caramel; pour milk mixture through strainer over caramel in cake pan. Discard solids. Let mixture in cake pan stand 10 minutes. Set cake pan in a medium roasting pan. Add enough hot water to roasting pan to come halfway up sides of cake pan. Carefully transfer roasting pan to preheated oven. Bake until bunet is set on the sides with just a slight wobble in the center, about 1 hour. Remove from oven. Carefully remove cake pan from roasting pan, and place on a wire rack; let cool at room temperature 1 hour.

4. Cover bunet with plastic wrap, and chill until cold and firm, at least 4 hours or up to 12 hours.

5. Fill a large skillet with water to a depth of ½ inch; bring to a simmer over medium. Unwrap bunet. Run a small offset spatula around edge of cake pan. Dip cake pan in simmering water until bunet releases from bottom of cake pan and spins when pan is rotated side to side, 3 to 5 seconds. (Don't leave it any longer or pudding will melt.) Invert bunet onto a large rimmed platter. (If bunet doesn't come out once inverted, keep inverted until it releases.) Garnish with whole cookies. Slice and serve. —FÀULA RISTORANTE, CERRETTO LANGHE, ITALY

MAKE AHEAD Bunet can be kept chilled up to 1 day.

WINE Herbal, lightly sweet Barolo Chinato: NV G.D. Vajra Barolo Chinato

Chocolate Puddings with Miso Caramel

ACTIVE 40 MIN; TOTAL 4 HR; SERVES 6

Miso-enriched caramel intensifies the deep, chocolaty flavor of these silky puddings from pastry chef Clarice Lam. A touch of cornstarch in the custard base helps thicken the puddings and keeps them from curdling or breaking. Be sure to bring the leftover caramel to the table; its savory, bitter, and sweet flavor will have guests reaching for more.

- 2 large eggs
- 1 large egg yolk
- 2 Tbsp. unsweetened cocoa
- 2 Tbsp. cornstarch
- ¼ tsp. kosher salt

- 2½ cups whole milk
- 1½ cups granulated sugar, divided
- 1 cup semisweet chocolate chunks
- ½ cup unsalted butter (4 oz.), cubed and softened, divided
- ¾ cup heavy cream, warmed
- ⅔ cup light corn syrup
- 2 Tbsp. water
- 2 Tbsp. red miso
- 1 Tbsp. fresh lemon juice
- ¼ tsp. vanilla extract
- Whipped cream, for serving

1. Whisk together eggs, egg yolk, cocoa, cornstarch, and salt in a heatproof bowl until smooth; set aside. Cook milk and ¾ cup sugar in a medium saucepan over medium, whisking occasionally, until milk is steaming and sugar is dissolved, 5 to 7 minutes. Remove from heat. Gradually drizzle hot milk mixture into egg mixture, whisking constantly, until well combined. Return mixture to saucepan; cook over medium-high, whisking constantly, until mixture thickens and begins to bubble, about 5 minutes. Remove from heat; whisk in chocolate and 2 tablespoons butter until smooth. Divide pudding among 6 (8-ounce) glasses; cover each with plastic wrap. Refrigerate until cold, 3 hours or up to overnight.

2. Cook cream in a small saucepan over medium-low, stirring occasionally, until steaming, 2 to 3 minutes. Remove from heat, and set aside. Cook corn syrup, 2 tablespoons water, and remaining ¾ cup sugar in a medium saucepan over medium-high, without stirring, until mixture is boiling and deep amber in color, 10 to 12 minutes. Remove from heat; gradually whisk in warm cream and remaining 6 tablespoons butter until smooth. Add miso, lemon juice, and vanilla; whisk until smooth. Set aside; let cool until warm but not hot, 15 to 20 minutes.

3. Pour 2 tablespoons caramel over each chilled pudding. Top each pudding with a dollop of whipped cream. Serve with remaining caramel. —CLARICE LAM

CHOCOLATE PUDDINGS
WITH MISO CARAMEL

RASBERRY-HIBISCUS SORBET

Raspberry-Hibiscus Sorbet

ACTIVE 25 MIN; TOTAL 2 HR; SERVES 8

The two main ingredients in sorbet are fruit and sugar—there's no dairy in sight. (In fact, the thing that differentiates a sorbet from a sherbet is that sherbet contains milk or cream.) This sorbet by chef and ice cream maker Fany Gerson has a creamy texture thanks to the addition of corn syrup or honey, which increases the sugar content and helps make the final product richer, less icy, and more scoopable. Bright and airy, with the perfect balance of creamy and tart from the raspberries, this sorbet makes for a great palate cleanser. With just the right amount of a floral hit from the hibiscus, this is a super-refreshing summertime treat.

- 1 heaping cup dried hibiscus flowers (about 1⅜ oz.)
- 1 cup water
- 1½ cups granulated sugar, divided
- 5 cups fresh raspberries (1 lb. 5 oz.)
- 2 Tbsp. light corn syrup or honey

1. Place hibiscus flowers and 1 cup water in a small saucepan; bring to a boil over high. Remove from heat; cover and let steep 30 minutes. Pour through a fine wire-mesh strainer into a bowl; discard hibiscus flowers, or reserve for garnish. Add 1 cup sugar to infused mixture, and stir until dissolved. Set aside until ready to use.

2. While hibiscus mixture steeps, stir together raspberries and remaining ½ cup sugar in a medium saucepan, and let macerate, stirring occasionally, 10 minutes. Cook over medium-low, stirring often, until sugar has dissolved, 3 to 4 minutes. Remove from heat, and let mixture cool to room temperature, about 20 minutes. Transfer mixture to a blender; process until smooth, about 1 minute. Pour through a fine wire-mesh strainer into a resealable container; discard solids. Add hibiscus liquid and corn syrup to raspberry puree; stir until well combined. Cover and refrigerate mixture until chilled, at least 1 hour or up to 12 hours.

3. Pour chilled sorbet mixture into frozen freezer bowl of an ice cream maker, and proceed according to manufacturer's instructions. Serve immediately for a soft-serve consistency, or transfer to a shallow container, cover, and freeze until firm, about 2 hours. Sorbet may be stored in an airtight container in freezer up to 3 weeks.
—FANY GERSON

NOTE Find dried hibiscus flowers at your local Latin grocery store or online at nuts.com.

Pistachio Stracciatella Gelato

ACTIVE 35 MIN; TOTAL 1 HR 35 MIN, PLUS 4 HR FREEZING; SERVES 8

Gelato is denser than ice cream, thanks in part to the larger amount of milk versus cream and the slower rate at which it's typically churned. The slower churning pace incorporates less air, yielding a texture that's less fluffy, and the lower percentage of fat makes the flavors taste more intense. "Stracciatella was always my go-to flavor," says chef and ice cream maker Fany Gerson. "In this recipe, I love putting that classic Italian flavor with another traditional Italian ingredient: pistachio. It just works." When the melted chocolate is added at the end of churning, it hardens right away, creating crunchy bits throughout the mixture for a fun take on two classic Italian flavors.

- 1½ cups whole milk
- 1 cup heavy cream
- ½ tsp. grated lemon or lime zest (from 1 lemon or lime)
- 4 large egg yolks
- ¾ cup granulated sugar
- ⅛ tsp. kosher salt
- 7 oz. unsweetened pistachio paste (not cream)
- 1½ oz. single-origin dark chocolate (60% to 75% cacao), chopped (about ¼ cup)
- ½ Tbsp. refined coconut oil or vegetable oil

1. Stir together milk, cream, and zest in a medium saucepan. Cook over medium-low, undisturbed, just until steaming, making sure mixture doesn't bubble, about

5 minutes. Remove from heat; cover and let infuse about 10 minutes.

2. Meanwhile, whisk together egg yolks, sugar, and salt in a medium bowl until smooth. Set aside until ready to use.

3. Pour infused milk mixture through a fine wire-mesh strainer into a separate bowl; discard solids. Gradually whisk infused milk into yolk mixture. Wipe saucepan clean.

4. Pour milk-yolk mixture back into cleaned saucepan. Cook over medium-low, stirring constantly using a wooden spoon, until mixture is thick enough to coat the back of a spoon, 6 to 10 minutes, making sure mixture doesn't bubble. Remove from heat. Pour through a fine wire-mesh strainer into a medium bowl; discard solids. Whisk in pistachio paste. Place medium bowl in a large bowl filled with ice water, and let stand, stirring occasionally, until mixture reaches room temperature, about 8 minutes. Transfer mixture to a resealable container; seal and chill at least 1 hour or, preferably, 12 hours.

5. Pour chilled pistachio mixture into frozen freezer bowl of an ice cream maker; proceed according to manufacturer's instructions for soft-serve consistency.

6. Meanwhile, microwave chocolate and oil in a small microwavable bowl on high until just melted, about 1 minute, stopping to stir every 15 seconds. Let cool about 5 minutes. Set aside until ready to use.

7. When gelato reaches soft-serve consistency and with maker running, gradually stream in chocolate until well combined, about 1 minute. Transfer to an 8-×4-inch loaf pan; cover with plastic wrap pressed directly on gelato surface. Freeze until firm, about 4 hours. Store gelato in an airtight container in freezer up to 1 week. To serve, transfer gelato to refrigerator until temperature reaches 16°F or gelato is easily scoopable, about 40 minutes. —FANY GERSON

NOTE Find pistachio paste online at fiddymentfarms.com.

Roasted Strawberry–Vanilla Ice Cream

ACTIVE 30 MIN; TOTAL 3 HR, PLUS 6 HR CHILLING; SERVES 8

This sweet, tart, and creamy confection is a beautiful homage to strawberries and cream. It's a French-style ice cream, adding egg yolks to cream and milk to form a custard base, giving rise to a thick, silky ice cream. According to chef and ice cream maker Fany Gerson, the key to French-style ice cream is making a base so good you could eat it without freezing it. In this recipe, Gerson wanted to celebrate the flavors she grew up eating. "My mom would take strawberries and put a little Mexican crema and sugar on top, and that became dessert," she recalls. "For this ice cream, roasting the strawberries gives a new dimension to the fruit."

ROASTED STRAWBERRIES

- 1 lb. fresh strawberries, stemmed and quartered (about 3½ cups)
- 2 Tbsp. granulated sugar
- 2 Tbsp. light corn syrup or golden syrup
- ⅛ tsp. kosher salt

ICE CREAM

- 2 cups heavy cream
- 1 cup whole milk
- 1 vanilla bean pod
- 6 large egg yolks
- ⅔ cups granulated sugar
- ¼ tsp. kosher salt

1. Make the roasted strawberries: Preheat oven to 300°F. Toss together strawberries, sugar, corn syrup, and salt in a 13- × 9-inch baking dish. Roast in preheated oven, stirring occasionally, until strawberries are soft and darker in color and juice is thickened, 30 to 40 minutes.

2. Using a potato masher, lightly crush strawberries in baking dish, making sure you have a chunky mixture. Let cool

completely, about 1 hour. Transfer to a resealable container, and refrigerate until ready to churn or up to 2 days.

3. Make the ice cream: Stir together cream and milk in a medium saucepan. Split vanilla bean pod lengthwise; scrape seeds. Add scraped seeds and vanilla pod halves to mixture in saucepan. Cook over medium-low, undisturbed, until mixture just comes to a simmer. Remove from heat. Cover and let steep 45 minutes to 1 hour.

4. Return steeped cream mixture to heat over medium-low; cook, undisturbed, until mixture just comes to a simmer. Meanwhile, whisk together egg yolks, sugar, and salt in a medium-size heatproof bowl.

5. Gradually whisk warm cream mixture into yolk mixture in bowl. Transfer cream-yolk mixture to saucepan. Cook over medium-low, stirring constantly, until mixture thickens and coats the back of a spoon, 6 to 10 minutes, making sure it doesn't bubble. Remove from heat. Pour through a fine wire-mesh strainer into a medium-size heatproof bowl; discard solids. Place bowl in a large bowl filled with ice water. Let stand, stirring often, until mixture reaches room temperature, about 8 minutes. Transfer to a sealable container; seal and refrigerate until cold, at least 6 hours or up to 12 hours.

6. Stir together strawberry mixture and ice cream base in a bowl. Pour mixture into frozen freezer bowl of an ice cream maker; proceed according to manufacturer's instructions. Serve immediately for a soft-serve consistency, or transfer to a shallow container, cover, and freeze until firm, about 2 hours. Store in an airtight container in freezer up to 3 weeks. —FANY GERSON

MAKE AHEAD Roasted strawberries can be made up to 2 days in advance and stored in an airtight container in refrigerator.

NOTE It's important to slowly add the hot cream mixture to the egg mixture, whisking constantly and never bringing to a boil, to ensure the eggs don't scramble.

Peach Ice Cream With Caramel-Bourbon Swirl

ACTIVE 40 MIN; TOTAL 3 HR, PLUS 24 HR STEEPING AND 4 HR CHILLING; SERVES 12

Tart, buttery, and sweet, the caramel-bourbon swirl here comes through in the best of ways, balancing the rich notes of the crème fraîche in this silky, swirled ice cream. Fresh, ripe peaches add a great bit of texture in every bite. American-style ice creams are eggless (unlike French-style ice creams, which contain eggs yolks) and usually made with a combination of milk and cream, sometimes containing cornstarch as a thickener. For this recipe, chef and ice cream maker Fany Gerson's version uses cream (no milk) and crème fraîche or sour cream to balance out the flavors and add creaminess to the fluffy texture.

CARAMEL

- 1 cup granulated sugar
- ¼ cup water
- 2 Tbsp. light corn syrup
- ¾ cup heavy cream
- ¼ cup unsalted butter, cubed
- ¼ cup (2 oz.) bourbon
- 1 tsp. fine sea salt

ICE CREAM

- 1 to 2 large (5-oz.) lemons
- 1½ cups heavy cream
- 2 lb. firm-ripe peaches (about 5 large peaches), peeled and cut into 1-inch chunks (about 4 cups)
- 1⅓ cups granulated sugar
- ¾ cups crème fraîche or sour cream
- ⅛ tsp. kosher salt

1. Make the caramel: Combine sugar, ¼ cup water, and corn syrup in a small saucepan, making sure to wipe down the sides of the pan so no crystals form. Bring mixture to a low boil over medium. Boil, undisturbed, until golden, 6 to 8 minutes. Continue cooking, gently swirling mixture occasionally in a circular motion (do not stir), until mixture turns a deep amber color, 2 to 4 minutes. Remove from heat. Carefully whisk in cream. (Caramel will seize but then sugar crystals will dissolve.) Add butter;

whisk until melted, about 1 minute. Stir in bourbon and salt; whisk again. Let cool to room temperature, about 1 hour. Cooled caramel can be stored in a resealable container in refrigerator up to 2 days; let come to room temperature before using, about 30 minutes.

2. Make the ice cream: Remove peel from 1 lemon; set peel aside. Juice peeled lemon to yield ¼ cup juice in a small bowl; if needed, juice remaining lemon to reach ¼ cup juice total. Discard seeds. Cover juice, and place in refrigerator until ready to use. Stir together cream and reserved lemon peel in a resealable container. Let steep in refrigerator until flavors meld, at least 24 hours or up to 48 hours.

3. Stir together peaches and sugar in a small saucepan. Let stand, stirring occasionally, until juices release, 10 to 15 minutes. Cook over medium, stirring often, until sugar is dissolved and mixture begins to boil, about 5 minutes. Remove from heat; let cool to room temperature, about 1 hour.

4. Pour lemon peel-cream mixture through a strainer into a medium bowl; discard peel. Transfer infused lemon cream to a blender; add cooled peach mixture, crème fraîche, reserved lemon juice, and salt. Pulse mixture until almost smooth but slightly chunky, about 10 pulses. Transfer mixture to a large resealable container; chill in refrigerator until cold, at least 4 hours or up to 12 hours.

5. Working in batches if needed, pour chilled peach mixture into frozen freezer bowl of an ice cream maker; proceed according to manufacturer's instructions. When mixture reaches soft-serve consistency and with ice cream maker running, gradually add 1 cup caramel to ice cream to create a swirl. Serve immediately for a soft-serve consistency, or transfer to a shallow airtight container, and freeze until firm, about 3 hours. Store ice cream in an airtight container in freezer up to 3 weeks.
—FANY GERSON

MAKE AHEAD Caramel can be made up to 2 days in advance and stored in an airtight container in refrigerator. Let come to room temperature before using.

Vegan Chocolate-Chipotle Ice Cream

ACTIVE 15 MIN; TOTAL 1 HR 45 MIN, PLUS 3 HR CHILLING AND 3 HR FREEZING; SERVES 8

This recipe is 100% vegan, but you would never know it: It's rich and decadent, like frozen ganache, with a bit of smoky tang from the chipotles. Nondairy ice cream is typically made with alternative milks or nondairy yogurt to achieve the creaminess of regular ice cream. Chef and ice cream maker Fany Gerson opts for a combination of both, calling for unsweetened oat milk or rice milk as well as coconut yogurt. "I don't love chocolate ice cream, but it's my husband's favorite, though he would never order a sorbet," she says. "So the challenge here was to make a chocolaty vegan ice cream that isn't a sorbet, has the creaminess of ice cream, and would appeal to both of us. The finished product is as creamy as it gets for being made without dairy, and the flavor combination of chocolate and chipotle, which is smoky and a bit hot, adds personality."

- 6 **medium-size dried chipotle chiles (about 1¼ oz.)**
- 1 **cup hot water**
- 14 **oz. vegan dark chocolate (70% cacao), chopped (about 2½ cups)**
- 1½ **cups plain unsweetened oat milk or rice milk**
- ¾ **cups organic granulated sugar**
- ½ **cup plus 2 Tbsp. unsweetened cocoa (about 2 oz.)**
- ¾ **tsp. kosher salt**
- ½ **cup plain coconut yogurt (such as Anita's)**

1. Toast chiles in a dry, heavy skillet over medium, turning occasionally, until fragrant, 1 to 2 minutes. Remove from heat. Remove and discard chile stems, seeds, and ribs. Place chiles and 1 cup hot water in a small heatproof bowl; let soak until softened, about 30 minutes. Drain, reserving soaking liquid. Process chiles in a mini food processor or a blender until a smooth paste forms, about 1 minute, adding 2 to 3 tablespoons reserved soaking liquid as needed and stopping to scrape down sides of bowl as needed. Set aside. (Mixture can be stored in an airtight container in refrigerator up to 6 days.)

2. Whisk together chopped chocolate, oat milk, sugar, cocoa, and salt in a medium saucepan. Cook over medium, whisking constantly, until chocolate is melted, about 3 minutes. Remove from heat; let mixture cool to room temperature, about 1 hour. Whisk in yogurt and 2 tablespoons chile paste, or more to taste. (Reserve remaining chile paste in freezer for another use.) Cover and refrigerate chocolate mixture until chilled, at least 3 hours or up to 12 hours.

3. Spoon chilled chocolate mixture into frozen freezer bowl of an ice cream maker, and proceed according to manufacturer's instructions. Transfer ice cream to a container; cover and freeze until firm, about 3 hours. Ice cream can be stored in an airtight container in freezer up to 1 week.
—FANY GERSON

MAKE AHEAD Chipotle paste can be frozen up to 1 month. Thaw before using.

SAUCES, SEASONINGS & CONDIMENTS

STRAWBERRY-VANILLA-
RHUBARB JAM (P. 315)
OPPOSITE: WHITE WINE PAN
SAUCE WITH CRÈME FRAÎCHE
AND SPRING HERBS (P. 308)

SMASHED GARLIC OIL

HOT HONEY

FANCY RANCH

GARLIC CONFIT

BASIC PIZZA SAUCE
(RECIPE P. 309)

Fancy Ranch

⏱ TOTAL 5 MIN; MAKES 1½ CUPS

Spiked with umami-rich anchovies, this is perfect for drizzling over pizza or tossing with salad greens. Chill overnight to thicken slightly and allow the flavors to meld.

- 1 to 2 oil-packed anchovy fillets (to taste), finely chopped
- ½ cup sour cream
- ½ cup mayonnaise
- ⅓ cup whole buttermilk, plus more if needed
- ¼ cup thinly sliced fresh chives
- 1 Tbsp. white vinegar
- 1 medium garlic clove, grated on a Microplane
- 1 tsp. black pepper
- ½ tsp. fine sea salt, plus more to taste
- ¼ tsp. onion powder

Using flat side of a knife, smash chopped anchovies into a smooth paste on a cutting board. Transfer to a medium bowl. Add remaining ingredients; whisk until well combined. Thin with additional buttermilk if needed to reach desired consistency. Season with additional salt to taste. Store in an airtight container in refrigerator up to 1 week. —PAIGE GRANDJEAN

Garlic Confit

ACTIVE 10 MIN; TOTAL 3 HR 10 MIN; MAKES 1½ CUPS

Garlic cloves become mellow and sweet as they bathe low and slow in buttery olive oil. Slather softened cloves over crusty bread, or whip garlicky oil into mashed potatoes.

- 1½ cups olive oil
- 2 garlic heads, cloves separated and peeled (about 26 cloves)
- 1 (6-inch) oregano sprig
- 2 chiles de árbol
- 2 (3- x 1-inch) lemon peel strips
- ⅛ tsp. fine sea salt

Preheat oven to 250°F. Combine all ingredients in a small lidded ovenproof saucepan. Cover and roast in preheated oven until garlic is softened and very lightly browned, about 2 hours. Uncover and let cool completely, about 1 hour. Store in an airtight container in refrigerator up to 1 week. —PAIGE GRANDJEAN

Pistachio Dukkah

PHOTO P. 183

⏱ TOTAL 5 MIN; MAKES ¾ CUP

Sprinkle this dukkah—a nut and spice blend from Egypt—over hummus, yogurt, roasted vegetables, or on bread dipped in olive oil.

- ¾ tsp. coriander seeds, toasted
- ¾ tsp. cumin seeds, toasted
- ½ cup raw pistachios, toasted and chopped
- 1 Tbsp. white sesame seeds, toasted
- ¼ tsp. crushed red pepper
- ¼ tsp. flaky sea salt

Coarsely crush coriander seeds and cumin seeds using a mortar and pestle. Transfer mixture to a small bowl; stir in pistachios, sesame seeds, crushed red pepper, and flaky sea salt. —GABY MAEDA

MAKE AHEAD Dukkah can be stored in an airtight container up to 5 days.

Hot Honey

⏱ TOTAL 5 MIN, PLUS 24 HR INFUSING; MAKES ⅔ CUP

Relying on time rather than heat to marry the flavors allows the fruity Calabrian chiles and floral clover honey to shine. For a milder spice, remove some or all of the Calabrian chile seeds.

- ½ cup clover honey
- 10 jarred whole Calabrian chiles (about 1½ oz.) (such as Tutto Calabria), finely chopped
- Pinch of fine sea salt

Stir together all ingredients in a small lidded jar. Cover tightly with lid, and let stand at room temperature at least 24 hours or up to 2 weeks. (Hot honey will get spicier the longer it infuses.) —PAIGE GRANDJEAN

NOTE Find Tutto Calabria chiles online at supermarketitaly.com.

Smashed Garlic Oil

⏱ TOTAL 5 MIN; MAKES ½ CUP

Pungent fresh garlic permeates the olive oil for a quick and easy finishing oil with big flavor.

- 6 medium garlic cloves
- ¼ tsp. fine sea salt
- ½ cup extra-virgin olive oil
- ½ tsp. finely chopped fresh oregano

Finely chop garlic, and sprinkle with salt. Using flat side of a knife, smash to form a paste-like consistency. Transfer mixture to a small bowl. Stir in oil and oregano. Store in an airtight container in refrigerator up to 1 day. —PAIGE GRANDJEAN

Pickled Carrots

PHOTO P. 183

ACTIVE 10 MIN; TOTAL 25 MIN, PLUS 24 HR REFRIGERATION; MAKES ABOUT 1¾ CUPS PICKLES PLUS ABOUT ½ CUP PICKLING LIQUID

These sliced pickled carrots add a little punch and crunch to any dish you add them to.

- 8 oz. small carrots, scrubbed, trimmed, and thinly sliced into ⅛-inch rounds (about 1½ cups)
- ½ tsp. grated jalapeño (from 1 small unseeded jalapeño)
- ½ tsp. grated garlic (from 1 small garlic clove)
- ½ tsp. grated peeled fresh ginger (from ½-inch piece peeled ginger)
- ½ cup Champagne vinegar
- 1 Tbsp. granulated sugar
- 1 tsp. kosher salt
- ½ tsp. fennel seeds
- ¼ cup carrot juice

Combine carrots, jalapeño, garlic, and ginger in a medium-size heatproof bowl; set aside. Bring vinegar, sugar, salt, and fennel seeds to a boil in a small saucepan over medium-high. Pour hot vinegar mixture over carrot mixture. Let cool 15 minutes. Stir in carrot juice. Cover tightly with plastic wrap, pressing plastic wrap onto carrots if needed to keep submerged. Chill at least 24 hours or up to 1 week. —GABY MAEDA

MAKE AHEAD Pickled carrots can be stored in refrigerator up to 1 week.

JAMAICAN GREEN SEASONING

HOUSE SPICE (RECIPE P. 306)

PEPPA SAUCE

CARIBBEAN-STYLE CURRY POWDER

Caribbean-Style Curry Powder

ACTIVE 10 MIN; TOTAL 30 MIN;
MAKES ABOUT 2½ CUPS

"What we call curry is at the heart of Caribbean cuisine. And, at the heart of curry is, naturally, curry powder," says 2019 F&W Best New Chef Kwame Onwuachi of this fragrant spice blend. "Brought to the Caribbean not by indentured Indian laborers themselves but by their colonial employers (curry powder, though obviously not curry, is a British, not Indian, creation), over time Caribbean curry has developed an identity of its own. In contrast to Madras curry powder, which was the most popular variation in the 18th century, this one features the distinctive flavor of anise seeds."

- 1¼ cups plus 1 Tbsp. coriander seeds (about 3 oz.)
- ¼ cup plus 1 Tbsp. anise seeds (about 1¼ oz.)
- ¼ cup plus 1 Tbsp. cumin seeds (about 1⅛ oz.)
- ¼ cup whole allspice (about ¾ oz.)
- 1 Tbsp. plus 1 tsp. yellow mustard seeds (about ½ oz.)
- 1 Tbsp. fenugreek seeds (about ½ oz.)
- ¾ cup plus 1½ tsp. ground turmeric (about 3⅛ oz.)

1. Preheat oven to 400°F. Spread coriander, anise, cumin, allspice, mustard seeds, and fenugreek in an even layer on a baking sheet. Toast in preheated oven until fragrant and deeply toasted, about 5 minutes. Remove from oven, and immediately transfer spices to a medium bowl. Let cool slightly, about 5 minutes.

2. Working in batches as needed, transfer toasted spices to a spice grinder or a blender; process until mixture becomes a fine powder, about 30 seconds. Return to bowl. Add turmeric, and whisk to combine.
—KWAME ONWUACHI

MAKE AHEAD Curry powder can be stored in an airtight container in a cool, dark place up to 4 months.

Peppa Sauce

ACTIVE 15 MIN; TOTAL 45 MIN, PLUS 24 HR STANDING; MAKES ABOUT 2½ CUPS

"The Scotch bonnet pepper is the star in this fiery but fruity hot sauce," says 2019 F&W Best New Chef Kwame Onwuachi. "Like most hot sauces, this one relies on the alchemy between vinegar and heat. To bump up the flavor, I use spice pickling liquid, an infused vinegar touched with ginger, thyme, and coriander. This recipe makes a quart, which is a lot, but trust me, this stuff goes fast. The French have their five mother sauces; I have my peppa sauce. I use it all the time, from jerk paste to curried chicken; I use it as a marinade and as a finishing sauce. It is always on my kitchen table and always in my pantry. And the best part is, like so many vinegar-based infused sauces, it gets better with age."

SPICE PICKLING LIQUID

- 1¾ cups white wine vinegar
- 1¼ cups water
- ¼ cup granulated white sugar
- 3 Tbsp. plus 1 tsp. kosher salt
- 1 Tbsp. plus 1 tsp. coriander seeds
- 2 tsp. chopped fresh habanero chile (from 1 stemmed and seeded small [⅓-oz.] habanero chile)
- 12 (4-inch) thyme sprigs
- 2 (2- to 3-inch) slices unpeeled fresh ginger

ADDITIONAL INGREDIENTS

- 25 fresh red Scotch bonnet chiles (about 12 oz.), stemmed and roughly chopped (about 1½ cups)
- ⅓ cup plus 2 Tbsp. peeled medium garlic cloves (from 1 to 2 garlic heads)

1. Make the spice pickling liquid: Combine vinegar, 1¼ cups water, sugar, salt, coriander, habanero, thyme, and ginger in a medium pot; bring to a boil over high. Remove from heat; let cool completely, about 30 minutes. Pour through a fine wire-mesh strainer into a bowl. Transfer to a sterilized 24-ounce jar with a tight-fitting lid.

2. Process Scotch bonnets, garlic, and 1 cup spice pickling liquid in a food processor until smooth, about 2 minutes, stopping to scrape down sides as needed. Transfer mixture to a separate sterilized

24-ounce jar with a tight-fitting lid. Place a sheet of wax paper on top of jar; seal lid. (The wax paper prevents the vinegar from reacting with the lid.) Let peppa sauce stand at room temperature in a cool, dark place 24 hours. Transfer jar to refrigerator.
—KWAME ONWUACHI

MAKE AHEAD Spice pickling liquid and peppa sauce can be kept in airtight containers in refrigerator up to 6 months.

Jamaican Green Seasoning

TOTAL 10 MIN; MAKES 1½ CUPS

"Green seasoning—also called marination or blend up in Jamaica—is a bright, vibrant, and versatile ingredient. I use it like an aioli, as a base for my curries, and to marinate everything from cucumbers to meat," says 2019 F&W Best New Chef Kwame Onwuachi. "For me, the mix of culantro (or shado beni, as it is also called), celery, and herbs, together with the kick of heat from the peppa sauce, define the core flavors of Caribbean cooking."

- ¾ cup packed fresh culantro (may substitute cilantro) (from 1 medium bunch), roughly chopped
- ½ cup canola oil
- 1 medium (2½-oz.) celery stalk, roughly chopped (about ⅓ cup)
- ⅓ cup roughly chopped yellow onion (from 1 small [5-oz.] onion)
- 2 medium (¾-oz.) scallions, roughly chopped (about ⅓ cup)
- 2½ Tbsp. Ginger-Garlic Puree (recipe p. 306)
- 2 Tbsp. plus 1 tsp. Peppa Sauce (recipe at left)
- 2 Tbsp. roughly chopped fresh thyme

Process all ingredients in a blender until smooth, about 2 minutes, stopping to scrape down sides as needed.
—KWAME ONWUACHI

MAKE AHEAD Green seasoning can be stored in an airtight container in refrigerator up to 1 week or in freezer up to 2 months.

House Spice

⏲ TOTAL 5 MIN; MAKES ABOUT 3¾ CUPS

"Nearly every kitchen I've been to in that stretch of Louisiana and Texas known as the Creole Coast has, somewhere in it, a jar of house spice," says 2019 F&W Best New Chef Kwame Onwuachi, who shared this recipe. "This mixture, made with varying degrees of heat, goes on everything: into the flour with which you fry chicken, onto a steak before it's seared, into the eggs in the morning. Growing up in the Bronx, we had it, too, made from scratch by my mom, whose roots are in the marshes of southern Louisiana. These flavors are the underpainting for my palette. House spice is as elemental in the kitchens I love as salt. This version is based on my mom's but kicked up a notch with Worcestershire powder for a touch of acidity and umami."

- ¾ cup plus 1 Tbsp. black pepper (about 3¼ oz.)
- ½ cup plus 2 Tbsp. kosher salt (about 3 oz.)
- ½ cup plus 1 Tbsp. plus 2 tsp. granulated garlic (about 3¼ oz.)
- ½ cup Worcestershire powder (about 2½ oz.)
- ¼ cup plus 3½ Tbsp. granulated onion (about 2⅛ oz.)
- 5 Tbsp. plus 2 tsp. cayenne pepper (about 1 oz.)
- 5 Tbsp. plus 2 tsp. sweet Hungarian paprika (about 1¼ oz.)

Whisk together all ingredients in a large bowl until combined. —KWAME ONWUACHI

MAKE AHEAD House spice can be stored in an airtight container in a cool, dark place up to 4 months.

NOTE Worcestershire powder can be found at spices.com.

Ginger-Garlic Puree

⏲ TOTAL 5 MIN; MAKES 2 CUPS

"Together with Peppa Sauce, ginger-garlic puree is a key ingredient in the majority of dishes that come out of my kitchen," says 2019 F&W Best New Chef Kwame Onwuachi. "The combination of the wake-up-your-mouth zing of ginger and the slightly softer garlic is common throughout the Caribbean, but I owe this particular preparation to my friend and former co-worker, Alex Sanchez, who developed it while running his fine dining restaurant in Mumbai."

- 1½ cups peeled garlic cloves (from about four garlic heads)
- ¾ cup canola oil
- 2 large (3-inch) pieces fresh ginger, peeled and thinly sliced

In a high-powered blender or a food processor, blend garlic cloves, canola oil, and ginger until smooth, about 1 minute, stopping to scrape down sides as needed. —KWAME ONWUACHI

MAKE AHEAD Ginger-garlic puree can be stored in an airtight container in refrigerator up to 1 week or in freezer up to 6 months.

Horn Rub

⏲ TOTAL 5 MIN; MAKES ABOUT ½ CUP

If you spend a lot of time barbecuing, you will try out literally hundreds of rubs, not to mention cooking sauces, table sauces, mops, binders, and pastes. Eventually, you will settle on an all-purpose rub that adds loads of flavor to just about anything you put in the smoker. This is chef Matt Horn's go-to rub, which he keeps close at hand at all times.

- ¼ cup packed dark brown sugar
- 2 Tbsp. kosher salt
- 1 Tbsp. coarsely ground black pepper
- 2 tsp. garlic powder
- 2 tsp. onion powder
- 1 tsp. paprika
- 1 tsp. cayenne pepper

Whisk together all ingredients in a medium bowl until well combined. —MATT HORN

MAKE AHEAD Rub can be stored in an airtight container in a cool, dark place up to 6 months.

Tomatillo Salsa Cruda

⏲ TOTAL 10 MIN; MAKES 2½ CUPS

Fermín Núñez's raw tomatillo salsa combines tart, fresh tomatillos; jalapeño and serrano chiles; tender scallions; and pungent fresh cilantro for a juicy, refreshing salsa perfect for topping tacos, eggs, or tortilla chips.

- 5 medium tomatillos (about 12 oz.), husks removed and roughly chopped (about 2½ cups)
- 1 small red onion (about 6 oz.), roughly chopped (about 1 cup)
- 1 cup packed fresh cilantro leaves and stems (from 1 [2-oz.] bunch)
- 2 medium jalapeño chiles (about 2 oz.) (unseeded), stemmed and roughly chopped (about ¾ cup)
- 2 medium scallions (about 1 oz.), trimmed and roughly chopped (about ½ cup)
- 1 medium-size fresh serrano chile (about ⅛ oz.) (unseeded), stemmed and roughly chopped (about 1½ Tbsp.)
- 2 Tbsp. pure olive oil
- 2 Tbsp. fresh lime juice
- 1 tsp. kosher salt, plus more to taste

Pulse tomatillos, onion, cilantro, jalapeños, scallions, and serrano in a food processor until finely chopped, 12 to 16 pulses, stopping to scrape down sides of bowl as needed. Transfer mixture to a medium bowl. Stir in oil, lime juice, and salt. Season with additional salt to taste. —FERMÍN NÚÑEZ, SUERTE, AUSTIN

MAKE AHEAD Store salsa in an airtight container in refrigerator up to 3 days.

NOTE For the best result, look for firm tomatillos. For a milder salsa, remove the seeds from the chiles.

TOMATILLO SALSA CRUDA

Amba (Pickled Mango Sauce)

ACTIVE 20 MIN; TOTAL 1 HR;
MAKES ABOUT 1 CUP

A blend of unripe green mango, white vinegar, and spices like fenugreek, cumin, and tart sumac punches up this sour condiment. Some versions of amba are fully pureed, but this recipe retains chunks of just-tender mango to give the sauce luscious body and bite. Try amba as a condiment for roasted meats, or do as Lucy Simon does and mix it with labneh for a fast-fix dip.

- 1 large (12-oz.) unripe green mango
- ½ cup white vinegar
- ¼ cup water
- 1½ Tbsp. agave
- 2 tsp. Dijon mustard
- 1½ tsp. kosher salt
- 1½ tsp. ground fenugreek
- 1 tsp. ground sumac
- ½ tsp. ground cumin
- ½ tsp. ground turmeric
- ¼ tsp. cayenne pepper
- 1 medium garlic clove, grated (about ¼ tsp.)
- Roasted meats or vegetables, for serving (optional)
- 1 cup labneh (optional)

1. Peel mango. Cut mango in half lengthwise; remove and discard pit. Chop 1 mango half into ¼-inch pieces; set aside. Bring vinegar, ¼ cup water, agave, mustard, salt, fenugreek, sumac, cumin, turmeric, cayenne, and garlic to a boil in a small saucepan over medium, stirring occasionally. Add chopped mango; return mixture to a simmer over medium. Simmer, stirring occasionally, 2 minutes. Remove from heat; let cool until some of the mango pieces are translucent, about 10 minutes. Meanwhile, chop remaining mango half into ½-inch pieces; set aside.

2. Transfer cooled mango-vinegar mixture to a blender; do not wipe saucepan clean. Process mixture until smooth, about

30 seconds. Add ½-inch mango pieces; using short pulses, pulse until sauce is a chunky consistency with a mix of small and large mango pieces, 1 to 2 pulses.

3. Scrape mango mixture into reserved saucepan. Bring to a gentle simmer over medium. Simmer, stirring often, until amba turns 1 or 2 shades darker, about 3 minutes. Remove from heat; let cool 30 minutes. Serve alongside roasted meats or vegetables, or stir in labneh for a tangy and creamy version of the condiment. —LUCY SIMON

MAKE AHEAD Amba may be stored in an airtight container in refrigerator up to 2 weeks.

Red Wine Pan Sauce with Cumin and Chiles

TOTAL 10 MIN; MAKES ABOUT ¾ CUP

Toasty cumin and piquant chiles, offset with fresh cilantro and lime zest, balance bold red wine in this quick pan sauce. After searing cuts of beef, such as hanger steak or filet mignon, or bone-in lamb chops, sweat the aromatics in the meat drippings before deglazing with wine.

- 1 Tbsp. beef or lamb pan drippings
- 1 Tbsp. finely chopped fresh red Fresno chile, or more to taste
- 2 medium garlic cloves, finely chopped
- 1½ tsp. ground cumin
- ⅓ cup bold red wine (such as Rioja or Bordeaux)
- 1 cup beef stock or lower-sodium beef broth
- 2 Tbsp. cold unsalted butter
- 3 Tbsp. chopped fresh cilantro
- ½ tsp. grated lime zest plus 1 Tbsp. fresh lime juice (from 1 lime)
- Kosher salt, to taste
- Black pepper, to taste

Heat drippings in a large skillet over medium-high. Add chile and garlic; cook, stirring constantly, until softened, about 20 seconds. Add cumin; cook, stirring constantly, until fragrant, about 10 seconds. Add wine. (Mixture will immediately come to a simmer.) Simmer over medium-high,

stirring occasionally to loosen browned bits on bottom of skillet, until liquid has reduced by about half, 1 to 2 minutes. Add stock; cook, stirring occasionally, until mixture has reduced to about ¾ cup and just barely coats the back of a spoon, 4 to 6 minutes. Reduce heat to low; add butter to mixture, stirring until just melted, about 30 seconds. Remove from heat. Stir in cilantro and lime zest and juice. Season with salt and black pepper to taste. —ANDREA SLONECKER

White Wine Pan Sauce with Crème Fraîche and Spring Herbs

PHOTO P. 300

TOTAL 10 MIN; MAKES ABOUT ⅔ CUP

This simple white wine pan sauce enriched with crème fraîche and a generous handful of tender fresh herbs like tarragon, dill, and chives makes smart use of the pan drippings from pan-roasted chicken breasts. Simply pan-roast airline chicken breasts, set them aside to rest, and then, while the chicken is resting, use the drippings to build the flavor-packed white wine pan sauce, which comes together in about 10 minutes and delivers an elegant, silky texture. The delicate flavors of the white wine pan sauce are also a good pair for thick fillets of trout, salmon, or halibut, which may be substituted for the chicken breasts.

- 1 Tbsp. chicken or fish pan drippings
- ¼ cup sliced spring onion bulb (from 1 large spring onion), sliced green garlic bulbs, or sliced ramp bulb and greens
- ⅓ cup dry white wine
- 1 cup chicken stock or lower-sodium chicken broth
- 2 Tbsp. crème fraîche
- 3 Tbsp. chopped mixed tender fresh herbs (such as tarragon, dill, chives, and parsley)
- 1 tsp. fresh lemon juice
- Kosher salt, to taste
- Black pepper, to taste

Heat drippings in a large skillet over medium-high. Add spring onion; cook, stirring often, until softened, about 1 minute. Add wine. (Mixture will immediately come to a simmer.) Simmer over medium-high, stirring occasionally to loosen browned bits on bottom of skillet, until reduced by about half, 1 to 2 minutes. Add stock; cook, stirring occasionally, until mixture has reduced to about ⅔ cup and just barely coats back of a spoon, 4 to 6 minutes. Reduce heat to low; stir in crème fraîche until just melted, about 30 seconds. Remove from heat; stir in herbs and lemon juice. Season with salt and black pepper to taste. —ANDREA SLONECKER

Basic Pizza Sauce

PHOTO P. 302

TOTAL 10 MIN; MAKES ABOUT 2 CUPS

Simple is best when it comes to tomato sauce. In our many rounds of testing, we tried cooked, raw, canned, and jarred tomato sauces and found the best flavor came from a raw sauce based on Muir Glen Organic Tomato Sauce. Open the can, grate in a little garlic, add a glug of olive oil, and stir in some fresh oregano, salt, and pepper. Spooned onto dough, it has bright acid and sweet-savory flavor that's the star of a cheese pizza and lets other toppings shine.

- 1 (15-oz.) can Muir Glen Organic Tomato Sauce
- 2 Tbsp. extra-virgin olive oil
- 2 medium garlic cloves, grated on a Microplane
- 1½ tsp. chopped fresh oregano
- ¾ tsp. fine sea salt
- ¼ tsp. black pepper

Stir together all ingredients in a bowl. Use immediately, or cover and refrigerate up to 2 days. —HUNTER LEWIS

Toum (Garlic Sauce)

TOTAL 10 MIN; MAKES ABOUT 1⅓ CUPS

Crushing garlic to a smooth paste in a mortar and pestle helps stabilize the emulsion for this airy, pungent whipped garlic sauce. It's a popular condiment at Mini Kabob in Los Angeles. Try it with Mini Kabob's Chicken Lule Kebab (recipe p. 127), Beef Shish Kebab (recipe p. 154) or with crudite or grilled vegetables.

- 1 medium head garlic, cloves separated and peeled (about 2 oz.)
- 1 cup sunflower oil, divided
- 2 Tbsp. fresh lime juice (from 1 lime), divided
- 1 large egg white
- 2 tsp. kosher salt, plus more to taste
- 1 to 2 Tbsp. cold water, if needed

1. Crush garlic cloves using mortar and pestle until smashed and softened, about 20 seconds. Transfer to food processor, and process until finely chopped, about 10 seconds, stopping to scrape down sides as needed. With processor running, slowly pour in ¼ cup oil, pouring in a thin, even stream, processing until well blended, about 2 minutes, stopping to scrape down sides as needed.

2. With processor running, gradually add 1 tablespoon lime juice to garlic mixture, processing until incorporated, about 20 seconds. With processor running, add egg white, processing until well combined, about 30 seconds. With processor running, gradually stream in remaining ¾ cup oil, processing until mixture is thick and fluffy, about 2 minutes. With processor running, gradually add remaining 1 tablespoon lime juice, processing until incorporated, about 20 seconds. Add salt and, if toum is very thick, add cold water, 1 teaspoon at a time, to thin into a smooth and spreadable consistency, pulsing 3 to 6 times after each addition. Add additional salt to taste. —OVAKIM AND ALVARD MARTIROSYAN

MAKE AHEAD Toum may be stored in an airtight container in refrigerator up to 3 days.

Pique

TOTAL 10 MIN, PLUS 3 DAYS MARINATING; MAKES ABOUT 3⅓ CUPS

This Puerto Rican hot sauce is made in-house at Boricua Soul, a Puerto Rican–Southern restaurant in Durham, North Carolina. The simple, fiery pepper vinegar condiment includes both jalapeño and habanero chiles for a more complex chile flavor. After you make this pique recipe, swirl it into a bowl of Vegan Collards, or add a spoonful over braised meats or anywhere else you like a hit of heat.

- 6 medium jalapeño chiles (about 10 oz.), stemmed, unseeded, and roughly chopped (about 2½ cups)
- 2 cups distilled white vinegar
- 6 medium habanero chiles (about 2¼ oz.), stemmed, unseeded, and roughly chopped (about ¾ cup)
- ½ tsp. coarse kosher salt (such as Morton's)
- 3 medium garlic cloves, smashed
- 10 whole black peppercorns

Combine all ingredients in a 1-quart wide-mouth jar with lid. Stir to dissolve salt. Cover with lid, and let stand at room temperature 3 days. Transfer to narrow-necked sealable bottles for easier pouring, if desired. —TORIANO FREDERICKS

MAKE AHEAD Pique can be refrigerated up to 2 weeks in a sealed container.

Salsa Taquera

ACTIVE 35 MIN; TOTAL 1 HR 35 MIN;
MAKES ABOUT 2½ CUPS

Sweetness from the tomato and tang from the tomatillos complement the mellow (but not overpowering) onion and garlic flavors in this salsa from the Philadelphia taco institution South Philly Barbacoa. Soaking the jalapeños and chiles de árbol tempers their piquancy without dulling their flavors.

- 2½ cups water, divided
- 2 Tbsp. plus 1 tsp. kosher salt, divided, plus more to taste
- 2 medium-size jalapeños (about 2½ oz.), seeded and ribs removed
- 3 small dried chiles de árbol (about ⅛ oz.), seeded
- 2 large tomatoes (about 1 lb.)
- 3 fresh tomatillos (about 12 oz.), husks removed
- ½ cup thinly sliced white onion (from 1 small onion)
- 1 large garlic clove, thinly sliced (about 1 tsp.)
- 3 cilantro sprigs (about ¼ oz.)
- ½ tsp. ground cumin
- ½ tsp. dried oregano
- ¼ cup extra-virgin olive oil
- 1 tsp. white wine vinegar, plus more to taste
- ¼ tsp. black pepper

1. Combine 2 cups water and 2 tablespoons salt in a small saucepan; bring to a boil over medium-high. Stir until salt is fully dissolved. Remove from heat. Let cool about 15 minutes. Add jalapeños and chiles de árbol; soak 1 hour.

2. Meanwhile, heat a comal or cast-iron skillet over medium-high. Add tomatoes and tomatillos; cook, turning occasionally, until charred in spots and starting to soften, about 15 minutes. Remove from heat, and set aside until ready to use.

3. Drain chile mixture, and transfer to a large pot. Add charred tomatoes and tomatillos, onion, garlic, cilantro, cumin, oregano, and remaining ½ cup water. Bring to a boil over medium-high; boil, stirring occasionally and breaking down tomatoes using the back of a wooden spoon, until tomatoes and tomatillos are soft and falling apart, about 5 minutes. Remove from heat.

4. Transfer mixture to a blender. Secure lid on blender, and remove center piece to allow steam to escape. Place a clean towel over opening. Process until smooth, about 30 seconds.

5. Wipe large pot clean. Add oil to pot; heat over medium-high. Carefully add pureed tomato mixture. (Sauce will splatter.) Using a long-handled wooden spoon, stir in vinegar, black pepper, and remaining 1 teaspoon salt. Bring to a boil, and boil, stirring often, until salsa thickens slightly and you can see bottom of pot when stirring, 8 to 10 minutes. Remove from heat. Season with additional salt and vinegar to taste. Serve hot or at room temperature. —CRISTINA MARTÍNEZ

MAKE AHEAD Salsa may be covered and refrigerated 5 to 7 days.

Salsa Verde Cocida

ACTIVE 25 MIN; TOTAL 40 MIN;
MAKES ABOUT 3½ CUPS

Cristina Martínez and Ben Miller of the beloved restaurant South Philly Barbacoa shared the recipe for this smooth salsa verde with serious depth of flavor. It packs a bit of piquancy from the jalapeños, but the heat is balanced by slightly sweet and tropical notes of green ground cherries (which may be substituted with small tomatillos), while epazote and cilantro give subtly earthy, pleasantly bitter flavors. South Philly Barbacoa served this fresh green salsa alongside lamb barbacoa at an iftar dinner for Ramadan, but it's equally delicious with chicken or beef.

- 1 small white onion (about 6 oz.)
- 2 cups fresh green ground cherries (about 9½ oz.), husks removed
- 2 cups water
- 8 medium jalapeños (about 10½ oz.), halved (seeded, if desired)
- 1 large bunch fresh epazote (about 5 oz.)
- 1 bunch fresh cilantro (about 2 oz.)
- 1 large garlic clove
- 2 tsp. kosher salt, plus more to taste
- ¼ cup extra-virgin olive oil

1. Cut onion in half lengthwise. Set aside 1 onion half; reserve remaining onion half for another use. Heat a comal or cast-iron skillet over medium. Add ground cherries; cook, stirring occasionally, until charred in spots and starting to soften, 6 to 8 minutes. Remove from heat.

2. Combine ground cherries, reserved onion half, 2 cups water, jalapeños, epazote, cilantro, garlic, and salt in a large pot. Bring to a boil over medium-high. Remove from heat. Let stand 5 minutes. Remove and discard epazote.

3. Transfer ground cherry mixture to a blender. Secure lid on blender, and remove center piece to allow steam to escape. Place a clean towel over opening. Process until smooth, about 30 seconds.

4. Wipe large pot clean. Add oil to pot, and heat over medium-high. Carefully add pureed ground cherry mixture. (Sauce will splatter.) Bring to a boil, and boil, stirring often, until salsa thickens slightly and you can see bottom of pot when stirring, 8 to 10 minutes. Remove from heat. Season with additional salt to taste. Serve hot or at room temperature. —CRISTINA MARTÍNEZ

MAKE AHEAD Salsa may be covered and refrigerated 3 to 5 days.

NOTE Green ground cherries and epazote can be found at mexgrocer.com.

SALSA VERDE COCIDA

SALSA TAQUERA

Cocktail Sauce

⏱ TOTAL 5 MIN SERVES 8

Food & Wine *Editor-in-Chief Hunter Lewis serves this zippy sauce with his very proper shrimp boil (recipe p. 108), along with whole-grain mustard.*

1 (8-oz.) jar cocktail sauce

2 Tbsp. prepared horseradish

2 Tbsp. fresh lemon juice

½ tsp. hot sauce (such as Tabasco)

Grated fresh horseradish, for serving (optional)

In a small bowl, stir together the cocktail sauce, prepared horseradish, lemon juice, and hot sauce. Store, covered, in the refrigerator for up to 5 days. Grate fresh horseradish on top for serving, if you like.

Bourbon Sauce

⏱ TOTAL 30 MIN; MAKES ABOUT 2 CUPS

Instead of vinegar, this thick, sticky sauce gets its kick from bourbon. For a classic sauce with Kentucky roots, use dark molasses in place of the honey. This recipe works well with any type of barbecue, and chef Matt Horn loves it in baked beans, too.

2 cups ketchup

1 cup (8 oz.) bourbon

¼ cup packed dark brown sugar

2 Tbsp. Worcestershire sauce

1 Tbsp. honey

1 Tbsp. kosher salt

1 Tbsp. black pepper

1 Tbsp. liquid smoke

Whisk together all ingredients in a medium saucepan until well combined. Bring to a boil over medium-high. Reduce heat to low; simmer, stirring occasionally, until sauce thickens and reduces by half, 25 to 30 minutes. —MATT HORN, HORN BARBECUE, OAKLAND, CALIFORNIA

MAKE AHEAD Bourbon sauce can be stored in an airtight container in refrigerator up to 1 month.

Shaved Onions with Sumac and Parsley
PHOTO P. 155

⏱ TOTAL 10 MIN; SERVES 8 TO 10

Paper-thin slices of onion, herbaceous parsley, and tart sumac come together in this refreshing salad-meets-condiment.

1 medium-size red onion (about 8 oz.), shaved on a mandoline into thin, translucent rings

1 medium-size yellow onion (about 8 oz.), shaved on a mandoline into thin, translucent rings

½ cup packed roughly chopped fresh flat-leaf parsley (about 1 large bunch)

1 Tbsp. ground sumac

Toss together onions, parsley, and sumac in a large bowl. Serve alongside kebabs. —OVAKIM AND ALVARD MARTIROSYAN

MAKE AHEAD Shaved onions with sumac and parsley may be stored in an airtight container in refrigerator up to 1 day.

Refrigerator Pickled Peppers

ACTIVE 15 MIN; TOTAL 1 HR 15 MIN, PLUS 2 DAYS CHILLING; MAKES 1 PINT

It's fun and easy to make your own pickled peppers. Part of the fun is choosing whatever variety of pepper you want: sweet, spicy, or a mix of the two. The easy part? All you need to do is put sliced peppers in a jar, pour a vinegar mixture over them, cover, and refrigerate. By layering the pepper slices into the jar first and then pouring the hot pickling brine over top, you use only enough liquid to submerge the slices and end up with a jar packed to the brim with delicious pickled peppers. Boiling the vinegar mixture not only dissolves the sugar, the heat slightly softens the peppers, mellows their burn and jump-starts the pickling process. Use these crisp-tender and acidic peppers to add flavor to Roasted Broccoli with Pickled Pepper Vinaigrette (recipe p. 185), and pile them onto sandwiches, tacos, or anywhere you want a bit of sweet piquancy and crunch. Don't throw away the pepper-infused vinegar left in the jar. Use it to amp up salad dressings, cocktails, or potato salad, or drizzle it over braised greens. With endless options, this recipe is the perfect excuse to hit the farmers' market and explore new varieties of colorful peppers.

2 cups stemmed, seeded, and thinly sliced (into rounds) fresh hot and/or sweet peppers

⅔ cup white wine vinegar or apple cider vinegar

⅔ cup water

¼ cup granulated sugar

1 Tbsp. kosher salt

Pack peppers into a sterilized pint jar (see Note). Bring vinegar, ⅔ cup water, sugar, and salt to a boil in a small pot over high; boil, stirring constantly, until sugar and salt dissolve, about 3 minutes. Pour hot brine over peppers in jar, filling jar to top. Let cool to room temperature, about 1 hour. Seal jar, and refrigerate 2 days before using. —MOLLY STEVENS

MAKE AHEAD Pickled peppers can be refrigerated in jars up to 3 months.

NOTE Submerge heatproof jar in boiling water for 10 minutes or run through the dishwasher on the hottest setting to sterilize.

Ikra (Eggplant Caviar)

ACTIVE 1 HR 15 MIN; TOTAL 2 HR 30 MIN; MAKES ABOUT 2½ CUPS

Twice-cooked eggplant provides the creamy base to this luscious, smoky condiment from Mini Kabob, a restaurant in Los Angeles. Seasoned with piquant hot pepper paste, fresh cilantro, and onion, it's delicious with lavash or as a dip for the restaurant's popular Mini Kabob Potatoes (recipe p. 215).

- 2 large red bell peppers (about 1 lb.)
- 1 large eggplant (about 1 lb.)
- ¼ cup canola oil
- 1 medium-size yellow onion (about 12 oz.), finely chopped (about 2 cups)
- 1 to 2 Tbsp. hot pepper paste (such as Öncü), to taste
- ¾ cup loosely packed finely chopped fresh cilantro (about 1 bunch)
- 1 tsp. kosher salt, plus more to taste
- ¼ tsp. black pepper, plus more to taste

1. Preheat grill to high (450°F to 500°F). Place bell peppers and eggplant on oiled grates, and grill, uncovered, turning occasionally, until blackened and charred all over, 15 to 20 minutes for peppers and 25 to 30 minutes for eggplant. Immediately transfer grilled peppers and eggplant to a large heatproof bowl, and cover tightly with plastic wrap. Let stand 15 minutes.

2. Remove and discard skins, stems, and seeds from peppers. Remove and discard peel and stem from eggplant. Process peppers and eggplant in a food processor until mixture forms a thick paste with small discernible pieces of pepper, about 15 seconds. Set aside.

3. Heat oil in a medium saucepan over medium-low. Add onion; cook, stirring occasionally, until very soft but not taking on color, 18 to 20 minutes. Stir in jarred hot pepper paste until well combined, about 1 minute, adding more paste for a spicier dip. Stir in pepper-eggplant mixture. Reduce heat to low; cook, uncovered, stirring often to prevent sticking, until mixture is mostly smooth, very soft, and thickened slightly, 20 to 30 minutes.

4. Remove from heat. Stir in cilantro, salt, and black pepper. Let cool to room temperature, about 1 hour. Season to taste with additional salt and black pepper. —OVAKIM AND ALVARD MARTIROSYAN

MAKE AHEAD Ikra can be stored in an airtight container in refrigerator up to 3 days; let come to room temperature before serving.

NOTE Find Öncü hot pepper paste at Middle Eastern grocery stores or online at basilgrocery.com.

TAMARIND-CHILE JAM

Tamarind-Chile Jam

ACTIVE 20 MIN; TOTAL 2 HR 10 MIN;
MAKES ABOUT 1½ CUPS

"Move over tomato ketchup, barbecue sauce, and mayonnaise," says cookbook author and recipe developer Lara Lee. "There's a new condiment-that-goes-with-everything in town!" Meet Tamarind-Chile Jam, a one-pot wonder that is sweet, spicy, sour, sharp, tangy, and pungent all at once. Savory, funky fish sauce balances the fruity sourness of the tamarind, while long red chiles add a pleasantly strong piquancy to this thick and sticky jam. Its uses are endless; spread it on a sandwich, serve it alongside sausage rolls, dollop it over eggs, dunk sweet potato wedges into it, or use it as a condiment for meat, chicken, or fish. For those who are heat adverse, seed the chiles before adding them for a milder jam. Use a wide, deep saucepan for faster reduction time—be careful of splattering jam—and take the pot off the heat as soon as the jam has reduced to 1½ cups; it will continue to thicken as it cools.

- 1 lb. tomatoes (about 3 medium tomatoes), cored and quartered
- 3 to 4 fresh red chiles (about 2 oz.) (unseeded) (optional), stemmed and roughly chopped (about ⅓ cup)
- 1½ Tbsp. roughly chopped peeled fresh ginger
- 4 medium garlic cloves, roughly chopped (about 4 tsp.)
- 1¼ cups superfine sugar
- 3 Tbsp. plus 1 tsp. Tamarind Water (recipe p. 330), divided
- 3 Tbsp. red wine vinegar
- 1 Tbsp. plus 2 tsp. fish sauce
- 1 whole star anise, toasted

1. Pulse tomatoes, chiles, ginger, and garlic in a food processor until finely chopped and well combined, about 8 pulses. Transfer mixture to a medium saucepan. Stir in sugar, 3 tablespoons tamarind water, vinegar, fish sauce, and star anise.

2. Bring to a boil over medium-high, stirring constantly to dissolve sugar. Reduce heat to medium-low; simmer, uncovered, stirring occasionally to prevent scorching, until jam is thickened and reduced to about 1½ cups, 1 hour to 1 hour and 15 minutes.

3. Remove mixture from heat; stir in remaining 1 teaspoon tamarind water. Let cool to room temperature, about 1 hour. —LARA LEE

MAKE AHEAD Store jam in an airtight container in refrigerator up to 1 month.

Strawberry-Vanilla-Rhubarb Jam
PHOTO P. 301

ACTIVE 50 MIN; TOTAL 2 HR 50 MIN;
MAKES 4 CUPS

When the blush red stalks of rhubarb begin to fill the market stalls, it's a sign that spring is finally here. Puckeringly tart, fibrous, and juicy, rhubarb is made for adding dimension and depth to sweets. Recipe developer Jasmine Smith likes to pair rhubarb with a classic partner, strawberries, to bring a brightening acidity to this luscious jam. Strawberries' natural sugars and pectin also help the jam set after boiling. Choose crisp, thin stalks of young rhubarb that are firm, not wilting or woody, for the best flavor and texture. This easy homemade jam replicates the classic sweet-tart pie filling of rhubarb and strawberries with an extra boost of flavor and aroma from real vanilla beans. To amp up that vanilla, leave the halved pod in the jam overnight before removing and discarding. Serve the jam on buttery biscuits, or drizzle it over sundaes. Fresh or frozen rhubarb works well here; freeze fresh stalks during their short spring season.

- 1½ lb. fresh rhubarb stalks, cut into ½-inch pieces, or frozen cut rhubarb (about 5½ cups)
- 4 cups quartered hulled fresh strawberries (from 1½ lb. fresh strawberries with tops)
- 3 cups granulated sugar
- 1 vanilla bean pod, halved lengthwise
- ½ tsp. kosher salt
- ½ tsp. grated orange zest plus 2 Tbsp. fresh orange juice (from 1 orange), divided

1. Stir together rhubarb, strawberries, sugar, vanilla bean pod halves, salt, and orange zest in a large saucepan. Bring to a boil over medium-high, stirring occasionally. Boil, stirring occasionally, until jam is thickened and reduced to about

4 cups, 25 to 30 minutes. Remove from heat; stir in orange juice. Using a wooden spoon, mash any large pieces of rhubarb and strawberries against side of pan.

2. Remove and discard vanilla bean pod halves. Pour jam evenly into 2 pint jars. Let cool to room temperature, uncovered, about 2 hours. Seal jars with lids, and store in refrigerator up to 3 weeks. —JASMINE SMITH

Wine Jelly

ACTIVE 10 MIN; TOTAL 55 MIN, PLUS 6 HR CHILLING; SERVES 8

Ask a chemist for a recipe, and they'll deliver, down to the microgram, a recipe that's been tested within an inch of its life for maximum consistency. Our senior editor's father—now retired from his lab career—used to make this jolly, loose-set wine jelly in batches for holiday gifts, and its glorious sweet-tart balance is a crucial part of the equation. Our testers tried—and loved—this recipe with Zinfandel and Shiraz; Donald Kinsman likes to make it with Dubonnet.

- 1 cup (8 oz.) sweet red wine (such as a sweet Zinfandel or sweet Shiraz)
- 1 Tbsp. pectin powder (such as Ball RealFruit Classic Pectin)
- 1 cup granulated sugar
- ½ tsp. citric acid

1. Bring wine to a rolling boil in a small saucepan over high. Whisk in pectin; boil, stirring constantly, 1 minute. Add sugar; return to a boil over high. Boil, stirring gently, until sugar completely dissolves and mixture thickens, about 1 minute. Remove from heat; stir in citric acid. Let stand 15 minutes.

2. Skim and discard any foam that has floated to surface of mixture. Pour mixture evenly into 8 small cups or an airtight container. Let cool, uncovered, to room temperature, about 30 minutes. Cover and chill until set, about 6 hours. —DR. DONALD V. KINSMAN

MAKE AHEAD Wine jelly can be stored in an airtight container in refrigerator up to 2 weeks.

NOTE Pectin powder and citric acid are available in the canning section of most grocery stores.

DRINKS

SURPRISE FIX (P. 329)
OPPOSITE: ABASOLO Y
TOPO CHICO (P. 324)

Cosmo Nouveau

⏱ TOTAL 5 MIN; SERVES 1

The Cosmopolitan is really just a vodka margarita with a splash of cranberry, notes Lynnette Marrero, head of education for the mixology conference Bar Convent and creator of all-female bartending competition Speed Rack. She uses that understanding of the DNA of the drink to create a light and refreshing citrus-forward Cosmopolitan that gets its sweetness from orange liqueur and pleasant tartness and color from a blend of lime and pomegranate juices. To further elevate the drink, she looks for special ingredients, using a citrus vodka infused with real fruit, and pomegranate juice (which she trades for the cranberry) to add complexity and body to the drink. "It has a nice tanginess that works well with the liqueur and lime," she says. Marrero garnishes her recipe with a twist of lemon peel, but you could use lime or another citrus peel for a different effect.

- **3 Tbsp. (1½ oz.) citrus vodka (such as Absolut Citron) or gin**
- **1 Tbsp. (½ oz.) orange liqueur (such as Grand Marnier, triple sec, or Cointreau)**
- **1 Tbsp. fresh lime juice**
- **1 Tbsp. refrigerated pomegranate juice**
- **Lemon peel twist**

Fill a cocktail shaker with ice. Add vodka or gin, orange liqueur, lime juice, and pomegranate juice; cover with lid, and shake well, about 15 seconds. Strain into a chilled martini cocktail glass; garnish with a lemon peel twist. —LYNNETTE MARRERO, COFOUNDER, SPEED RACK

NOTE For a less tart and citrus-forward version, use gin instead of citrus vodka.

Frozmopolitan

⏱ ACTIVE 5 MIN; TOTAL 35 MIN; SERVES 10

Cocktail savant Toby Cecchini is credited with inventing the internationally recognized version of Cosmopolitan — a drink he codified while bartending at the Odeon. These days, as the owner of The Long Island bar in Brooklyn, he continues to come up with distinctive drinks that taste like instant classics, including this frozen Cosmopolitan that's great for a crowd. Fruity and citrusy, Cecchini's "froze-mopolitan" tastes so much like a delicious fruit punch that you might not notice there's alcohol in it. Serving the drink in well-chilled glasses straight from the freezer helps it stay frozen a little longer. If not serving right away, cover the blender and freeze, stirring the drink occasionally, for up to 30 minutes.

SIMPLE SYRUP

- **½ cup granulated sugar**
- **½ cup water**

FROZMOPOLITAN

- **8 cups ice cubes**
- **¾ cup cranberry juice cocktail (such as Ocean Spray)**
- **½ cup simple syrup**
- **½ cup (4 oz.) citrus-flavored vodka (such as Absolut Citron)**
- **⅓ cup fresh lime juice (from 3 limes)**
- **¼ cup (4 oz.) orange liqueur (such as Grand Marnier, triple sec, or Cointreau)**
- **¼ cup fresh lemon juice (from 2 lemons)**
- **¼ cup fresh orange juice (from 1 orange)**

1. Make the simple syrup: Stir together sugar and ½ cup water in a small saucepan. Cook over medium-high, stirring constantly, until sugar dissolves, about 2 minutes. Let cool completely, about 30 minutes.

2. Make the cocktail: Process all cocktail ingredients and simple syrup in a blender until completely smooth and slushy, 30 seconds to 1 minute. Pour evenly into 10 chilled martini cocktail glasses. —TOBY CECCHINI, THE LONG ISLAND BAR, NYC

MAKE AHEAD Frozmopolitan can be stored in the freezer up to 30 minutes, stirring occasionally to maintain texture. Simple syrup can be stored in an airtight container in refrigerator up to 2 weeks.

Gin Toasty

⏱ TOTAL 5 MIN; SERVES 1

All it takes is a bit of hot water to give this warm alcoholic drink—a riff on a gin and tonic—a hot toddy–like edge: When heated, the botanicals in gin act like mulled spices. Using tonic syrup instead of tonic water is crucial to the drink; hot water does the same trick that effervescent bubbles do to ferry the aromatics in the gin and the syrup right up to your nose. The result is an ingeniously simple warm cocktail, perfect for a snowy winter day.

- **¼ cup plus 3 Tbsp. hot water (3½ oz.)**
- **3½ Tbsp. (1¾ oz.) gin**
- **1½ tonic syrup (¾ oz.) (preferably Jack Rudy Cocktail Co. Classic)**
- **Orange peel twist**

Stir together ¼ cup plus 3 tablespoons hot water, gin, and tonic syrup in a mug until combined. Garnish with orange peel twist. —BROOKS REITZ

Martini Miniature Shot

⏱ TOTAL 5 MIN; SERVES 8

Clean and herbal with a slightly sour note at the finish, this shot mimics the flavor of a dry and dirty gin martini. The salty, buttery olives on the side cut through the alcoholic heat of the drink.

- **½ cup (4 oz.) dry gin**
- **½ cup (4 oz.) fino sherry**
- **½ cup (4 oz.) dry vermouth**
- **Green olives, for eating after shooting**

Combine gin, sherry, and vermouth in an ice-filled mixing glass or shaker. Stir with a cocktail stirrer until cocktail is very cold, about 15 seconds. Strain into shot glasses. Serve shots with olives. —REBEKAH PEPPLER

MARTINI MINIATURE SHOT

Plum Gin Fizz

ACTIVE 20 MIN; TOTAL 55 MIN; SERVES 1

This fruity gin fizz isn't overly sweet, allowing the flavor of the caramelized plums to shine. A botanical gin works well with the fruit in this cocktail, adding herbaceous and fruity notes. To play up the deep color of the plums, try Empress 1908, a royal purple–hued, botanical-style spirit. For a vegan version, in place of the egg white, substitute 3 tablespoons unsalted or low-sodium aquafaba. (Note that you won't get quite as much foam.) The same roast-and-puree technique can be used for more stone fruits, such as apricots and sour cherries.

PLUM PUREE

- **2 lb. fresh plums, halved and pitted**
- **⅓ cup granulated sugar**

COCKTAIL

- **¼ cup (2 oz.) gin (such as Empress 1908, The Botanist, or Hendrick's Midsummer Solstice)**
- **1 large egg white**
- **1 Tbsp. fresh lemon juice**
- **Ice cubes**
- **¼ cup club soda**
- **1 lavender sprig, for garnish**

1. Make the plum puree: Preheat oven to 400°F. Toss together plums and sugar on a large rimmed baking sheet until fully coated; spread in a single layer. Roast in preheated oven until fruit is soft and juicy, about 10 minutes, stirring halfway through roasting time. Let cool 5 minutes. Scrape fruit and any liquid on baking sheet into a food processor or blender; pulse until smooth, 5 to 8 pulses. Pour through a fine wire-mesh strainer into a medium bowl, pressing puree using a rubber spatula. (This may take about 10 minutes.) Discard pulp. Refrigerate, uncovered, until completely cool, about 20 minutes. (You should have about 2 cups plum puree, enough for 9 cocktails.)

2. Make the cocktail: Combine gin, egg white, lemon juice, and 3½ tablespoons plum puree in a dry cocktail shaker without ice. Place lid on shaker; shake vigorously to combine, about 15 seconds. Add enough ice to shaker to fill three-fourths of the way up. Place lid on shaker, and shake until well chilled, about 10 seconds. Strain into a chilled highball glass filled with ice. Top with club soda, and garnish with lavender sprig. —HANNAH SELINGER

MAKE AHEAD Plum puree may be stored in an airtight container in refrigerator up to 1 week.

Ho-Ho-Jito

TOTAL 5 MIN; SERVES 1

Bartender Anh Ngo's Winter Mojito (playfully named Ho-Ho-Jito on the cocktail menu at Kata Robata in Houston) riffs on a classic mojito. Sage and rosemary infuse the simple syrup, adding savory flavor to the sweet, fresh drink, and dark spiced rum (instead of a classic mojito's white rum) brings richer flavor. Garnishes of rosemary, sage, and mint provide the final touches that transform a summery mojito into a cozy, cold-weather sipper.

- **¼ cup (2 oz.) spiced rum**
- **2 Tbsp. fresh lime juice (1 oz.)**
- **1½ Tbsp. Herb-Infused Simple Syrup (¾ oz.) (recipe follows)**
- **10 to 12 fresh mint leaves**
- **⅓ cup club soda**
- **Fresh herb sprigs (such as sage, rosemary, and mint)**

Combine rum, lime juice, syrup, and mint leaves in a cocktail shaker filled halfway with ice. Cover and shake vigorously until chilled, about 20 seconds. Strain into a 12-ounce Collins glass filled with ice. Top with club soda. Garnish with herb sprigs. —ANH NGO

Herb-Infused Simple Syrup

ACTIVE 5 MIN; TOTAL 35 MIN; MAKES ABOUT 1½ CUPS

This twist on classic simple syrup infuses the sweetener with fresh, piney rosemary and sage to add an aromatic depth.

- **1 cup granulated sugar**
- **1 cup boiling water**
- **5 rosemary sprigs (about ½ oz.)**
- **5 sage sprigs (about ½ oz.)**

Stir together sugar and 1 cup boiling water in a heatproof measuring cup until dissolved. Add herb sprigs; press with a spoon until submerged. Steep, uncovered, 30 minutes. Pour through a fine wire-mesh strainer into a 2-cup glass jar; discard solids. Cover and refrigerate up to 2 weeks. —ANH NGO, KATA ROBATA, HOUSTON

HO-HO-JITO

MIAMI VICE

Miami Vice

TOTAL 30 MIN, PLUS 4 HR FREEZING;
SERVES 4

*This summery cocktail from frozen drink
expert Thomas Houston of Superior
Seafood and Oyster Bar in New Orleans
swirls frozen strawberry daiquiri and
piña colada in one glass for a creamy,
sweet, and frothy fruity drink. Instead
of using ice, strawberries and pineapple
are frozen prior to blending to achieve
a plush frozen consistency without
watering down the drink.*

BITTERS-SOAKED FROZEN STRAWBERRIES

- 3 cups halved fresh strawberries
  (from 1 qt. strawberries)
- ¼ cup (2 oz.) Regans' Orange Bitters

PIÑA COLADA

- 2 cups drained canned crushed
  pineapple in juice (from 2 [20-oz.]
  cans)
- 1 cup well-shaken and stirred cream
  of coconut (such as Coco López)
  (from 1 [15-oz.] can) (see Note)
- ½ cup (4 oz.) Don Q Piña rum
- 4 dashes Angostura bitters

STRAWBERRY DAIQUIRI

- ½ cup (4 oz.) Don Q Añejo rum
- ¼ cup turbinado sugar

ADDITIONAL INGREDIENTS

- 4 fresh strawberries, hulled
- 4 pineapple leaves (from 1 pineapple)

**1. Make the bitters-soaked frozen
strawberries:** Stir together strawberries
and bitters in a medium bowl. Let stand at
room temperature until strawberries have
absorbed bitters flavor, about 10 minutes,
stirring once after 5 minutes. Drain and
transfer soaked strawberries to a gallon-
size ziplock plastic freezer bag. Seal bag,
and freeze until strawberries are frozen, at
least 4 hours or up to 3 months.

2. Meanwhile, make the piña colada:
Place crushed pineapple in a gallon-size
ziplock plastic freezer bag. Seal bag; spread
pineapple in an even layer. Freeze until
pineapple is frozen, at least 4 hours or up
to 3 months.

3. Remove frozen pineapple from freezer;
remove from bag. Using your hands or a
knife, break pineapple into small (about
1-inch) pieces. Combine cream of coconut,
rum, bitters, and pineapple pieces in a
blender, adding pineapple last. Process until
smooth, about 1 minute. Pour piña colada
into a small pitcher; place in freezer until
ready to use.

4. Make the strawberry daiquiri: Remove
bitters-soaked frozen strawberries from
freezer. Combine rum, sugar, and frozen
strawberries in a blender, adding frozen
strawberries last. Process until smooth,
about 1 minute, stopping to scrape down
sides as needed. (The room-temperature
alcohol will begin melting the strawberries.)

5. Pour piña colada evenly into 4 glasses
(about ½ cup each); top evenly with
strawberry daiquiri (about ½ cup each),
and stir mixtures in each glass until swirled
together. Spear each hulled strawberry with
1 pineapple leaf; place 1 speared strawberry
in each glass for garnish. —THOMAS HOUSTON

NOTE Cream of coconut is thick, syrupy
sweetened coconut cream and may not be
substituted with coconut cream.

Sour-Cherry Mezcal Margarita

ACTIVE 15 MIN; TOTAL 45 MIN; SERVES 1

*This fruity spin on a margarita combines
smoky mezcal, citrusy Cointreau, and
sweet-tart cherry puree in a vibrant red
drink perfect for late-summer sipping.
Bright, pleasantly tart sour cherries are in
season for a limited window, so this simple
roasted puree is an easy way to preserve
their flavor. Try it on ice cream, too.*

SOUR CHERRY PUREE

- 2 lb. fresh sour cherries, stemmed
  and pitted
- ⅔ cup granulated sugar

COCKTAIL

- Smoked coarse salt (such as
  Olsson's Red Gum Smoked Salt)
  (optional)
- ¼ cup (2 oz.) mezcal joven espadín
  (such as Ilegal Joven)
- 1 Tbsp. (½ oz.) orange liqueur (such
  as Cointreau)
- Ice cubes
- 1 large (about 2½-inch) ice cube

1. Make the sour cherry puree: Preheat
oven to 400°F. Toss together cherries and
sugar on a large rimmed baking sheet until
fully coated; spread in a single layer. Roast
in preheated oven until fruit is soft and juicy,
about 10 minutes. Let cool 5 minutes. Using
a silicone spatula, scrape fruit and any
juices on baking sheet into a food processor
or a blender; pulse until smooth, 8 to
10 pulses. Pour through a fine wire-mesh
strainer into a medium bowl. Discard solids.
Refrigerate, uncovered, until completely
cool, about 20 minutes. (You should have
about 2 cups sour cherry puree, enough for
10 cocktails.)

2. Make the cocktail: If using the smoked
salt, sprinkle some on a small plate.
Lightly moisten rim of a rocks glass with
water; dip rim in smoked salt. Combine
mezcal, orange liqueur, and 3 tablespoons
sour cherry puree in a cocktail shaker
filled three-fourths full with ice. Place
lid on shaker; shake vigorously until well
combined, about 15 seconds. Strain
into a rocks glass with a large ice cube.
—HANNAH SELINGER

TO PREPARE 10 COCKTAILS Combine
2½ cups mezcal, 1¾ cups plus
2 tablespoons sour cherry puree, and ¼ cup
plus 2 tablespoons orange liqueur in a large
pitcher filled with ice; stir until chilled. Pour
into rocks glasses with large ice cubes
(rimmed with smoked salt, if desired).

MAKE AHEAD Sour cherry puree may be
stored in an airtight container in refrigerator
up to 1 week.

Ti' Punch

⏱ TOTAL 5 MIN; SERVES 1

Don't be fooled by the simplicity of this Guadeloupean cocktail—it packs a ton of flavor from vegetal, grassy white rhum agricole, which is made from sugarcane juice, unlike sweeter white rums made from molasses or sugarcane byproducts. Serving this drink at room temperature, as is traditional, opens up the aromatic, herbal notes. If you prefer, you can serve it chilled for a smoother drink; just be sure to dissolve the sugar before adding the ice.

- 2 lime wedges (from 1 quartered lime)
- 2 Tbsp. (1 oz.) blanc rhum agricole (such as Rhum J.M or Rhum Clément), plus more to taste
- 1 tsp. unrefined granulated cane sugar, plus more to taste

Squeeze 1 lime wedge into an old-fashioned glass or a small wide-mouthed stemmed glass. Add blanc rhum agricole and sugar to glass; stir until sugar is dissolved, 1 to 2 minutes. Taste and adjust rhum and sugar as desired. Garnish with 1 lime wedge, if desired. Serve at room temperature or chilled over ice if you prefer. —JESSICA B. HARRIS

NOTE Rhum J.M and Rhum Clément white agricole rums are both available online at totalwine.com.

Royal Paloma Cocktail

⏱ TOTAL 5 MIN; SERVES 1

Tart grapefruit juice, floral orange liqueur, blanco tequila, and a hint of anise-flavored Pernod are topped with lemon tonic water in this tasty cocktail.

- ¼ cup (2 oz.) blanco tequila (such as Lobos 1707)
- 2 Tbsp. (1 oz.) orange liqueur (such as Cointreau)
- 2 Tbsp. fresh lemon juice (from 1 lemon)
- 2 Tbsp. fresh grapefruit juice (from 1 grapefruit)
- 1 tsp. anise-flavored liqueur (such as Pernod)
- Cracked ice
- 1 thin grapefruit half-moon slice
- ¼ cup lemon tonic water (such as Fever-Tree Lemon Tonic)
- Fennel frond, for garnish

1. Stir together tequila, orange liqueur, lemon juice, grapefruit juice, and anise-flavored liqueur in a cocktail mixing glass. Add cracked ice to mixing glass to fill about two-thirds of the way full. Stir until well chilled, about 15 seconds.

2. Arrange grapefruit half-moon slice against the inside of a large Collins glass (at least 12 ounces); fill glass three-fourths of the way full with cracked ice. Strain cocktail into prepared glass, and top with lemon tonic water. Garnish with fennel frond. —CARLTON MCCOY

NOTE To make cracked ice, place 1 ice cube at a time in the palm of your hand, and tap with the back of a bar spoon to break apart. Alternatively, place about 2 cups ice cubes in a quart-size ziplock plastic bag, and tap each cube 1 time with a meat mallet to break apart.

Abasolo y Topo Chico

PHOTO P. 316

⏱ TOTAL 5 MIN; SERVES 1

"Because Abasolo is not a heavily oaked whiskey," says distiller Iván Saldaña Oyarzábal, "it works well in refreshing drinks like this highball. I love mixing it with Topo Chico, another amazing Mexican product. It brings out the sweet, floral notes of corn in our whiskey."

- ¼ cup (2 oz.) Abasolo El Whisky de Mexico
- Large, clear ice cubes
- ½ cup Topo Chico Mineral Water
- 1 (6-×1-inch) orange peel strip, ends cut on an angle

Pour Abasolo into a highball glass filled with large, clear ice cubes. Top with Topo Chico, and garnish with orange peel strip. —IVÁN SALDAÑA OYARZÁBAL

Gingerbread Margarita

⏱ TOTAL 5 MIN; SERVES 1

This winter margarita has a warm, cozy, cake-spice panache that wouldn't be out of place at a holiday party. The spiced syrup is key: It intensifies the orange flavors of the cocktail while adding a seasonal spice hit that brings much-needed warmth during the winter months.

- ¼ cup (2 oz.) añejo tequila
- 1½ Tbsp. fresh lime juice (¾ oz.)
- 1½ Tbsp. Spiced Orange Syrup (¾ oz.) (recipe follows)
- ½ oz. orange liqueur (such as Gran Gala)
- Orange peel twist
- Cinnamon stick

Fill a mixing glass halfway with ice. Add añejo tequila, lime juice, spiced orange syrup, and orange liqueur; stir until chilled, about 20 seconds. Strain tequila mixture into a coupe glass. Wrap orange peel twist around cinnamon stick, and lay across coupe glass to garnish. —DAVID MARZORATI JR.

Spiced Orange Syrup

TOTAL 15 MIN, PLUS 12 HR MACERATION; MAKES ABOUT 1⅔ CUPS

Layers of oranges and sugar spiced with cloves, cinnamon, allspice, and nutmeg macerate to yield this versatile syrup.

- 1½ cups granulated sugar
- ¼ tsp. ground cloves
- ¼ tsp. ground cinnamon
- ¼ tsp. ground allspice
- ¼ tsp. ground nutmeg
- 2 large navel oranges, sliced ¼-inch thick (about 3 cups)
- ⅓ cup classic simple syrup

Stir together sugar, cloves, cinnamon, allspice, and nutmeg in a medium bowl. Layer oranges and sugar mixture in a large lidded container. Seal; let stand at room temperature 12 hours. During final hour, shake vigorously every 15 minutes until sugar is mostly dissolved. Pour through a fine wire-mesh strainer into a 2-cup glass jar. Press oranges with back of spoon; discard solids. Stir until sugar is dissolved. Stir in simple syrup. Cover and refrigerate up to 2 weeks. —DAVID MARZORATI JR.

GINGERBREAD MARGARITA

Jilo Old-Fashioned

TOTAL 5 MIN; SERVES 1

In Jilotepec, Mexico, distiller Iván Saldaña Oyarzábal makes Abasolo El Whisky de Mexico from nixtamalized corn. "My favorite stirred cocktail with Abasolo is our Jilo Old-Fashioned, named after our distillery," he says. "This cocktail uses two products from our distillery: Abasolo and its sister brand Nixta Licor de Elote. Nixta adds sweetness, instead of a traditional sugar cube, and also adds a silky texture, giving even more depth to this old-fashioned."

- ¼ cup (2 oz.) Abasolo El Whisky de Mexico
- 1 Tbsp. (½ oz.) Nixta Licor de Elote
- 3 dashes Angostura bitters
- Large, clear ice cubes
- 1 (4-×1-inch) orange peel strip, ends cut on an angle
- 1 (4-×1-inch) lemon peel strip, ends cut on an angle

Pour Abasolo, Nixta Licor de Elote, and bitters into a mixing glass filled with ice. Stir 10 seconds, and strain into a rocks glass filled with large, clear ice cubes. Garnish with orange and lemon peel strips. —IVÁN SALDAÑA OYARZÁBAL

Apricot-Nectarine Julep

ACTIVE 15 MIN; TOTAL 1 HR 5 MIN; SERVES 1

A puree of roasted apricots and nectarines brings out bourbon's notes of vanilla and nutmeg, making for the ultimate late-summer cocktail. Pour some of the reserved puree on top of the crushed ice for a cocktail that almost resembles a Hawaiian shave ice. The same roast-and-puree technique can be used for more stone fruits, such as plums and sour cherries.

APRICOT-NECTARINE PUREE

- 1 lb. fresh apricots, halved and pitted
- 1 lb. fresh nectarines, halved and pitted
- ⅓ cup granulated sugar

COCKTAIL

- 15 fresh mint leaves (about ¼ loosely packed cup)
- ¼ cup (2 oz.) bourbon
- Finely crushed or pebbled ice
- 1 mint sprig, for garnish

1. Make the apricot-nectarine puree: Preheat oven to 400°F. Toss together apricots, nectarines, and sugar on a large rimmed baking sheet until fully coated; spread in an even layer. Roast in preheated oven until fruit is soft and juicy, about 20 minutes, stirring halfway through roasting time. Let cool 5 minutes. Scrape fruit and any liquid on baking sheet into a food processor or blender; pulse until smooth, 5 to 8 pulses. Pour through a fine wire-mesh strainer into a medium bowl. Refrigerate, uncovered, until completely cool, about 20 minutes. (You should have about 2 cups apricot-nectarine puree, enough for 8 cocktails.)

2. Make the cocktail: Muddle mint leaves and ¼ cup apricot-nectarine puree in bottom of a julep cup. Add bourbon and crushed or pebbled ice to cover; stir until chilled, about 20 seconds. Fill cup with additional ice, adding enough to form a small mound on top. Pour 2 to 4 tablespoons apricot-nectarine puree over ice. Garnish with a mint sprig, and serve with a short julep straw. —HANNAH SELINGER

TO PREPARE 8 COCKTAILS Muddle 2 cups loosely packed fresh mint leaves and 2 cups apricot-nectarine puree in a pitcher. Add 2 cups bourbon and crushed or pebbled ice to cover, and stir until chilled, about 20 seconds. Serve drinks over ice, and garnish with mint sprigs.

MAKE AHEAD Apricot-nectarine puree may be stored in an airtight container in refrigerator up to 1 week.

Cognac-Almond Shot

TOTAL 5 MIN; SERVES 8

A pleasantly strong almond flavor permeates this sweet shot from the orgeat syrup, a nutty, creamy syrup made with orange flower and almonds. It's citrusy and faintly bitter, with light floral notes and a smooth finish.

- ¾ cup (6 oz.) cognac
- 6 Tbsp. fresh orange juice
- 3 Tbsp. (1½ oz.) orgeat syrup
- 3 Tbsp. (1½ oz.) orange liqueur (such as Cointreau)
- 6 dashes Angostura bitters

Combine cognac, orange juice, orgeat, orange liqueur, and bitters in a cocktail shaker filled with ice. Cover with lid, and shake vigorously until cold, about 15 seconds. Strain into shot glasses, and serve. —REBEKAH PEPPLER

Hawksmoor Apple Martini

⏱ ACTIVE 5 MIN; TOTAL 35 MIN; SERVES 1

Adam Montgomerie, bar manager of English steakhouse Hawksmoor's buzzy outpost in New York City, has a smart and elevated riff on the appletini. Think of the Hawksmoor Apple Martini as the love child between the nostalgic, sweet appletini of the 1990s and the booze-forward dry martini that sweet-up drink is derived from. In place of apple liqueur and sour mix, this recipe calls for the highest quality eau-de-vie — a clear fruit brandy — and a splash of homemade malic acid eau-de-vie that delivers a crisp apple finish. Malic acid is an organic acid found in fruit that is often used as an additive in beverages and desserts to give a richer aroma and clean acidic flavor. "The idea was to do a more modern, more elegant version," Montgomerie says. "The eau de vies are very good quality. There is no citrus: The malic acid gives you that fresh, bright green apple bite but keeps things clean. And the drink itself is clear, which is a nice surprise. It looks like a classic martini."

MALIC ACID EAU-DE-VIE

- ½ cup (4 oz.) apple eau-de-vie (such as Neversink)
- 2 tsp. malic acid

2-to-1 simple syrup

- 1 cup granulated sugar
- ½ cup water

MARTINI

- 3½ Tbsp. (1¾ oz.) apple eau-de-vie (such as Neversink)
- 1½ Tbsp. (¾ oz.) pear eau-de-vie (such as Clear Creek)
- 1½ Tbsp. (¾ oz.) Lillet Blanc
- ¾ tsp. verjus (such as Wolffer Estate)
- ¾ tsp. malic acid eau-de-vie
- ¾ tsp. 2-to-1 simple syrup
- Edible apple blossom flower (optional)

1. Make the malic acid eau-de-vie: Combine apple eau-de-vie and malic acid in a small bowl; stir until malic acid is fully dissolved.

2. Make the simple syrup: Combine sugar and ½ cup water in a small saucepan. Cook over medium-high, stirring constantly, until sugar dissolves, about 2 minutes. Let cool completely, about 30 minutes.

3. Pour apple eau-de-vie, pear eau-de-vie, Lillet Blanc, verjus, malic acid eau-de-vie, and 2-to-1 simple syrup in a cocktail mixing glass, and fill nearly to the top with ice cubes. Stir mixture until well combined and chilled and ice is slightly melted, about 20 seconds. Strain into a Nick and Nora cocktail glass. Garnish with an edible apple blossom flower. —ADAM MONTGOMERIE, HAWKSMOOR BAR, NYC

MAKE AHEAD Malic acid eau-de-vie can be made up to 1 month in advance and stored in an airtight container in refrigerator. Simple syrup may be stored in an airtight container in refrigerator up to 2 weeks.

NOTE Find malic acid online at modernistpantry.com.

Frosé

TOTAL 10 MIN, PLUS 6 HR FREEZING; SERVES 6

This zesty frosé starts with a homemade, fruity, and fragrant strawberry simple syrup made with fresh strawberries. Combined with a floral rosé and a splash of tart lemon juice, it all adds up to a boozy yet balanced and elegant slushy. You'll want to keep your freezer stocked with this frosé to keep you refreshed all summer long. The strawberry simple syrup keeps the slushy smooth, not icy. It isn't just delicious in this frosé, either — try it in other cocktails and mocktails, drizzle the pink syrup over fresh fruit salad, or brush it over layers of cooled cake before frosting to add a rosy hue and luscious sweetness.

- 1 (750-ml.) bottle Space Age rosé
- 1 cup plus 2 Tbsp. Strawberry Simple Syrup (recipe right)
- ¼ cup plus 2 Tbsp. fresh lemon juice (from 2 lemons)
- ¼ cup plus 2 Tbsp. (3 oz.) tequila, vodka, or gin
- Aperol (optional)

1. Combine rosé, strawberry simple syrup, lemon juice, and tequila in a large freezer-safe container; stir to combine. Cover and freeze until almost solid (mixture won't freeze completely because of the alcohol), at least 6 hours or up to 10 hours, stirring mixture once every hour.

2. Remove from freezer. Divide frosé evenly among 6 chilled glasses. Top glasses with Aperol for a little extra fun, if desired, and serve. —JOSH PHELPS

MAKE AHEAD Frosé can be stored in an airtight container in the freezer up to 1 month.

NOTE Find Space Age rosé, made on the Central Coast of California, online at groundedwineco.com.

Strawberry Simple Syrup

⏱ TOTAL 5 MIN; MAKES 1½ CUPS

Juicy, ripe strawberries are pureed with sweet syrup to create a fragrant and fruity base perfect for cocktails and mocktails. Try drizzling the pink syrup over fresh fruit salad or brushing it over layers of cooled cake before frosting to add a rosy hue and luscious sweetness.

- 1 cup plus 2 Tbsp. granulated sugar
- 1 cup plus 2 Tbsp. water
- 5 large fresh strawberries (about 7½ oz.), hulled

1. In a small saucepan, bring sugar and 1 cup plus 2 tablespoons water to a boil; simmer until the sugar is dissolved, about 3 minutes. Remove from heat, and let cool completely.

2. Process strawberries and 1 cup plus 2 tablespoons simple syrup in a blender until smooth, about 1 minute. Pour syrup through a fine wire-mesh strainer into a measuring cup; discard solids. —JOSH PHELPS

MAKE AHEAD Syrup can be made up to 3 days in advance and stored in an airtight container in refrigerator.

Sakura Martini

⏱ TOTAL 5 MIN; SERVES 1

This elegant, modern take on the saketini was created by Kenta Goto, owner of Manhattan's Bar Goto and Brooklyn's Bar Goto Niban. Goto uses aged genshu sake and gin in the drink, and garnishes it with a salt-pickled sakura, or cherry blossom.

- 5 Tbsp. (2½ oz.) ginjo sake (such as Ryujin Kakushi Ginjo Namazume Genshu)
- 5 tsp. (¾ oz.) gin (such as Roku)
- ⅛ tsp. maraschino cherry liqueur (preferably Maraska brand)
- Salt-pickled cherry blossom

Combine sake, gin, and cherry liqueur in a cocktail mixing glass filled with ice; stir until chilled, about 50 times. Strain into a chilled martini or coupe glass; garnish with a salt-pickled cherry blossom. —KENTA GOTO, BAR GOTO, NEW YORK CITY

NOTE Salt-pickled cherry blossoms can be found in Japanese grocery stores or online at kokorocares.com. Maraska Maraschino Cherry Liqueur is a clear liqueur made from Croatian cherries; order from totalwine.com.

Amaro Negroni Shot

⏱ TOTAL 5 MIN; SERVES 8

This throat-warming, rich, and delicious shot is reminiscent of a full-strength Negroni. Amaro, red bitter, and sweet vermouth round out its pleasantly bitter edge.

- ½ cup (4 oz.) amaro (such as China-China)
- ½ cup (4 oz.) red bitter (such as Campari or Cappelletti)
- ½ cup (4 oz.) sweet vermouth
- 1 (1-×2-inch) orange peel strip

Combine amaro, red bitter, and vermouth in an ice-filled mixing glass or shaker. Hold orange peel by its long edges, skin facing down into the glass, and pinch peel to express citrus oils; drop peel into glass. Stir with a cocktail stirrer until cocktail is very cold, about 15 seconds. Strain into shot glasses, and serve. —REBEKAH PEPPLER

Bitter Orange Shot

⏱ TOTAL 5 MIN; SERVES 8

With a balance of spicy and citrusy notes from the blend of Amer Picon, an orange-based bitter aperitif, and sweet vermouth, this shot is nicely bittersweet, with a warming, but not hot, finish.

- 1 cup (8 oz.) Amer Picon
- 5 Tbsp. (2½ oz.) sweet vermouth
- 3 Tbsp. fresh lemon juice
- 10 dashes orange-flavored bitters

Combine Amer Picon, vermouth, lemon juice, and bitters in a cocktail shaker filled with ice. Cover with lid, and shake vigorously until very cold, about 15 seconds. Strain into shot glasses, and serve. —REBEKAH PEPPLER

Surprise Fix

PHOTO P. 317

⏱ TOTAL 5 MIN; SERVES 1

Floral, sweet St-Germain and bittersweet fresh grapefruit juice round out a shot of Waterpocket Distillery's Long Lost Minthe, an unsweetened peppermint botanical spirit with minty, herbal, and citrus pith notes. While Long Lost Minthe can only be sourced at Utah state liquor stores or directly from Waterpocket Distillery, it can be substituted with a range of liqueurs, including Vicario Monk's Secret and Dampfwerk Distilling's The Helgolander.

- 2 Tbsp. (1 oz.) Waterpocket Distillery Long Lost Minthe
- 2 Tbsp. fresh grapefruit juice (from 1 grapefruit)
- 2 Tbsp. (1 oz.) elderflower liqueur (such as St-Germain)
- 1 Tbsp. fresh lime juice (from 1 lime)
- Cracked or crushed ice
- Mint sprig or orange peel strip

Combine Long Lost Minthe, grapefruit juice, elderflower liqueur, and lime juice in a 10-ounce tumbler or highball glass; stir to combine. Top with cracked or crushed ice. Garnish with a mint sprig or an orange peel strip; serve immediately. —RYAN EARL MANNING, WATERPOCKET DISTILLERY, WEST VALLEY CITY, UTAH

Tamarind Cocktail Base

⏱ ACTIVE 10 MIN; TOTAL 40 MIN; MAKES ABOUT ⅔ CUP (ENOUGH FOR ABOUT 4 COCKTAILS)

Aromatic lemongrass, makrut lime leaves, and spicy ginger combine with tart fruity tamarind and rich, sweet coconut sugar to create a potent and delicious Tamarind Cocktail Base that can be used in all kinds of concoctions.

- 1 medium (about 10-inch-long) lemongrass stalk
- 1¼ cups water
- 1 (1-inch) piece fresh ginger, peeled, cut crosswise into ¼-inch slices, and smashed
- ¼ cup plus 2 Tbsp. coconut sugar or packed light brown sugar
- 2½ oz. wet seedless tamarind block (about ¼ cup), torn into about 1-inch pieces
- 4 makrut lime leaves, torn in half

1. Trim and discard top 2 inches from lemongrass stalk. Leaving root end attached, cut lengthwise down center of stalk. Place on a work surface, and hit firmly using the back of a chef's knife until bruised, 6 to 8 times. Combine bruised lemongrass, 1¼ cups water, and ginger in medium saucepan. Bring to a boil over medium-high. Remove from heat. Add coconut sugar, tamarind, and makrut lime leaves; using a whisk or fork, smash tamarind to break up as much as possible. Let stand 30 minutes.

2. Pour mixture through a fine wire-mesh strainer into a blender; reserve tamarind and ginger in strainer, and discard lemongrass and lime leaves. Add tamarind and ginger to mixture in blender. Process until smooth, about 25 seconds. Place strainer over a medium bowl; pour blended mixture through strainer, pressing with the back of a spoon to strain as much of solids as possible. Scrape underside of strainer into bowl. Discard remaining solids in strainer. —LARA LEE

MAKE AHEAD Store tamarind cocktail base in an airtight container in refrigerator up to 1 week.

Tamarind Daiquiri

⏱ TOTAL 5 MIN; SERVES 1

Sugary rum, floral lime leaves, and fresh lime juice get a hit of complexity from zippy tamarind cocktail base in this daiquiri.

- ¼ cup (2 oz.) white rum
- 1 Tbsp. Tamarind Cocktail Base (recipe left)
- 1½ tsp. fresh lime juice (from 1 lime) Makrut lime leaves, for garnish

Combine rum, tamarind cocktail base, and lime juice in a cocktail shaker; fill shaker with ice. Place lid on shaker, and shake until very cold and outside of cocktail shaker is thoroughly frosted, about 30 seconds. Strain into a coupe or daiquiri glass. Garnish with lime leaves. —LARA LEE

Tamarind Cooler

⏱ TOTAL 5 MIN; SERVES 1

This cooler goes down well with a generous pour of tequila but is equally refreshing as an effervescent, delightfully sour mocktail.

- ¾ cup club soda
- ¼ cup (2 oz.) tequila (optional)
- 2 Tbsp. Tamarind Cocktail Base (recipe left)
- Lime wedge, for garnish

Fill a cocktail glass with ice. Add club soda, tequila (if using), and tamarind cocktail base; stir to combine. Garnish with a lime wedge. —LARA LEE

Tamarind Arnold Palmer

⏱ TOTAL 5 MIN; SERVES 1

Lara Lee swaps lemonade for the complexly sour, lemongrass-laced tamarind cocktail base in her riff on the classic non-alcoholic refresher.

- 1 cup brewed iced tea
- 2 Tbsp. Tamarind Cocktail Base (recipe left)

Fill a cocktail glass with ice. Add iced tea and tamarind cocktail base; stir to combine. Serve. —LARA LEE

Tamarind Water

⏱ ACTIVE 5 MIN; TOTAL 25 MIN; MAKES ABOUT ½ CUP

Tamarind water makes a refreshing drink in warm weather, but it's also a crucial flavor agent in many recipes. Blocks of tamarind pulp wrapped in cellophane are widely available online and at Asian food markets.

- ¾ cup boiling water
- 2¼ oz. wet seedless tamarind block (about 3 Tbsp.), torn into about 1-inch pieces

1. Stir together ¾ cup boiling water and tamarind pieces in a medium-size heatproof bowl. Using a fork, mash tamarind to dissolve pieces as much as possible. Stir well. Let stand 20 minutes.

2. Pour tamarind mixture through a fine wire-mesh strainer over a medium bowl. Using a spatula, push out as much liquid as possible, working any remaining pulp with spatula to continue to break it down, 1 to 2 minutes. Scrape pulp from underside of strainer, and add to mixture in bowl. Discard remaining solids in strainer. —LARA LEE

MAKE AHEAD Tamarind water may be stored in an airtight container in refrigerator up to 1 week or frozen in ice cube trays up to 2 months.

NOTE Tear leftover tamarind block into 1-inch pieces, and freeze in a ziplock plastic bag up to 2 months.

TAMARIND ARNOLD PALMER

TAMARIND COOLER

TAMARIND COCKTAIL BASE

TAMARIND DAIQUIRI

CAFÉ BRÛLOT

Café Brûlot

⏱ TOTAL 5 MIN; SERVES 10

Scholar and cookbook author Jessica B. Harris has been a part-time resident of New Orleans for many years. She shared her shortcut recipe for a Café Brûlot, which she likes to serve after a meal at her summer home on Martha's Vineyard. Café Brûlot is a signature cocktail of New Orleans, where it's prepared tableside at restaurants in an elaborate process that culminates in pouring flaming, citrus- and cinnamon-infused brandy down a clove-studded orange peel into a special silver-lined punch bowl, then dousing the flames with chicory-flavored coffee. Instead, Harris eschews the fireworks and special equipment, opting for a greatly streamlined drink that's much easier to prepare at home. In her version, warmed orange liqueur and cognac, fresh lemon and lime juice, cinnamon, cloves, and hot coffee come together in a simple but satisfying warming, boozy after-dinner cocktail that can be quickly prepared, served, and savored. You can serve the drink directly from the heatproof bowl it's prepared in, or do as Harris does: "I mix it all and pour it out of an antique Victorian tea pot." Note this is a very potent drink. "The booze doesn't burn off," Harris cautions. "Serve in demitasse cups. No seconds."

- 1 Tbsp. fresh lemon juice (from 1 lemon)
- 1 Tbsp. fresh orange juice (from 1 orange)
- 1 (3-inch) cinnamon stick
- 4 whole cloves
- ¾ cup (6 oz.) orange liqueur (such Grand Marnier, Cointreau, or triple sec)
- ¼ cup (2 oz.) cognac
- 4 cups brewed strong coffee, hot

Stir together lemon juice, orange juice, cinnamon stick, and cloves in a large heatproof bowl until combined; set aside. Heat orange liqueur and cognac in a small saucepan over medium, stirring occasionally, until heated through, about 2 minutes. Add cognac mixture to lemon juice mixture in bowl. Stir in hot coffee, and serve immediately. —JESSICA B. HARRIS

NOTE Remove the cinnamon stick and cloves before storing leftovers to prevent bitterness from overlong steeping.

Yemeni Pour-Over Coffee

⏱ TOTAL 10 MIN; SERVES 1 TO 2

This is coffee as a meditative process and tradition as opposed to a quick way to caffeinate. Slowly pouring the water over the grounds in a circular motion three different times pulls out the flavors of the beans and results in a drink unlike anything you'll find at a coffee cart. Try sipping this black before adding anything to it in order to fully experience the flavors.

- 20 grams Yemeni coffee beans (such as Al Mokha) (about ¼ cup)
- 400 grams water (about 1⅔ cups plus 1 Tbsp.)

1. Using a burr grinder, grind coffee beans into a medium grind. Set aside.

2. Heat 400 grams water in an adjustable-temperature electric pour-over kettle with a gooseneck spout to 205°F according to manufacturer's instructions. (Alternatively, bring water to a boil in a stovetop pour-over gooseneck kettle. Remove from heat, and let cool 30 seconds.)

3. Place coffee dripper from pour-over set on top of coffee server. Place 1 bleached paper filter in dripper, and place the entire pour-over set on a digital food scale. Pour 30 grams hot water onto filter to wet it. (This step will eliminate any flavor from the bleached paper, as well as preheat the coffee server.) Once water has passed through filter, discard water in server. Return dripper with filter to top of server.

4. Add ground coffee to filter. Start a timer. Slowly pour 50 grams hot water over ground coffee in a circular motion to saturate all the coffee grounds. Give server a little circular shake to evenly distribute coffee grounds, or stir using a spoon to mix quickly. This process should happen in 15 seconds. When timer reaches 30 seconds, slowly pour 150 grams hot water over coffee in a circular motion. At 1 minute and 30 seconds, slowly pour remaining hot water (about 160 grams) over coffee in a circular motion.

5. Let coffee drain. Remove and discard filter. Enjoy, preferably black. —HAKIM SULAIMANI, YAFA CAFÉ, BROOKLYN

NOTE Find Yemeni coffee beans at Middle Eastern markets or online at kalustyans.com.

Midori Shochu Sour

⏱ TOTAL 5 MIN; SERVES 1

This Midori Sour, which melds the best qualities of Midori with Shochu, was created by Julia Momosé, owner of Kumiko, a Japanese dining bar in Chicago, and author of The Way of the Cocktail: Japanese Traditions, Techniques & Recipes. This dazzling cocktail comes together quickly in a shaker, and dry-shaking the drink without ice aerates without overchilling. Though a juicy, chilled melon ball might be the perfect garnish for any cocktail, its fragrant acidity plays off of the melon liqueur and fresh citrus juice for a perfectly quenching bite.

- 3 Tbsp. (1½ oz.) Mizu Green Tea Shochu (see Note)
- 2 Tbsp. (1 oz.) melon liqueur (such as Midori)
- 1 Tbsp. fresh lemon juice (from 1 lemon)
- 1 Tbsp. fresh lime juice (from 1 lime)
- 1 Tbsp. simple syrup
- ¼ cup club soda
- Honeydew melon ball

Combine green tea shochu, melon liqueur, lemon juice, lime juice, and simple syrup in a cocktail shaker. Cover and shake 15 seconds. Pour mixture over fresh ice in a highball glass; top with club soda. Carefully slide a spoon down inside wall of glass, and scoop upward to nuzzle the ice up, allowing ingredients to come together. Top with additional ice if desired. Garnish with a honeydew melon ball, and serve. —JULIA MOMOSÉ, KUMIKO, CHICAGO

NOTE If you can't find green tea shochu, substitute with another rice-based shochu, such as Hakutake Shiro Shochu or Chiyonosono 8,000 Generations. Shochu can be found at Japanese grocery stores, liquor stores, or online at mizushochu.com.

RECIPE INDEX

Page numbers in **bold** indicate photographs.

BUNET (CHOCOLATE CRÈME
CARAMEL WITH AMARETTI)
(RECIPE P. 294)

SCALLION PANCAKES
(RECIPE P. 238)

GRILLED MAHI-MAHI WITH
LEMONGRASS-LIME AIOLI
(RECIPE P. 98)

**BLACKENED FISH SANDWICHES
WITH HORSERADISH TARTAR SAUCE
(RECIPE P. 228)**

CONTRIBUTORS

KAREN AKUNOWICZ is the chef/owner of Fox & the Knife in Boston and a 2018 James Beard Foundation Award winner.

KIKI ARANITA was chef/owner of the beloved, award-winning Poi Dog in Philadelphia. She continues to cook through chef residencies, creates content for numerous companies, and teaches recipe development at Drexel University.

VISWAEH BHATT is an Oxford, Mississipppi–based James Beard Award–winning chef and author of *I Am From Here: Stories and Recipes from a Southern Chef.*

SYLVIE BIGAR is a New York City–based food and travel writer and author of *Cassoulet Confessions: Food, France, Family, and the Stew That Saved My Life.*

TRIGG BROWN is the co-founder of Brooklyn's Win Son and co-author of *Win Son Presents: A Taiwanese American Cookbook.*

AMBER BURLING is the culinary director of Goodnight Hospitality, a restaurant consortium in Houston, Texas, that includes Rosie Cannonball, MARCH, and Montrose Cheese & Wine.

KATIE BUTTON is a four–time James Beard–nominated chef of Cúrate in Ashevhille, North Carolina. Cúrate was named one by *Food & Wine* as one of "40 Most Important Restaurants in the Past 40 Years" in 2018.

EDGAR CASTREJÓN is a San Francisco–based chef, photographer, and writer. He is the author of *Provecho: 100 Vegan Mexican Recipes to Celebrate Culture and Community.*

TOBY CECCHINI is a writer, mixologist, and co-owner with Joel Tompkins of The Long Island Bar in Brooklyn, New York.

LAN SAMANTHA CHANG is an American writer of novels and short stories. She is the recipient of fellowships from the National Endowment for the Arts, the John Simon Guggenheim Foundation, and the American Academy in Berlin. She is the director of the University of Iowa Writers' Workshop.

JUSTIN CHAPPLE is a chef, food writer, and cookbook author. He is the Culinary Director–at–Large of *Food & Wine.*

BRANDON CHAVANNES is executive chef of The Betty, located in the Kimpton Sylvan Hotel in Atlanta.

CAMILLE COGSWELL is a James Beard Award–winning pastry chef and *Food & Wine* Best New Chef 2020 based in Asheville, North Carolina.

NINA COMPTON is the James Beard Award–winning chef/owner of Compère Lapin and CL Raw Bar in New Orleans.

TOM CUNANAN is chef and co-owner with Palo Dungca of Pogiboy in Washington, DC.

CASSIDEE DABNEY is the executive chef of The Barn at Blackberry Farm in Walland, Tennessee.

CLARE DE BOER is co-head chef and owner with Jess Shadbolt of New York City's King and a *Food & Wine* Best New Chef 2018.

GENOVA DELICATESSEN is a classic Italian deli—open since 1926—with two locations in Napa and Walnut Creek, California.

THESSA DIADEM is chef/owner of All Day Baby in Los Angeles and a *Food & Wine* Best New Chef 2020.

JASON DIAMOND is an author, editor, speaker and self-proclaimed "big eater" based in New York City.

FELIPE DONNELLY is chef/owner with his wife, Tamy Rofe, of Colonia Verde, Cómodo, and Disco Tacos in New York City.

MARY DUMONT is a *Food & Wine* Best New Chef 2006 and co-owner of Plantpub in Cambridge, Massachusetts.

PAOLO DUNGCA is chef and co-owner with Tom Cunanan of Pogiboy in Washington, D.C.

KAREN FINLEY is a friend of food scholar and writer Jessica B. Harris and a fellow summer resident of Martha's Vineyard

TIMOTHY FLORES is chef and co-owner with Genie Kwon of Kasama in Chicago and a *Food & Wine* Best New Chef 2022.

SAM FORE is chef/owner of Tuk Tuk Sri Lankan Bites in Lexington, Kentucky.

TORIANO FREDERICKS is chef and co-owner with his wife, Serena, of Boricua Soul in Durham, North Carolina.

LAUREN FRIEL is a sommelier and owner of Rebel Rebel natural wine bar in Somerville, Massachusetts.

EVAN FUNKE is executive chef of Felix Trattoria in Los Angeles. His first cookbook, *American Sfoglino*, won the IACP Award for Best Cookbook in 2020.

SHAWN GAWLE is the executive pastry chef for Goodnight Hospitality, in Houston, Texas.

ANDREA GENTL is an award-winning travel and food photographer and author of *Cooking with Mushrooms* (Workman, 2022).

FANY GERSON is the chef and co-owner of Fan-Fan Doughnuts in New York CIty and the author of *My Sweet Mexico* (2010), *Paletas* (2011), and *Mexican Ice Cream* (2017).

KENTA GOTO is a mixologist and owner of Bar Goto, a Japanese-style cocktail bar in New York City.

PAIGE GRANDJEAN is an associate food editor at *Food & Wine.*

SARAH GRUENEBERG is a James Beard Award–winning chef and co-owner of Monteverde in Chicago, named a *Food & Wine* "Best Restaurant" in 2016.

BRIDGET HALLINAN is an associate food editor at *Food & Wine*.

MATTHEW HAMILTON is the executive sous chef of March in Houston, Texas.

ALEXANDER HARDY is a writer and mental health educator based in New York City.

JESSICA B. HARRIS is an American culinary historian, college professor, cookbook author, and journalist.

MARY-FRANCES HECK is a food writer, chef, recipe developer, and frequent contributor to *Food & Wine*.

CHRISTIAN HERNANDEZ is the chef de cuisine of March in Houston, Texas.

MATT HORN is the chef/owner of Horn Barbecue in Oakland, California, and a *Food & Wine* Best New Chef 2021.

THOMAS HOUSTON is a mixologist and bar manager of Superior Seafood & Oyster Bar in New Orleans.

DAMIRA INATULLAEVA is a cooking instructor specializing in Uzbek cuisine in Brooklyn, New York.

RAY ISLE is the executive wine director at *Food & Wine*.

THOMAS KELLER is the James Beard Award–winning chef/owner of several restaurants, including the Michelin-starred French Laundry in Yountville, California, and Per Se, in New York City.

ERIC KIM is a *New York Times* food writer and author of *Korean American: Food That Tastes Like Home*.

DR. DONALD V. KINSMAN is a retired chemist and the father of *Food & Wine* Executive Features Editor Kat Kinsman.

LEAH KOENIG is a Brooklyn-based food writer and author of six cookbooks, including *The Jewish Cookbook* and *Modern Jewish Cooking*.

JONATHAN KUNG is a chef, social media star, and owner of Kung Food Market Studio in Detroit, Michigan.

GENIE KWON is chef and co-owner with Timothy Flores of Kasam in Chicago and a *Food & Wine* Best New Chef 2022.

CLARICE LAM is the chef/proprietor of The Baking Bean pop-ups and pastry chef for Kimika in New York City.

CARLO LAMAGNA is the chef/owner of Magna Kusina in Portland, Oregon, and a *Food & Wine* Best New Chef 2021.

CHRISTINE LAU is executive chef of Kimika in New York City.

KERRIN LAZ is the owner of LAZ Wine in Napa Valley, California.

KATE LEAHY is a San Francisco–based food and wine writer and the author or co-author of multiple cookbooks. Her first cookbook, *A16 Food + Wine*, was the 2008 IACP Cookbook of the Year.

LARA LEE is a Sydney, Australia–based chef, food writer, and author of *Coconut & Sambal: Recipes from My Indonesian Kitchen* and *A Splash of Soy: Everyday Food from Asia*.

HUNTER LEWIS is editor-in-chief of *Food & Wine*.

ANITA LO is a Michelin-starred chef, *Food & Wine* Best New Chef for 2001, and author of *Cooking without Borders and Solo: A Modern Cookbook for a Party of One*.

BUDDHA LO is executive chef of Huso and Marky's in New York City.

OTTO LUCÀ is executive chef of Longotto Ristorante in Novello, Piedmont, Italy.

ANDRÉ MACK is a sommelier, winemaker, and proprietor of & Sons, a ham bar in Brooklyn, New York.

GABY MAEDA is chef de cuisine at State Bird Provisions in San Francisco and a *Food & Wine* Best New Chef 2021.

RYAN EARL MANNING is owner of BarDaddy, a Salt Lake City–based bar and restaurant consulting firm.

LYNNETTE MARRERO is a James Beard Award–winning bartender and mixologist based in New York City.

CRISTINA MARTINEZ is a James Beard Award–winning chef and chef/owner of South Philly Barbacoa and Casa Mexico in Philadelphia.

DAVID MARZORATI JR. is bar manager of Baldamar in Roseville, Minnesota.

OVAKIM MARTIROSYAN is a chef and co-owner along with his wife, Alvard Martirosyan, of Mini Kabob in Los Angeles.

ALVARD MARTIROSYAN is a chef and co-owner along with her husband, Ovakim Martirosyan, of Mini Kabob in Los Angeles.

CARLTON MCCOY is the master sommelier at Stony Hill Vineyard in Napa Valley, California.

MELISSA MIRANDA is chef/owner of Musang in Seattle, and a *Food & Wine* Best New Chef 2020.

SAMIR MOGANNAM is head chef at Beit Rima in San Francisco.

JULIA MOMOSÉ is a bartender, writer, and creative force behind Kumiko, the Japanese dining bar in Chicago. In 2022, Momosé received the Chicago Exceptional Cocktails Award from the Michelin Guide.

ADAM MONTGOMERIE is the bar manager of the New York outpost of London's Hawksmoor restaurant.

SHOTA NAKAJIMA is a Seattle-based chef and semi-finalist for the national James Beard Award in 2018, 2019, and 2020.

ANH NGO is a bartender at Kata Robata in Houston, Texas.

ANDREA NGUYEN is a San Francisco–based chef, food writer, and cookbook author. In 2018, she received the James Beard Award for Best Cookbook for *The Pho Cookbook*.

FERMÍN NÚÑEZ is the executive chef of Suerte in Austin, Texas, and a *Food & Wine* Best New Chef 2021.

KWAME ONWUACHI is a James Beard Award–winning chef, *Food & Wine* Best New Chef 2019, and author of *Notes from a Young Black Chef* and *My America: Recipes from a Young Black Chef*.

CARINE OTTOU is a London-based chef and owner of Marie's Little Jar, which produces West African–inspired sauces, marinades, and dips.

CHINTAN PANDYA is executive chef of New York City's Dhamaka.

REBEKAH PEPPLER is a Paris-based food writer, cookbook author, and food stylist. Her most recent book *À Table*, was published in 2021 by Chronicle Books.

MELISSA PERELLO is executive chef of two San Francisco restaurants, Octavia, and the Michelin-starred Frances.

JOSH PHELPS is owner and winemaker of Grounded Wine Company in St. Helena, California.

BROOKS REITZ is a Charleston, South Carolina–based restaurateur, designer, entrepreneur, and founder of Jack Rudy Cocktail Co.

FELIPE RICCIO is a chef-partner with Goodnight Hospitality in Houston, Texas.

FÀULA RISTORANTE is the restaurant in the Casa Langa Hotel in Cerretto Langhe, Piedmont, Italy.

SONOKO SAKAI is a food writer, cookbook author, and teacher based in California. Her book, *Japanese Home Cooking: Simple Meals, Authentic Flavors* won the IACP International Cookbook Award in 2019.

IVÁN SALDAÑA OYARZÁBAL is a distiller and creator of Montelobos Mezcal, Abasolo corn whisky, Nixta Licor de Elote corn liqueur, and Ancho Reyes chile liqueur.

NOAH SANDOVAL is chef/owner of the Michelin-starred Oriole in Chicago.

HANNAH SELINGER is an award-winning travel, food, and lifestyle writer based in East Hampton, New York, and Boxford, Massachusetts. Her essay, "In My Childhood Kitchen, I Learned Both Fear and Love" appears in the *2022 Best American Food Writing* collection.

JESS SHADBOLT is co-head chef and owner with Clare de Boer of New York City's King and a *Food & Wine* Best New Chef 2018.

SEAN SHERMAN is co-founder and chef of the James Beard Award–winning Owamni in Minneapolis. His book, *The Sioux Chef's Indigenous Kitchen*, won the James Beard Award for Best American Cookbook in 2018.

LUCY SIMON is a New York–based wine, spirits, and food writer and editorial assistant at *Food & Wine*.

LUCAS SIN is chef at Nice Day in Melville, New York, and a *Food & Wine* Best New Chef 2021.

ANDREA SLONECKER is a Portland, Oregon-based food writer and cookbook author. Her book, *The Picnic*, won the 2016 IACP award for Best General Cookbook.

JASMINE SMITH is a recipe developer and tester based in Birmingham, Alabama.

T.J. STEELE is head chef of Claro in Brooklyn, New York.

HILLARY STERLING is head chef at Ci Siamo in New York City.

MOLLY STEVENS is a cooking instructor, food writer, recipe developer, and cookbook author. Her cookboks *All About Braising: The Art of Uncomplicated Cooking* (2004) and *All About Roasting: A New Approach to a Classic Art* (2011) each won both James Beard and IACP cookbook awards.

HAKIM SULAIMANI is the owner of Yafa Café in Brooklyn, New York.

NOK SUNTARANON is chef/owner of Kalaya Thai Kitchen in Philadephia.

ANNA SWANN is chef/owner of Ulam, a Dallas-based Filipino pop-up concept.

ANN TAYLOR PITTMAN is a James Beard Award–winning recipe developer, editor, cookbook author, and writer based in Birmingham, Alabama.

ANNA THEOKTISTO is a recipe developer and tester based in Birmingham, Alabama.

PIERRE THIAM is a New York City–based chef, author, and social activist. He is executive chef co-founder of Teranga, a fine-casual food chain in New York and executive chef of Nok by Alara in Lagos, Nigeria, and signature chef of the five-star Pullman Hotel in Dakar, Senegal.

HETEL VASAVADA is a San Francisco–based baker and author of *Milk & Cardamom: Spectacular Cakes, Custards and More Inspired by the Flavors of India.*

KELSEY YOUNGMAN is a New York City–based cook, baker, writer, and editor for *Food & Wine.*

CLAUDETTE ZEPEDA is an award-winning San Diego–based chef and culinary entrepreneur with food concepts in the US, Australia, and Mexico.

PHOTO CREDITS

MEASUREMENT GUIDE

basic measurements

GALLON	QUART	PINT	CUP	OUNCE	TBSP	TSP	DROPS
1 gal	4 qt	8 pt	16 c	128 fl oz			
½ gal	2 qt	4 pt	8 c	64 fl oz			
¼ gal	1 qt	2 pt	4 c	32 fl oz			
	½ qt	1 pt	2 c	16 fl oz			
	¼ qt	½ pt	1 c	8 fl oz	16 Tbsp		
			⅞ c	7 fl oz	14 Tbsp		
			¾ c	6 fl oz	12 Tbsp		
			⅔ c	5⅓ fl oz	10⅔ Tbsp		
			⅝ c	5 fl oz	10 Tbsp		
			½ c	4 fl oz	8 Tbsp		
			⅜ c	3 fl oz	6 Tbsp		
			⅓ c	2⅔ fl oz	5⅓ Tbsp	16 tsp	
			¼ c	2 fl oz	4 Tbsp	12 tsp	
			⅛ c	1 fl oz	2 Tbsp	6 tsp	
				½ fl oz	1 Tbsp	3 tsp	
					½ Tbsp	1½ tsp	
						1 tsp	60 drops
						½ tsp	30 drops

us to metric conversions

The conversions shown here are approximations. For more precise conversions, use the formulas to the right.

VOLUME			WEIGHT			TEMPERATURE			CONVERSION FORMULAS
1 tsp	=	5 mL	1 oz	=	28 g	475°F	=	246°C	tsp × 4.929 = mL
1 Tbsp	=	15 mL	¼ lb (4 oz)	=	113 g	450°F	=	232°C	Tbsp × 14.787 = mL
1 fl oz	=	30 mL	½ lb (8 oz)	=	227 g	425°F	=	218°C	fl oz × 29.574 = mL
¼ c	=	59 mL	¾ lb (12 oz)	=	340 g	400°F	=	204°C	c × 236.588 = mL
½ c	=	118 mL	1 lb (16 oz)	=	½ kg	375°F	=	191°C	pt × 0.473 = L
¾ c	=	177 mL				350°F	=	177°C	qt × 0.946 = L
1 c	=	237 mL	LENGTH			325°F	=	163°C	oz × 28.35 = g
1 pt	=	½ L	1 in	=	2.5 cm	300°F	=	149°C	lb × 0.453 = kg
1 qt	=	1 L	5 in	=	12.7 cm	275°F	=	135°C	in × 2.54 = cm
1 gal	=	4.4 L	9 in	=	23 cm	250°F	=	121°C	(°F − 32) × 0.556 = °C